Corneliu C. Simuț

The Doctrine of Salvation in the Sermons of Richard Hooker

Arbeiten zur Kirchengeschichte

Begründet von
Karl Holl† und Hans Lietzmann†

herausgegeben von
Christian Albrecht und Christoph Markschies

Band 94

Walter de Gruyter · Berlin · New York

Corneliu C. Simuţ

The Doctrine of Salvation in the Sermons of Richard Hooker

Walter de Gruyter · Berlin · New York

∞ Printed on acid-free paper which falls within the guidelines
of the ANSI to ensure permanence and durability.

ISBN-13: 978-3-11-018498-3
ISBN-10: 3-11-018498-2

Library of Congress Cataloging-in-Publication Data

A CIP catalogue record for this book is available from the Library of Congress.

Bibliographic information published by Die Deutsche Bibliothek

Die Deutsche Bibliothek lists this publication in the Deutsche Nationalbibliografie;
detailed bibliographic data is available in the Internet at < http://dnb.ddb.de >.

Printed in Germany
Cover design: Christopher Schneider, Berlin

To my children,
Ezra and Lara

Foreword

Richard Hooker (1554-1600) has been an unquestioned authority in Anglican ecclesiastical theology for centuries. In the present book, the young Baptist scholar Dr. Corneliu Simuț, lecturer in historical and dogmatic theology at Emanuel University of Oradea (Romania), examines a wide range of contemporary studies in which the assessment of Hooker's theology has become ambivalent. Some authors even think that Hooker is more Catholic than Reformed in his theology. Dr. Simuț wants to show quite the opposite. According to him, Hooker follows in the steps of his Protestant predecessors, especially as far as the doctrine of salvation is concerned. A detailed study of some of the most important English reformers under the reign of Henry VIII, Edward VI and Mary I is followed by an even more profound research of Hooker's early sermons. This line of inquiry differs from the usual Hooker-research, which is almost exclusively concentrated on the five or eight books of the *Lawes of the Ecclesiasticall Politie*. It also differs from the earlier book written by Dr. Simuț, *Richard Hooker and his Early Doctrine of Justification. A Study of his* Discourse of Justification (Aldershot: Ashgate, 2005), in which the connection between Hooker and the great Continental reformers was at the centre of his attention.

Hooker's sermons turn out to be a lively testimony of careful theological reflections on faith, righteousness, justification, forgiveness of sins, election and perseverance, all of which are essential elements of the key concern of the Reformation: how do I acquire lasting salvation? Dr. Simuț points to the genuinely Reformed stress on the sovereignty of God, on faith alone, on the imputation of the merits of Christ, on the sanctification by the Holy Spirit which is found in all of Hooker's sermons. He also discovers a logical sequence in Hooker's successive sermons, in which not only the doctrine of justification – considered to be the *articulus stantis et cadentis ecclesiae* in the Protestant tradition – is presented but also the broader doctrine of salvation. Firstly, there is the necessity of faith, then the epistemology of faith, namely the certainty and doubt that go with faith. In the next sermon, which – compared to Hooker's other sermons – is evidently an elaborate theological discourse rather than an address from the pulpit, the foundation of faith is

dealt with. In this particular sermon, Hooker comes to his most fundamental distinctions and to his most sympathetic presentation of Catholic doctrines, referring to the *Decretum de justificatione* of the Council of
Trent. With the help of these insights, the controversy between Hooker
and his Puritan fellow-preacher, Walter Travers, can be explained and
reproduced more easily. Finally, the sermon on the nature of pride
gives Dr. Simuţ the opportunity to reconstruct Hooker's anthropology
of faith, with its main elements such as the relation of grace and nature,
the lasting impact of sin, the spiritual life of the believer and the
presence of Christ, and eventually, the concept of justice.

Dr. Simuţ's main purpose in analysing and evaluating these sermons is to show the links which connect Hooker's rich theological
insights with the martyrs of the Protestant faith in England, such as
William Tyndale, John Frith, Robert Barnes, Thomas Cranmer, John
Bradford and John Foxe. I think that Dr. Simuţ is very convincing when
he points to the many parallels existing between the theological views
which Hooker carefully elaborates and the passionate insights of his
predecessors. Thus, I must say that I am impressed by Dr. Simuţ's
analytical power, which gives the reader a comprehensive entrance into
Hooker's world. I am equally certain that his analysis will give rise to a
broader perspective on Hooker's theology within the wider reception
of his thought in contemporary religious culture. For the same reason,
however, I doubt that Hooker's significance can or should be restricted
to the Reformed tradition, as generally claimed nowadays. Being a
Catholic theologian, I can easily recognise and appreciate many Catholic starting-points and trains of thought in Hooker's doctrine of salvation. A careful study of the Council of Trent and the recent *Declaration
on the Doctrine of Justification*, issued by the Vatican and the Lutheran
World Federation (1999), will show that the differences are not
insurmountable. Dr. Simuţ's rich study has only strengthened this
conviction.

Prof. Dr. Nico Schreurs
Emeritus Professor of Dogmatic Theology
University of Tilburg

Acknowledgements

It is my delight to express my profound gratitude to Professor Dr. Nico F. M. Schreurs from the Faculty of Theology within the University of Tilburg, the Netherlands, who has always been supportive in encouraging my research as well as in providing useful insights into Richard Hooker's complex soteriology. Professor Schreurs did not only help me academically but also financially because I stayed in his home during most of my journeys to the Netherlands. Together with his wife, Lucia, Professor Schreurs was a wonderful host, so my trips to the Netherlands were not only intellectually challenging but also socially pleasant.

I am also thankful to Dr. Dick Akerboom from the Titus Brandsma Institute within the Radbout University of Nijmegen who read my work diligently and provided careful suggestions whenever necessary. His willingness to help me in any way he could meant a lot to my studies in Tilburg.

I wish to say thank you to my friend Prof. Dr. Wim Janse of Leiden University and the Free University of Amsterdam who, in spite of his countless duties, has managed to remain an endless source of constant encouragement and a competent advisor in academic matters.

Miss Charmian Widdowson has undertanken once again the most demanding task of correcting my manuscript. Her dedication to master the details of the text was essential for the publication of this work. I am greatly indebted to my friend, Mr. Iulian G. Necea, for doing the typesetting of the manuscript besides his daily teaching and pastoral activities. My sincerest thanks also go to my friend, and former student, Mr. Trevin Wax, for diligently checking important sections of this volume.

My book would not have been published without the permanent advice and support of Dr. Albrecht Döhnert, Editor at Walter de Gruyter Publishing House in Berlin, Germany. I am equally grateful to Dr. Claus-Jürgen Thornton, Editor-in-Chief of the Theology, Judaism and Religion Section of Walter de Gruyter Publishing House, who authorised the publication of my thesis.

I owe my deepest thanks to my family. Despite her time-consuming duties as mother and doctoral student, my wife, Ramona, has never ceased to stay by me and my work. As far as I am concerned, the most delightful part of writing this book was the awareness that hard work is always rewarded by spending my time with my children, Ezra and Lara. I dedicate this book to both of them in full admittance that it would have been infinitely more difficult for me to write this book without their neverending smile, joy, and love.

Corneliu Simuţ
Oradea, July 2005

Contents

1. Reading Richard Hooker Today:
A Historical Study

Richard Hooker (1554-1600) is best known for his *Lawes of the Ecclesiasticall Politie* which were written towards the end of his life.[1] In the four hundred years since his death, the vast majority of books about Hooker focused on his *Lawes* to the detriment of other works which he penned during his early career. Hooker's early works are not so elaborate as his later *Lawes* and they are considerably shorter. Unlike his *Lawes*, which is made up of eight separate books, most of Hooker's early writings are in fact sermons which he delivered as part of his pastoral ministry. Generally known as "Tractates and Sermons", they include *The Two Sermons Upon Part of S. Judes Epistle* (1582-1583), *A Learned and Confortable Sermon of the Certaintie and Perpetuitie of Faith in the Elect* (1585), *A Learned Discourse of Justification, Workes and How the Foundation of Faith is Overthrown* (1586), *Master Hooker's Answer to the Supplication that Master Travers Made to the [Privy] Counsell* (1586),[2] and *A Learned Sermon of the Nature of Pride* (1586).[3]

---

1   In his last years, Hooker also wrote some responses to various attacks on the *Lawes*. For instance, he wrote a response to *A Christian Letter*, published anonymously in 1599 (allegedly by a group of Puritan opponents who accused him of disseminating teachings which are contrary to the *Thirty-Nine Articles*). Later on, Hooker decided he should write a thorough defence of his *Lawes*. This work, now called *The Dubling Fragments*, was left unfinished as he died after a short illness in 1600. For details, see Nigel Voak, *Richard Hooker and Reformed Theology: A Study of Reason, Will, and Grace* (Oxford: Oxford University Press, 2003), 10.

2   This is not a sermon but it helps us understand how Hooker clarified Travers's accusations. In his *Answer*, Hooker explains what he meant by some teachings from previous works.

3   The Folger edition also includes the following writings within Hooker's "Tractates and Sermons": *A Remedie Against Sorrow and Feare, delivered in a funeral Sermon, John 14:27*, *A Sermon of Richard Hooker Found in the Study of the late Learned Bishop Andrews* (which seems not to have been written by Hooker), and three sermon fragments on *Matthew 27:46*, *Hebrews 2:14-15*, and *Proverbs 3:9-10*. These will not be treated in this book because they cannot be dated accurately and they are not essentially relevant to Hooker's doctrine of salvation. See W. Speed Hill (ed.), *The Folger Library Edition of the Works of Richard Hooker*, vol. V ("Tractates and Sermons"), hereafter referred to as *Works V*.

The purpose of this book is twofold: firstly, to investigate Hooker's sermons with a critical eye on his doctrine of salvation, which is a recurrent theme throughout his early theology, and secondly, to identify the connections between Hooker's doctrine of salvation and the most important theologians of the early Reformation in England. Thus, it will be argued that Hooker continues the soteriological tradition of the early English Reformation represented by William Tyndale, John Frith, Robert Barnes, Thomas Cranmer, John Bradford and John Foxe. My interest in the connection between Hooker's understanding of salvation and the writings of the first English reformers was triggered after reading an article by Arthur P. Monahan published in 1997.[4] In this article, Monahan attempts to prove Hooker was a Counter-Reformation (namely Catholic) political thinker. This could mean that while Hooker's theology may still be Protestant, his political ideas are Catholic. Monahan, however, is not saying this. What he does say is that Anglicanism, of which Hooker is a respected representative, "retained the greatest resemblance in theology, ecclesiology and institutional structure to the medieval Church of Rome from which it was separating."[5] By affirming this, Monahan is trying to argue that Hooker's entire theology, which evidently encompasses his soteriology, is more Catholic than Protestant. This would imply that Hooker's doctrine of salvation is not in line with the teachings of the early English reformers. To counter Monahan's argument, I will identify the most important dogmatic connections between the soteriology of the early English reformers and Hooker's doctrine of salvation as reflected in his sermons.

Before doing this, however, it is necessary to understand how Hooker has been perceived and how his works have been read since he died in 1600.[6] To begin with, it should be highlighted that in recent years the scholarly interest in the theology of Hooker increased significantly after the completion and publication of the Folger Library Edition of his works almost a decade ago, under the general super-

---

4   Monahan, "Richard Hooker: Counter-Reformation Political Thinker", in A. S. McGrade (ed.), *Richard Hooker and the Construction of Christian Community*, 203-218.

5   Monahan, "Richard Hooker: Counter-Reformation Political Thinker", 218.

6   It should be said here that this introductory chapter contains some information from my previous work on Hooker. For details, see Corneliu C. Simuţ, "Continuing the Protestant Tradition in the Church of England: The Influence of the Continental Magisterial Reformation on the Doctrine of Justification in the Early Theology of Richard Hooker as Reflected in his *A Learned Discourse of Justification, Workes, and How the Foundation of Faith is Overthrown* (1586)", PhD thesis, Aberdeen (2003), 4-35, or Corneliu C. Simuţ, *Richard Hooker and his Early Doctrine of Justification. A Study of his* Discourse of Justification (Aldershot: Ashgate, 2005), 1-12.

vision of Professor W. Speed Hill.[7] This excellent critical edition was preceded by another voluminous publication also edited by Professor Speed Hill, which marked the beginning of academic investigation of Hooker scholarship in the early 1970s.[8] Since then, some very important and well-informed studies in Hooker scholarship have been written by W. Cargill Thompson,[9] Egil Grislis,[10] Robert Eccleshall,[11] Nigel Atkinson,[12] Bruce Kaye,[13] Damian Grace,[14] John Gascoigne,[15] and Nigel Voak.[16] Within the last four hundred years, however, investigations focused on major interpretations of Hooker, and the pattern of research was either historical or philosophical. The various attempts to offer a clear picture of what has been written in Hooker scholarship have scanned the whole history of research in this field, and finally tried to come up with a special image of Hooker and his place within the history of human thought. Accordingly, Hooker has been generally viewed as either a distinguished theologian or a reputed philosopher. What kind of theologian Hooker is, and to which particular theological tradition he belongs, is still a debated issue. Likewise, the attempts to classify him as philosopher or theologian and to incorporate him within a specific philosophical or theological movement are equally uncertain.

---

7   W. S. Hill (ed.), *The Folger Library Edition of the Works of Richard Hooker* (1977-1993).
8   W. Speed Hill (ed.), *Studies in Richard Hooker. Essays Preliminary to an Edition of His Works* (Cleveland: The Press of Case Western Reserve University, 1972).
9   W. D. J. Cargill Thompson, "The Philosopher of the 'Politic Society'. Richard Hooker as a Political Thinker", in W. Speed Hill, *Studies in Richard Hooker: Essays Preliminary to an Edition of His Works* (Cleveland: The Press of Case Western Reserve University, 1972), 3-76.
10   Egil Grislis, "The Hermeneutical Problem in Richard Hooker", in W. Speed Hill, *Studies in Richard Hooker: Essays Preliminary to an Edition of His Works* (Cleveland: The Press of Case Western Reserve University, 1972).
11   Robert Eccleshall, "Richard Hooker and the Peculiarities of the English: The Reception of the *Ecclesiastical Polity* in the Seventeenth and Eighteenth Centuries", *History of Political Thought* II/1 (1981), 63-117.
12   Nigel Atkinson, *Richard Hooker and the Authority of Scripture, Tradition, and Reason: Reformed Theologian of the Church of England?* (Carlisle: Paternoster Press, 1997).
13   Bruce Kaye, "Authority and the Shaping of Tradition: New Essays on Richard Hooker", *The Journal of Religious History* 21/1 (1997), 3-9.
14   Damian Grace, "Natural Law in Hooker's *Of the Laws of the Ecclesiastical Polity*", *The Journal of Religious History* 21/1 (1997), 10-22.
15   John Gascoigne, "The Unity of Church and State Challenged: Responses to Hooker from the Restoration to the Nineteenth-Century Age of Reform", *The Journal of Religious History*, 21/1 (1997), 60-79.
16   Nigel Voak, *Richard Hooker and Reformed Theology. A Study of Reason, Will, and Grace* (Oxford: Oxford University Press, 2003), 1-21.

It is not within the goal of this chapter to produce a strictly final classification of Hooker according to the general categories of theology or philosophy. This chapter is a historical approach to Hooker scholarship, which also intends to foster critical insights on what has been produced regarding Hooker's life and work. It should be mentioned, however, that its investigation is highly selective. The finality of this historical survey is to investigate the most pre-eminent works that saliently emerge as decisive within Hooker scholarship. Accordingly, Hooker scholarship has been divided into three major views on Hooker's life and work. Firstly, the traditional view of Hooker's thought fosters the classical, non-critical image of Hooker, and it might be historically settled between Hooker's death and the first two decades of the twentieth century. Secondly, the modern view of Hooker's thought is fundamentally analytical and partially corrects the traditional view of Hooker, especially in historical and biographical matters. This ranges historically until the 1970s, when a particular interest in Hooker suddenly developed.[17] Thirdly, the contemporary view of Hooker's thought is mainly critical of Hooker's works and even of his motivation for writing, and it is probably the most prolific in divergent interpretations of Hooker, not necessarily in academic research. Nevertheless, all these three views of Hooker offer a diverse and comprehensive image of the most important works that investigated Hooker's life and thought.

1.1 The Traditional View

The traditional view of Hooker's thought is primarily a reference to all the works that appeared immediately after his death at the end of the sixteenth century until the first two decades of the twentieth century. Even though the analysis encompasses a long period of time of over three centuries, it should be taken into account as a whole because the works that were published within these historical boundaries share at least two common characteristics. Firstly, the works are essentially neither analytical, nor critical regarding Hooker's thought but rather descriptive. Secondly, there is a bias towards a certain degree of appre-

---

17   This interest in Hooker is obvious, especially with the appearance of Speed Hill's *Studies in Richard Hooker: Essays Preliminary to an Edition of His Works* (Cleveland: The Press of Case Western Reserve University, 1972).

ciation of Hooker, despite the controversial aspects of his theology, and the diverse theological positions of the writers that tackled it.

There are mainly four different perspectives on Hooker's thought in the traditional view. Each of them corresponds to the specific interest of the writer approaching Hooker's thought, and displays a large variety of themes that the English reformer diligently analysed in his work.

1.1.1 The Historical Perspective

The historical perspective within the traditional view of Hooker's thought is concerned mainly with the person and the work of the reformer. Biography and bibliography were the very first interests of the writers who tried to portray an image of Hooker. This traditional portrait of Hooker lasted for more than three centuries without being seriously challenged.[18] On the other hand, this particular traditional historical perspective generally produced a rather sympathetic and non-critical image of Hooker, which seems to be the feature of the whole traditional view.

Thomas Fuller was the first historian who wrote about Hooker.[19] His story is characterised by imprecision and a very simplistic description of Hooker's life and work. In his *Church History*, Fuller argues that Hooker was a bachelor, but he changes his mind a few years later, when he wrote in his *Worthies* that Hooker's wife and children "were neither to his comfort when living, nor credit when dead."[20] He offers the classical image of Hooker, a "stone-still" theologian, "unmovable in his thoughts and opinions."[21] His style of preaching was long and complicated, and it had "many closes till the end of the statement."[22] Fuller discloses an obvious preference for Travers, Hooker's puritan opponent, who is described in a much more

---

18 The first serious attempts to question and solve the uncertainties and the erroneous information regarding Hooker's life and work were written only in the first half of the twentieth centuries. For more detailed information, cf. C. J. Sisson, *The Judicious Marriage of Mr. Hooker and the Birth of "The Laws of Ecclesiastical Polity"* (Cambridge: Cambridge University Press, 1940), and David Novarr, *The Making of Walton's "Lives"* (New York: Cornell University Press, 1958).

19 Thomas Fuller, *The Church History of Britain, from the Birth of Jesus Christ until the Year MDCXLVIII*, vol. I-III (London: William Tegg, 1868). The first edition, however, was published in 1655.

20 Thomas Fuller, *Worthies*, vol. I, 1662.

21 Thomas Fuller, *The Church History of Britain*, vol. I, 141.

22 *ibid.* 141.

vivid imagery. Accordingly, Travers had a "graceful utterance, harmonious gestures, and a clear methodology of preaching."[23] Nevertheless, it seems that Fuller's description of Travers proved to be another classical image that other historians and theologians later confirmed.[24]

John Gauden's *Life of Hooker* is a rather misleading piece of historiography than a plain narrative of his thought. There are some things that must be mentioned about Gauden, as they help a better understanding of his work. John Gauden was a strange prelate, who had an ambiguous ecclesiastical career.[25] He apparently was unscrupulous and ambitious. He claimed a bishopric, then wanted to move to Exeter, and eventually complained of his stay at Exeter.[26] Accordingly, it is not very difficult to believe Shirley's description of Gauden as being completely untrustworthy and a blackmailer.[27] Gauden had Low Church positions, but he was appointed bishop in the High Church. Thus, he published Hooker's *Book VII* to show that he was in favour of the High Church doctrine.[28] Gauden's *Life* is a historiographical work, which contains literary defects, historical inadequacy, and a vulgar manner of writing.[29] The need for a better informed and a more urbane historical work became apparent soon after Gauden published his book.

Shortly after the appearance of Gauden's work, Gilbert Sheldon, Archbishop of Canterbury, commissioned another historical work that was supposed to correct Gauden's misleading attempt. This task was undertaken by Izaak Walton, who provided an idealistic and romantic

---

23   *ibid.* 142.

24   Fuller is interested in the debate between Hooker and Travers. After Hooker was appointed Master of the Temple, it normally happened that Travers would confute in the afternoon what Hooker preached in the morning. Fuller explains the reasons that triggered the controversy between Hooker and Travers. Firstly, Hooker held that the Church of Rome was a true Church, even though not perfect and pure. Secondly, he said that those who lived and died in it, i.e. the Church of Rome, might be saved if they repented of all their sins committed out of ignorance. Travers' answer did not cease to appear, and he determinedly stated that the Church of Rome was not the true Church, and those who live and die in it cannot be saved if they think they should earn justification by works.

25   F. J. Shirley, *Richard Hooker and Contemporary Political Ideas* (London: SPCK, 1949), 45.

26   *ibid.* 47.

27   *ibid.* 48.

28   David Novarr, *The Making of Walton's "Lives"* (New York: Cornell University Press, 1958), 222.

29   C. J. Sisson, *The Judicious Marriage of Mr. Hooker and the Birth of "The Laws of Ecclesiastical Polity"* (Cambridge: Cambridge University Press, 1940), x-xi.

picture of Hooker.[30] Walton is exceedingly preoccupied to portray Hooker as a child-like English divine, a sort of an abstract-minded and gentle-hearted human being, who elegantly dismisses any controversy, and blissfully confutes his opponents. Walton's *Life* is prone to a boastful description of the High Church, and an obvious negativistic understanding of Puritan theology and practice.[31] In spite of his lack of objectivity, Walton made some useful corrections to Gauden's *Life of Hooker*. Even if these corrections seem theologically insignificant, they are historically vital for a proper understanding of Hooker. Accordingly, Walton corrected Gauden's picture of Hooker's mediocrity in college, he strongly defended Hooker's last three books (he actually attempted to provide a reasonable High Church perspective over the theological ambiguity of these books), and he lastly stated Hooker's position from a High Church standpoint.[32] Even if Walton's *Lives* had been the standard historical description of Hooker's life and work for over three centuries, it was becoming increasingly criticised by the beginning of the twentieth century,[33] until it was definitively replaced by David Novarr's book, which became the authorized *Life* of Hooker.[34]

J. H. Parker describes the historical conflict of late sixteenth century England and tries to place Hooker within it, by explicitly stressing the

---

30 Izaak Walton, *The Lives of Dr. John Donne, Sir Henry Wotton, Mr. Richard Hooker, Mr. George Herbert, and Dr. Robert Sanderson* (London: 1825). The first edition was published in 1664.

31 Even if Walton himself admits that among the Puritans, whom he calls nonconformists, there might be some people of good intentions, the rest are "possessed with a high degree of spiritual wickedness" or "with an innate restless pride and malice." Walton, *The Lives*, 192.

32 Novarr, *The Making of Walton's "Lives"*, 226. For a totally different view, I am indebted to Professor Diarmaid MacCulloch, who strongly disagrees with Novarr. For instance, in a discussion we had on the 5th February 2001, Professor MacCulloch said that Gauden, for all his faults, had a more accurate vision of Hooker than Walton. As far as Walton is concerned, in Professor MacCulloch's opinion, it is a mistake to say that Walton strongly defended the last three books of Hooker's, because, on the contrary, Walton made every effort to cast doubt on their reliability in their existing form.

33 Cf. Richard Hooker, *Of the Laws of the Ecclesiastical Polity*, vol. I-II (Books I-IV), Introduction by Christopher Morris (London: J. M. Dent & Sons Ltd, 1907). Christopher Morris is not particularly enthusiastic about Walton's work, which he describes as "unreliable gossip" that "generally moulded his subjects to fit a ready-made pattern" (vi). Neither is Douglas Bush very sympathetic to Walton. He considers that Hooker's life described by Walton is the result of error and prejudice. Walton is also charged "with excessive idealization and with recreating five different men", among whom one is Hooker. Cf. Douglas Bush, *English Literature in the Early Seventeenth Century 1600-1660* (Oxford: Clarendon Press, 1952), 223-224.

34 Novarr, *The Making of Walton's "Lives"*.

divine working in having Hooker as protector of Anglican theology. Parker's preface to some *Selections from the Fifth Book of Hooker's "Ecclesiastical Polity"* is very simplistic in description and it offers a devotional argument rather than a historical one for Hooker's theological activity. Parker also provides us with a firm Anglican position that evidently reflects a certain fear of Calvinism. Actually, Parker writes of the danger of a turning towards Calvinism. According to Parker, if it were not for Hooker, "we might have been where Geneva and Holland are now."[35] Another important statement of Parker will be taken over and used as a theological foundation for the essential interpretation of Hooker. This position infers the fact that Hooker took the "good and middle way", obviously in response to the so-called "extreme" positions of both Calvinism and Roman-Catholicism.

1.1.2 The Political Perspective

The political perspective within the traditional view of Hooker's thought is primarily focused on a specifically political reading of Hooker's entire theology. This political reading is either applied to the whole of Hooker's system or it depicts certain areas of it, mainly his view of the Church and of Church government, the relation between Church and state, and the theory of a Christian society. Again, the perspective is neither analytical nor critical, but rather descriptive or even apologetic. The theologians that upheld this political reading wanted to justify Hooker's views within their original historical context and advance them as prescriptive for the contemporary religious settlement.

The Whig interpretation of Hooker promotes both a radical and a moderate Erastian position. Bishop Benjamin Hoadley, a supporter of the radical Erastian interpretation, suggests that, according to Hooker, the Church is entirely a human institution which should be organised by the state. The moderate Erastian interpretation, promoted by Bishop William Warburton, is based on the presupposition that Church and state are fundamentally separate. However, an alliance is permitted between the Church and the state, although the state is not allowed to control the temporal affairs of the Church. Warburton criticised Hooker, who says that the Church and the state are one and the same society. Warburton was convinced that the state is an entirely secular

---

35   J. H. Parker, *Selections from the Fifth Book of Hooker's "Ecclesiastical Polity"* (Oxford: 1839), vii.

institution, and criticises Hooker who claimed that the state, like the Church, is an instrument of the divine will, and the goal of the state is identical to the goal of the Church. The Whigs strongly opposed the Tory party, which upheld a hierarchical conception of society, within which the king was appointed by divine right. Such an interpretation makes the Church subordinate to the state and to the decision of the king. Thus, royal supremacy is the authority which coordinates even the life of the Church.[36]

W. E. H. Lecky's stated intention is to talk about Hooker as a political thinker.[37] According to Lecky, Hooker is "the ablest [divine] that Protestantism has ever produced." Moreover, Hooker's works are featured by a "splendid eloquence", "a tendency to elevate the principles of natural light", and a "desire to make the Church independent from the state."[38] Lecky briefly describes Hooker's *Lawes* as having two main aspects. Firstly, the *Lawes* examine the origins and functions of government, and secondly, they explain the way government normally functions. As far as the first aspect is concerned, Lecky notices that Hooker hardly ever appeals to the Church Fathers or Scripture, and uses his own reason to elaborate his argument. Regarding the second aspect, Lecky enumerates briefly some basic ideas, which Hooker displayed in his argument, and which form his fundamental view of civil government.[39] According to Lecky, Hooker is an exponent of modern liberalism (politically, not theologically). It was Hooker who came up with the idea that the power of the government should be greatly restricted. The government he points to should be constitutional

---

36 For details about the Whig and Tory interpretation of Hooker, see John Gascoigne, "The Unity of Church and State Challenged: Responses to Hooker from the Restauration to the Nineteenth-Century Age of Reform", *The Journal of Religious History* 21/1 (1997), 63-66, and Robert Eccleshall, "Richard Hooker and the Peculiarities of English: The Reception of the *Ecclesiastical Polity* in the Seventeenth and Eighteenth Centuries", in *History of Political Thought* II/1 (1981), 95-101.

37 W. E. H., Lecky, *History of the Rise and Influence of the Spirit of Rationalism in Europe*, vol. II (London: 1865), 198.

38 *ibid*. 198.

39 Lecky starts by noticing that, according to Hooker, individuals in a society created kings to govern them. In the beginning, royal power was absolute, which caused misery for all people. Individuals then created laws so that everybody should observe his own duty. The king receives his authority from people, but this does not mean that the office of the king is less sacred; on the contrary, it is sacred because everything men do, they do according to the divine right. At the same time, the king is subject to the law, and must conform to it, as the power of enacting laws belong to the people. Finally, tyranny appears when the king tries to enact all laws for his own purposes; thus invalidating all laws. See *ibid*. 199.

(and this is a direct reference to the king's office), as this political system is superior to despotism.[40]

Though primarily concerned with examining Hooker as the first great systematic English theologian, Alfred Barry nevertheless extensively describes the principles of the Elizabethan settlement, which places him within the political perspective to Hooker, rather than within the theological perspective.[41] According to Barry, Hooker's political thinking has three main goals. Firstly, Hooker's goal is to criticise Presbyterian government, even if the attack is directed more against Rome, not against Geneva. In this context, Hooker writes about Church discipline, confession, and absolution. The auricular confession and private absolution are not a sacrament of penance. Secondly, Hooker's goal is to defend Episcopalian government. The promises and blessings of the Church belong to it as a whole. No rule of Church polity is described in the Holy Scripture. Accordingly, the Church has the power to determine its own polity of government. From the very beginning, the polity of Church government has been Episcopalian. Episcopalian government is divinely instituted, as bishops are invested with power from above. Thirdly, Hooker's goal is to define the right function of royal supremacy. The Church and state are not two separate bodies, they are coextensive. The member of the commonwealth is necessarily a member of the Church and vice-versa. Both in Church and state, royal supremacy is a constitutional authority. All laws of the Church must be passed by the whole society (the clergy in the Convocation, and the laity in the Parliament). The crown must express its assent to both clergy and laity.[42]

Christopher Morris has a manifold interest in Hooker, but for the time being it is his political considerations regarding Hooker's thought that should be at issue.[43] Morris primarily notices that Hooker "had a strong sense of historical development",[44] an idea that is crucially

---

40 *ibid.* 200-201.
41 See Alfred Barry, *Masters of English Theology* (London: 1877), 22-46. However, Barry is also interested in Hooker's theology. Main theological themes tackled by Barry: the doctrine of laws in the Church, the doctrine of the harmony of the natural and of the supernatural in truth and grace, the epistemology (the doctrine of the knowledge of God), the theological distinction between transitory and permanent in the Holy Scripture, worship in the Church of England, and the doctrine of the sacraments.
42 *ibid.* 47-57.
43 One can easily notice that, beside his political interest, Christopher Morris discusses Hooker both theologically and literally. See Richard Hooker, *Of the Laws of the Ecclesiastical Polity*, vol. I-II (Books I-IV), Introduction by Christopher Morris (London: J. M. Dent & Sons LTD, 1907), vii-ix.
44 *ibid.* ix.

important for his political system. This means that Hooker respected the past and tried to establish a way to reform the changeable things in the Church, the so-called "things indifferent." Morris remarks that there is a need of a Sovereign in Hooker's theology. This necessity of a Sovereign derives out of the possible rise of anarchy in any given society. Hooker supported and developed the idea of a constitutional monarchy that must accept the rule of law. This proves to be utterly important, because the king or the queen has his or her power by law.[45] In his attempt to counter the ecclesiology of the Puritans, Hooker opposed their vision of the Church as a "gathered Church" of the elect. This is definitely an important ecclesiological view, because such a definition of the Church separates Church and state in two different directions, but for Hooker, it was vital that the Church and state should be the same. According to Hooker, the membership in the commonwealth is the same as the membership in the Church. Then king and Parliament are representative for both state and Church.[46] Morris remarked that Hooker had tried to reconcile Protestant theology with the tradition of natural law (this can be traced back to the Catholic scholasticism and to the Stoic philosophy). According to Morris, Hooker accepted the Reformation and retained some Renaissance beliefs, such as the confidence in human reason.[47]

Francis Paget is another theologian whose interest in Hooker is manifold, but his political view of Hooker is representative for the whole scholarship in this field.[48] According to Paget, Hooker investigates the political and religious situation in England, namely that many people accepted the Puritan religion, together with its system of discipline. Hooker sketches two main reasons for this situation. Firstly, the understanding of the controversy between the Anglican and the Puritan Churches requires a special training and knowledge, so many uninformed people fell prey to the Puritan position. Secondly, the method used by the Puritans to convince the multitudes does not give credit to their final conviction. Hooker's opinion is that the Puritans informed the people of the mistakes and faults existing in England, and all these mistakes and faults were attributed to political and Church government. Accordingly, the

---

45 ibid. x.

46 ibid. xi.

47 Richard Hooker, *Of the Laws of the Ecclesiastical Polity*, vol. I-II (Books I-IV), Introduction by Christopher Morris (London: J. M. Dent & Sons LTD, 1907), xii.

48 Beside the political theory of Hooker, Paget's concern also encompasses the theology of the English reformer. See Francis Paget, *An Introduction to the Fifth Book of Hooker's Treatise of the Laws of Ecclesiastical Polity* (Oxford: Clarendon Press, 1907), 119-122.

Puritans held that Church discipline was thought to be the only help against these evils. Ultimately, from the Puritan perspective, English men and women were deeply persuaded that resisting the Puritan system of Church discipline meant resisting the will of God.[49] At a political level and from the Anglican perspective, resisting the Puritan system of Church discipline would have meant adherence to the specifically Anglican Church government and to the English political settlement. Again, politically the fundamental principle of Hooker's treatise is that societies have the right to impose and enforce laws on the individual (by means of the Convocation and the Parliament, and with the approval of the king or queen). Nevertheless, Paget draws attention to the fact that this right is limited and cannot overcome express revelation and demonstrative proof.[50]

1.1.3 The Theological Perspective

The theological perspective within the traditional view of Hooker's thought is probably the most important. Although evidently biased and appreciative of Hooker, the theological perspective nonetheless offers important insights into Hooker's entire system of thought. The most important issues of the theological perspective are the doctrine of episcopacy, the doctrine of Scripture, the doctrine of salvation (with special reference to justification and sanctification), the doctrine of authority, and the doctrine of the sacraments (especially the Eucharist). As all perspectives within the traditional view, the theological one is not highly critical or analytical, but its main feature is the description of Hooker's theology so that it might be easier to be read and understood. A basic characteristic of the theological perspective is the attempt to ascribe Hooker's theology to the wider dogmatic framework of the Church of England.

The name of Richard Hooker is linked inextricably to the Oxford Movement. The most prominent theologian of the Oxford Movement who showed an obvious interest in the works of Richard Hooker was John Keble. Theologically, his most important characteristic is the attempt to accommodate Hooker's theology to the High Church claims. Keble was a High Church clergyman of the Oxford Movement and he earnestly tried to describe Hooker's theology so that it might appear totally Anglican, or at least dogmatically closer to the English Church

---

49   *ibid.* 117-119.
50   *ibid.* 122.

than to the Calvinist doctrine.[51] Keble's methodological enterprise was a diligent attempt, but it did not produce the expected results as later scholarship plainly contends.[52] Keble is primarily interested in the doctrine of the divine origin of episcopacy, in the doctrine of the Eucharist, and in the doctrine of salvation. He does not hesitate to say that Hooker belongs to "the same school of ecclesiastical opinions" that say that "episcopacy grounded on apostolical succession was of supernatural origin and divine authority, whatever else was right or wrong."[53] Keble explains that in Hooker's theology the Eucharist is based on the incarnation of the Son of God.[54] Accordingly, Hooker

---

51 On the relationship between Hooker and Calvin, Keble is very pessimistic: "He [i.e. Hooker] saw in Calvin a disposition to treat irreverently, not only the creeds, the sacred guards provided by the Church for Christian Truth, but also that holiest Truth itself, in some of his articles." John Keble, *The Works of that Learned and Judicious Divine, Mr. Richard Hooker, with an Account of his Life and Death by Izaak Walton*, vol. I-III (Oxford: Oxford University Press, 1836), lxxviii.

52 "John Keble has been at great pains to prove that he defended the divine origin of Episcopacy, in opposition to the claim of Cartwright for the divine origin of the Presbytery. That Keble has succeeded none will admit but those who are of Keble's party." Cf. John Hunt, *Religious Thought in England from the Reformation to the End of Last Century. A Contribution to the History of Theology*, vol. I (London: Strahan & Co. Publishers, 1870), 57. For further details, cf. Alfred Barry, *Masters in English Theology* (London: 1877), 4; Novarr, *The Making of Walton's "Lives"*, 215; Stanley Archer, "Hooker on the Apostolic Succession: The Two Voices", *The Sixteenth Century Journal* XXIV/1 (1993), 73; Atkinson, *Richard Hooker and the Authority of Scripture, Tradition, and Reason*, xii-xv.

53 Keble, *The Works*, lxxv.

54 Another theologian who is concerned with Hooker's doctrine of the Eucharist is Darwell Stone. There are some key aspects of the Eucharist that Stone identified in Hooker. Firstly, Hooker rejects transubstantiation. He does not say whether or not the body and blood of Christ are present in the elements of the Eucharist or whether or not they are only communicated to those who receive the sacrament. Anyway, affirming or denying transubstantiation is not important for Hooker. What is important is that the elements of the Eucharist are the body and blood of Christ to the recipient. Secondly, regarding the real presence of Christ in the Eucharist, this should not be sought in the sacrament itself, but in the recipient. The real presence of Christ is described in terms of the participation of the body and blood of Christ, which is the true fruit of the Eucharist. Thirdly, the importance of the Eucharist is due to the true and real participation of Christ, who imparts Himself as mystical head to all the recipients, and who gives the Holy Spirit to all the Christians that are united with him for their sanctification. Fourthly, Stone notices that in Hooker the Eucharist has a sacrificial aspect, although Hooker repeatedly claims that there is no sacrifice in the ministry of the Church. Nevertheless, this sacrificial aspect is not a reference to a real sacrifice, but to a sacrifice of thanksgiving. However, this sacrifice of thanksgiving is of the same importance as the ancient sacrifices of the Mosaic Law. For the whole discussion on the Eucharist, see Darwell Stone, *A History of the Doctrine of the Holy Eucharist*, vol. I-II (London: Longmans and Co., 1909), 239-247.

upholds the ubiquity of Christ's glorified body in the elements of the Lord's Supper, which sounds more Lutheran than Calvinist. He also agrees with the real presence of Christ's body at the Eucharist.[55] Concerning soteriology, Keble has Hooker distinguishing *in re* between justification and sanctification, when in reality, *in tempore*, the two processes cannot be separated, for they take place simultaneously. Furthermore, Hooker uses the phrase "imputed righteousness" and employs a dual hermeneutic, arguing that Paul speaks more of the righteousness of justification while James the righteousness of sanctification.[56] Finally, Keble notices that English theology was greatly influenced by Hooker: "...the gradual but decisive change which English theology underwent in the hands of Hooker."[57]

The theologians of the Oxford Movement claimed that the state had abandoned its traditional function of being the Church's protector. The Church must, therefore, reaffirm its autonomy and break all ties with the state. As the Oxford Movement was essentially anti-Erastian,[58] Keble insisted that the English state promoted liberalism which was hostile to the true religion of the Church. Thus, Keble supports the Episcopal government of the Church and uses Hooker to prove his ideas. Keble notices that Hooker did not highlight the importance of bishops because he gave too much power to the monarch as fundamental representative of the union between the Church and the state. It is evident that the monarch represents the whole Church and overrules even the authority of the Apostles of Christ. Though this position is thoroughly Erastian, Keble tries to accommodate Hooker to his own theology and explains that there were not fundamental differences between Hooker's view and his own. He argued that Hooker ascribed such a great power to the monarch only because he had believed in the complete communion between the Church and state. Based on Hooker's thought, Keble himself was not entirely determined to say that the Church should divorce the state.

Unlike Keble, his follower, Hurrel Froude, plainly said that the Church should separate from the increasing liberal state. Thus, he openly admits that he disagrees with Hooker and urges the clergy to take on a more visible role. Froude regarded the Anglican tradition as being too submissive to the state; the Church should separate from the

---

55   Keble, *The Works*, lxxx.

56   *ibid.* xcviii-xcix.

57   *ibid.* ciii.

58   Peter Nockles, "The Oxford Movement: Historical Background 1780-1833", in Rowell, Geoffrey (ed.), *Tradition Renewed. The Oxford Movement Conference Papers* (London: Darton, Longman and Todd, 1986), 24-50.

state and assert its individual identity. John Henry Newman had an even more radical perspective. He suggested that one should abandon the Church of England, which is irremediably embedded with Erastianism, and turn to the Catholic Church of Rome. Less combative, Eduard Bouverie Pusey promoted the idea that the union between Church and state might be revigorated if the power of Parliament were to diminish and the power of the monarch to increase; the monarch, however, must be a Christian.[59]

For Hooker, the Church was more than the clergy: Hooker intended to make reference to the Church in its spiritual aspect, the English people at prayer. Thus the civil magistrate could exercise authority in the Church as truly as any bishop. Hooker stated that the Church has the right to choose its own form of government (namely, non-Episcopalian Churches are true Churches) but he also said that the Holy Spirit instituted bishops. The logical inference (which Hooker did not have in mind) is that the Church has no power to change what God had ordained. No human legislation can, in any way, change what God had decreed by his divine law. In this respect, the theologians of the Oxford Movement believed Hooker's doctrine should be revised because, according to Hooker's teachings, "the Church Establishment looked less like an eternal embodiment of divine law than a historical compromise which was now being swept away."[60] However, the Church has its own authority given by Christ's commission to the apostles, the very source of the apostolic succession. The civil power does not have any jurisdiction over the Church. In the end, concerning the doctrine of salvation in particular, it should be mentioned that the theologians of the Oxford Movement conceded that Hooker's sermon on justification was not in line with their own teaching.[61]

John Hunt investigated the theological foundation of Hooker's doctrine of the Church. According to Hunt, the basic ecclesiological principle in Hooker is that the Church must be free from state, because the polity of the Church must be free. Another important idea in Hooker ecclesiology is that the rites and ceremonies of the Church must be observed, even though they might be corrupted. Nevertheless, the order established in the Church is an expression of divine order.

---

59   For details, see Gascoigne, "The Unity of Church and State Challenged: Responses to Hooker from the Restoration to the Nineteenth-Century Age of Reform", 72-75.

60   S. W. Sykes, and S. W. Gilley, "'No Bishop, No Church!' The Tractarian Impact on Anglicanism", Geoffrey Rowell (ed.), *Tradition Renewed. The Oxford Movement Conference Papers* (London: Darton, Longman and Todd, 1986), 123-125.

61   Peter B. Nockles, *The Oxford Movement in Context. Anglican High Churchmanship, 1760-1857* (Cambridge: Cambridge University Press, 1994), 257.

Accordingly, episcopacy is an ancient way of governing the Church. By contrast, presbytery is a modern way of governing the Church. In this context, both ways of Church polity seem to coexist, and Hooker is not a fierce advocate of uniformity, according to Hunt.[62] However, should Hooker adhere to episcopacy, which he did, it was because of his belief that he was faithful to the ancient Church order that was divine and rational. In this respect, Hooker's natural theology is at issue, as he advocated the natural light, but not to the detriment of Scripture. The use of reason has its limits, because it is firstly the supernatural light that presupposes the natural – a fundamental idea in Hooker's theology.[63]

It has been already noted twice that Morris has a manifold interest in Hooker's theology. I mention him again because his reading of Hooker is performed both politically and literally, on the one hand, and theologically, on the other hand, as it shall be proved next. Morris' theological reading of Hooker encompasses mainly the doctrine of the Church. According to Morris, Hooker earnestly tackles some essentials of Anglicanism. Firstly, the Church of England continued many practices of the Roman Church that were not found in the Holy Scripture. From this perspective, and according to the Gospel of Christ – but not to the doctrine and tradition of the Church – the word "presbyter" was more relevant than the word "priest." Episcopacy is a custom established by the Church, and it may be changed should it be proved not to work. Nevertheless, all the above-mentioned things are "indifferent" and therefore they do not affect the salvation of human souls as the essentials of Christianity always do. In Hooker's opinion, it was desirable to follow all these things indifferent according to the Church

---

62   Hunt, *Religious Thought in England*, 60.

63   This principle of Hooker's theology is extended to his doctrine of Scripture. According to Hunt, in Hooker's theology, Scripture enlightens reason, which means reason is effective, but needs assistance from Scripture. Thus reason is a valid theological method, but it must be used within certain limits and we should always take into account the fact that Scripture helps reason, not vice-versa. Although Hooker defends reason and the light of nature, it is characteristic of his theology to maintain that God has not given men such a natural reason that could lead *per se* to the knowledge of salvation. It is only the light of Scripture that informs us about salvation. The ultimate truth can be found only by means of supernatural revelation, namely Scripture. Reason and the light of nature teaches us our duty, but is unable to teach us anything about salvation. On the other hand, according to Hooker, we know that Scripture is the Word of God by reason. Thus epistemologically and in strictly human terms, reason is the first, and Scripture is the second. There is no Gospel without reason. In this respect, the first outward reason to believe Scripture is the authority of the Church. For further information on Hunt's interpretation of Hooker, see *ibid.* 60.

tradition, authority and reason. Obviously, the Puritans did not appro-
ve of this argument, and Hooker tried to offer a basic response. Firstly,
we should not rely on Scripture alone. Beside Scripture, there are other
means of knowledge and of discovering God's law and will. Unless
these means of knowledge contradict reason, they should be used in
the theological enterprise. Reason was given by God to help at a better
understanding of his revelation. This is the reason why some of the
Church practices have been kept through history, namely because they
conformed to reason.[64]

Having identified a political reading of Hooker in Paget's work, as
already mentioned, his theological reading of Hooker approaches the
question of authority in theology with special reference to Church
discipline. Regarding the authority of Scripture, Paget argues that
Hooker's position is not very well developed and it consists of saying
that the Holy Scripture does not contain any information on a certain
prescribed polity of Church discipline. Therefore, according to Hooker,
is it curious why some adopted it as if it were of divine origin.
Regarding the authority of the primitive Church, Hooker contends that
the Puritans returned to apostolic authority without any trust in the
doctrine of the Church that followed the apostolic times. Historically,
however, the appeal to apostolic practice and Church government is
futile, because the knowledge of those times is partial and thus
imperfect. Accordingly, the return to apostolic time in terms of any
given practical matter is an attempt that ultimately becomes theologically futile. Hooker's conclusion is that the practice of the apostolic
time cannot be applied to contemporary issues, because the historical
context has changed. Regarding the authority of contemporary
theologians, Hooker is not particularly interested in defending his
position by using their arguments. One of the theologians that Hooker
frequently cited was Calvin, whose idea of Church discipline was
accepted – at least according to Hooker – because his theology gained
the sympathy of many people.[65]

For L. S. Thornton, Hooker was not an Erastian because he believed
in a divinely-appointed ministry.[66] Within Hooker's general theology,
the doctrine of the incarnation is of fundamental importance because
Christ inaugurates a new type of humanity. Regarding Hooker's soteri-

64 For further details, see Richard Hooker, *Of the Laws of the Ecclesiastical Polity*, vol. I-II
    (Books I-IV), Introduction by Christopher Morris (London: J. M. Dent & Sons LTD,
    1907), viii ff.

65 Paget, *An Introduction to the Fifth Book of Hooker's Treatise of the Laws of Ecclesiastical
    Polity* (Oxford: Clarendon Press, 1907), 119-120.

66 L. S. Thornton, *Richard Hooker. A Study of his Theology* (London: SPCK, 1924), 91.

ology, the guarantee for the union of Christ with the believer is brought about through the crucial role that faith plays and also the hypostatic union between humanity and divinity in Christ.[67] Thornton believes that Hooker took great care in seeing the work of Christ in terms of his role as mediator, a role that stresses the union that exists between Christ and the justified believer. Thornton claims that Hooker grounds salvation in the person and work of Christ, but even though God takes the initiative in man's salvation, man must still display a rational faith or a faith that informs his reading of Scripture.[68] Even though the justified believer shares a union with Christ, the nature of neither the believer nor Christ changes. Christ remains God, eternal and unchanging, while man remains a human being.[69]

1.1.4 The Literary Perspective

The literary perspective within the traditional view of Hooker's thought makes particular reference to the style of Hooker's entire work. It is within this specific framework that Hooker's books and treatises are regarded as an utterly significant part of the English Church literature, and generally as a part of the whole of English literature. The literary perspective takes into discussion the literary style and the literary devices of Hooker's work. The theologians that took this approach are very sympathetic to and appreciative of Hooker's contribution to the development of English literature overall.

Thus, Benjamin Kennicott's book is a summary and a commentary of Hooker's Fifth Book of the *Lawes*. He does not display a particular bias towards a literary discussion of Hooker's work, but shows none-theless some brief general remarks concerning the entire *corpus* of Hooker's books. According to Kennicott, the author of the *Lawes* is "learned", and "the subjects of the books are amply discussed." In addition, "the nature of the subjects is profound", and the books are deemed to be "a celebrated defence of the Church of England."[70] Kennicott holds the opinion that Hooker's work is characterized by "deep and solid reasoning", "important arguments", "perspicuity and force", and a "spirit of exalted piety". As far as the language is concerned, this is "pure, solemn, and energetic". Moreover, it contains

---

67   *ibid.* 54-61.

68   *ibid.* 26.

69   *ibid.* 66-67.

70   Benjamin Kennicott, *An Analysis of Hooker's Ecclesiastical Polity being a Particular Defence of the Church of England* (London: 1819), iii.

the "seeds of eternity", and it "will live till the last fire shall consume all learning."[71]

Richard Cattermole manifested a specific interest in Hooker as literary writer. Cattermole holds the opinion that Hooker's books and treatises form a "great theological work, of a highly literary character in our language."[72] Cattermole is also very appreciative of Hooker because, from a strictly literary viewpoint, the English reformers did not have a distinguished literary style before the reign of Elizabeth.[73] As far as Cattermole is concerned, Hooker overcame Bacon in literary skill: "The style of Hooker is richer, more uniformly sustained, more homogenous than Bacon's, more nearly the best English of all periods." And again, "his vast learning is more thoroughly fused, and more effectively taken up by the force of his own genius."[74] As Cattermole is interested in Hooker's works as English Church literature, but English literature nonetheless, he notices some important aspects. Firstly, the spirit of the age required authoritative quotations from ancient sources, but Hooker seldom quotes such authorities. Secondly, Hooker's work reflects a patristic bias. Thirdly, one essential mark of Hooker's work is the use of reason.[75] However, the last three books of Hooker bear the mark of inferiority compared to the first five. Cattermole is obviously influenced by the traditional view of Hooker's "unhappy marriage", so he blames Hooker's wife for the lower literary craftsmanship of the last three books.[76]

Contrary to the trend of his contemporary scholarship, George Philip Krapp is not interested in discussing Hooker form the standpoint of theology or philosophy. According to Krapp, Hooker's work has the characteristics of the Elizabethan epoch: firstly, it is a work with largeness of conception and of execution, and secondly, it is a work "of the age of giants, worthy of its place in the rank with the writings of

---

71 *ibid*. iv.

72 Richard Cattermole, *The Literature of the Church of England Indicated in the Selections from the Writings of Eminent Divines: With Memoirs of Their Lives, and Historical Sketches of the Times in Which They Lived*, vol. I-II (London: 1844).

73 *ibid*. 1. According to Cattermole, it was only Archbishop Parker and Bishop Jewell that qualified as "literary craftsmen" during the reign of Elizabeth I.

74 *ibid*. 22.

75 "Majestic, but not unfamiliar, calmly pouring out the light of reason, but often touched with that imaginative colouring which, in men on genius, is the natural utterance of reason." *ibid*. 22.

76 "They were destroyed, through the stupidity and connivance of his wife, shortly after his decease." *ibid*. 23.

Bacon, Shakespeare, and other great Elizabethans."[77] It is distinguished of Hooker that his technique of style is to be commended, and that he wrote his entire work in order to be understood by the average English mind. Krapp advanced a rather peculiar opinion regarding Hooker's work as literary enterprise, as he noted that "Hooker was consciously and intentionally literary."[78] The dignity of his style may also be found in other major ancient writers like Aristotle, Cicero, Chrysostom, Augustine, and Aquinas. Hooker wrote in the "epigrammatic and aphoristic brevity of Bacon," and mainly worked with concepts, not with images. This is one of the reasons why his work is so difficult to read and understand.[79] Krapp's approach to Hooker's work is important because it explains many characteristics of Hooker's style, which are of Latin origin. Hooker's English topic very much resembles of the Latin topic, and many literary devices are the actual translation of Latin formulae.[80] Krapp finds a reasonable excuse for Hooker, and writes that he "was not following a model of English style, but constructing one," even if he does not coin new words according to the normal practice of the day.[81] On the contrary, Hooker accepted the English language of the day, and used the then existing literary resources in order to obtain the best possible result.[82]

As mentioned before, Morris has a multiple interest in Hooker which extends to the literary aspect of the latter's work.[83] In his introduction to one of Hooker's editions of the *Lawes*,[84] Morris makes a brief description of Hooker's style, and openly appreciates his work: "He did as much perhaps for English prose as he did for the Anglican

---

77 George Philip Krapp, *The Rise of English Literary Prose* (New York: Oxford University Press, 1915), 142.

78 *ibid.* 145.

79 *ibid.* 145.

80 Some literary devices of Latin origin used by Hooker: the omission of the verb or of all verbs, except the past participle; the separation of the verb and the past participle, and the placing of the latter at the end of the sentence or clause; the predicate nominative precedes the governing word; an adjective or substantive is placed at the end of the sentence; the adjective follows the noun it modifies. For detailed examples regarding these literary devices, see Krapp, *The Rise of English Literary Prose*, 146-147. For the influence of Latin grammar in Hooker's works, see Vickers, Brian, "Hooker's Prose Style", in Richard Hooker, *Of the Laws of the Ecclesiastical Polity*, A. S. McGrade and Brian Vickers eds. (London: Sidgwick and Jackson, 1975), 41-59.

81 Krapp, *The Rise of English Literary Prose*, 148.

82 *ibid.* 149-150.

83 Morris' manifold interest in Hooker consists of the fact that he reads Hooker politically, literally, and theologically.

84 Richard Hooker, *Of the Laws of the Ecclesiastical Polity*, vol. I-II (Books I-IV), Introduction by Christopher Morris (London: J. M. Dent & Sons LTD, 1907).

religion and for political philosophy."[85] According to Morris, Hooker never lost control of sentences and of argument. Having a remarkable bias for cadence, Hooker uses emphatic devices that underline the main ideas of his statements. Hooker's style is melodious, his discourse is urbane, and is characterized by a delicate irony.[86]

To conclude, the traditional view of Hooker's thought has four main perspectives that shape the classical image of Hooker's life and work. Even if these four perspectives are not primarily analytical or critical, the resulting descriptive methodology covers a wide range of important aspects of Hooker's entire work. The historical perspective tackles the biography and bibliography of Hooker, as it is especially focused on personal facts and the development of his work within the historical context of the age. The historiographical writings that pertain to this perspective are neither highly academic, nor altogether historically accurate, but they still offer valuable information on Hooker's life and work. The political perspective encompasses specific issues to do with public life in the Elizabethan period. Matters of Church government, the relation between Church and state, English society as Christian society, and royal supremacy are all aspects of Hooker's political thought. The main idea that takes shape after a careful consideration of the political perspective on the traditional view of Hooker is that the English theologian was a Renaissance man, a forerunner of political liberalism, rather than an insightful successor of scholastic theology. The theological perspective encompasses certain issues that are obviously part of Hooker's theological system. One might argue that polity and theology are interwoven in Hooker, but ultimately they are distinct parts of his thought. The divine origin of episcopacy, the authority of Scripture, the mystery of the sacraments, the real presence of Christ in the Eucharist, the righteousness of justification and sanctification, the general question of authority, and the profoundly human character of Church discipline are all theologically different from any other major aspect of Hooker's thought. The literary perspective is somehow unexpectedly present within the larger framework of the discussions regarding Hooker's thinking, because it investigates his works not as being particularly a part of English theological literature, but as being a specific part of the whole of English literature. The literary inquiry over Hooker's works makes reference to the style and literary devices used in the composition of Hooker's prose as revelatory for his exquisite linguistic

---

85   *ibid*. vii.
86   *ibid*. vii-viii.

training, especially in Latin. It was this traditional view that shaped
Hooker scholarship till almost the second half of the twentieth century.
In spite of its powerful image of Hooker, the traditional view finally
gave up in the face of the serious analytical research that emerged as an
earnest reassessment of Hooker's entire thought.

1.2 The Modern View

In the last two decades of the first half of the twentieth century, the
traditional view of Hooker underwent a sudden challenge, and a
modern, specifically analytical trend in Hooker scholarship appeared.
The novelty of the modern view of Hooker's thought consists of
questioning the very authorities that established the traditional view of
Hooker. Even if it only lasted for just under forty years (namely until
the early 1970s), the modern view of Hooker's thought shook the very
foundation that the previous scholarship had laid over more than three
hundred years. The modern analytical view is not only descriptive, but
also prone to further investigation in all areas of Hooker scholarship.
More or less sympathetic to Hooker's person and work, the modern
view was methodically built by theologians that were not highly critical
of Hooker's motivations in writing his work. Nevertheless the earnest
character of their research reflects an objective desire to display
Hooker's thinking, especially as a representative part of human invest-
tigation.

The modern view of Hooker's thought mainly encompasses a
reassessment of the traditional view in almost all its major approaches:
historical, political, and theological. The traditional literary perspective
has not been challenged, which might confirm the efficiency of some
older theological and literary investigations. Nevertheless, a new
perspective comes at this stage and it analyses the philosophical aspect
of Hooker's thought.

1.2.1 The Historical Perspective

The historical perspective within the analytical view of Hooker's
thought reassesses the traditional view by means of solid historical
research and of new documentary sources. The modern historical
perspective is backed up by new material regarding both the biography
and the bibliography of Hooker, and it represents a correction of the

traditional historical perspective. Old data must give way to new evidence and over more than forty years a more reliable and trust-worthy image of Hooker has emerged, in the light of newly discovered historical documents.

C. J. Sisson's work is the first radical reassessment of the traditional view of Hooker. Sisson is interested not merely in discussing Hooker, but he carefully investigates the history of the biography and bibliography of Hooker. This was clearly a difficult task, as he had to dismiss many of Walton's claims that laid the basis for a firmly history-rooted view of Hooker. Even though he was working with new valid documentary sources found in the Court of Chancery (the so-called Chancery records), Sisson tried to keep the fragile balance between the Walton's story, and the new available information. Much of the old information used by Walton was not genuine,[87] argues Sisson, and it was only the Chancery records that could have challenged the traditional picture of Hooker. It was not Walton's fault that his work was inaccurate (unlike Gauden and his books).[88] The Chancery records revealed a totally new picture of Hooker's married life that radically shifted the traditional view of his "unhappy marriage". Thus Sisson traces the history of Hooker's family for many years after his death and investigates the life and actions of most members of Hooker's family.[89] In this respect, the entire analytical investigation of Sisson is based on his deep conviction that Hooker was a man that "loved the truth and pursued it." Moreover, the "beauty of his life" and the "attempt to furnish the truth in important matters" for him was eventually confirmed by all new documentary sources.

Unlike Sission, Peter Munz does not reflect a special interest in Hooker's biography but in Hooker's thought. The actual history of Hooker's life is not the main concern of Munz, who focuses primarily on placing Hooker within the larger framework of the history of thought. In this respect, Munz presents a detailed study of some major

---

87 In the same period of time, Sisson was not alone in challenging the historical accuracy of Walton's *Lives*. Douglas Bush noted that Hooker's life described by Walton is the result of error and prejudice. According to Bush, Walton's High Church informants wanted to discredit the last three books of Hooker, and they did this by inventing the story of Hooker's "unhappy marriage". Discrediting Hooker directly would have been conspicuous, argues Bush, so they thought of destroying the reputation of Hooker's wife. For further details, see Douglas Bush, *English Literature in the Early Seventeenth Century 1600-1660* (Oxford: Clarendon Press, 1952), 223-224.

88 C. J. Sisson, *The Judicious Marriage of Mr. Hooker and the Birth of "The Laws of Ecclesiastical Polity"* (Cambridge: Cambridge University Press, 1940), xi.

89 For further details, see *ibid.* 17-44.

ideological influences that impacted Hooker's thought. Working from the wider perspective of the history of ideas, Munz firstly analyses Hooker's thought under the influence of Thomas Aquinas' reason based methodology. The essence of this discussion is the authority of reason. According to Munz, reason is the only necessary authority is settling the problem of episcopacy. Human reason dictated that bishops be appointed, and it was experience that proved they were needed.[90] Secondly, Munz directs his study towards the influence that Marsilius of Padua had upon Hooker.[91] This touches the relationship between Church and state, which – according to Hooker – are identical within the historical context of late sixteenth century England. The Church is a natural society that needs law for its preservation.[92] Thirdly, Munz discusses the influence of Aristotle upon Hooker. Aristotle's theory of the natural origin of society shaped Hooker's theology, according to which the state is the result of sin, and was instituted by God to appease the worst effects of sin by means of God's perfect law, the only effective instrument against sin.[93]

Using the same analytical methodology, Christopher Morris scrutinises Hooker's thought in order to place it within the history of ideas. According to Morris, Hooker was firstly influenced by Aristotle with his variability of human institutions, man's natural sociability, and the theory of law as disembodied wisdom. Secondly, Hooker was influenced by the Stoic philosophy that upheld man's capacity to discern a universal moral law. Thirdly, another influence in Hooker is Augustine with his theory of man's insufficiency without a government to remedy his sin. Fourthly, Hooker's theology adopted the theory of the harmony between man's natural and supernatural endings. Fifthly, Hooker had a good knowledge of Marsilio of Padua, and he used his theory of the identity of Church and state. Another theory of Marsilio is present in Hooker's theology, namely the community as the ultimate source of law. Sixthly, the Roman law supplied Hooker with the concept of political sovereignty. Seventhly, it was the feudal law that

---

90 Peter Munz, *The Place of Hooker in the History of Thought* (Connecticut: Greenwood Press, 1952), 47-60.

91 Munz identifies a logical flaw in Hooker's argument, because he begins with Aquinas and ends with Marsilius of Padua. Actually, Hooker could not reconcile the political theory of Aquinas with the political reality of Tudor monarchy. Accordingly, he softly changes the logic and adopts Marsilius' arguments that the state is a totally secular institution. For further information, see W. D. J. Cargill Thompson, "The Philosopher of the 'Politic Society'. Richard Hooker as a Political Thinker", in W. Speed Hill, *Studies in Richard Hooker*, 3-76.

92 Munz, *The Place of Hooker in the History of Thought*, 47-61-85.

93 *ibid.* 116.

inspired Hooker to operate with the notions of "contract", and "consent".[94] Morris advances two interesting conclusions regarding Hooker's achievements. The first conclusion is that Hooker maintained the balance between Protestant theology and the tradition of natural law. The second conclusion is that Hooker managed to restore the belief in man and in reason, a belief that – according to Morris – the Protestants had lost.[95]

After Sisson, David Novarr is the second historian who wrote an annotated historical biography of Hooker, based on extensive historical research. Thus he seriously challenged and corrected the traditional historical perspective on Hooker's life and work. His historical investigation is far too detailed to be synthesised merely in some basic ideas, but some main characteristics may be underlined. Firstly, Novarr admits his dependence on Sisson, who had already provided a remarkably new image of Hooker. Secondly, it is quite interesting for Novarr the historian to display a keen theological interest in Hooker. Thus he competently analyses Hooker's views on episcopacy, Church prerogatives, and a constitutionally limited monarchy. In this respect, he remarks that Hooker's approach to these aspects, and especially to kingship, is wholly historical.[96] Thirdly, he has done a tremendous work of historical research, even if his investigation is based – to a rather large extent – on many works of contemporary scholars.[97] Novarr has also made useful inquiries into the works of Hooker's first biographers, Gauden and especially Walton. His extensive commentary on Walton's *Lives* (with special reference to Hooker's *Life*) is very important, as it confirms Sisson's research and offers many other useful historical insights regarding Hooker's life and work.

1.2.2 The Political Perspective

The political perspective within the modern view of Hooker's thought is not radically different from the traditional one, and the areas of investigation encompass the same classic aspects: the theory of the Church, the theory of the state, the relation between Church and state,

---

94 Christopher Morris, *Political Thought in England: Tyndale to Hooker* (London: Oxford University Press, 1953), 196.
95 *ibid.* 195.
96 Novarr, *The Making of Walton's "Lives"*, 212-213.
97 This should not imply that Novarr did not use primary sources. Nevertheless, recent historical and theological scholarship plays an important role in Novarr's historical investigation.

royal supremacy, etc. It is, however, a fresh research study in the field, which is more than merely descriptive in methodology, and rather ambitious in reassessing Hooker's thought in an epoch when the paradigm of interpretation has changed in less then a couple of decades. The modern political perspective on Hooker is more focused, and attempts to "isolate" a specific "political system" within Hooker's thought, primarily to be studied apart from his theology.[98] Unlike the traditional political perspective, the modern political perspective on Hooker's thought tends to be academically sober, allowing little room for more or less sympathetic appreciation of Hooker.

According to George Sabine, Hooker's *Lawes* was intended to refute Puritanism and its criticism of the established Church of England, even if it does not reflect the main characteristics of a controversial treatise. The basic political idea of the *Lawes* is the theory of Church government. Thus, Hooker carefully constructs an examination of the philosophy of law and of government. He considers that Church

---

98   One of the first scholars who considered that Hooker's *Lawes* was important for the history of political thought was W. K. Jordan. According to Jordan, the purpose of the *Lawes* is mainly political, because Hooker wanted to show that the Puritan ideas were in conflict with the political structure of England. Moreover, the Puritans, argued Jordan, denied the claims of political obedience. Jordan further explains that in Hooker, Church and state are distinguishable entities. But in a Christian state, like England of the late sixteenth century, the two entities are one, so the Church and state are both represented in the Parliament. The argument is developed in the direction of royal supremacy, with the king being the representative of both Church and state. Accordingly, subjection to the king means subjection to the Church and vice-versa, so that anyone who rebels against the national Church system must be punished. On the other hand, the state magistrates must be good orthodox Christians, who are in communion with the Church, of which they are the lay governors. When this close relationship is no longer valid, the Church is free to repair this problem without any political interference from the state. the king, however, is the representative of the headship of Christ, but Jordan notices that Hooker has never mentioned to what extent a Christian king has the power to settle the doctrine and discipline in the Church. For further details, see W. K. Jordan, *The Development of Religious Toleration in England from the Beginning of the English Reformation to the Death of Queen Elizabeth* (London: 1932), 222-232. Another scholar who read Hooker theologically was Gottfried Michaelis. His study, although not very large, is an ambitious project, because it tackles a wide range of aspects of Hooker's political thought. For example, Michaelis is firstly interested in the origins of Hooker's political theory. Under this heading, he analyses the theory of law, the theory of the construction of the state (society) together with the theory of the state, the theory of the constitutional state, the theory of state and Church. Michaelis also analyses Hooker's perspective on the state within the context of the sixteenth century. The study ends with Michaelis' examination of Hooker's influence on the political thought of the seventeenth century in England. Gottfried Michaelis, *Richard Hooker als politischer Denker* (Berlin: Verlag Dr. Emil Ebering, 1933).

government is only one aspect of civil society. In Sabine's opinion, the *Lawes* represent the last statement of the medieval tradition concerning the theory of the state. The political aspect of the controversy between Hooker and the Puritans refers to Church polity. The Puritans rejected the polity of the established Church, which meant, in Hooker's view, that they rejected the current political system.[99] According to Sabine, Hooker's political theory is mainly medieval, but it is mixed with nationalism. He reached this conclusion because, in Hooker's thought, the English Church and the English nation are identical in membership. Society in its entirety is simultaneously Church and state, and has both an ecclesiastical and a secular constitution.[100]

Alexandre Passerin D'Entrèves is definitely one of the most important scholars who read Hooker politically.[101] D'Entrèves begins his political analysis of Hooker by offering a definition of law. Hooker's theory of law is dependent on that of Thomas Aquinas, but not identical to it. Generally, the doctrine of natural law leads to the secularisation of politics.[102] This was not the case with Hooker, whose political theory led to the identity between Church and state. According to Hooker, laws are made by politic societies. On the one hand, the civil society issues laws of a civilly joined society, and on the other, the Church issues laws of a spiritually joined society.[103] These two kinds of laws must coexist. Within the Christian community there must be a coincidence of state and Church. For this to last, the state must accept the true religions professed by the Church, and the state must be based on religious uniformity (this does not necessarily entail dogmatic conformity, but strictly external conformity).[104] Nevertheless, the laws of ecclesiastical and civil polity should be conceived rationally (by means of reason, not on the grounds of reason), so that they be

---

99   G. Sabine, *A History of the Political Thought* (London: G.G. Harrap & Co., 1937), 439.

100   *ibid.* 441.

101   Cargill Thompson is right to say that d'Entrèves radically changed the perspective from which Hooker had been seen. D'Entrèves stresses the medieval character of Hooker's thought and claims it is anachronistic to interpret Hooker in terms of Locke and Hooker's theory of natural law in terms of Grotius and of the seventeenth century. See W. D. J. Cargill Thompson, "The Philosopher of the 'Politic Society'. R. Hooker as a Political Thinker", in W. Speed Hill, *Studies in Richard Hooker*, 3-76.

102   d'Entrèves, *The Medieval Contribution to Political Thought* (Oxford: Oxford University Press, 1939), 117-118.

103   *ibid.* 120.

104   *ibid.* 139.

historically convenient.[105] Thus, according to d'Entrèves, Hooker is prone rather to medieval political theory than to classic rationalism.[106]

F. J. Shirley's book is important for the modern political perspective, because he investigates Hooker's theory of the state, and his view of the relationship between Church and state. According to Shirley, the basis of Hooker's theory of the state is Aristotelian. Hooker elaborates his theory of the state out of a real preoccupation for contemporary English reality. He advocates the necessity of the social contract, and of a state constitution. The monarch reigns for the public good, but tyrants must not be got rid of, because monarchical rule is of divine origin. Nevertheless, the monarch must rule according to the law of reason and of God. Passive obedience is the highest form of protest should the political rulers exceed their duty in Christian society.[107] The Church is a divine society, originating with Christ and the apostles. The identity between Church and state in England is justifiable, because the political and religious conditions allow it. Church and state are both societies that differ in function, but they are organically one. In order to preserve the unity and identity of both of them, there must be a supreme head over both. Accordingly, the supreme head, which is the king or the queen, is the origin of the law and the source of authority within both Church and state. Because political society is natural and divine, the supremacy of the state is divine. Hence, obedience is necessarily part of the divine plan.[108]

In the *History of Political Philosophy* which they edited, Leo Strauss and Joseph Cropsey tackle Hooker's view of political power and his opinion regarding the relationship between Church and state. According to Hooker, political power belongs to people and is entrusted to the government by contract and consent. The action of the political body represents the will of the whole community, by means of lay representatives in the Parliament and of clerical representatives in the Convocation. As far as the relationship between Church and state is concerned, the principles of ecclesiastical and civil power are to be reached by reason. Matters of Church polity, unlike matters of dogma,

---

105 *ibid.* 125.
106 There are four main reasons according to which Hooker is a medieval political thinker rather then a classic rationalist. Firstly, Hooker maintains the traditional theological concepts. Secondly, he sets certain limits to the independence and autonomy of human reason. Thirdly, rational constructs must resist the test of history. Fourthly, rational constructs must not contradict the evidence of tradition and the evidence of historical development. *ibid.* 120.
107 F. J. Shirley, *Richard Hooker and Contemporary Political Ideas* (London: SPCK, 1949), 100-110.
108 *ibid.* 112-113.

must be arranged by means of reason, because Scripture is not sufficient for specific issues of polity.[109] Another aspect of Hooker's political theory is the inseparability of Church and state. In this context, religion is politically useful. Church and state have the same substance in all Christian commonwealths. But, in nations where Christians are a minority, the Church is essentially separated from the state.[110] Ultimately, Church and state are complementary, and they both direct man towards his supernatural destiny.[111]

1.2.3 The Theological Perspective

The theological perspective within the analytical view of Hooker's thought does not present a remarkable novelty compared to the previous traditional theological perspective. Generally, the theological aspects under discussion are mainly the doctrine of Scripture, the doctrine of the nature of the Church, the doctrine of the sacraments, especially the Eucharist, and the doctrine of justification. The directions of the modern theological perspective range from acknowledging the Reformation heritage of Hooker to ascribing a Catholic tendency to Hooker's theology.

---

109 Leo Strauss and Joseph Cropsey (eds), *History of Political Philosophy* (Chicago: Rand McNally & Co.: 1966), 319. At this point, there are some aspects of Hooker's theory of law that must be mentioned. It is important to notice that Scripture is not sufficient for specific issues of polity because the fundamental purpose of Scripture is to teach supernatural duties. In this respect, Scripture *is* sufficient to teach supernatural duties. But, for Hooker, the natural and the supernatural order complement each other, and men must fulfil both natural and supernatural duties. Accordingly, natural duties may be discovered by reason, but supernatural duties are beyond the reach of reason because of the Fall. *ibid.* 318.

110 For further details, see A. L. Rowse, *The England of Elizabeth: The Structure of Society* (London: MacMillan, 1951), 484-487, and J. W. Allen, *A History of Political Thought in the Sixteenth Century* (London: Methuen & Co. LTD, 1957), especially chapter VI.

111 Strauss and Cropsey (eds), *History of Political Philosophy*, 320. In this context, the distinction between opinion and action must be analysed. In Hooker's opinion, nobody can control the theological opinions of all individuals living within a nation. Therefore, all opinions that are contrary to the established doctrine must be tolerated, but all actions taken against the established doctrine and polity must be stopped. All actions that are subversive to the already settled polity – either of the Church or of the state – cannot be tolerated. Doctrinal diversity is inevitable, but politically there must be uniformity of action. Theological opinions do not affect the polity of the state until they take the shape of political action, which can profoundly affect the political and religious establishment. Order is the characteristic of state and must be enforced if in danger of being lost by subversive actions that originate in different theological opinions. For further details, see *ibid.* 321.

Gordon E. Rupp analyses much of Hooker's theology; however, it is the doctrine of justification which is most relevant to this research. Rupp notes that Hooker sees justification as forensic, namely consisting of the remission of sins and God's acceptance of the sinner. Justification is realised solely on the basis of Christ's imputed merits and perfect righteousness, not by man's efforts to be righteous, which are defiled by sin. Rupp points out the seeming influence that Luther had upon Hooker, since justification comes from the theology of grace and the theology of the cross. The end effect is that justification is proclaimed to be the work of God from the beginning to the end of the salvation process. Rupp believes that Hooker managed to maintain the delicate balance between the objective doctrine regarding Christ's merits and the subjective doctrine regarding faith as existing in all matters of justification. Vital for the justified believer is the subsequent union with Christ. Every believer can take comfort in the fact that Christ is in him, and the believer is in Christ. Hooker's theology places the righteousness of Christ outside humanity, but this belief does not annul the important implication that justification brings about new life and fundamental changes for the believer.[112]

E. T. Davies approaches Hooker's doctrine of Scripture. Christians should not look in Scripture for the things that belong to reason, and whatever they discover by reason – which does not contradict Scripture – must be trusted. For Hooker, Scripture teaches theology, and reveals to men the supernatural law of God. Nevertheless, the law of God is not completely revealed in Scripture, because nature also reveals God. It is not dishonouring to God if we learn about him by looking at nature. Nothing dishonours God except sin. In this respect, nothing is irrelevant to man's salvation. But, Christians should know that Scripture does not teach everything. Moreover, Scripture does not reveal the basis for its own authority. Christians only accept its authority because they have been taught so in the Church.[113] Generally, two extremes must be avoided. Firstly, the Catholic view of Scripture, which claims that both Scripture and tradition are necessary for salvation (too little attributed to Scripture). Secondly, the Puritan view of Scripture, which affirms that everything we need for salvation must be found in Scripture (too much attributed to Scripture). Scripture leaves enough room for the Church to decide on many aspects of Christianity. It is not theologically necessary that Scripture should

---

112 E. G. Rupp, *Studies in the Making of the English Protestant Tradition* (Cambridge: Cambridge University Press, 1949), 166-191.

113 E. T. Davies, *Episcopacy and the Royal Supremacy in the Church of England in the XVI Century* (Oxford: Blackwell, 1950), 45.

explicitly teach us particular things regarding any form of Church government.[114] Hooker makes a very important distinction that Davies notices. There are things necessary to salvation that must be found in Scripture, and there are things accessory to salvation that are not be found in Scripture (but these things must not be contrary to Scripture).[115]

J. R. Parris' short essay on Hooker's doctrine of the Eucharist displays a clear understanding of his sacramental theology.[116] Parris uses an analytical methodology with a slightly critical accent, and he suggests that Hooker did not understand correctly the difference between Calvin and Zwingli regarding their understanding of the Eucharist. According to Parris, Zwingli does not allow that human nature be present in the Eucharist, but Hooker's interpretation is that, according to Zwingli, Christ's presence in the Eucharist is whole, perfect, and entire. Nobody can tell for sure whether this is because of Hooker's theological tolerance or because of a real dogmatic mistake.[117] Hooker's foundation of the doctrine of the Eucharist is threefold: Scripture, tradition, and reason. Even if Hooker claims that transubstantiation is not essential to the truth of the Eucharist, he nevertheless writes that the practice of the adoration of the elements and transubstantiation are heresies.[118] Moreover, the efficacy of the Eucharist is pragmatic and experiential, rather than theoretical. Arguing from effect to cause, Hooker thinks that we experience grace, then we know that Christ is present in the sacrament. The Eucharist and the sacraments generally do not contain grace in themselves. The sacraments are profitable to us, but their efficacy is in God. For the sacrament to be valid and efficient we must trust God.[119]

C. F. Allison puts Hooker's doctrine of justification in light of the decrees of the Council of Trent. Hooker's theology and the Trent formula agree in several key places. First, both claim that all men have sinned and do not have the righteousness of God. Second, God is the one who offers justification and the only one who can justify a sinner.

---

114 *ibid.* 47.

115 *ibid.* 49.

116 J. R. Parris, "Hooker's Doctrine of the Eucharist", *Scottish Journal of Theology* XVI (1963), 151-165.

117 *ibid.* 155.

118 *ibid.* 156-157.

119 In this context, Hooker also discusses the limits of reason in demonstrating the ultimate mystery of God's work in the Eucharist. The way Christ and the Holy Spirit enter a human soul cannot be fully apprehended or expressed. The blessings of God cannot be wholly understood, even though they are communicated by palpable means. For further information, see *ibid.* 160-163.

Only Christ has attained God's justice, so it is his work that must be applied to sinners in order for justification to take place. Allison does note, however, two major areas of disagreement between the Council of Trent and Hooker: the essence of justification and the manner in which justification is applied to sinners. Hooker believes that the righteousness of Christ makes justification attainable for the Christian, since the Christian dwells in him and thus is seen as having a right standing before God. Once Christians are in Christ, they grow in grace, according to the righteousness of justification. Hooker sees the formal cause of justification as being Christ's righteousness which is imputed to us when we are accepted into Christ's body, the Church. The Trent formula sees the formal cause of justification as being the inherent righteousness infused in man through sacramental grace. Hooker strongly disagrees with the Trent formula, stating that understanding the righteousness of justification in this manner perverts the truth of Christ. It must be remembered, however, that Hooker does not negate that an inherent righteousness does exist in man but this righteousness is that of sanctification, not of justification.[120]

J. S. Marshall is one of the most important theologians in Hooker scholarship. According to Marshall, Hooker's concept of ministry is sacramental, and preaching is secondary. Thus the main responsibility of men is to celebrate the Holy Eucharist, which – in fact – is central to Roman-Catholicism. Marshall's interpretation is an attempt to demonstrate Hooker's continuity with Rome and Catholic theology. Marshall does not see or is not interested in noticing Hooker's basic commitment to the Reformation.[121] According to the Catholic interpretation of Hooker, the Church is the mystical body of Christ, and is invisible. Thus the Church is only known to God. The mark of the visible Church is: one Lord, one faith, and one baptism. Obviously, the authorities that informed Hooker are Aristotle, and scholastic theology, especially Thomas Aquinas. The Catholic interpretation of Hooker claims that the apology of the English Church polity is a response to Puritanism, although Hooker makes more references to Rome rather than to the Puritans. Even if it basically attempts to cut off the dogmatic distance between Hooker and Rome, the rest of Catholic interpretation is fairly balanced.[122]

---

120 C. F. Allison, *The Rise of Moralism. The Proclamation of the Gospel from Hooker to Baxter* (London: SPCK, 1966), 2-5.

121 J. S. Marshall, *Hooker and the Anglican Tradition: An Historical and Theological Study of Hooker's Ecclesiastical Polity* (London: Adam & Charles Black, 1963).

122 For further details on the Catholic interpretation of Hooker, see Joseph Lecler, *Toleration and the Reformation*, vol. II (London: Longmans, 1960), 398-401.

1.2.4 The Philosophical Perspective

The philosophical perspective within the modern view of Hooker's thought basically makes reference to reason, as both authority and methodological instrument in Hooker's theology. The philosophical perspective may well be considered a part of the theological perspective, because – in Hooker – reason is always a philosophical category that has a certain theological application. Actually, in Hooker's thought, reason is interwoven not only with theology, but with politics and even history. The modern philosophical perspective has been singled out for the simple reason that some theologians presented Hooker's theology from a philosophical point of view.[123]

Gunnar Hillerdal is concerned with philosophical ideas in Hooker and he suggests that Hooker's thought is not entirely coherent from the standpoint of logic. According to Hillerdal, Hooker's thesis is a "philosophical failure", and in his thought reason is supposed to clarify revelation, even though it needs God's grace to understand revelation. Because he questions Hooker's logical coherence, Hillerdal writes that there is a slight doubt whether Hooker manages to reconcile the two opposing traditions of thought (the Aristotelian-Thomist philosophy of reason and the Protestant theology of grace and predestination).[124] Thus, he infers that Hooker's thought is circular.[125] Hillerdal is sternly criticised by Nigel Atkinson, who thinks Hillerdal was "frustrated" by the essential distinction in Hooker, "the way of nature" – "the way of grace".[126]

According to Robert Hoopes, Hooker wanted to build a rational basis for all the practices of the English Church that could not be found in Scripture.[127] He also attempted to rehabilitate the concept of *right*

---

123 One of the main debates on Hooker, is whether he managed to reconcile two opposing traditions of thought: the Aristotelian-Thomist philosophy of reason and the Protestant theology of grace and predestination.

124 Cargill Thompson, "The Philosopher of the 'Politic Society'. Richard Hooker as a Political Thinker", 12.

125 Egil Grislis, "The Hermeneutical Problem in Richard Hooker", in W. Speed Hill, *Studies in Richard Hooker*, 159-206.

126 See Gunnar Hillerdal, *Reason and Revelation in Richard Hooker* (Lund: C. W. K. Gleerup, 1962). For further details about Atkinson's critique of Hillerdal, see Atkinson, *Richard Hooker and the Authority of Scripture, Tradition, and Reason*, 32.

127 "[Hooker] was motivated primarily by a desire to provide a rational warrant for existing extra scriptural practices of the Church." Robert Hoopes, *Right Reason in the English Reformation* (Cambridge: Harvard University Press, 1962), 123.

reason, and asserts the "ontological reality and harmony of nature, reason, and morality."[128] Hoopes notices three main philosophical themes in Hooker. Firstly, there is the essential rationality of God. Secondly, the essential rationality of man. Thirdly, the ability of human reason to know the natural and supernatural things. Hooker is an advocate of the rational character of God. Hoopes contrasts Hooker with Calvin. Hooker's God is the God of absolute Reason, while Calvin's God is the God of absolute Will.[129] In Hoopes' opinion, Hooker uses Aquinas' ethical knowledge and moral action within the virtue of prudence. This functions as a proof of salvation. In Hooker, salvation is conditioned by the acceptance of right reason. The elect are those who work hardest in God's service. Salvation is not cheap; there must be an effort to know God in the right manner. Nature needs grace, and grace uses nature.[130] Justification must encompass the whole man. Moreover, for Hooker justification is not merely a divine acknowledgement of man's faith. The certainty of faith must be accompanied by the assent of reason.[131] Reason is present within the entire thought of Hooker. Nothing escapes reason, not even the doctrine of the Holy Scripture, as special divine revelation.[132] Hoopes writes that for Hooker Scripture may contain all the things necessary to salvation, but it cannot teach its own authority. Thus the Church should be interested in spreading Christianity, not merely Bibles. In this respect, right reason may lead to the discovery of truth. Thus truth must be confirmed and fortified by the revealed Word.

As far as theological methodology is concerned, H. R. McAdoo thinks Hooker was interested in establishing a liberal method, which holds reason in high esteem in matters of Church practice and

---

128 *ibid.* 123.
129 *ibid.* 124.
130 *ibid.* 127.
131 *ibid.* 130.
132 On the necessity of reason, see Bethell's summary of Hooker. According to Bethell, reason is necessary for at least three motives. Firstly, reason is necessary for natural knowledge. Secondly, reason is necessary to authenticate Scripture. And thirdly, reason is necessary to apprehend truths above reason. The doctrine of revelation is, however, important, and can be seen in Hooker's doctrine of Scripture, but generally reason is impossible without reference to natural reason. In this respect is important to notice, in Hooker, the special grace of the Holy Ghost is the enlightening of our minds, but the testimony of the Spirit in the believer must be conformed to reason. For further details, cf. S. L. Bethell, *The Cultural Revolution of the Seventeenth Century* (London: Dennis Dobson, 1963), 22-23.

doctrine.[133] The foundation of the liberal methodology in Hooker consists of two main elements: nature and reason as means of knowledge. In Hooker's opinion, there is a problem with using Scripture as the only authority in matters of polity and liturgy, as well as in matters nonessential. This problem consists of the fact that each individual interpretation of Scripture with regard to all these matters becomes an authority in itself.[134] Nevertheless, Scripture is important, but in things of the supernatural, and even these supernatural things include much of the natural law.[135] How should be Scripture interpreted if things supernatural contain elements of the natural law? Hooker tried to find a solution. Even if reason is limited and not sufficient to teach man all that is necessary for everlasting life, reason and human authority should not be restricted or denied in ecclesiastical matters. Thus, according to McAdoo, Hooker is deeply indebted to Aquinas: "Hooker's writings on law and reason stem from the *Summa Theologica*."[136] McAdoo also claims that Hooker is concerned with practical issues, not primarily with academic matters. This is why Hooker's methodology, and generally the methodology of Anglicanism, has always been compelled to take into account at least two aspects: firstly, the freedom of reason, and secondly, the visible Church.[137]

Robert Orr introduces the discussion on the importance of reason in Hooker by starting with the problem of episcopacy. Hooker rationally advances some arguments for the episcopacy. Firstly, the office of bishops is from heaven, even from God. Secondly, the Holy Ghost is the author of episcopacy. Thirdly, all questions of Church government are, however, matters accessory rather than matters necessary.[138] But Orr writes that, for Hooker, the rational foundation of episcopacy cannot ultimately be distinguished from the divine mandate that instituted this form of Church government.[139] From this standpoint, Orr introduces some of the main aspects of Hooker's theology that tackle the issue of reason. Firstly, the Bible contains all beliefs necessary to

---

133 According to McAdoo, Hooker's theological enterprise is "an attempt to establish a liberal method which holds reason to be competent to deal with questions of ecclesiastical polity, and to be itself an ultimate factor in theology." H. R. McAdoo, *The Spirit of Anglicanism. A Survey of Anglican Theological Method in the Seventeenth Century* (London: Adam & Charles Black, 1965), 5.

134 *ibid.* 6.

135 *ibid.* 7.

136 For further details, see *ibid.* 8-9.

137 For further details, see *ibid.* 9, 22.

138 Robert Orr, *Reason and Authority: The Thought of William Chillingworth* (Oxford: Clarendon Press, 1967), 143.

139 *ibid.* 145.

Christianity. Secondly, Scripture cannot solve the controversies regarding its own authority. Thirdly, the moral nature of God demands that salvation be available to all people. Fourthly, the moral law is apprehended by reason. To reason as methodological instrument, Hooker ascribes a great deal of importance as he fifthly contends that reason is supplemented by faith, and is not contradicted by faith.[140] Accordingly, men are taught by nature, Scripture, and experience. The practical use of reason should control the passions and direct the will. At this point, Hooker introduces an important factor that might obscure the proper use of reason. This factor is sin, which hinders man from correctly perceiving the law of reason.[141]

In Philip Harth's opinion, reason and revelation provide the foundation of religion for Hooker,[142] who makes an important distinction between natural religion and divine revelation. Granted that divine religion is directly taught by Scripture, natural religion can be discovered by reason. There are at least three major roles of reason in Hooker's theology. Firstly, reason proves the existence and attributes of God. Secondly, reason teaches of the immortality of the soul. Thirdly, reason discloses the natural law.[143] But nevertheless, reason is not almighty. Accordingly, Hooker develops his theory of the necessity of divine revelation to mankind. There are two main reasons why divine revelation is vital for humanity. Firstly, divine revelation is important because reason is not equally powerful in all men. Faith nevertheless is a sort of support for reason. God has repeated the natural truths in his revelation, so that all men may know by faith what some know by reason. Secondly, divine revelation is important because man has a supernatural end, and the supernatural duties of man cannot be perceived and performed by reason. The goal of Scripture is to reveal the supernatural duties of man that nobody could have discovered by natural means. At this point, Harth makes an important comment and states that Hooker is rather ambiguous: either revelation has disclosed things impossible to be fathomed by reason, or reason has the power to penetrate into God's transcendence and perceive it.[144]

---

140 *ibid.* 147.

141 *ibid.* 151-158.

142 Phillip Harth, *Swift and Anglican Rationalism. The Religious Background of "A Tale of a Tub"* (Chicago: The University of Chicago Press, 1969), 23.

143 *ibid.* 25.

144 This is the basis of Hooker's theory of reason. However, Harth continues his analysis, and discusses the relationship between reason and Scripture, which is ultimately important for Hooker's epistemology. In Hooker, reason is fundamentally necessary for the interpretation of Scripture, because it is reason that teaches Christians that Scripture is the Word of God. Hooker's reason-oriented epistemology

To conclude, the modern view of Hooker's thought is different from the traditional view mainly in terms of historical research. The traditional view offered a distorted image of Hooker's life and work, primarily because of the faulty methodology used by Hooker's main biographers. Things changed towards the end of the first half of the twentieth century, when a new generation of scholars emerged. The fresh interest in Hooker's biography and bibliography led to earnest historical research that challenged and corrected the traditional view. The most important correction regarding Hooker's life was the theory of his "unhappy marriage", which had spotted his biography for more than three centuries. The historical perspective on the analytical view of Hooker encompasses not merely the biography of Hooker, but also his works from the wider perspective of the history of ideas. The political perspective within the modern view of Hooker's thought is the result of a new reassessment of Hooker's political thinking. The academic investigation in this regard led to the conclusion that Hooker was predominantly a theologian who had been influenced by medieval scholasticism rather than by Renaissance philosophy. The reassessment of Hooker's political thought encompasses the same traditionally settled aspects like the theory of the Church, the theory of the Christian society, the identity between Church and state, and royal supremacy. The theological perspective within the modern view of Hooker' thought does not necessarily break the traditional pattern, but it discloses a vivid interest in some major theological aspects of Hooker's entire system. The theological investigation tackled the nature of the Church and its visible part, the role of Scripture in relation to reason, the sacraments with Christ's real presence in the Eucharist, and the doctrine of salvation with special reference to the righteousness of justification and sanctification. The theological perspective consists of two perspectives: on the one hand, the acknowledgment of Hooker's use of his Reformation heritage, and on the other hand, the attempt to ascribe Hooker a Catholic bias. The philosophical perspective within the modern view of Hooker's thought could be a part of the theological

---

is heavily influenced by scholastic theology, especially by the thomistic epistemological conception of understanding and belief, or science and faith. According to the thomistic conception, understanding (science) is a matter of reason, which offers the "certainty of evidence", and belief (faith) is a matter of faith, which offers the "certainty of adherence". Eventually, Harth notices that for Hooker, reason and faith complement each other, but remain fundamentally distinct. Accordingly, Harth's conclusion is that in Hooker the concept of "rational faith" is impossible. The things discovered by faith are not so evident as those discovered by reason, but their truth is more certain, as they depend on the testimony of God, who cannot deceive. For further details, see *ibid.* 26-43.

perspective, but it was investigated separately only because some scholars have shown a particular interest in Hooker's concept of reason. Although reason is present in Hooker's entire work, a special investigation of it proved to be a desired academic exercise. Accordingly, the research focused on reason and its influence on particular aspects of Hooker's thought, namely general and special revelation, and the doctrine of justification. The distinguishing characteristic of the modern view of Hooker's thought was its somehow objectively oriented methodology of investigation. The research was mainly directed towards Hooker's theories, and the scholars were not particularly interested in refuting each other's opinions. The academic spectrum changed, however, by the beginning of the 1970s. A new generation of scholars began seriously to question both Hooker's motivations in writing, and his proper work. Given this newly oriented research focus, the interaction between the different opinions on Hooker suddenly increased.

1.3 The Contemporary View

The 1970s were obviously a turning point in Hooker scholarship. The content and methodology of writing changed, in the sense that the previous earnest and objective analysis of Hooker made room for a sharp and, sometimes, incisive critique from scholars that began open confrontations among themselves in books, articles or other research materials. This is not the main characteristic of this contemporary view of Hooker, but it is surely a constant element that singles it out. It is not Hooker that is primarily at issue now, but opinions about Hooker. It so happened that these opinions slowly attracted the methodology of research, and consequently produced a wide variety of well-informed and learned studies. Hooker gradually became a pretext for study, instead of being a text that should be studied. Moreover, it is the contemporary view that finally broke the attitude of pious reverence towards Hooker. Even if Hooker's thought has been criticised frequently, it is a known fact that until relatively recently, nobody has openly dared criticise Hooker's motivation for writing the way he did. As the present study will prove, the critical view of Hooker's thought varies from iconoclastic opinions to quite sympathetic and even appreciative remarks concerning Hooker as both person and writer.

Like the modern view, the contemporary view is a contribution to Hooker scholarship in the four main fields already mentioned: history, politics, theology, and philosophy. Whether Hooker was a Reformed pastor or a Catholic-biased theologian is still a debated issue, as one can easily notice in all these different perspectives on Hooker's thought.

1.3.1 The Historical Perspective

The historical perspective within the contemporary view of Hooker's thought is focused more on the historical development of Hooker scholarship than on Hooker himself, as person or writer. Biography and bibliography regarding Hooker are no longer at issue; what is important proves to be the very way they have been historically analysed. The main feature of the contemporary historical perspective is its interest in placing Hooker scholarship within the larger ideological framework of the history of human thought.

As many other Hooker scholars, W. D. J. Cargill Thompson's interest in Hooker is manifold, but the historical aspect of his research can be grasped from the very beginning. He drafts a critical analysis of Hooker scholarship from a historical standpoint. Cargill Thompson is quite sceptical regarding modern Hooker scholarship. Although advances have been made at least historically (both in biography and bibliography), critical and historical studies in the twentieth century are not too many. According to Cargill Thompson, modern writing about Hooker is mainly uncritical and every writer repeats the same stereotypical ideas. As a result, genuine research has been hindered because of the overstress on Hooker's political thought.[145] Anglican theology did quite a bit of harm to Hooker scholarship, because it presented Hooker as a great pacifist, only preoccupied with laws, not with conflicts and theological disputations, and did not see Hooker's subjectivity in purposely refuting the Puritan claims as being utterly wrong. Thus Anglican theology tended to ignore the polemical character of Hooker's works. It was taken for granted that Hooker was a remarkable philosopher and, until quite recently, the logic of his thought has not been questioned. This is why, according to Cargill Thompson, the task of Hooker scholarship in the twentieth century is to break up with the stereotypical ideas of the past.[146]

---

145 Cargill Thompson, "The Philosopher of the 'Politic Society'. Richard Hooker as a Political Thinker", in W. Speed Hill, *Studies in Richard Hooker*, 4.
146 This is apparently a false alarm. By the time Cargill Thompson launched it, the traditional view of Hooker had already been decisively challenged and corrected by at least two notable historians, Charles Sisson and David Novarr. Accordingly, there is no need of a reassessment of the preconceptions of the traditional researchers of

P. D. L. Avis tried to moderate the opinion of Cargill Thompson, who was critical of Hooker's objectivity. Actually, Cargill Thompson accused Hooker of not being ready to admit that the Puritan claims might have been true at least in some respects. In trying to give an answer to Cargill Thompson, Avis takes into consideration some historical facts that might offer a balanced answer.[147] Firstly, Avis suggests that Hooker understood the seriousness of the problems that the Elizabethan Church faced in that particular historical context. Secondly, the Church did not always have the power to initiate reform and tackle abuses. Thirdly, Hooker held a different opinion regarding the marks of the Church to the Puritan use of the classical *notae ecclesiae*. Accordingly, Hooker defended the Anglican Church rather than refuting the Puritans.[148] There is another historically important aspect that Avis tried to approach, namely the way Hooker perceived Calvin. On the grounds that Hooker criticised the Lutheran view of justifycation, Avis attempts to create a more Reformed-biased image of Hooker. Even if Hooker had a high regard on Calvin's greatness, industry, influence, achievement, and personal authority, he nevertheless elegantly criticised Calvin for rejecting royal supremacy.[149] Eventually, Hooker's conclusion is that Calvin was a great but fallible human being. Nevertheless, Avis sees in Hooker a Reformed theologian, and this conclusion is predominantly historical in nature.

The relatively short article written by Avis produced an immediate reaction from Richard Bauckham, who wrote an even shorter confutation.[150] Bauckham doubts the efficiency of Avis' arguments regarding Hooker's view of Calvin. Actually, Bauckham seeks to demonstrate that Hooker did not have any ties with Calvinism, either historical or dogmatic. Bauckham's first argument is rather mathematical. According to him, in the *Lawes*, Hooker cites Calvin nine times: six times in his support, and three times to disagree with him.[151] Briefly,

---

Hooker, as Cargill Thompson claimed. For a complete view of Cargill Thompson's suggestions, see *ibid.* 5-13.

147 P. D. L. Avis, "Richard Hooker and John Calvin", *The Journal of Ecclesiastical History* 32 (1981), 19-28.

148 *ibid.* 20.

149 Actually, Hooker's opinion is that Calvin had not been properly informed when he accused the Church of England of blasphemy for granting Henry VIII the title of Supreme Head of the Church. See Cargill Thompson, "The Philosopher of the 'Politic Society'. Richard Hooker as a Political Thinker", in W. Speed Hill, *Studies in Richard Hooker*, 23.

150 Richard Bauckham, "Richard Hooker and John Calvin: a Comment", *Journal of Ecclesiastical History* 32/1 (1981), 29-33.

151 *ibid.* 29.

according to Bauckham, Hooker wanted to escape Calvin's relevance in matters of Church polity in England, so that he might build his own theory.[152] In conclusion, Bauckham thinks that Hooker's theology reflects an obvious independence of mind, and no essential Calvinistic influence. On the other hand, Bauckham is ready to make a slight concession, but not in regard to Hooker, but to the other English theologians, who all were – in his opinion – influenced by Calvin and depended on the Swiss theology. Bauckham also suggests that Hooker's view of Calvin must not be looked upon in the field of history or Church polity, but in the field of soteriology (which encompasses justification, predestination, and the Eucharist) – the only one that establishes a powerful link between Hooker and Calvin. Bauckham's opinion is that, in soteriology, Hooker barely cites Calvin, but had read Calvin in order to formulate his own theological view.[153]

Robert Eccleshall offers an extended critical and historical presentation of the way Hooker's work was interpreted during the seventeenth and the eighteenth centuries, with special references to the political aspect of his thought. The study is far too long and detailed to be briefly and, at the same time, competently summarized, but some basic remarks are, however, necessary. First of all, from a historical perspective, the *Lawes* do not belong to a specific ideological tradition. Despite the fact that it had been used for different purposes in specific historical situations, the *Lawes* had only one main goal which responded to a particular historical context, namely that the English system of government is fully equipped to issue and enforce sound ecclesiastical and civil regulations. Openly professing an appreciative view of Hooker, Eccleshall advocates the internal coherence of the *Lawes*, and contends that all the eight books are authentic. Moreover, from a historical viewpoint, the *Lawes* show that Hooker was deeply rooted in the social, political, and historical realities of the Elizabethan society which he knew well enough to defend in such an extensive work. Eccleshall wants to place the *Lawes* not merely in factual history, but ultimately in the history of human thought. In his opinion, Hooker

---

152 Bauckham wrote that in the Preface to the *Lawes*, the goal of Hooker was "to dispose once and for all of Calvin's relevance to the discussion of Church polity in England and to leave himself free to develop his own argument in his own way without kowtowing to Calvin's authority." *ibid*. 31.

153 *ibid*. 32-33. See also, Richard Bauckham, "Hooker, Travers and the Church of Rome in the 1580s", *Journal of Ecclesiastical History* 29/1 (1978), 37-50.

laid the basis of a "robust and consistent political theory", drawing especially from the medieval intellectual tradition.[154]

1.3.2 The Political Perspective

The political perspective within the contemporary view of Hooker's thought does not radically change the pattern of modern political perspective, but in terms of serious research, one might rightly conclude that books and articles in this particular field are not lacking. Hooker's political system was extensively studied, and the different perspectives bear witness of the interest in Hooker as a political thinker. The main themes that the scholars analysed remained the same as in the modern political perspective: the theory of the law and its importance for the Church, the theory of state, the theory of the Christian society, the relation and identity between Church and state, and the problem of royal supremacy. It is hard precisely to delineate each one of these theories, but one can single out for certain some main theologians interested in Hooker's political thought.

W. Speed Hill was definitely interested in Hooker's political system.[155] He approaches Hooker by starting from the Puritan theory of Church government. According to Hooker, the Puritan system of Church government was modelled on Calvin's Church of Geneva. Obviously, the Puritans claimed that their theory of the Church government is in conformity to Scripture, so the English Church should be blamed for keeping the Episcopalian system of Church government, which is characteristic to Rome. Hooker's response is that the polity of the Church of England is rooted in the natural law, which is given by God.[156] So, the authority of natural law stands level with the authority of Scripture in matters of organisation of the Church polity. There are essential differences between the Church of England and the Church of Rome, and the superficial resemblances between them do not cover up what is doctrinally different in perspective.[157] Speed Hill is generally

---

154 Robert Eccleshall, "Richard Hooker and the Peculiarities of the English: The Reception of the *Ecclesiastical Polity* in the Seventeenth and Eighteenth Centuries", *History of Political Thought* II/1 (1981), 63-117.

155 Other useful insights over Hooker's political system may be found in J. P. Sommerville, "Richard Hooker, Hadrian Savaria, and the Advent of the Divine Right of Kings", *History of the Political Thought* IV/2 (1983), 229-245.

156 W. Speed Hill, "The Evolution of Hooker's *Laws of Ecclesiastical Polity*", in Cargill Thompson, *Studies in Richard Hooker*, 135.

157 *ibid.* 136.

sympathetic to Hooker. According to Speed Hill, the Puritan attack had "subversive implications" and Hooker was "far from blind" not to see them. Hooker did not respond in a contentious manner, but he wanted to emphasise the logical inconsistencies of the Puritan position. It is a mistake to blend politics with salvation, in other words it is a mistake to identify individual salvation with disciplinary reform. Thus the salvation of the individual does not depend on the reformation of a Church political, disciplinarian or dogmatic system. On the one hand, the concern of individual Church members should be faith and doctrine, which may be known easily, even if they are more difficult to performe. On the other hand, the concern of the Church as corporate body should be the administrative organisation, the ceremonies and the worship, the essence of its laws and substance of its jurisdiction, and especially its relationship to the state.[158]

Robert Faulkner produced a very good and comprehensive critical study of Hooker. Even though he treats a variety of different themes of Hooker's thought, the main focus of the study is political. Faulkner's book begins with Hooker's concern to defend the Church of England by opposing its enemies. A chapter on ethics follows, which is somehow unique within the larger framework of Hooker scholarship. As far as Hooker's ethics are concerned, Faulkner is interested in the law of reason, philosophy, and moral virtue. Hooker actually investigates the character of Christian ethics. Although Hooker is influenced by Aristotle in construing his ethical theory, he nonetheless make an obvious distinction between ethics and politics, which is not characteristic of Aristotle. But from a larger theological perspective, God's comprehensive governance encompasses both ethics and politics. Faulkner's political focus is evident as he concludes that ultimately, the doctrine of Christian salvation, specifically Protestant, models Hooker's understanding of philosophical ethics and politics.[159] Faulkner's chapter on Hooker's ethics continues with an examination of the prominence of reason, and with a discussion on will and choice. Hooker's Christian politics is then closely investigated, with special stress on the law of Christian politics, the divine authority of public or state government, the theory of consent, and the rule of law. The next step is the analysis of the role of faith within the context of Church and true religion. According to Faulkner, the English Church polity rests on two main

---

158 *ibid.* 148.

159 Robert Faulkner, *Richard Hooker and the Politics of a Christian England* (Berkeley: University of California Press, 1981), 61.

pillars: the discipline of faith, and Episcopal authority.[160] Faulkner's study ends with an approach to royal supremacy,[161] the Christian commonwealth, and the Christian governance.[162]

Arthur S. McGrade stresses the originality of Hooker in political matters. Thus for Hooker, the basis for legitimate political power is the consent of the governed, which is a break with Aristotle. The problem of royal supremacy is tackled within a socially oriented analysis. Accordingly, royal supremacy becomes a matter of socio-political effectiveness. The argument runs as follows: should everybody profess the same religion, they will have the basic idea of living well, which will coordinate their secular and spiritual goals. This coordination of the secular and spiritual is viewed as a communal task.[163] In Hooker's

---

160 A recent analysis of Hooker's view of episcopacy was done by Stanley Archer. He begins with an interesting remark regarding the fact that Hooker's patrons, bishop John Jewell and bishop John Whitgift, denied the apostolic succession in favour of doctrinal succession. For Hooker, however, the clergy is a separate and distinct order (following the Old Testament), and the bishop is a clergyman of superior rank (Hooker makes the distinction of rank among clergy, based on the theology of Irenaeus and Ignatius). The office of bishop is upheld by tradition, and is alterable for urgent use. Anyway, episcopacy is still the best form of Church polity, even if alterable. For further information, see Stanley Archer, "Hooker on Apostolic Succession: The Two Voices", *The Sixteenth Century Journal* XXIV/1 (1993), 67-74. See also M. R. Sommerville, "Richard Hooker and his Contemporaries on Episcopacy: an Elizabethan Consensus", *The Journal of Ecclesiastical Studies* 35 (1984), 177-187.

161 A useful particularization of the problem of royal supremacy had been previously discussed by P. G. Stanwood, in his very short but comprehensive article "Stobaeus and Classical Borrowing in the Renaissance, with special reference to Richard Hooker and Jeremy Taylor", *Neophilologus* 59 (1975), 141-146. Stanwood investigates the role of the king as both secular and ecclesiastical head. Thus according to Hooker, it is God who sometimes designates the king as he did in ancient Israel. In this case, the power of the king immediately originates in God merely by divine right. People are left free by God to choose their own leader. In this respect, the king is approved by God, and everyone must confess that his power is, in fact, God's power. The king is the mediator between God and men, an idea that obviously follows the pattern of the Old Testament. The counterbalance to the theory of royal supremacy is the right of the Church to issue and enforce laws. In Hooker's opinion, all free and independent societies make their own laws. The power should belong to the whole society, not to a single political body. Nevertheless, a certain part of the same society may have greater freedom in action than the rest. For further discussion, see P. G. Stanwood, "Stobaeus and Classical Borrowing in the Renaissance, with special reference to Richard Hooker and Jeremy Taylor", *Neophilologus* 59 (1975), 141, 143.

162 For an analysis of Faulkner, especially in comparison to Cargill Thompson, see Brendan Bradshaw, "Richard Hooker's *Ecclesiastical Polity*", *The Journal of Ecclesiastical History* 34 (1983), 438-444.

163 Richard Hooker, *Of the Laws of Ecclesiastical Polity*, Arthur S. McGrade ed. (Preface, Book I, Book VIII) (Cambridge: Cambridge University Press, 1989), xxiii.

thought, the political community is more than merely an economic association, as in Aristotle. The pursuit of psychological good (with special reference to the needs of the soul) is a basic characteristic of such a community. As far as the identity between Church and state is concerned, royal supremacy is the only solution for this proposal. The king is superior to every member of the political society, but he is not superior to the community as a whole.[164] Thus, the whole community is the source of political power. The role of the Parliament is the embodiment of this doctrine. Notably, the Parliament includes clergy, and any decision of the Parliament will eventually reflect the will of the Church, as completely identified with state. The community is politically active in legislation, in issuing and enforcing laws.[165] For Hooker, the integrative principle of Christian society is obedience towards the law, and he is not talking about intellectual consent, but about social and political conformity.[166] In McGrade's opinion, Hooker has a rather optimistic or even idealistic view of English political life. It has often happened that society made laws that gave power to the king, but it has not always been the case that the king used the power

---

164 *ibid.* xxv.

165 *ibid.* xxvii. Another useful investigation on Hooker's theory of law was made by Paul Forte. In his sympathetic study of Hooker, Forte proves Hooker's philosophical orientation (with special reference to the legal theory) by his critical use of legal sources like Judeo-Christian tradition, Aristotle, Cicero, Roman civil law, Thomas Aquinas, Henri de Bracton, Christopher St. German, Richard Cosin, and some political philosophers, among whom he mentions Sir Thomas Smith, and John Hooker, Richard's uncle. According to Forte, law is an ultimate cause or first principle in Hooker political theory. Law encompasses all beings and informs all reality. Law is also a product of reason, even if it requires force in some of its applications. Forte concludes that Hooker produced a coherent theory of law, and stresses the need for authority and the benefits of obedience. Human law must be in accordance to the eternal laws of God and reason. For further details, see Paul Forte, "Richard Hooker's Theory of Law", *The Journal of Medieval and Renaissance Studies* 12 (1982), 133-157. On of the most recent contributions to Hooker scholarship in respect to his political theory is a brief article of Tod Moore. According to Moore, the basis of Hooker's political theory is the philosophy of law. The article is particularly interesting because Moore refutes the theory according to which Hooker was mainly influenced by Thomas Aquinas and suggests that his primary influence was Aristotle. Following this line of thought, Moore makes a brief analysis of Aristotle's influence within the history of thought, especially in the Renaissance and Reformation (with reference to the importance of Philipp Melanchthon and Pierre Ramus in trying to include Aristotle within the Christian tradition). Moore's conclusion is that Hooker was a forerunner of political liberalism. Tod Moore, "Recycling Aristotle: The Sovereignty Theory of Richard Hooker", *History of Political Thought* XIV/3 (1993), 345-359.

166 Richard Hooker, *Of the Laws of Ecclesiastical Polity*, Arthur S. McGrade ed. (Preface, Book I, Book VIII) (Cambridge: Cambridge University Press, 1989), xxx.

according to that law.[167] McGrade edited a volume on Hooker's theology, which comprises articles of various interprettations.[168] One of the articles of interest is that of Arthur P. Monahan.

Monahan places Hooker among the Counter-Reformation political thinkers for three main reasons. To begin with, Hooker emphasised popular consent as the basis for his political authority. Furthermore, he believed the element of limit to be the essential qualifier of legitimate authority. Finally, Hooker promoted the medieval corporation theory elaborated in 14th- and 15th-century conciliarist thought. Monahan believes Hooker to qualify better as a Counter-Reformation theologian, than a Protestant "in terms of his general theory of the nature and origins of temporal polity", namely his political thinking. This conclusion might lead some to believe that Hooker's theology was Protestant while his politics were Catholic, but this is not Monahan's point. By seeing Hooker as a respected representative of Anglicanism and Anglicanism as being the Church that "retained the greatest resemblance in theology, ecclesiology and institutional structure to the medieval Church of Rome from which it was separating" Monahan's goal is to establish the idea that Hooker's theology is closer to Catholicism than Protestantism.[169]

Eve Lurbe has produced one of the most recent studies on Hooker's political thought. In her opinion, Hooker promotes a dual conception of society. According to Hooker, Christian society is formed by both Church and state. There are two basic aspects behind this dual conception of society. Firstly, there is no society without laws. Secondly, Hooker has a holistic notion of the community. To exemplify his theory, Hooker uses the notion of participation between head and limbs. The head is not the one that always gives orders, which the limbs merely accept obediently.[170] Hooker also uses the analogy of Christ and the king, but he does not refer to a perfect identity between them. Thus the power of the king is subordinate to the power of Christ. The power of the king is limited by space and time, but the power of Christ is not. The power of the king only has jurisdiction over the external function of the Church, but it cannot modify the doctrine of the

167 *ibid.* xxviii.
168 Arthur S. McGrade (ed.), *Richard Hooker and the Construction of Christian Community* (Tempe: Medieval and Renaissance Texts and Studies, 1997).
169 Arthur P. Monahan, "Richard Hooker: Counter-Reformation Political Thinker", in McGrade (ed.), *Richard Hooker and the Construction of Christian Community*, 203-218.
170 Eve Lurbe, "Political Power and Ecclesiastical Power in Richard Hooker's *Laws of the Ecclesiastical Polity*", *Cahiers Elisabéthains* 49 (1996), 16.

Church.[171] Lurbe notices another important aspect of Hooker's political thought, namely the distinction between the Church as natural society ("body politic"), and the Church as supernatural society ("body mystic"). As far as the relationship between Church and state in concerned, political society consists of Christians only. Lurbe's conclusion is that "the notion of profane is foreign to Hooker", and that he holds a "fairly optimistic vision of human life."[172]

1.3.3 The Theological Perspective

The theological perspective within the critical view of Hooker's thought has been developed within the main lines settled by the modern theological perspective. The research in this particular field focuses on the doctrine of Scripture, on the doctrine of justification, and on the doctrine of the sacraments. Generally, the doctrine of Scripture seems to have been of interest for almost all theologians who tackled Hooker within the contemporary theological perspective. Another aspect of interest, which varies according to different writers, is the attempt to place Hooker clearly within a certain theological tradition, especially the Reformed.

According to Egil Grislis, Hooker's theological system[173] is neither exclusively biblical, nor merely rational. Grislis is interested in Hooker's doctrine of Scripture, and in the methodology of biblical interpretation used by Hooker. From Grislis' viewpoint, Hooker has a high regard of Scripture. Thus Grislis draws the attention on the fact that Hooker repeatedly underscores the absolute perfection of Scripture. Nevertheless, the extra-biblical Christian heritage, namely Christian tradition, must not be avoided in a proper hermeneutical task. But, for Hooker, Scripture is a supernaturally given revelation.[174] Grislis notices three major hermeneutical presuppositions in Hooker.

---

171 *ibid.* 17.

172 *ibid.* 19-21.

173 One of the attempts to approach extensively Hooker's entire theological system was produced by the French Olivier Loyer. Actually, Loyer's book is a Ph.D. dissertation that approaches a wide variety of theological themes in Hooker. It is not a deep analysis of Hooker's work, but rather a large systematic presentation and a good summary of his thought. The book is especially useful in quickly getting a grasp of Hooker's work, but is not particularly helpful in disclosing further insights of Hooker's theology. For further information, see Olivier Loyer, *L'Anglicanisme de Richard Hooker* (Paris: 1977).

174 Egil Grislis, "The Hermeneutical Problem in Richard Hooker", Cargill Thompson (ed.), *Studies in Richard Hooker*, 182.

Firstly, Scripture is the Word of God and absolutely necessary for salvation. Secondly, Scripture does not consist exclusively of supernatural laws. And thirdly, Scripture has a divine author.[175] What is interesting in Grislis' study is the fact that he identifies a christo-centric principle at the foundation of Hooker's biblical interpretation. Thus literal interpretation is always subordinated to this christocentric principle. Accordingly, the Church is indwelt by the redeeming presence of God in Jesus Christ, and it is this presence that bears witness to the power of reason and revelation. Ultimately, both reason and revelation are to inform Christians, as well as transform them.[176]

Patrick Collinson believes Christology to be the most important aspect of Hooker's doctrine of justification. All that traditionally pertains to salvation is centred in the person and work of Christ. An example would be Hooker's belief that faith is valid and the believer's salvation efficient only when he or she is found in Christ. In other words, salvation is always seen as the work of God in Christ, not the work of the sinful human being. God finds man, but he finds man *in Christ*. No one can place man in Christ apart from God. This clearly indicates that Hooker's soteriology is strongly rooted in grace, not human justice. The human's responsibility is to have a true and lively faith. But even that faith which exists in man is not a part of man, but is also a gift from God himself. Collinson takes note of the dual aspect of Hooker's soteriology – justification first, followed by the sanctification process that consists of good works based on faith, hope and love. Hooker believes good works to be the result of justification, not its cause. Up to this point, Collinson has acknowledged all the Protestant features in Hooker's doctrine of salvation. The remainder of his interpretation of Hooker's thought revolves around predestination and election, which according to Hooker, are expressions of God's grace and reveal that his theology is ultimately Reformed.[177]

Lee Gibbs argues that Hooker's doctrine of justification is more complex, incorporating insights from both Catholic and Protestant theology. Hooker is seen as advancing a *via media* between Rome and the Reformation. Gibbs admits that Hooker criticises the Catholic doctrine of justification by inherent righteousness because it inevitably dismisses any comfort of salvation, turning Christ's righteousness into a superfluous aspect and thus undermining the very foundation of

175 *ibid.* 186-187.

176 *ibid.* 197-198.

177 Patrick Collinson, *Archbishop Grindal 1519-1583. The Struggle for a Reformed Church* (London: Jonathan Cape, 1979), 41.

Christian faith.[178] Hooker identifies three aspects in regard to righteousness. First, a glorifying righteousness exists, perfect and inherent, in the world to come. Secondly, a justifying righteousness exists in this world, perfect though not inherent. Thirdly, a sanctifying righteousness exists in this world, imperfect but inherent. Gibbs calls this "a synthesis between Paul's doctrine of justification by faith alone without works and James' doctrine of works and not only faith."[179] Hooker believes the internal righteousness of sanctification and the external righteousness of justification of Jesus Christ, which is imputed, to be united *in tempore* and received simultaneously.[180] The righteousness of justification is necessarily inferred by the habitual righteousness of sanctification. At the same time, the righteousness of justification necessarily presupposes the habitual righteousness of sanctification. Hooker believes that human merits cannot attain the justification of righteousness, even if these good works are an inseparable part of the justified person's life.[181]

Philip E. Hughes paints a portrait of Hooker that is Protestant and specifically Reformed. He argues that John Jewel influenced Hooker and that this is the reason why Hooker takes great care in not ascribing any importance to works of human merit that have no power to justify a person before God. Even if a man wishes to do something in addition to that which God requires from him, those works that are supposed to bring about a surplus of additional merit, do not count as helping him towards salvation. The only way that God accomplishes justification is through the imputation of Christ's perfect righteousness that is able to save the unworthy sinner on the basis of faith. Hughes points out Hooker's double language of justification, namely the imputation of Christ's righteousness to the believer and the consequent non-imputation of the believer's righteousness, which are too unworthy to aquire merits before God. The justified believer, however, does not remain idle. After he is justified, he will begin to perform good works, not so

---

178 Lee Gibbs, "Richard Hooker's *Via Media* Doctrine of Justification", *Harvard Theological Review* 74/1 (1981), 212-213.

179 *ibid.* 216.

180 Gibbs explains Hooker's *via media* doctrine of justification. Firstly, the righteousness of justification and the righteousness of sanctification differ in essence. Secondly, the righteousness of justification and the righteousness of sanctification differ in order and dignity. Thirdly, the righteousness of sanctification has two distinct aspects: *habitual* righteousness, and *actual* righteousness. For further information, see *ibid.* 217-219.

181 *ibid.* 220.

that he can earn or maintain his salvation, but so he can prove that salvation in love.[182]

Stanley Archer shows how Hooker strongly emphasised faith and remained firm in his belief. Also to be noted is the importance of grace in Hooker's theology, which Archer believes that Hooker proclaimed was available to all. For Archer, sanctification is one of the most important aspects of salvation, because it requires the person's life in order to develop. Archer insists that Hooker understood the person and work of Christ as being the only foundation of faith. That is why Hooker continually directs our attention to Christ himself, described as Saviour because he was crucified for the salvation of the whole world. Archer does not shy away from Hooker's controversial argument surrounding the salvation of certain Catholics. He believes that, according to Hooker, in Catholic theology, there was nothing that explicitly denied Christ his rightful place as the foundation of faith. This appears to be a subject where Calvin's influence on Hooker is noticeable. Archer also discusses Hooker's thoughts on the nature of pride and the nature of justice. He presupposes that Hooker's view of God was influenced by Aquinas, and that explains why he describes God as being consistent, reasonable and just. Archer sees Hooker as being in line with the main Magisterial reformers, because he promoted faith as the necessary component required by God for personal salvation.[183]

William Haugaard contends that Hooker has an inclusive view of the Church. He also agrees that there must be Christian unity in the whole Church of Christ, and in this sense he is ecumenical. This view extends to his notion of truth. Thus truth is ultimately related to the revelation of God, and it cannot be exclusively the property of one particular Church. If revelation is universal, then truth should be universally at the disposal of any Church, not of one particular Church.[184] The discussion goes on with Hooker's view of Scripture, which contains the knowledge of the salvation offered by God to humankind. Scripture contains all revealed and supernatural truth, so it is sufficient, and it does not need tradition to complete its revealed information. Accordingly, Scripture contains all the things necessary for salvation, but not every single thing for daily life. Simple things in

182 Philip E. Hughes, *Faith and Works. Cranmer and Hooker on Justification* (Wilton: Morehouse-Barlow, 1982), 40-45.

183 Stanley Archer, *Richard Hooker* (Boston: Twayne Publishers, 1983), 22-33.

184 William Haugaard, "Richard Hooker: Evidences of an Ecumenical Vision from a Twentieth Century Perspective", *Journal of Ecumenical Studies* XXIV/3 (1987), 432.

daily life are regulated by natural law, which is of divine origin.[185] As far as the sacraments are concerned, Hooker has a Reformed perspective on them and holds that they are the means of grace for eternal life, but grace is only represented or signified. Hooker develops his doctrine of the sacraments in the wider context of the doctrine of Trinity, Christ, and Church. Moreover, they should be understood by means of the all-encompassing doctrine of participation.[186] Christ dwells in the inner person of the Christian who celebrates the Eucharist.[187]

Peter Lake points out that Hooker believes a correct understanding of doctrine to be necessary for salvation. Before salvation can become effectual for the believer, he must correct understand doctrines such as the Trinity, the coeternity of the Father with the Son, and infant baptism, which Hooker admits cannot be proved literally from a specific Scriptural passage but rather from a profound study of all the Scriptural witness. Lake seeks to place Hooker in his rightful place within English Protestant theology from the ecclesiological standpoint. Thus, Hooker occupies the middle ground between John Whitgift, who believed the English Church should stand between Rome and Anabaptism, and Richard Bancroft, who wished to see the English Church as being located between Roman and Genevan-style Protestants. Hooker sought to distance himself from a Church which had Calvinist leanings but which enjoyed being on the verge of sectarianism. The theology of the English Church, however, is clearly

---

185 *ibid*. 434.

186 One of the best studies that analyse the doctrine of participation in Hooker's thought was written by William Wolf, John Booty, and Owen Thomas. According to their research, Hooker does not agree with participation as *theosis* (deification, complete or ontological unity), and with participation as *syngeneia* (kinship). Participation may be defined by some other terms, like *metousia* (to share, to partake in), or *metalambano* (to partake, to share), but the best word that encompasses Hooker's view of participation is *koinonia* (the two sided relationship, with accent on giving and receiving). The basis of participation is the doctrine of the Trinity, and the doctrine of the hypostatic union of the two natures in Christ. The reality of participation in Christ is the real issue in the Church, not the mode of participation. Moreover, participation in Christ takes place in the community, the society of the people of God. Participation of all the people of God in Christ as Saviour is made effective by means of the Spirit through the Word and sacraments. For further details on participation in Hooker's thought, cf. William Wolf, John Booty, Owen Thomas, *The Spirit of Anglicanism: Hooker, Maurice, Temple* (Edinburgh: T&T Clark, 1982), 3-41.

187 Haugaard, "Richard Hooker: Evidences of an Ecumenical Vision from a Twentieth Century Perspective", *Journal of Ecumenical Studies* XXIV/3 (1987), 436.

Reformed.[188] Nonetheless, Hooker stands within the Reformed tradition, although his theology is not classical Reformed and as a Calvinist, he comes close to arminianism. Lake came to this conclusion after wrestling with Hooker's strong christocentric approach to salvation, which implies that Christ's death for all men opens the door to seeing every person as a potential member of Christ's Church.[189]

W. J. Torrance Kirby describes Hooker as a Reformed theologian, paralleling Hooker's thought to Luther and Calvin. Through this, he manages to show vital Reformed features in Hooker's theology, namely his insistence on man's depravity, the work of Christ as mediator, and man's union with Christ which is an actual incorporation in Christ. Torrance Kirby rightly notes Hooker's breakdown of righteousness into three forms (of justification, sanctification, and glorification) and Hooker's two modes of grace (by imputation for justification, and infusion for sanctification). He also thoroughly analyses how Hooker's justification and sanctification oppose the theology of Thomas Aquinas, who held that grace was a habit of the soul.[190] Favouring the Reformed reading of Hooker, Torrance Kirby emphasises Hooker's bringing together *Sola Scriptura*, the belief that Scripture contains all things necessary to salvation, and the informed understanding of reason's role in biblical interpretation.[191]

One of the most interesting aspects of Crerar's assessment of Hooker is concerned with the problem of grace. Thus Crerar writes that, in Hooker, grace redeems the soul in the form of love, and this idea is available to Hooker from the works of Thomas Aquinas. Hooker, however, does not copy Aquinas but modifies his theory. The result is that Hooker agrees with Aquinas in saying that grace dwells in us through the work and presence of the Holy Spirit. According to

---

188 Peter Lake, *Anglicans and Puritans? Presbyterians and English Conformist Thought from Whitgift to Hooker* (London: Unwin Hyman, 1988), 151-163.

189 Peter Lake, "Calvinism and the English Church 1570-1635", in Margo Todd (ed.), *Reformation to Revolution. Politics and Religion in Early Modern England* (London: Routledge, 1995), 179-207.

190 W. J. Torrance Kirby, *Richard Hooker's Doctrine of the Royal Supremacy* (Leiden: E. J. Brill, 1990), 41-53. See also Kirby, "*Supremum Caput*: Richard Hooker's Theology of Ecclesiastical Dominion", *Dionysius* XII (1988), 94-109; Kirby, "Richard Hooker as an Apologist of the Magisterial Reformation in England", in Arthur Stephen McGrade (ed.), *Richard Hooker and the Construction of Christian Community*, 219-233; Kirby, "Richard Hooker's Theory of Natural Law in the Context of Reformation Theology", *Sixteenth Century Journal* XXX/3 (1999), 681-703, and Kirby, "The Paradigm of Chalcedonian Christology in Richard Hooker's Discourse on Grace and the Church", *Churchman* 114/1 (2000), 22-39.

191 For details, see Kirby, "Richard Hooker as an Apologist of the Magisterial Reformation in England", 219-233.

Crerar, Hooker even uses the model of infusion to describe the presence of the Spirit within the human being. Nevertheless, unlike Aquinas, Hooker places a significant amount of stress upon the difficulty of the work of grace, through the Holy Spirit, to fight our stubbornness and persistence in sloth. Crerar suggest that Hooker, like Aquinas, uses the hylomorphic concept of substance but with one significant difference. While Aquinas displays such a high degree of reverence towards grace that he assumes grace alters the human soul just by his presence within it, Hooker is more sceptical and really suspicious about our bias to indifference and sin. Thus, grace must do more that just be present within the soul of the sinner if the sinner is to be inwardly changed.[192]

Nigel Atkinson agrees with Torrance Kirby that Hooker should be considered a Reformed theologian. Atkinson, however, believes this can be better proved by showing how Hooker defended the full sufficiency and authority of Scripture. Christians must obey Scripture as the supreme source of authority, even if the Church says otherwise. Atkinson believes that "Hooker was most concerned to protect the supreme and final authority of Scripture."[193] Accordingly, Hooker sought to refute both the Catholic and Puritan views of Scripture. Hooker saw the Catholics as considering Scripture to be insufficient due to the emphasis placed on supplementary tradition. On the other hand, Hooker believed the Puritans were adding things to Scripture as well. Atkinson thinks that Hooker's doctrine of Scripture has a pastoral touch that concerns itself with the consciences of weaker people. If Scripture were to contain only simple things, it would become an instrument of psychological and spiritual torment.[194] In addition, Scripture's purpose is soteriological, that is to provide fallen humanity the knowledge necessary to obtain salvation. Therefore, Atkinson argues that for Hooker, Scripture is clearly above nature, teaching things that reason cannot perceive.[195] A crucial aspect of Hooker's doctrine of Scripture and one that takes into account his Reformed theology is that special revelation, or the Holy Scripture, must be obeyed by Christians who desire to glorify God as Saviour and Redeemer.[196]

---

192 Douglas Crerar, *Positive Negatives. A Motif in Christian Tradition* (New York: Peter Lang, 1991), 178-179.
193 Atkinson, *Richard Hooker and the Authority of Scripture, Tradition, and Reason*, 99.
194 *ibid.* 100.
195 *ibid.* 101.
196 *ibid.* 28.

Anthony Milton thinks that the core difference between the theology of the Church of England and that of the Church of Rome is the doctrine of justification. Richard Hooker had an innate understandding of this doctrine, and so he treated the subject extensively, seeking to reconcile the conflict between the two Churches. Hooker explained the manner in which God's salvation takes place within history, reflecting both the Church of Rome as well as the Protestant Churches.[197] Milton believes it important to take note of how Hooker was regarded immediately after his death. According to Milton, Hooker's theology was respected by Calvinists during the Jacobean period, although the ceremonialist elements of his theology were not highly appreciated until the 1630s.[198] Calvinist theologians in England came to conclude that Hooker had indeed been an apologist for the Church of England, even though they did not utilize his works in doctrines of crucial importance. Milton does not see Hooker as being particularly interested in Lutheran theology and believes that Hooker used Luther's viewpoints only to complete his case against the Church of Rome.[199]

1.3.4 The Philosophical Perspective

The philosophical perspective within the contemporary view of Hooker's thought is mainly concerned with reason. Again, exactly like the previous modern philosophical perspective, the contemporary philosophical perspective is not so much a self-evident methodological enterprise, as an appendix to the contemporary theological perspective. In Hooker, reason cannot be thought of in isolation, but in relation to history, politics, and theology. Regarding the specifically critical aspect of this philosophical perspective, it is clear that research in the field is not merely analytical, but often triggers a subjective reaction in the scholars involved, concerning either Hooker's position or even his philosophy of writing, and his inward motivation.

W. D. J. Cargill Thompson is evidently biased when he questions Hooker's motivation for writing the *Lawes*, which is only incidentally a political work or a work of political theory. According to Cargill Thompson, the *Lawes* is not even a work of theology in the sense of being an exposition of Christian principles. It is rather a work of apologetics, a defence of the constitution and practice of the Church of

---

197 Anthony Milton, *Catholic and Reformed. The Roma and Protestant Churches in English Protestant Thought 1600-1640* (Cambridge: Cambridge University Press, 1995), 211.

198 *ibid.* 533.

199 For details, *ibid.* 440.

England. The book has a polemical purpose, even if this aspect has been played down.[200] Hooker's temperate language is more a stylistic device, even if it might be a feature of character. Hooker's Preface is a "skilful exercise of denigration which sets the tone for the rest of the book."[201] Hooker's aim in the Preface is to discredit the Puritan movement, and only partially to refute theologically the beliefs of the Puritans. According to Cargill Thompson, "Hooker's account of Calvin is a calculated misrepresentation, a deliberate attempt to undermine Calvin's reputation among his readers."[202] Again, Cargill Thompson suggests that Hooker professes a high respect for Calvin as theologian and distinguished person, but in fact he implies that Calvin has come up with a "pious fraud." Moreover, Hooker could have inferred that Calvin talked about the discipline of the Church as being divinely instituted in order for the people of Geneva to accept it easily. As far as the Puritans are concerned, Hooker would have exaggerated their biblicism and made it more extreme than it really was. According to Cargill Thompson, Hooker was methodologically eclectic, and he never referred to the books written by his contemporaries. Their influence upon his thought may nonetheless be traced quite easily (Bancroft, Saravia, etc.).[203]

According to John Booty, in Hooker reason is the ultimate human authority. Even Scripture as special revelation must be authenticated by this ultimate human authority, namely reason. Moreover, Scripture is interpreted by means of this ultimate human authority, which is reason. But Scripture is not self-evident. We know by experience that the authority of the Church is the first to attest the true character of Scripture.[204] Nevertheless, the reason of mature Christians goes beyond the authority of the Church. Reason is a fallible authority, and it must operate in relation to Church and Scripture. Reason is an authority in theology in the sense that it helps the apprehension and interpretation of Scripture. This means that Scripture presupposes the existence of a recipient of revelation. The recipient of revelation must be living and thinking, in other words he must possess reason, as an analytical (not critical) faculty of the mind. This recipient of revelation accumulates experience and reason. Moreover, he lives within the context of society,

---

200 Cargill Thompson, "The Philosopher of the 'Politic Society'. Richard Hooker as a Political Thinker", in W. Speed Hill, *Studies in Richard Hooker*, 13.

201 *ibid*. 14.

202 *ibid*. 14.

203 *ibid*. 15-16.

204 John Booty, "Hooker and Anglicanism", in W. Speed Hill, *Studies in Richard Hooker*, 217.

formed by other living, thinking, and reasoning recipients of revelation who testify to the true character of their accumulative experience. Thus revelation is given so that it should be understood. The giver of the revelation offers it as reasonable and understandable information, and the receiver of the revelation appropriates it in a reasonable and understandable manner.[205] So reason, together with tradition and Church authority helps Scripture in informing men with the proper knowledge of salvation. In Hooker, reason is not unbridled, but it is that which receives the divine truth. Ultimately, reason is not a critical faculty of the mind.[206]

W. Speed Hill investigates Hooker's theory of reason in the context of the controversy with Travers. Hooker affirms the authority of reason in the whole debate. For him, the doctrine of predestination, that he discussed with Travers, had the apostle Paul as authority, but the authority in reading Paul's writings was reason.[207] Thus, the issue of the debate was not the proper interpretation of Paul, but the matter of

---

205 *ibid.* 217-222.
206 As a traditional Anglican, Booty is concerned with many more aspects of Hooker's thought both theological and political. For details, see John E. Booty, "The Quest for the Historical Hooker", *The Churchman* 80/3 (1966), 185-193; Booty, "Contrition in Anglican Spirituality: Hooker, Donne, and Herbert", 25-48, in William J. Wolf (ed.), *Anglican Spirituality* (Wilton: Morehouse-Barlow, 1982); William Wolf, John Booty, Owen Thomas, *The Spirit of Anglicanism: Hooker, Maurice, Temple* (T&T Clark: Edinburgh, 1982); Booty, "The English Reformation: A Lively Faith and Sacramental Confession", in Paul Elmen, (ed.), *The Anglican Moral Choice* (Wilton: Morehouse-Barlow, 1983), 15-32; Booty, "Hooker's Understanding of the Presence of Christ in the Eucharist", in John E. Booty (ed.), *The Divine Drama in History and Liturgy. Essays Presented to Horton Davies on his Retirement from Princeton University* (Allison Park: Pickwick Publications, 1984), 131-148; Booty, "The Judicious Mr. Hooker and Authority in the Elizabethan Church", in Stephen W. Sykes, (ed.), *Authority in the Anglican Communion* (Toronto: Anglican Book Centre, 1987), 95-101; Stephen Sykes, John Booty, *The Study of Anglicanism* (London: SPCK, 1988); Booty, "An Elizabethan Addresses Modern Anglicanism. Richard Hooker and Theological Issues at the End of the Twentieth Century", *Anglican Theological Review* LXXI/1 (1989), 8-24; Booty, "The Law of Proportion: William Meade and Richard Hooker", *St. Luke's Journal of Theology* XXXIV/2 (1991), 19-31; Booty, "Elizabethan Religion: Disorder Ordered", *Anglican Theological Review* 73/2 (1991), 123-138; Booty, "Hooker and Anglicanism: Into the Future", *Sewanee Theological Review* 36/2 (1993), 215-226; Booty, "*Foreword*: Richard Hooker, Anglican Theologian", *Sewanee Theological Review* 36/2 (1993), 185-186; Booty, "The Spirituality of Participation in Richard Hooker", *Sewanee Theological Review* 38/1 (1994), 9-20; Booty, "Anglican Identity: What is This Book of Common Prayer?", *Sewanee Theological Review* 40/2 (1997), 137-145; Booty, "Understanding the Church in Sixteenth-Century England", *Sewanee Theological Review* 42/3 (1999), 269-289.
207 W. Speed Hill, "The Evolution of Hooker's *Laws of the Ecclesiastical Polity*", in W. Speed Hill, *Studies in Richard Hooker*, 127.

ultimate authority in theology. According to Hooker, the ultimate authority in theology is reason. The controversy between Hooker and Travers contained the very issue of the English Reformation: the English Church lacked a single, authoritative tradition (which was formerly Rome) to regulate biblical interpretation. In this case, what authority should theology resort to where there are different interpretations to the same doctrine? This single authority is reason.[208] According to Speed Hill, Hooker's most effective weapon was not his philosophical acumen or his reason-based judgement, but his "capacity to speak to the Puritan as a man who appreciated the essential inwardness of this religious experience." This is the novelty of Speed Hill's interpretation: Hooker as existentialist philosopher (not historically, of course, because it would have been an anachronism, but merely ideologically).[209] Hooker tries to find a proper reasonable answer to the spiritual need of the individual in search of the certainty of faith.[210] Thus he analyses this spiritual need within the context of human reason and human aspirations. Actually, Hooker argues for the reasonable character of theology (with special reference to salvation) for the individual seeking certainty.[211]

Nigel Voak suggests that the main philosophical influences in Hooker were Aristotle and Aquinas. Thus, while Aquinas mentioned that sin affected the will, rather than the reason, Hooker stated that sin affected both the will and the reason. This is why human reason needs the support of God's grace. Due to the grace of God, man is able to become united with God in a gradual manner and attain a state of incorruption. Grace perfects human reason and human being so that this state of incorruption affects both the mind and the body, and, Voak

---

208 *ibid.* 128.
209 *ibid.* 149.
210 Hooker offers a remarkable balance in talking about certainty, because he also approaches the problem of doubt. One of the theologians that investigated the notion of doubt in Hooker's thought was Marianne Micks. For Hooker, once we taste the sweetness of faith, we never really lose it. Doubt, however, exists in our lives. Hooker's analysis of doubt is made in relation to his understanding of the importance of reason in theology. Man doubts not only because of sin, but also because of psychosomatic realities. Besides, man doubts because God gives him periods of spiritual darkness. According to Micks, reason in Hooker is the sister of Wisdom in the Bible; it is not the reason of the eighteenth century theology. The conclusion advanced by Micks is that Hooker is part of the Augustinian and Anselmian tradition of reason (*fides quaerens intellectum*, "faith seeking understanding") rather than part of rationalism. For further details, see Marianne Micks, "Richard Hooker as Theologian", *Theology Today* XXXVI/4 (1980), 560-563.
211 W. Speed Hill, "The Evolution of Hooker's *Laws of the Ecclesiastical Polity*", in W. Speed Hill, *Studies in Richard Hooker*, 150.

infers, man's reasoning powers, "since virtue exists through rational choice of the good."[212] Voak does not seem willing to put Hooker alongside the mainline Magisterial reformers because of Hooker's rationalist theology. Actually, Voak argues that Hooker's theology, heavily influenced by rationalism, was an "effective weapon" against the reformers. Voak accuses Hooker for promoting an inadequate doctrine of grace, because he allegedly restricts grace to the sacraments and pays no heed to conversion or the necessity of prevenient grace. However, in Voak's opinion, this is not the most serious fault of Hooker's theology. That is the fact that he does not manage to include grace in the psychology of man's reason, which, according to Voak, leads to the "error of Pelagianism."[213]

Subsequently, Voak published his doctoral thesis as *Richard Hooker and Reformed Theology. A Study of Reason, Will and Grace*. Along with this, he provided an excellent guide to Hooker's theology of salvation that is particularly useful because it helps the reader understand how Hooker's theology developed over time.[214] Voak distinguishes between Hooker's early theology of justification (as presented in his *A Learned Discourse of Justification*) and his later theology of justification (as contained in the *Lawes*, his marginal notes to *A Christian Letter* and the so-called *Dublin Fragments*). Voak claims that Hooker's early theology is decisively Reformed (Calvinist), but he emphasises that his later theology clearly steps outside the Reformed tradition.[215] Voak admits that his understanding of Hooker's thought differs from that of Torrance Kirby and Atkinson and that his beliefs line up closer to that of Peter Lake (one of Voak's doctoral examiners). In attempting to establish his own position, Voak claims that Hooker should not be forced into a mould that makes him either "thoroughly 'Anglican' or as thoroughly Reformed." Instead, he suggests that Hooker "should be taken on his own terms, in all his complexity, as a major if somewhat enigmatic contributor to the theological self-understanding of the Anglican Communion."[216] Voak concedes that Hooker can be considered "at least in part a Reformed theologian" but only because of his early doctrine of justification. In Voak's view, Hooker's later works clearly distance him from the Reformed tradition.[217] Voak's identify-

---

212 Nigel Voak, "Reason and Grace in Richard Hooker" (M.Phil. Dissertation: The University of Oxford, 1994), 33-35.

213 *ibid*. 41.

214 Voak, *Richard Hooker and Reformed Theology*, 321.

215 *ibid*. 190.

216 *ibid*. 324.

217 *ibid*. 319.

cation of the development of Hooker's theology is correct, but I do not believe that one should make this distinction sharper than it is. When all is said and done, one must come to terms with whether or not Hooker was a Reformed theologian. We must not lose sight of the fact that in his later theology of the *Lawes*, Hooker never mentioned explicitly that his view of justification expressed in his early theology of the *A Learned Discourse of Justification* was incorrect, in need of revision or that it should be understood in a different way.

According to Atkinson, the controversy he had with the Puritans drove Hooker to develop this theory of reason. Hooker clearly differentiates between "the way of nature" and "the way of grace." The Puritans had been wrong epistemologically for failing to distinguish between the different nature of laws belonging to men in their distinct associations, spiritual or natural.[218] Hooker believed that the Puritans were correct in claiming that God should be glorified by all the actions of men, actions which must be modelled according to the law of God. The Puritans were wrong, though, in their belief that Scripture is the only law of God that shapes human actions. God must receive glory for both natural and spiritual things. This means that he must be praised both as the Creator who gives us life and health, and as the Saviour who grants us salvation and eternal hope. We must not forget, however, that we have to take into account and obey God's special revelation, Scripture, if we hope to glorify God as Saviour and Redeemer.[219] According to Atkinson, Hooker accepted the Reformed doctrine of total depravity and, in this respect, reason has not all the power to penetrate the truths of the supernatural kingdom. Reason is limited in searching the depths of truth in the heavenly kingdom.[220] But, it is noticeable that, in Hooker's thought, there is a moral imperative pertaining to the earthly kingdom. Thus humans have the power and responsibility to perform good works, in accordance with the exercise of their reason.[221]

William J. Bouwsma writes that Hooker was interested in the philosophy of both Aristotle and Aquinas but he was neither the first, nor the only English Protestant to have manifested such a preoccupation during that time. One other famous case is that of Philip Melanchthon. Bouwsma attempts to place Hooker within the broader context of the European culture, and to attach to him the label of a

---

218 Atkinson, *Richard Hooker and the Authority of Scripture, Tradition, and Reason*, 27.
219 *ibid*. 28.
220 *ibid*. 30.
221 *ibid*. 31.

capable humanist-rhetorician.[222] Thus, besides Aristotle and Aquinas, Pico della Mirandola was another major influence in Hooker's thought, especially from the perspective of the freedom of will which ascends from sensual to spiritual existence. Hooker was also influenced by Erasmus and Calvin, because he attacked the degeneration of Christianity from a religion of the heart into external forms and hypocrisy. In his defense of human desires, which were traditionally suspect because of theirassociation with the sinful body, Hooker seems to have been acquainted with Boccaccio and Lorenzo Valla. As for his principle of moderation, Hooker may have been indebted to Machiavelli and his principle of equilibrium.[223]

Edmund Newey seems convinced that Hooker's doctrine of participation is essentially a Platonic concept. Thus, he explains that Hooker followed Aquinas in utilizing the Platonic and Aristotelian tradition and not forcing a rigid dichotomy between the two philosophers. Newey suggests that Hooker followed Aquinas by using analogy to reconcile the Platonic notion of participation with the Aristotelian interpretation of causality. This causes Newey to consider Hooker to be pre-modern, sharing with Aquinas the medieval thesis that *causa est in causato* (the cause is in the thing caused). Newey goes on to claim that in his definition of participation, Hooker utilized a dual concept of grace: the grace of union and the grace of unction. Newey writes, based on his analysis of Hooker's Book V of the *Lawes*, that to Christ alone belongs the grace of union, though the grace of unction is shared by us together with Christ. Put simply, we receive from Christ the grace of unction and we are confronted with Christ by the grace of unction. In this manner, humanity participates in God. This participation is the action of grace, imputed and imparted (or infused). Reason allows us to understand this reality, and reason is the faculty given to us by God that assures a passive reception of God's grace.[224]

To conclude, the contemporary view of Hooker's thought did not entirely break with the previous traditional and modern views, but it surely produced a rich academic research within Hooker scholarship. Even if it is not a new perspective on Hooker concerning his life, the opinions of scholars differ in many respects. It is notable however that,

---

222 William J. Bouwsma, "Hooker in the Context of European Cultural History", in Claire McEachern and Deborah Shuger (eds), *Religion and Culture in Renaissance England* (Cambridge: Cambridge University Press, 1997), 144-146.

223 *ibid.* 149.

224 Edmund Newey, "The Form of Reason: Participation in the Work of Richard Hooker", in Benjamin Whichcote, Ralph Cudworth and Jeremy Taylor", *Modern Theology* 18/1 (2002), 1-26.

although there is a consensus regarding Hooker's life, the research in this field raised issues in many aspects of Hooker's thought, on which scholars have not reached full agreement yet. Despite of the variety of different perspectives on Hooker, there is a certain common attempt to place Hooker in the larger context of the history of thought or specifically of the history of Christian theology. As in the previous traditional and modern views, the contemporary view of Hooker's thought has been examined from four different angles that reflect the special interest of each scholar that approached Hooker: history, politics, theology and philosophy. The historical perspective within the contemporary view of Hooker's thought displays a somehow new interest in Hooker scholarship, not in his biography or work. The problems regarding Hooker's life and work have already been solved by modern analytical scholarship, so now the interest shifts to what has been written on Hooker. Now historians and theologians do not critically examine Hooker, but each other's research on Hooker. The result of the historical interest in Hooker offers a balanced Reformed-oriented image of Hooker, who is now thought to be a theologian of the Reformed tradition, deeply rooted in the historical, social and political realities of the Elizabethan England. As far as the political perspective within the contemporary view of Hooker's thought is concerned, the research is prone to connect Hooker to Aristotle, rather than to medieval scholasticism, especially Thomas Aquinas. In this respect, Hooker is regarded as being a forerunner of political liberalism. A brief conclusion of the political perspective reveals the fact that, at least in matters of Church, state, and royal supremacy, Hooker created a rather too optimistic and idealistic view. This political theory is based on the notion of participation that has been extensively approached as an encompassing and integrative conception. The theological perspective within the contemporary view of Hooker's thought consists of research that tackled the doctrine of justification, the doctrine of the sacraments, and especially the doctrine of Scripture. The main conclusion of the section is that Hooker is a Reformed theologian in all these major doctrines. In matters of justification he holds the righteousness of justification that is offered by Christ. For Hooker, the sacraments only convey grace, they do not have grace in themselves, and they are effective on the grounds that God makes them useful for men. Scripture is necessary in all things supernatural, but is not concerned with any of those simple things, that wholly belong to the natural life, and so it needs reason as a complementary authority in theology. The philosophical perspective within the contemporary view of Hooker's thought is a particularization of the contemporary theological perspective, because it investigates reason with special reference to different aspects of Hooker's theology. The research in this particular domain offers a salient image of Hooker that ranges from the shrewd controversialist to the mild pastor, and from the existentialist philosopher to the Reformed theologian. Opinions concerning the importance of reason as authority in theology beside Scripture obviously differ. On the one hand, reason is of uttermost importance for Scripture, and there is no real knowledge of the supernatural without reason, because it is reason that proves the veridical character of Scripture. On the other hand, reason is important, but not vitally decisive, because Scripture is the sole authority that informs and transforms human life.

Having described how Hooker's works were read up to the present time, it is now appropriate to resume the theme of this book, namely the doctrine of salvation in Hooker's sermons. Though a most distinguished theologian, Hooker was not the first to write about salvation in English Protestantism but followed in the footsteps of the early English reformers as indicated in the following chapters.

2. The Doctrine of Salvation in the Early English Reformation

The purpose of this chapter is to present the doctrine of salvation in the early English Reformation which Hooker continued in his sermons. To this end, I selected some of the most representative English theologians from the first half of the sixteenth century, spanning from the early reign of Henry VIII to the first years of the reign of Elizabeth I. It is important to connect Hooker to the soteriology of the early English reformers because by means of their theology, he continues the soteriology of the Continental Magisterial Reformation, most notably of the Reformed understanding of salvation.[1] To be sure, this chapter contains some of the most significant soteriological ideas of the early English Reformation which will be later reflected in the sermons of Richard Hooker.

2.1 The Early Reign of Henry VIII

Early English Protestant thought evidently borrowed a significant amount of theological insights from the Lutheran Reformation, but not always in great detail or with minute accuracy. Thus, concepts like righteousness, faith and forgiveness of sins could be easily identified in the writings of the first English Protestant theologians. In this respect, righteousness is opposed to merits, faith fundamentally apprehends Christ and forgiveness of sins is basically identified with justification.

---

1   For more details about the links between Hooker and the Magisterial reformers, see Corneliu C. Simuţ, "Continuing the Protestant Tradition in the Church of England: The Influence of the Continental Magisterial Reformation on the Doctrine of Justification in the Early Theology of Richard Hooker as Reflected in his *A Learned Discourse of Justification, Workes, and How the Foundation of Faith is Overthrown* (1586)", PhD thesis, Aberdeen (2003), or Corneliu C. Simuţ, *Richard Hooker and his Early Doctrine of Justification. A Study of his* Discourse of Justification (Aldershot: Ashgate Publishing, 2005), 22-47.

Although essentially christological, the soteriology of the early English reformers was not based on a very elaborate Christology, which probably led to a more anthropological view of salvation and particularly of justification. It is clear that justification is not the work of man, but the initiative of God; nonetheless, in terms of the substance of justification, early English theologians suggested that justification was primarily a divine work that affected man's entire life and not necessarily his status before God. Thus, justification does not mean to consider righteous but rather to make righteous. Justification is not primarily a matter of forensic declaration but of effectual transformation.

Another important theological aspect of the early English Protestant theology of justification is the doctrine of predestination. Accordingly, justification is tackled within the broader context of predestination, which belongs to the inscrutable will of God. The doctrine of predestination was intentionally used in order to detach justification and salvation from the realm of human possibilities. The importance of morality, however, still remains a fundamental feature of soteriology. Justification is oftentimes equalled to Christ himself, who must be faithfully followed. Thus, salvation, including predestination and justification, must have a practical finality and constitute the basis for daily moral life.

2.1.1 William Tyndale

In Tyndale, the doctrine of justification is scattered throughout all his writings, especially in his *Prologues* to various books of the Holy Scripture, of which the most important is the *Prologue to the Epistle of Saint Paul to the Romans*. Tyndale begins his assessment of justification from the fact that justification is totally separated from the law. Nobody can be justified by the works of the law. Justification is not from man, but from God, through the Holy Spirit who gives the true faith of Christ. Actually, good works are the result of a new heart, which is always the working of the Holy Spirit.[2] The Spirit of God is present where true faith is present. The Spirit of God is given to us by faith so that we might believe the promises of God regarding salvation. When we exercise our faith, the Spirit enters our heart and loosens the bonds of the devil, which had kept our heart in captivity. Thus, justification

---

2   William Tyndale, *Prologue to the Epistle of Saint Paul to the Romans*, in G. E. Duffield (ed.), *The Work of William Tyndale* (Appleford: The Sutton Courtenay Press, 1964), 123.

comes by faith, which is given by the Holy Spirit, who comes from God. Ultimately, our justification is directly from God, not from any inward work of our human nature. Tyndale wrote that our faith brought the Spirit, but it did not deserve the Spirit. Faith itself is not a work, but the gift of the Holy Spirit. Faith and the Spirit must not be separated. It is the Spirit that produces faith in us, but this process begins by the preaching of the Word of God, which brings us the good news of salvation. Tyndale wrote:

> All our justifying then comes from faith and faith and the Spirit come of God and not of us. When we say faith brings the Spirit, it is not to be understood that faith deserves the Spirit or that the Spirit is not present in us before faith, for the Spirit is ever in us and faith is the gift and working of the Spirit, but through preaching the Spirit begins to work in us.[3]

Tyndale's doctrine of justification is analysed within the more encompassing theology of the covenant, whereby those who believe enter the covenant of God and they are sure of the presence of the Spirit within themselves. God has promised this and we know that the Spirit is within us when we have faith. The theology of the covenant is founded on the promises of God, which he bestows upon us together with the gift of the Spirit, who produces true and justifying faith in us. Tyndale further explains that once we enter this covenant with God, we know for sure that by faith we shall increase in our salvation. Actually, it is God who works out the rest of our salvation until the completion of history and the entering into the everlasting life. Accordingly, it is only faith which justifies. In Tyndale's theology faith has a threefold function. Firstly, faith justifies, which primarily means that our sins are forgiven. Secondly, faith makes us righteous and thirdly, faith fulfils the law. All these three functions of faith are accomplished through the Spirit, which is given to us on the basis of Christ's merits. The Spirit produces an inward desire and strength in us, which enables us to perform good works in love. Tyndale wrote:

> Faith only justifies, makes righteous, and fulfils the law, for it brings the Spirit through Christ's deservings; the Spirit... looses the heart, makes him free, sets him to liberty and gives him strength to work the deeds of the law with love, even as the law requires; then at the last out of the same faith, so working in the heart, spring all good works by their own accord.[4]

Justification is by faith, which also brings the Spirit, who produces in us an inward desire to perform outward good works. But although a man is justified and begins to do good works, it is nevertheless possible for anyone to fall into sin again. The primary objective cause of relapsing

3 Tyndale, *Romans*, 124.
4 *ibid.* 125.

into sin is sin itself, namely our sinful nature which is impregnated with sin. There is, however, a subjective cause of falling again into sin. For Tyndale, this is human negligence, which stops the work of the Spirit in us and hinders our meditation of God. Tyndale explains:

> If any man that has forsaken sin and is converted to put his trust in Christ and to keep the law of God, do fall at any time, the cause is, that the flesh through negligence has choked the Spirit and oppressed her, and taken from her the good of her strength; which food is her meditation in God and in his wonderful deeds and in the manifold covenants of his mercy.[5]

Tyndale also places justification in connection to the concept of grace. Grace is God's favour or his benevolent attitude towards us. By grace, God chose to save us, without us having done anything that might have deserved grace. It was by grace that God sent Christ to die for our sins:

> Grace properly is God's favour, or kind mind, which of his own self, without deserving of us, he hears to us, whereby he was moved and inclined to give Christ unto us, with all this other gifts of grace.[6]

The main gift of grace is the Holy Spirit, who is given to all those whom God favours. A slight formula of predestination might be detected at this point of Tyndale's argument, but it should be said that he was more preoccupied with the forensic aspect of God's justification. Because of his grace, God counts us perfect before him for the sake of Christ. Through faith, men must appropriate this forensic justification, by which God counts us righteous in his sight, on the basis of his grace and for the sake of his Son. When we have faith in Christ, God does not take into account our sins, but he approaches us in accordance with our faith in Christ and with his promises. True faith is worked within us only by the Holy Spirit and it changes us by giving us a new nature. Actually, true faith causes us to be born again in God and transfers us into the status of being considered sons of God. Every aspect of our humanity is radically changed by faith. When we have faith, it means that the Holy Spirit takes control over our mind, emotions and will. Faith works for the increasing improvement of our moral life. Tyndale wrote:

> Right faith is a thing wrought by the Holy Ghost in us, which changes us, turns us into a new nature and begets us anew in God and makes us the sons of God, as you read in the first of John; and kills the old Adam and makes us altogether new in the heart, will, lust and in all our affections and

---

5   *ibid.* 127.
6   *ibid.* 128.

powers of the soul; the Holy Ghost ever accompanying her and ruling the heart.[7]

Justifying faith must necessarily produce good works, because it is alive and always driven by the Holy Spirit. Tyndale then defines faith as a fundamental trust in God's benevolent attitude towards humanity; a trust which consists of commitment to God, a joyful life and sincerity towards both God and our fellow men. It is virtually impossible to separate good works from faith, because the new lifestyle that faith imposes and actually produces within us, influences us in such a manner that we must be ready and willing to do good things to our neighbours:

> Faith is, then, a lively and a steadfast trust in the favour of God, wherewith we commit ourselves altogether unto God; and that trust is so surely grounded and sticks so fast in our hearts, that a man would not once doubt it, though he should die a thousand times therefore.[8]

When he introduces the idea of righteousness, Tyndale apparently equals it to faith. Like faith, righteousness is ultimately a gift of God and true justifying righteousness belongs completely to God. Therefore, the righteousness of God changes human nature into a new spiritual nature. Man is made free by this righteousness, in order to offer a pattern of new behaviour towards his fellow men. Although he made reference to righteousness, Tyndale slightly changes his argument towards another analysis of faith, which forgives the sins of men. In Tyndale's theology, righteousness and faith are used interchangeably with reference to justification. For Tyndale, justification is basically the forgiveness of sins. Faith must be placed in Christ and in his sacrifice, which warranties our justification. Tyndale highlights the profound Christological essence of his doctrine of justification:

> Christ is our righteousness, our justifying, our redemption, our atonement, that has appeased God and cleanses us from our sins and all in this blood, so that his blood is the satisfaction only.[9]

Justification is through faith in Christ. Faith is not only an intellectual assent to the historicity of Christ or to the orthodoxy of Christian doctrine. Tyndale argued that even Satan and the devils might be doctrinally orthodox, but still lacking in personal saving faith. Accordingly, the personal dimension of faith is linked to the person and work of Christ in justification:

---

7   *ibid.* 128-129.

8   *ibid.* 129.

9   Tyndale, *Exposition of the First Epistle of St. John*, in James McGoldrick, *Luther's English Connection. The Reformation Thought of Robert Barnes and William Tyndale* (Milwaukee: Northwestern Publishing House, 1979), 117.

The devil believes that Christ died, but not that he died for his sins. Neither does anyone who consents in the heart to continue in sin, believe that Christ died for him. For to believe that Christ died for us is to see our horrible damnation and… to be sure that we are delivered therefrom through Christ. In that we have power to hate our sins and to love God's commandments. All such repent and have their hearts loosed out of captivity and bondage of sin and are therefore justified through faith in Christ.[10]

Like Melanchthon, Tyndale uses a "psychological" approach to faith and justification, in the sense that he defines faith as the assurance of our conscience that we are delivered from sin and its consequences:

The faith of the true believers is that God justifies or forgives and Christ deserves it; and the faith or trust in Christ's blood receives it and certifies the conscience thereof and saves and delivers her from the fear of death and damnation. And this is that we mean, when we say faith justifies: that faith (I mean in Christ and not in our own works) certifies the conscience that our sins are forgiven us for Christ's blood sake.[11]

Faith receives justification. Thus, it appears that justification is something completely independent of human intervention and consequently is entirely the work and plan of God. Justification is the forgiveness of our sins and the imputation of the righteousness of Christ to us. God forgives us and considers us righteous, as if we really were righteous. For the sake of Christ, God devised this justification, which is imputed to us. Commenting on Psalm 32, Tyndale wrote that the blessing of God essentially consists of the fact that man is justified not by works, but by the fact that "his sin is not reckoned." Consequently, it means that, if justification is described by Scripture as being the non-imputation of sin, justification also consists of the fact that righteousness, particularly God's righteousness, is imputed to us and we are considered righteous, as in Luther's famous definition of the righteousness of faith.[12] However, the line between being considered righteous and being made righteous is thin enough to be easily crossed, because Tyndale continues to mention that we are justified and given the Holy Spirit with the clear finality of doing good works.[13] We receive justification by faith and the result is that our conscience is fully aware of its content, the forgiveness of sins and consequently, the performance of good works:

---

10   Tyndale, *First John*, 121.
11   Tyndale, *Exposition of Matthew V, VI, VII. Exposition to the Reader*, Duffield (ed.), *The Work of William Tyndale*, 189.
12   See Martin Luther, *The Bondage of the Will*, in Jaroslav Pelikan (ed.), *Luther's Works*, vol. 33 (Philadelphia: Fortress Press, 1972), 270-271.
13   Tyndale, *Romans*, 133.

Our deeds are the effect of righteousness and thereto an outward testimony and certifying of the inward righteousness, as sourness is of leaven. And when I say faith justifies, the understanding is that faith receives the justifying. God promises to forgive us our sins and to impute us for full righteous. And God justifies us actively: that is to say, forgives us and reckons us for full righteous. And Christ's blood deserves it; and faith in the promise receives it and certifies the conscience thereof.[14]

In his *Answer to Sir Thomas More's Dialogue*, Tyndale provides a sort of *ordo justificationis*, as he lists a number of stages, which match the various events that make up the whole process of justification. Thus, the initiator of justification is evidently God, who gives us light to see that the law is good and righteous. On the other hand, the same light from God helps us see our sin and our unrighteousness. The knowledge of both the righteousness of the law and the unrighteousness of human nature produces true repentance.[15] Although repentance is produced within human nature, it is not of human nature. Repentance originates in God and is the work of the Holy Spirit. The same Spirit that works out repentance in us produces trust and confidence in our hearts. This trust is given to us by the Spirit in order that we should believe the mercy and the truth of God, which will be accomplished according to his promises. The trust of faith is the spring of love for he law of God. Thus, justification cannot be without repentance, although repentance is not that which justifies. Repentance must be accompanied by trust in God, which immediately produces love for God's law. Thus, it is righteousness which produces the inward desire to fulfil the law of God in order that we should behave properly among other men. On the other hand, Tyndale mentions that nobody can produce faith in or by himself, because faith is fundamentally a gift of God. For Tyndale, is clear that faith does not justify. Actually, justification consists of the "right way unto righteousness by what means men must be made righteous and safe." It appears that, for Tyndale, justification means to make one righteous. What Lutheran theology, especially Luther and Melanchthon, termed "forensic justification" (with special reference to man being considered righteous) is an aspect that Tyndale only inferred. In fact, Tyndale repeatedly speaks of man being made righteous and particularly of Abraham, who "was justified and made righteous." In justification, we are made righteous by faith in Christ, who achieved this righteousness for us, in order that our sins be remitted. It is only the righteousness of Christ, given to us by faith, that

---

14 Tyndale, *Exposition of Matthew V, VI, VII. Exposition to the Reader*, 267.
15 Tyndale, *The Answer to Sir Thomas More's Dialogue*, in Duffield (ed.), *The Work of William Tyndale*, 369.

effectively helps in justification. Justification is from God, but it necessarily changes man inwardly, through faith and through the Holy Spirit, which was given to us on the basis of Christ's death at the cross and to which we are supposed to respond in love.[16]

It is not love, however, which justifies. Faith alone justifies through preaching. Faith alone receives the mercy with which God justifies and forgives us. True faith is directed towards the work of Christ and particularly to his atoning sacrifice at the cross. Justification consists of the strong belief that God had promised to forgive the sins of humanity for the sake of Christ. Faith alone justifies and it justifies before God. This is true justification, the one worked out before God, by faith in the promise of God to forgive our sins on the grounds of Christ's atoning sacrifice. Good works, however, are very important and, in his *Prologue Upon the Epistle of Saint James*, Tyndale even wrote that they also justified. It is true, good works do not justify in the true sense of the word, namely before God, but they nevertheless justify before the world. Thus, through justification by faith, man is inwardly righteous before God, and through justification by works, one is outwardly righteous before the world, because he willingly performs the will of God before his fellow man as true testimony of his own faith.[17] Faith in the blood of Christ justifies us actively and the very love which originates in faith is only a passive manifestation of our justification. Thus, the righteousness of God or the righteousness of Christ is active, while the righteousness of the believer is passive.[18]

In Tyndale's theology, the whole process of justification is entirely the work of God. Tyndale is very careful to mention clearly that God's mercy and promises in Christ save us by moving us to faith, whereby we receive justification, which is totally the work of God. Justification, however, becomes effective by means of faith, which necessarily produce good works. Every man is justified without works and without the help of the law, but by Christ alone. Justification "comes of grace promised us of God, through the deserving of Christ, by whom, if we believe, we are justified without help of the works of the law."[19]

Tyndale often links justification, faith and the Spirit to the correct preaching of the Word of God, which is obviously a Lutheran

---

16   Tyndale, *Romans*, 132-133.

17   Tyndale, *The Prologue Upon the Epistle of Saint James*, in Duffield (ed.), *The Work of William Tyndale*, 161-162. See also Tyndale, *Prologue to the Book of Numbers*, 69.

18   Tyndale, *The Answer to Sir Thomas More's Dialogue*, in Duffield (ed.), *The Work of William Tyndale*, 380.

19   Tyndale, *The Prologue Upon the Epistle of Saint Paul to the Galatians*, in Duffield (ed.), *The Work of William Tyndale*, 149.

theological influence. In this respect, it becomes clear that, although justification is objectively the work of God, it nevertheless has a subjective aspect, which consists of the correct and faithful preaching of the Gospel, which must be accepted for one's justification, as prescribed by Melanchthon.[20] Nonetheless, the primary soteriological interest of Tyndale is to ascribe justification to God alone. In order to do this, Tyndale uses the concept of predestination, by which justification is taken out of the realm of humanity and placed into the sphere of God's action.[21]

2.1.2 John Frith

The most important and original soteriological writing of John Frith is *A Disputation of Purgatory*, published in 1531, in which he polemically confutes the Catholic doctrine of purgatory.[22] In this work, Frith promotes the so-called concept of "two purgatories." Basically, Frith's idea is that, in terms of soteriology, the existence of two purgatories is evident: the first is the Word of God, and the second is the cross of Christ. The first purgatory, the Word of God, cleans the heart from original sin and from daily sins. Frith clearly explains that the Word of God must be appropriated and understood by means of faith. The result of believing the Word of God is the forgiveness of sins. The second purgatory, which is the cross of Christ, is revealed through the Word of God. Actually, the Word of God informs us on the reality and historicity of Christ's death. The soteriological outcome of Christ's death consists of the satisfaction offered for our sins and for our reconciliation with God the Father. The individual believer must personally appropriate the death of Christ by means of faith in order to be transformed and given a will which allows him to lead a life in accordance with the commandments of God. Frith explains his doctrine of the two purgatories:

> God hath left us two purgatories; one to purge the heart and cleanse it from the filth which we have partly received of Adam (for we are by nature

---

20   Pauck (ed.), *Melanchthon and Bucer*, 125.

21   Tyndale, *Romans*, 134-141.

22   In this work, Frith attacks John Rastell's *New Book on Purgatory* (1530), which contains some rational arguments for the existence of purgatory and secondly he rejects Thomas More's *The Supplication of Souls* (1529), which is an attempt to use texts from Scripture in order to prove the existence of purgatory. Carl Trueman, *Luther's Legacy. Salvation and the English Reformers 1525-1556* (Oxford: Clarendon Press, 1994), 128.

children of wrath, Ephesians 2) and partly by adding thereto by consenting unto our natural infirmity. This purgatory is the Word of God, as Christ saith (John 15) Now are ye clean for the word which I have spoken unto you. This purgation obtaineth no man but through faith, for the unfaithful are not purged by the Word of God, as the Scribes and Pharisees were nothing the better for hearing his Word, but rather the worse, for it was a testimony against them unto their condemnation. And because we receive this purgation only through believing the Word, therefore is the virtue of this purging applied also unto faith; for Peter saith (Acts 15) That the Gentiles' hearts were purged through faith, that is to say, through believing the Word. And what word is that? Verily the preaching that Christ's death hath fully satisfied for our sins and pacified for ever the Father's wrath towards us etc. This faith purifies the heart and giveth us a will and gladness to do whatsoever our most merciful Father commandeth us.[23]

This text is of particular importance, because it reflects three major aspects of Frith's soteriology: firstly the centrality of Christ; secondly, the importance of faith; and thirdly, the existential effects of salvation. The centrality of Christ is emphasised by the fact that he has done the work of salvation, which Frith approaches primarily in terms of redemption. Early in his theological career, Frith began his soteriology from the fact that God the Father manifested grace and love to sinful humanity. Due to his sinful nature, man cannot do anything for his salvation; all the deeds of man are pure vanity, because he participates in the sin of Adam in such a way that his own free will is distorted to the point of being entirely incapable of moving towards God. God offers his love to man, who actually lives in this serious predicament. For Frith, is important to note that God offers his love freely to man, who does not deserve it. The love of God is revealed through the work of salvation in Christ. If man has anything good in this world, he has the gifts of grace, whereby God has chosen a certain people for salvation before the creation of the world. This incipient formula of election is important for Frith's theology, as it establishes the foundation of justification and of God's work in his love and grace. Consequently, the decree of God the Father in election is not an arbitrary decision, but a clear manifestation of God's love and grace. The work of God the Son marvellously displays the love and grace of God.[24]

Thus, Christ is the mediator between God and man and the very fact that he is both divine and human is essential to salvation. By his

---

23 John Frith, *A Disputation of Purgatory*, in N. T. Wright (ed.), *The Work of John Frith* (Appleford: The Sutton Courtenay Press, 1978), 90.

24 Frith, *Patrick Places*, in Wright (ed.), *The Work of John Frith*, 29.

work, Christ actually merits salvation and communicates it to those who trust him.[25] The centre of Frith's theology is the work of Christ, which was done once and for all. The sufficiency and the completion of the work of Christ is the very origin of his entire theology. God offers salvation to humanity in Christ and in Christ alone. Salvation was worked out in two ways. Firstly, the death of Christ on the cross provided a full satisfaction for our sins and secondly, the righteousness of Christ provided righteousness for us. This transfer of righteousness is achieved by the union with Christ, whereby the believer unites himself with God the Son by means of faith. Frith explains that there is an interchange between Christ and the believer. The righteousness of Christ becomes ours, we clothe ourselves in the justice of Christ, in such a manner that whatever Christ deserved comes to us by faith. What is true of Christ is considered true of us. Frith wrote:

> This Christ is become our righteousness... so that the justice of God is not to give us that we ourselves have deserved, ...but to clothe us with another man's justice (that is Christ's) and to give us that which Christ hath deserved for us. And this justice of God, through the faith of Jesus, cometh unto all and upon all them that believe.[26]

As far as Christ's work is concerned, his incarnation must necessarily be accompanied by his death in order that the remission of sins should be completed. Sin has offended the righteousness of God to such a degree that it requires a remedy through the satisfaction offered by the death of Christ. Frith explains that the work of Christ was entirely for us and it substituted what we should have done in order to have our sins remitted. The essence of the work of Christ was humility, because Christ humbled himself and accepted death on the cross so that we should have our sins totally forgiven. The work of Christ was only for our sake, not for his. It is, however, interesting that Frith promotes the universality of Christ's death, although he had mentioned election as the manifestation of God's grace and love in salvation. Frith wrote:

> Christ humbled himself and was made obedient unto the death, even to the death of the cross... This obedience and death was not for himself, but for us, for he alone suffered and died for us all... Now since he was obedient unto the death for us, that is even as good as though we ourselves had been obedient every man for himself unto the death; and since he died for us, that is even as good as though we had died ourselves for us our own sins.[27]

---

25 For more details, see Trueman, *Luther's Legacy*, 131.

26 Frith, *Patrick Places*, 30.

27 *ibid.* 30.

The specific purpose of Christ's satisfaction is the appeasing of God's wrath.[28] The role of faith is given by the death of Christ, which results in certain benefits for the believer, and by the concept of *formed* faith. The specific outcome of Christ's death is the non-imputation of original sin and consequently the imputation of Christ's righteousness to the believer, as if it were his own.[29] It should be said that this resembles very much Luther's statements about the imputation of righteousness on account of Christ.[30] The concept of *formed* faith is apparently a concession that Frith makes to his Catholic opponents. It is a known fact that Catholic theology promotes a twofold definition of faith, which consists of *fides informis*, or incomplete faith, which is essentially an intellectual assent, and *fides formata*, or complete, formed faith, which is faith accompanied by *charitas*, or love expressed in good works. Other reformers, Melanchthon for instance, have rejected this twofold definition, on the grounds that faith without love is a hypocritical concept. Moreover, writes Melanchthon, the twofold definition of faith in Catholic theology is utterly useless because faith accompanied by love does not justify as it is a mere expression of the intrinsic value of man. True faith is trust in the promises of God.[31]

In Frith's theology, however, formed faith only refers to saving faith, in contrast with an intellectual apprehension or recognition of Christ's work.[32] The existential implications of faith for the believer consist of the work of the Holy Spirit, who changes the believer's will so that he should be conformed to God's requirements.

For Frith, justification has an essentially pneumatological aspect. The Holy Spirit is deeply involved in justification and his work specifically begins with the union of the believer with Christ. This is actually the personal or subjective appropriation of justification, which has basically three necessary results. Firstly, justification provides the assurance of salvation for all believers, because salvation has a secure foundation in the person and work of Christ. Secondly, the nature of the Christian life should be a clear fact. The Christian believer is righteous because he is in Christ, not because he is becoming more righteous through the growing work of the Spirit within him. Thirdly, in order that faith be true, it must be accompanied by good works. The point of performing good works, although justification is by faith alone,

---

28   Trueman, *Luther's Legacy*, 131-132.
29   Frith, *A Disputation of Purgatory*, in Wright (ed.), *The Work of John Frith*, 179.
30   See Luther, *Lectures on Galatians*, in Pelikan (ed.), *Luther's Works*, vol. 26 (St. Louis: Concordia Publishing House, 1963), 235.
31   For details, see Pauck (ed.), *Melanchthon and Bucer*, 92.
32   Trueman, *Luther's Legacy*, 134.

is the commandment of God, whereby we are urged to manifest our love towards our fellow men. Faith must necessarily be manifested in love, which is practically expressed in good works. Good works are the sign of faith and of the believer's life in Christ. For Frith, true faith is "the faith which worketh through charity and not that dead historical faith, which the devils have and tremble." The truth of faith is only confirmed by personal involvement and the liveliness of faith is obviously shown in action for the benefit of our neighbours. Faith is a gift of God and pleases God. Faith is the only means by which the believer may appropriate justification for himself. The works of love or good works must not be performed for the reward that they actually earn, but out of love for Christ.[33]

The second purgatory described by Frith is the cross of Christ:

> Nevertheless, because our infirmity is so great and our members so weak and frail that we cannot eschew sin as our heart would and as our will desireth; therefore, hath God left us another purgatory, which is Christ's cross: I mean not his material cross that he himself died on, but a spiritual cross, which is adversity, tribulation, worldly depression, etc. And this is called the rod or scourge of God, wherewith he scourged every son that he received, that he remember his law and mortify the old Adam and fleshly lust, which else would wax so rebellious that it would subdue us, reign in us and hold us thralled under sin.[34]

Another work in which Frith wrote about the relationship between justification and the atoning death of Christ was *The Revelation of Antichrist* and especially its first part, *An Epistle to the Christian Reader*. Frith begins to explain his doctrine of salvation by establishing its objective foundation in the person and the work of Christ. Human sin had to be remitted and replaced by an appropriate righteousness before God. God himself dealt with this situation and sent Christ to die as a substitutive sacrifice for our sin in order that he should be the necessary righteousness unto salvation before God the Father. Frith wrote:

> But thanks be unto God, which hath given us victory through our Lord Jesus Christ, which by sin damned sin in the flesh, for God made him to be sin for us (that is to say, a sacrifice for our sin and so is sin taken in many places of the two Tetaments), which knew no sin that by his means should be that righteousness before God is allowed.[35]

At his point, the role of faith is vital, as faith requires a visible, true and real personal trust in the substitutive death of Christ unto salvation,

33   Frith, *Patrick Places*, 31-34.
34   Frith, *A Disputation of Purgatory*, 90-91.
35   Wright (ed.), *The Work of John Frith*, 460.

which primarily consists of our redemption from sin. Frith makes clear that faith is not effective if it only consists of an intellectual apprehension and understanding of salvation, but it must contain a purely subjective and personal involvement by showing forth an inner trust in Christ as the believer's own Saviour and Redeemer. In the words of Frith:

> It is not therefore sufficient to believe that he is a Saviour and a Redeemer, but that he is a Saviour and a Redeemer unto thee; and this canst thou not confess, except thou knowledge thyself to be a sinner, for he that thinketh himself no sinner, needeth no Saviour and Redemer.[36]

Only those who admit that they are sinners may be justified. Frith's deep conviction is that God gave us eternal life through the work of Christ, which was decreed and performed for our own benefit, but for the sake of Christ. Satisfaction and atonement for our sins is made in Christ, who died for us, so that God could make us alive in Christ, by offering us his salvation which we receive by faith. Faith presupposes that the believer accepts his own sinfulness before God and wholeheartedly trusts that his salvation depends entirely on Christ's work.[37]

God's salvation in Christ must have a practical end in the life of the believer, which implies an actual fight for righteousness. Frith does not refer to a justifying righteousness, but to the inner righteousness of the believer, which is the proof of justification. While the first purgatory, the Word of God, is primarily concerned with man's status before God, the second purgatory, the cross of Christ, approaches man's morality. Frith is very careful to underline the two basic aspects of salvation: forgiveness of sins and sanctification, represented by his theory of the two purgatories. He wrote:

> Let us do our diligence, calling for the Spirit of God, that this concupiscence reign not in our mortal body, ever knowledging, with a mild heart, our iniquities to our Father which is in heaven, for he is faithful and just to remit us our sins and to purge us from all iniquity, through the blood of Jesus Christ his Son."[38]

Should there be any justification at all by means of Christ's righteousness imputed to us, as in Melanchthon for instance,[39] human nature must be compulsorily transformed so that subsequent behaviour should please God. Frith applies the paradigm of suffering both to

---

36   ibid. 461.
37   ibid. 462. Trueman, *Luther's Legacy*, 124.
38   Frith, *An Epistle to the Christian Reader*, in Wright, *The Work of John Frith*, 466.
39   See Melanchthon's *Apology of the Augsburg Confession* in Philip Schaff (ed.), *The Creeds of Christendom*, vol. 3 (Grand Rapids: Baker Books, 1996), 8.

Christ and the believer, who are thus united. Christ suffered on the cross in order to defeat sin objectively. In the same way, the believer must suffer on the spiritual cross of his daily tribulations, in order subjectively and personally to defeat the desires of his own sinful nature.[40]

In the theology of Frith, justification by faith is represented by the union of the believer with Christ. From God's perspective, justification is a free gift, but from the believer's perspective, it is a complete trust in the promises of God concerning salvation in Christ. In Frith, justification has three major aspects: it is by grace, in Christ, through faith. The faith of the believer does not count for his inner righteousness, but it actually unites him with Christ, who shares with him his perfect righteousness accomplished by his atoning death. Nonetheless, inner righteousness is utterly important. Frith strongly believed that justification must be clearly reflected in the life of the believer in such a way that it involves distinct moral obligations. The duty of the justified believer is to mortify his sin in daily sanctification and to perform good works for the benefit of his neighbour. Frith was convinced that salvation must provide a firm basis for a daily moral life.[41]

Towards the end of his life, in *A Mirror to Know Thyself*, Frith wrote that self-knowledge implies the understanding that every good gift comes from God. Thus, Frith interprets the text from James 1:17 in terms of a twofold benefit, which completes his soteriology. The good gifts of God do not relate only to salvation, but also to creation. Frith then places the whole discussion of salvation within the broader paradigm of God's sovereignty and grace, which is manifested in both creation and salvation. Due to his mercy and love, God's sovereign choice is to save men. In Frith's theology, Christ is both the instrumental cause and the revelation of salvation, which consists of predestination, election, vocation and justification. Frith is very specific in his analysis of predestination. For him, predestination makes reference to three important aspects. Firstly, God's election of some individuals is not based on foreseen merits; secondly, God's election is based on his sovereign grace; and thirdly, God's election is dictated by his inscrutable will, which should not and cannot be investigated. This reasoning makes justification totally dependent on predestination and on God's unfathomable will.[42]

---

40 For a very informative discussion, see Trueman, *Luther's Legacy*, 135.
41 Trueman, *Luther's Legacy*, 149.
42 For more information, see Trueman, *Luther's Legacy*, 146.

2.2 The Late Reign of Henry VIII and
the Reign of Edward VI

In this historical period of the English Church, the doctrine of salvation continued to be assessed within the lines that had already been established by previous reformers, with a particular stress on two fundamental soteriological aspects. Firstly, an increasingly concentration on the doctrine of justification and grace could be detected, in the sense that justification was thought of in terms of its external character in relation to men. Thus, justification is essentially an act of God, which is totally detached from any human intentions or capabilities of accomplishment. Justification originates in God and is not determined by any human action. In this respect, justification is entirely of grace. This inevitably led to a certain focus on the idea of imputation, which involved the righteousness necessary to salvation. Whether it is the righteousness of Christ or the righteousness of the believer that is actually imputed has not practical importance; the vital aspect of the imputation is that God himself performs it, which is a clear delineation of God's work from human work.

Secondly, the definition of faith and its role in justification became significantly important especially as an answer to Catholic theology. Faith is fundamentally described as a rather passive factor in the process of justification. Faith does not fulfil anything in justification; faith only receives justification. At the same time, the fact that justifycation is by faith alone, not merely by faith, was another preoccupation in this period. Catholic theology might have conceded justification was by faith, but not by faith alone. English reformers had a very important reason for underlining that justification is by faith alone, because this definition implied the total absence of works as grounds for justification. The reality of salvation infers a total active involvement of God, which excludes any human merit.

2.2.1 Robert Barnes

According to *The Supplication of 1531*, the soteriology of Barnes has two main aspects: firstly, that only faith justifies before God and secondly, that fallen human will can only sin. Thus, the first major doctrine of Barnes' soteriology is justification by faith alone, which he deals with separately from the doctrine of free will. When he describes justification, Barnes chooses to express it negatively, by denying any soteriological importance that might be attributed to good works. After he clarifies this point, Barnes proceeds by defining justification positively. Barnes does not lose sight of the importance of the doctrine; consequently he underlines the centrality of justification in Paul's teaching and its importance for Christian tradition in a manner similar to that of Luther, in the sense that justification is essentially the work of God through faith in Christ.[43] Barnes' authorities are Scripture and the patristic writings, from which he identifies the christological essence, its gracious nature and its anteriority to good works.[44]

From Scripture, Barnes promotes the vital importance of Christ in salvation. Thus, the work of Christ consists of salvation, redemption, justification and reconciliation. Christ is sufficient for salvation; we need nothing and nobody but him in order to be justified. Barnes develops his understanding of the role of Christ in salvation by analysing the relationship between the historical person of Jesus and the divine work of salvation. The link between the historical person of Jesus, and God's plan of salvation is the incarnation of Christ, which is the ultimate purpose of reconciliation between God and man. Within this context, Barnes offers a definition of saving faith. For him, true faith is not primarily the intellectual acceptance of Christ's historicity or divinity, but rather a genuine belief in the purpose and outcome of his incarnation. In the theology of Barnes, the crucial role of Christ's incarnation is visibly decreased unless we believe the very purpose of incarnation, which is reconciliation with God. Likewise, the resurrection of Christ is of considerable disinterest unless we sternly affirm its outcome, which is justification before God. The true importance of salvation is revealed only by the testimony that Christ is the only Saviour. Thus, Christ is the firm ground of justification. Barnes is very well aware of the christological duality of salvation. For him, Christ as the basis of justification is both an objective truth and a subjective reality. Hence, justification is, on the one hand, a totally transcendent enterprise, but on the other hand, it is also a reality that fundamentally transforms humanity. Barnes is not very preoccupied with elaborate explanations regarding the objective aspect of justification, which he rather assumes than analyses. Surprisingly enough, he does not insist on the cross of Christ when he describes justification. He prefers to underline the resurrection of Christ as the reason for our justification.

---

43   See Luther, *Lectures on Romans*, in Pelikan (ed.), *Luther's Works*, vol. 25, 172.
44   Trueman, *Luther's Legacy*, 159.

The immediate consequence of the fact that Barnes in not particularly interested in explaining the objective aspect of justification is a relatively feeble affirmation of Christ's atoning work on the cross and an unclear expression of God's righteousness and wrath. Barnes, however, held that salvation is objectively accomplished in the person of Christ.[45]

The next stage in Barnes' theology of justification is the definition of grace, which is essentially a free gift of God. Grace is God's favour that humanity does not deserve. Thus, justification is an active process only because God accomplishes it. From the standpoint of human beings, justification is passive, because no work of man is ever soteriologically important for justification. In this respect, Barnes defines justification as the remission of sins, which is accomplished through faith. He also mentions the imputation of righteousness. For him, justification is essentially an act of God, which originates in him and is determined by no human action. Justification is entirely of grace. God's grace in salvation, or particularly in justification, is Barnes' first interest. Justification involves the imputation of righteousness, but it is difficult to assess whether he infers the imputation of the righteousness of Christ or the imputation of the righteousness of the believer considered in advance. Trueman explains that the conclusion depends on the interpretation of the following text from Barnes:

> I pray you, what good works doth the wicked man? Mark also how he saith that righteousness is imputed onto him. Ergo, it is not deserved. For that that is deserved is not imputed of favour, but it must be given of duty.[46]

Although an elaborate and clarifying conclusion is difficult to reach because of the ambiguity of Barnes' statement, Trueman insists on two important aspects. Firstly, he mentions Barnes' chief preoccupation with the graceful nature of salvation and justification. Now, Barnes uses the analogy of the king's council, which supposedly granted salvation on the basis of the king's favour, not of individual competency or merit. Secondly, Trueman raises the issue of a rather puzzling theological arrangement in Barnes' theology. Apparently, Barnes did not develop the doctrine of the believer's union with Christ, which at least in Luther – with whom Barnes was well acquainted – is the very root of the doctrine of imputation. Although Barnes briefly mentions the relationship between Christ's unconditional love and the sinful life of the believer, which he compares to marriage, Trueman is very

---

45   For more details, *ibid.* 159-162.
46   Barnes, *A Supplication* (1531), xliii.a.

careful and writes only that "it is just not possible to reach firm conclusions on Barnes's doctrine of imputation based on this isolated statement."[47] Unlike Trueman, Clebsch is quite certain that the accomplishment of reconciliation is actually justification by the imputation of Christ's righteousness to man, who by his own fallen nature cannot attain such righteousness.[48] McGrath does not seem to be bothered by this uncertainty and he only writes that the *Supplication of 1534* unequivocally affirms the imputation of righteousness. He does not say, however, whose righteousness. It should be said that whether it is the righteousness of Christ, as Clebsch naturally mentions, or the righteousness of the believer considered proleptically, as Trueman notices, it is only a matter of dogmatic decision. At least, according to the *A Supplication of 1534*, the answer appears to be the righteousness of Christ. Barnes wrote:

> Wherefore we say with S. Paul, that faith only justifies imputative; that is, all the merits and goodness, grace and favour, and all that is in Christ, to our salvation, is imputed and reckoned unto us.[49]

It is clear, however, that justification has a twofold aspect: firstly, the objective foundation in Christ and the grace of God, and secondly, the believer's subjective appropriation of these. Thus, Barnes describes the relationship between saving faith and good works. For Barnes, justification is by faith. The nature of faith is twofold, as it has both an objective level and a subjective significance. Objectively, faith involves a belief in Christ's historical existence and theological truth. Subjectively, faith implies the personal significance of Christ for the individual believer. Barnes wrote:

> The very true way of justification is this: first cometh God for the love of Christ Jesus and alonely of his mere mercy and giveth us freely the gift of faith whereby we do believe God and his holy Word, and stick fast by the promises of God, and believe that though heaven and earth and all that is in them should perish and come to nought, yet God shall be found true in his promises: for this faith's sake be we the elect children of God.[50]

The very nature of faith is its quality as a gift. We do nothing in order to obtain faith. It is only the love and grace of God that actually provide faith for us. True and justifying faith is given to us freely. Saving faith is always directed towards God and his Word. Barnes admits that human reason can only produce intellectual faith, whereby even pagans can

---

47 Trueman, *Luther's Legacy*, 163.
48 William Clebsch, *England's Earliest Protestants 1522-1535* (New Haven: Yale University Press, 1964), 67.
49 For more details, see Barnes, *A Supplication* (1534). See also McGrath, *Iustitia Dei*, 227.
50 Barnes, *A Supplication* (1531), lviii.b-lix.a.

acknowledge the historical existence of Christ and the value of his teachings. Nevertheless, justifying faith must be directed towards God's revelation, namely towards God himself and his Word. A strong trust in the promises of God regarding salvation is another essential component of justifying faith. It is also important to notice that justification is directly linked to election. We are the children of God if we believe. Although Barnes apparently makes election dependent on justification, he only wants to underline the centrality and importance of faith. It would have been logically inconsistent if Barnes had said that election was the outcome of justification. He had clearly stated that God chose some to election and some to damnation before the foundation of the world. Accordingly, it is within the logical boundaries of his theological reasoning to conclude that election is proved by justification or by the faith of justification. In spite of the objective fact of God's election, the individual believer must necessarily exercise his faith, which is the essence of salvation. The initiative of salvation belongs entirely to God and man has no active role in it. Although he denies good works as part of justification, he is not an antinomian. Barnes shows that justification produces good works, which are not optional, but compulsory for every justified believer. Faith changes both the believer's status before God and his inner human being. The outcome of a transformed humanity is good works. By grace, God has actively intervened in our lives in order that we should be justified and saved; therefore, our lives are changed by faith and they must follow the same pattern of active involvement in the lives of our fellow men. It is important to notice the pneumatological aspect of faith. The believer receives God's gift of faith by the Holy Spirit, who thus becomes actively involved in our justification. Accordingly, Barnes' conclusion is that faith actively leads to good works, as also explained by Melanchthon.[51] Although good works are the necessary result of faith, so that faith is logically the cause of good works, it is incorrect to infer that this is a mere causal sequence. Faith must be understood as the essence of Christian moral behaviour. Barnes wrote:

> Finally, of a fleshly beast it maketh me a spiritual man; of a damnable child it maketh me a heavenly son. Of a servant of the devil, it maketh me a free man of God's, both delivered from the law, from sin, from death, from the devil and from all misery that might hurt me. My Lords, this is the faith that doth justify and because it is given from heaven in to our hearts by the Spirit of God, therefore it can be no idle thing.[52]

---

51   See Melanchthon in Pauck (ed.), *Melanchthon and Bucer*, 105-106.
52   Barnes, *A Supplication*, xlix.b.

Man, however, will necessarily produce good works, but not as the cause of justification, but as an outward testimony. Accordingly, nobody should try to perform good works in order to prove his justification. Every believer will do good works as a grateful response to God's free justification.

> Therefore those men that will do not good works because they be justified alonely by faith be not the children of God nor the children of justification, and of that is this a sure and evident token; for if they were the very true children of God, they would be the gladder to do good works because they are justified freely. Therefore should they also be moved freely to work, if it were for no other purpose nor profit but alonely to do the will of their merciful God that hath so freely justified them.[53]

Thus, justification is by faith and every believer will gladly perform good works as a result. This idea is also based on Barnes' interpretation of *The Epistle of James*. Although not very happy with the canonicity of the epistle, as he only allows for a hypothetical canonicity, Barnes nevertheless defends the principle that justification by faith alone must be and actually is the normative principle for biblical hermeneutics. Justification cannot be through works. Thus, Barnes draws a distinction between the works performed before justification and those performed after justification. It is clear from Barnes that neither option counts for salvation. Salvation is not by works. A sinner who comes to Christ just before his death will not be able to perform good works as a result of his conversion. This, however, underlines the graceful aspect of salvation. We are saved by God's grace, which is objectively shown in the death of Christ, not by works, regardless of whether they are performed before or after justification. Barnes concludes that, if James speaks of justification as involving works, he must have had in mind the works which are the outcome of justification.[54]

Barnes' doctrine of justification by faith does not have a theological aspect only, whereby he affirms the objectivity of justification due to God's grace in the work of Christ. Justification has also an anthropological aspect, which highlights its subjective appropriation by faith. Barnes thinks that the idea of faith as a gift is necessary not only because God has chosen to accomplish salvation in this way, but also because the nature of fallen man demands it.[55] Fallen humanity can do nothing to gain salvation, because sin affects the whole human being. Man must have Christ within him, if he really wants to do anything worthwhile for his salvation. The whole of a man is corrupted, there is

---

53   *ibid.* l.b.
54   See Trueman, *Luther's Legacy*, 170.
55   *ibid.* 171.

nothing good left in him, so he cannot perform good works unless the Holy Spirit is within him. Consequently, justification is by grace, because man is essentially incapable of initiating his salvation, as he has not soteriological motivation within himself.[56] In order that man should be aware of his inability to save himself, God gave him the law, which reveals man's pride. Man cannot even fulfil the demands of the law without the external help of God:

> Thy maker knoweth that they be impossible for thee. He knoweth also thy damnable and presumptuous pride that rekonest how thou canst do all things that be good of thine own strength without any other help; and, to subdue this presumptuous pride of thine, and to bring thee to knowledge of thine own self, he hath given thee his commandments; of which thou canst not complain, for he be both righteous and good.[57]

At this point, Barnes promotes a very sharp doctrine of predestination. Because God is righteous and good, he saves a few people, whom he had previously predestined, and damns many more, whom he had also predestined. In spite of this predestination, God remains good and just. The strong belief in God's goodness and righteousness is true justifying faith. Barnes wrote:

> Moreover, thou believest that God is righteous, that God is wise and that God is merciful. Now faith is of those things that do not appear, nor that can be proved by exterior cause. Hold thee fast to this faith, then all thy fleshly reasons be afoiled. For, when God saveth so few men and damneth so many, and thou knowest no cause why, yet must thou believe that he is merciful and righteous. This is faith, which, if it could be proved by exterior cause, then were it no need to believe it.[58]

In his later theology, and especially in the *Supplication of 1534*, Barnes reaffirms the primacy of Christ in justification. Christ only is the one who justifies. Despite the significant differences between the *Supplication of 1531* and the *Supplication of 1534*, the doctrine of justification is explained within the same theological foundation.[59] Thus, in the theology of Barnes, the doctrine of justification consists of the following basic truths: Christ is the objective cause of justification, free grace is the basis of foundation, faith is the gift of God, justification is seen as remission of sins and good works are the necessary outcome of faith.

---

56   *ibid.* 173.
57   Barnes, *A Supplication*, lxxxvii.a.
58   *ibid.* xciiii.b.
59   For the differences, see Trueman, *Luther's Legacy*, 192.

2.2.2 Thomas Cranmer

One of the most important writing of Cranmer regarding salvation is his *Notes on Justification*. Although it is impossible to establish a certain date for their writing, it is clear that they reflect Cramer's firm conviction on justification, so they should not be dated too soon in his career. In the end, the date of writing is not important; the relevance of the *Notes on Justification* is given by their methodology. Cranmer makes clear that this doctrine of justification is based on authorities from Scripture, the Fathers and the Schoolmen. This is Cranmer's primary concern, as he mainly quotes from the apostle Paul for the witness of Scripture, then from Irenaeus, Origen, Basil the Great, Ambrose, Jerome, Theodoret, Augustine and Chrysostom for the witness of patristic writings, and finally from Peter Lombard, Thomas Aquinas, Anselm and Bernard de Clairvaux for the witness of scholastic works.[60]

From the very beginning, Cranmer points out that it is not faith which should be considered the ground of justification, because ultimately justification is not even by faith but solely by grace. Following Luther, Cranmer wrote that the doctrine of justification should not underline faith as the greatest or the necessary work of man, but highlight the fact that justification is possible only by the grace of God, which is expressed in the work of God.[61] Human works do not deserve the remission of sins. It is only Christ and his gracious work at the cross that deserve forgiveness and the total remission of sins. For Cranmer, it was clear that the doctrine of justification in Scripture is not contradictory. It is a known fact that *The Epistle of James* caused many reformers either to reject it from the canon of Scripture, like Martin Luther for instance, or elegantly to express their willingness to consider it part of Scripture, although no firm conviction is this respect was involved, like Robert Barnes. It was not, however, the case with Cranmer. He was convinced that James did not contradict Paul, but only described that kind of justification which is the continuation of Paul's doctrine of justification. Actually, Cranmer wrote that James

---

60 See also Geoffrey W. Bromiley, *Thomas Cranmer Theologian* (London: Lutterworth Press, 1956), 28.

61 For details, see Althaus, *The Theology of Martin Luther* (Philadelphia: Fortress Press, 1966), 232-234.

referred to a justification which is "the declaration, continuation and increase of that justification Paul spake of before."[62]

Justification by faith emphasises the ultimate importance of Christ for justification. Actually, the doctrine of justification by faith should be a means of glorifying our Saviour Jesus Christ, who was offered on the cross for the sins of humanity and who rose again for our justification. Cranmer points out that justification is achieved by Christ and received by faith. It is only by faith that man knows the mercy and grace of God, which were promised by God's work. The mercy and grace of God in Christ and for the sake of Christ accomplished justification. Man receives it by faith, which is the means whereby he knows all this. For Cranmer, man's appropriation of justification by means of faith should be interpreted as a transfer of the glory of justification from man to Christ. By faith, we acknowledge that the glory of our justification should not be ours, but should be completely ascribed to the merits of Christ.[63]

In his *Homilies*, Cranmer develops the doctrine of justification with a very strong emphasis on the grace and glory of God, which are revealed in the person and the work of Jesus Christ.[64] Cranmer stresses again that justification by faith should not praise faith itself, but the work of Christ, which is ultimately the source of our justification. Apparently, Cranmer interprets justification as being a means whereby man is made righteous, because he totally excludes good works as the foundation of justification. It is clear that justification consists of a certain righteousness, but this is not the righteousness of man. It is rather an alien righteousness, a righteousness which is totally external to humans. This alien righteousness is realised by the atoning work of Christ, so it is the righteousness of Christ. Thus, the righteousness of Christ, which is the objective foundation of justification is the unique factor that manifests God's grace and appeases God's wrath. Cranmer describes justification by means of the imagery of a ransom, which is fully paid in Christ to the satisfaction of God's justice:

> Our justification doth come freely by the mere mercy of God and of so great and free mercy that whereas all the world was not able of themselves to pay any part towards their ransom, it pleased our heavenly Father, of his infinity mercy, without any our desert of deserving, to prepare for us the

---

62 Some of Cranmer's quotations are from the Parker Society editions of his works (hereafter *Works*). This quotation is from *Works* II, 208.

63 Bromiley, *Thomas Cranmer Theologian*, 29-30.

64 Cranmer's *Homilies* include *The Homily of Salvation, The Homily of the True, Lively and Christian Faith* and *The Homily of Good Works*. Fore more details, Bromiley, *Thomas Cranmer Theologian*, 30.

most precious jewels of Christ's body and blood, whereby our ransom might be fully paid, the law fulfilled and his justice fully satisfied.[65]

Cranmer further explains that justification is given to man by faith. At this point, Cranmer offers a definition of faith, which is in line with his previous theology. Basically, faith is the sincere acknowledgment of the human predicament. Man is sentenced to death because of his sin and he has no intrinsic power to change this situation. Faith is the admission of the fact that should there be any salvation at all, it is only God who wills and accomplishes it. The very nature of faith points to the essence of justification. If man has justification by faith alone, it means that justification is ultimately by grace, which is clearly shown in Christ. Thus, according to Cranmer, justification is through faith alone, by grace alone, in Christ alone. At his point, his imagery of ransom becomes relevant. Justification is a gift, which was freely given to us by God. From this perspective, justification involves a ransom, which humanity is unable to pay. God alone was the one who solved this problem, as he settled the way this payment should be made. Cranmer is very careful to indicate that man did not deserve anything, but that it was God's will that he should arrange the way of dealing with this ransom. The solution to justification is the body and blood of Christ, namely his atoning work at the cross. For Cranmer, justification consists of three main aspects: firstly, the payment of the ransom whereby we were redeemed from sin; secondly, the fulfilment of the law which mankind was incapable of performing completely and thirdly, the satisfaction of God's justice which was not within the power of human nature to achieve perfectly.[66]

The explicit language of imputation is not thoroughly present in Cranmer, but it is nevertheless occasionally mentioned in relation to the righteousness of the believer. Thus, Cranmer mentions that justification is the remission of sins, but also the acceptance or the reconciliation of the believer with God, which is equated with renewal in Christ. The pneumatological aspect of justification is present in Cranmer's theology with special reference to the work of the Holy Spirit within the believer in order that he should perform good works towards God and his fellow men. Justification is through faith, whereby we believe that we have been received in God's grace and that our sins have been remitted for the sake of Christ. For Cranmer, this faith is imputed as righteousness in the sight of God, which is in accordance with Melanchthon's *Augsburg Confession* (Article IV)[67]:

---

65   Cranmer, *Works* II, 130.
66   Bromiley, *Thomas Cranmer Theologian*, 31.
67   Melanchthon, *The Augsburg Confession*, in Schaff, *The Creeds of Christendom*, vol. 3, 8.

> On justification, we teach that its proper meaning is remission of sins and acceptance or reconciliation of us into the grace and favour of god, that is, true renewal in Christ. And we teach that though sinners do not obtain this justification without repentance and a good and well-inclined outgoing (*bono et propenso motu*) of heart, wrought by the Holy Spirit, towards God and their neighbour, yet they are not justified in virtue of the worth or merit of their repentance, or of and of their works or merits, but they are justified freely for Christ's sake through faith, when they believe that they are received into grace and their sins are remitted for the sake of Christ, who by his death made satisfaction for our sins. This faith God imputes for righteousness in his sight (*coram ipso*).[68]

Christ is actually the righteousness required for justification for all those who believe in him. This is a clear affirmation of the fact that the inner righteousness of the believer cannot suffice for justification. Only the external righteousness of Christ, which by faith belongs to the believer, is consequently the factor that offers the ground for justification. By his atoning death, Christ paid the necessary ransom to God, perfectly fulfilled the law and fostered the required justice to God. Cranmer wrote:

> Christ is now the righteousness of all them that truly do believe in him. He for them paid their ransom by his death: he for them fulfilled the law in his life: so that now in him and by him, every true Christian man may be called a fulfiller of the law; forasmuch as that which their infirmity lacketh, Christ's justice hath supplied.[69]

Actually, Cranmer analyses the doctrine of justification taking into account two realities. The first reality is that man is sinful and cannot do anything to change his position. He cannot do God's will and he consequently reaches a state of personal failure, guilt and condemnation. The second reality is God's mercy towards sinners. The mercy of God is manifested in his love, whereby he sent Christ, his Son, to die for the sins of all men so that we have the remission of sins, as in Bucer.[70] Thus, J. I. Packer writes that, in Cranmer, justification is "the bestowal upon them of righteousness (forgiveness and acceptance) for Christ's sake."[71] For Cranmer, justification consists of the fact that the believer is considered righteous on the basis of the righteousness of Christ:

---

68 Thomas Cranmer, *The 1538 Articles*, in G. E. Duffield (ed.), *The Works of Thomas Cranmer* (Appleford: The Sutton Courtenay Press, 1964), 4.

69 Cranmer, *Works* II, 130.

70 See also Martin Bucer, *Romans*, 12.51-56, in the translation of Stephens, *The Holy Spirit*, 51-52.

71 J. I. Packer, "Introduction" to Duffield (ed.), *The Works of Thomas Cranmer*, xxiv.

[...] Those [...] which will not knowledge the justness or righteousness which will not knowledge the justness or righteousness which cometh by God, but go abut to advance their own righteousness, shall never come to that righteousness which we have by God; which is the righteousness of Christ: by whom only all the saints in heaven and all other that have been saved have been reputed righteous and justified. So that to Christ our only Saviour and Redeemer, on whose righteousness both their and our justification doth depend, is to be transcribed all the glory thereof.[72]

The object of justifying faith is the person of Christ. Faith is trust in Christ, not in ourselves. One of the most difficult problems Cranmer faced was to delineate between faith manifested in man and the total otherness of God's work. Cranmer had a strong conviction that faith was not a work of justification or a self-justifying work. Justification is entirely the work of God. Man cannot produce justification; he can only receive it by the grace of God, which is manifested in the work of Christ, described as Redeemer, Saviour and Justifier. The distinguishing character of Cranmer's definition of faith is that faith actually belongs to the believer. He does not insist on faith as a gift of God, although he is not far from this definition. For Cranmer, our faith in Christ is within us. After this assessment, Cranmer immediately writes that faith does not justify us and it should not be regarded more than a mere work of virtue, like for instance hope, charity, repentance, fear of God, which are all within us. Although faith is within the believer, Cranmer has a firm conviction that the object of faith is not within the believer, but outside him, in the person of Christ.[73] We have faith when we fully trust that it is only Christ who takes away our sins. Within the broader discussion on justification, faith is only a passive factor. Justification is by faith alone if this particular faith directs our trust towards Christ and his death for our salvation.

Cranmer strove to clarify another aspect of faith, which although clear from Scripture, did cause misinterpretations and attacks from the traditional Churches, namely the Catholic or the Catholic-oriented Churches. He insisted that salvation and particularly justification was by faith alone or by faith only. The word "only" was at the heart of the matter. Traditionalist theology might have agreed that salvation was by faith, but not by faith only. It was possible to argue that we were saved by faith, but also by hope, charity or repentance. The role of the word "only" attached to faith was to underline that justification is "without works." Although we have faith, it is within the essence of justifying

---

72 Cranmer, *Annotations on the King's Book*, in Duffield (ed.), *The Works of Thomas Cranmer*, 12.

73 Geoffrey W. Bromiley, *Thomas Cranmer Theologian* (London: Lutterworth Press, 1956), 32.

faith to be oriented towards Christ and his works, not towards us and our works. In order to clarify this aspect, Cranmer writes that faith must not be regarded as a personal work or merit of the believer:

> And because all this is brought to pass through the only merits and deservings of our Saviour Christ, and not through our merits or through the merits of any virtue that we have within us, or of any work that cometh from us, therefore, in that respect of merit and deserving we renounce, as it were, altogether again faith, works and all other virtues.[74]

In Cranmer, true justifying faith includes two aspects. Firstly, faith is the acceptance of the facts and doctrines of Christianity. Secondly, faith involves a trust in the promises of God, which necessarily expresses itself in a life of daily obedience. This element of personal conviction makes faith the only means whereby we appropriate the justification of God. Cranmer writes:

> The true Christian faith [...] is not only knowledge of the articles of the faith, or a mere historical belief of Christian doctrine; but, together with that knowledge and belief, it is a firm trust in the mercy of God promised for Christ's sake, whereby we maintain and conclude with certainty that he is merciful and propitious even to us.[75]

In Cranmer's theology, faith also has an epistemological role. By faith, the believer knows God and this knowledge of God produces good works. Thus, good works are the test by which true and justifying faith should be discerned from a false belief in God. Cranmer promotes a rather sober definition of faith, which must be intellectual, volitional and emotional. Thus faith includes a belief in the historicity of Christ, a firm trust in the work of Christ for us, a personal disposition towards the acceptance of the work of Christ and a lively attitude which flows from the appropriation of God's work. In spite of these intellectual, volitional and emotional aspects of faith, which are characteristic of human psychology, Cranmer once again underlines that faith is passive in relation to the work of God. Faith cannot create, but only receive the justifying righteousness of Christ, which is entirely the gift of God. Faith, however, must be active from the perspective of human conduct. The believer who exercises his faith in Christ must necessarily perform good works, which are the outward expression of justification. True faith will always compel the believer to do good works, which are the necessary outcome of justification. Cranmer wrote:

> For good works are necessary to salvation, not because they make an ungodly man righteous, nor because they are a price for sins or a cause of justification; but because it is necessary that he who is already justified by

---

74   Cranmer, *Works* II, 133.
75   Cranmer, *The 1538 Articles*, in Duffield (ed.), *The Works of Thomas Cranmer*, 4.

faith and reconciled to God through Christ should have a care to do the will of God.[76]

Although he defines faith in terms of human psychology, Cranmer is faithful to the witness of Scripture and he also asserts the *extra nos* character of faith, which is the gift of God to the elect as, for instance, in Zwingli.[77] Due to his understanding of election, Cranmer describes faith as bringing the assurance of the believer's final preservation. Sinful human nature may cause the believer to fall again, but God's faithfulness will restore him, which will cause the believer to perform good works as a sign of thankfulness for God's grace.[78]

2.3 The Reign of Mary I and the Early Reign of Elizabeth I

The reign of Mary I marked a decisive step in the history of the English Reformation, when Protestant teaching and practical life came under severe persecution. Apparently, this situation led to an increasingly obvious presence of election in the theology of the day as a sign of assurance that God is the one who secures salvation. Justification is kept within the same doctrinal framework, but is especially approached within the more encompassing doctrine of election. Thus, the doctrine of justification in election grows to be a clear sign of God's sovereignty over salvation and the entire creation. The doctrine of election generates a strong orientation towards an absolute predestination. In predestination, election and justification God acts according to his otherness, which subsists beyond the physical boundaries of creation. The sovereignty of God is clearly manifested in his decrees of predestination, election and justification, which are subsequently applied in execution.

On the other hand, the reign of Elizabeth I brought a certain period of stability, which was manifested in theology and religious life. The English reformers reoriented theological debates towards the claims of Catholic theology and the concept of faith became of crucial importance in doctrinal formulations regarding justification. In line with previous soteriological definitions, faith was identified as the sole means by

---

76   *ibid.* 4.

77   Ulrich Zwingli, *Early Writings* (Durham: The Labyrinth Press, 1987), 199.

78   For more details, see J. I. Packer, "Introduction" to G. E. Duffield (ed.), *The Works of Thomas Cranmer* (Appleford: The Sutton Courtenay Press, 1964), xxv.

which justification is granted to humanity, totally apart from any human capacity to fulfil the righteousness required for justification. In this respect, the doctrine of Christ directed soteriology towards the primacy of God in salvation and justification. The preservation of a healthy balance between God's promise of justification and man's responsibility in sanctification was another major preoccupation of the English Reformation in this historical period.

2.3.1 John Bradford

The first work in which Bradford discusses the doctrine of salvation is *A Treatise of Election and of the Free Will*. He begins his treatise by writing that salvation starts with election, which is made in Christ before creation. Bradford proves his point by enumerating some texts from Scripture, which include Ephesians 1 and Romans 8-11. He then links election to the nature of God. The certainty of the being and nature of God results in the certainty of his creation. Despite its existence in time, no element of creation can do anything but simply exist because of the nature of God. Part of the nature of God is his knowledge, which is the direct foundation of election. Creation exists because God had previously had knowledge of it and this is due to his nature. The knowledge of God must not be separated from the wisdom and the will of God, all of which cause things to exist within creation. Trueman writes that Bradford infers a doctrine of absolute predestination from the being of God by the very fact that he links God's foreknowledge to his will and by emphasising the unity of that will.[79] Bradford does not promote a fatalistic approach to creation and salvation; on the contrary, he is against the opinion that holds a fatalistic necessity in connection to both creation and salvation. According to Bradford, God is a free agent, actually he is "the most free agent" and he cannot be tied to second causes. He is the very creator and he cannot be bound within the limits of his own creation. God decrees all parts of creation in accordance with this wisdom, which perceives and determines in advance the being and action of all things. Then, by his power, God puts every element of his creation in execution, according to what he had previously decreed. Using the language of the execution of God's decree, Bradford wrote in a manner which resembles that of Beza:[80]

---

79 See Trueman, *Luther's Legacy*, 253.
80 See Beza, *Letter to John Calvin, the 29ᵗʰ of July 1555*, in Holtrop, *The Bolsec Controversy*, 739.

We should certainly know that it is God which is the ruler and arbiter of all things, which of his wisdom hath foreseen and determined all things that he will do and now of his power doth in his time put the same in execution, according as he hath decreed with himself.[81]

The next step in Bradford's argument is the distinction between necessity and constraint. Thus, he contrasts constraint with willingness, which is consequently attached to the concept of necessity. The very nature of God, and particularly his goodness, as in Bucer's definition of justification,[82] is of necessity or willingness and not of constraint. God is good because he chooses to be good; nobody can enforce anything on God. As Bradford extends his definition to human goodness or wickedness, so that men do good and evil of necessity or according to their own nature, not of constraint, his main idea is apparently that nature determines the action of both God and men. Good and evil nature determines good and evil actions of necessity, not of constraint. The distinction between necessity and constraint is of uttermost importance in matters pertaining to salvation, because Bradford clearly delineates the nature and the action of God, who is essentially good, from the nature and action of the devil, who is essentially evil. If all things exist of necessity in accordance with their own nature, it is evidently clear that any action of God, who is good by nature, is substantially good. Thus, God cannot be the source of evil, because his nature and will are good. Although Bradford does not list election among the actions of God, which he performs of necessity in accordance with his own good nature, he nevertheless infers it, thus leading his argument to the likely conclusion that election cannot be but a good action of God. Bradford further explains that necessity should be equated to providence. All things that are done of necessity are consequently done by God's providence, which is a clear reflection of the will of God. At this point, Bradford introduces the concept of the Word of God, which is a revelation, but not the revelation of the will of God. The Word of God does not disclose the will of God entirely. In his Word, God only reveals "so much of his will as we should with diligence search and observe." As the will of God reflects his nature, we should only contemplate God as he is described in his Word, not as he is in himself. The same truth should be applied to the actions of God, which must be assessed in accordance with the revelation in the Word of God. Thus, the providence of God should be evaluated according to the revelation displayed in the Word of God. On the other hand, any

---

81 John Bradford, *The Writings of John Bradford* (Cambridge: Cambridge University Press, 1848), 211.

82 See Bucer, *Romans*, 119.A.16-B.8 in Stephens, *The Holy Spirit*, 52-53.

action of man which is performed outside the prescriptions of the Word of God is sin. We can only know the Word of God, not the entire providence of God. This is why man has to perform those actions, which are required by the Word of God, otherwise his actions are rightfully considered transgressions. Original sin is the result of Adam's evil action, which reflects his evil will, because he did not act in accordance with the prescriptions of the Word of God that he knew. God, however, turned the whole situation round in order that it should serve his providence. Due to his good nature and will, God could not tolerate sin and he consequently punished the action and its doer. Thus, God displayed his good nature in accordance with this providence, which is not totally revealed in his Word. This is why men should not question God's reasons in acting consequently when he actively punishes sin.[83] Trueman notices this vitally important aspect of Bradford's theology and writes that Bradford "takes the scriptural revelation concerning God's eternal decree of election as the ultimate foundation for the doctrine. Thus he anchors election primarily in God's scriptural revelation and not in his being."[84]

The nature of God is essentially different from the nature of man. On the one hand, the nature of God is the only essence that cannot commit sin. The perfect justice, wisdom and holiness of God cannot perform any action which is against his own nature and precepts. On the other hand, the nature of man, although created in the image of God, cannot be perfect as the nature of God. Adam's sinful action changed human nature so drastically, that the original immortality, wisdom, righteousness and holiness gave way to death foolishness, unrighteousness and corruption. For Bradford, it is clear that the author of sin is man, while God is the author of all the things in creation, apart from sin. Moreover, it is due to his good nature and will that God decreed the election of his children of necessity, not of constraint, in order that he should save them from their sin. Bradford has a firm conviction that man cannot do anything in matters pertaining to his salvation from sin. There is no such thing as free will concerning any human performance that could bring man closer to salvation. For Bradford, we could say we have free will only in respect to this life, not in respect to the new life, given by God's salvation. Should anyone consider a possible *ordo salutis* in the theology of Bradford, the first step is certainly God's decree of election. Election is followed by justification. The next step is regeneration, which is clearly seen in

---

83   Bradford, *Writings*, 213-214.
84   Trueman, *Luther's Legacy*, 255-256.

sanctification.[85] However, election of necessity, not of constraint, is actually the work of justification:

> By this which I have already spoke, I think the diligent reader may see how that there is election of God's children and how that God's providence stretcheth itself to all things; so that all things in respect thereof come of necessity, but yet nothing thereby to be done by constraint and enforcement: wherethrough God is seen to be the author of all things and yet of no evil or sin [...] Justification in Scripture is taken for the forgiveness of sins and consisteth in the forgiveness of sins. This is only God's work and we nothing else but patients and not agents.[86]

Although very brief, Bradford's definition of justification contains some very important aspects, such as the forgiveness of sins, the exclusive initiative of God in salvation and man's passive role in receiving it. For Bradford, man has no contribution in justification. Moreover, man has no contribution in regeneration either, as this is completely the work of God through the Holy Spirit. Bradford is not particularly explicit in delineating justification from sanctification and they are apparently one and the same work of God, which man receives passively and which marks his transfer from death to life by means of God's gracious intervention. By the work of the Spirit, we make progress in sanctification, which apparently results in a growth of our justified position. Like Calvin, who believed in our justification in the sight of God,[87] Bradford wrote that:

> Afore we be justified and regenerated of God, we are altogether dead to God and to all goodness in his sight; and therefore we are altogether patients till God have wrought this his only work, justification and regeneration. Which work, in respect of us and our imperfection and falls, in that it is not so full and perfect but it may be more and more, therefore by the Spirit of sanctification (which we receive in regeneration as the seed of God) we are quickened to labour with the Lord and to be more justified.[88]

In Bradford, justification is by faith, which is actually the means whereby justification and sanctification are made effective within the believer. He does not elaborate his definition of faith, but other parts of his writings offer the essentials of his view on faith, which is from God, in Christ and leads to the sanctification of everyday life. In his *Prayer for the Obtaining of Faith*, Bradford writes that faith comes from God and is the proof of God's goodness and love towards the believer in Christ. Faith brings assurance of the forgiveness of sins and acknowledges this

---

85 Bradford, *Writings*, 215-216.
86 *ibid.* 217-218.
87 Calvin, *Institutes*, 3.9.2.
88 Bradford, *Writings*, 218.

fact due to the work of Christ. It is obvious that faith is not an empty concept, as it is always directed towards Christ and his work. As far as the believer is concerned, faith produces within him an inner holiness and righteousness for sanctification. Bradford wrote:

> [...] Gracious Father, I am bold to beg of thy mercy, through thy Son Jesus Christ, one sparkle of true faith and certain persuasion of thy goodness and love towards me in Christ; wherethrough I being assured of the pardon of all my sins, by the mercies of Christ thy Son, may be thankful to thee, love thee and serve thee in holiness and righteousness all the days of my life.[89]

Bradford's second work which contains a brief discussion on justification is *A Defence of Election*. In this treatise, Bradford reaffirms that the will of God is revealed in his Word, from which we know that, for the sake of Christ, he elected some people, but not everybody. In connection with the elect, Bradford writes that God had predestined them, called them, justified them and glorified them in such a way that they will be preserved in salvation forever.[90] In order to explain what election is, Bradford makes an elaborate exegesis on Ephesians 1. Firstly, he establishes the cause of God's election, which is his good will expressed in love, as in Calvin.[91] Secondly, election was decreed before creation. Thirdly, election was decreed in Christ. Bradford explains that election was decreed and realised in Christ, because he was the only one who was able to deal with the justice of God. The elect could not have solved the problem of God's justice. It was only Christ who was able to satisfy God's justice, but not necessarily for the sake of divine justice. Christ satisfied God's justice for the elect. Again, Bradford makes a direct connection between election and justification, writing that Christ justified God's children, namely the elect, by means of the mercy and the justice of God. When he writes about election, Bradford is very careful to mention it within the context of Christ's death.[92] Fourthly, by his election, God singled out only some people, not all of them. This specific point is important, as Bradford attaches to election the forgiveness of sins, holiness and union with Christ. As in Calvin,[93] election is proved by faith, because Bradford points out that not all people believe. If only some believe, the logical outcome is that those who believe had been elected. One should not forget, however, that Bradford makes a distinction between sufficiency and efficiency. The death of Christ is sufficient for all, but is efficient only for the elect. The

---

89   *ibid*. 210.
90   *ibid*. 311.
91   Calvin, *Institutes*, 3.24.3.
92   Bradford, *Writings*, 312.
93   Calvin, *Institutes*, 3.24.5.

logical inference is that justification too is efficient only in the elect. According to Trueman, this is one instance when Bradford does not offer a satisfactory solution to the problem of election. If God wants everybody to be saved, but the death of Christ is only effectual for the elect, the reliability of Scripture becomes questionable. Trueman rightly notices that Bradford emphasises the particularity of God's election, rather than the universality of God's desire to save. Bradford, however, has a problem in showing, in Trueman's words, "how God can will all men to be saved in view of the fact that he has already elected only some to eternal life."[94] Trueman writes that the only solution to Bradford's problem regarding the universality of God's will to save and the elective character of his salvation is faith.[95] The paradox between the universality of God's desire to save and the limited nature of the decree of election must necessarily be accepted by faith, although Bradford comes up with a linguistic solution. Thus, he writes that whenever Scripture mentions the fact that God wills the salvation of all, the term "all" makes direct reference to all the elect or to all kinds of people: "Yea, when Scripture saith that God will have all men saved, it speaketh either of all the elect, or of men of all sorts states and conditions."[96] Despite these arguments, one thing is clear: the practical proof of God's work in salvation, which includes election, predestination and justification, is faith. True faith is the firm conviction that God alone has secured salvation for us.

Thus, only the elect receive the forgiveness of sins and live in holiness because of their regeneration and union with Christ. Fifthly, God predestined the elect unto everlasting life. The predestination unto eternal life of the elect was decreed by God in Christ.[97] The purpose of predestination is that the elect should grow in the likeness of Christ. Sixthly, the purpose of election is the manifestation of the glory and grace of God. This way, election and predestination were decreed unto the sanctification of the elect. Seventhly, although predestination is a decree which had been issued before creation and time, it is actually linked to creation and time. The reflection of predestination in time and history is justification. At this point, Bradford does not offer any definition of justification, but he connects it to the hearing of the Word of God, to faith, to receiving of the Holy Spirit and to the remission of sins. Eighthly, election is the guarantee of eternal life, because all those who had been elected would be preserved in grace until they reach

---

94 Trueman, *Luther's Legacy*, 259.
95 *ibid*. 260.
96 *ibid*. 325.
97 Bradford, *Writings*, 313.

their final salvation. Again, Bradford mentions that election is the manifest proof of God's glory and grace.[98] Bradford carefully underlines all these points in order to show that salvation is entirely the initiative of God, which is practically supported and carried on in history by God alone.

The third work where Bradford approaches justification is *A Declaration Concerning Religion*. The definition of justification is not highly elaborate, but it contains some critical aspects, which are significant to his soteriology. Bradford writes:

> We believe and confess concerning justification that, as it cometh only from God's mercy through Christ, so it is perceived and had of none which be of years of discretion otherwise that by faith only. Which faith is not an opinion, but a certain persuasion wrought by the Holy Ghost in the mind and heart of man; wherethrough, as the mind is illuminated, so the heart is suppled to submit itself to the will of God unfeignedly, and so sheweth forth an inherent righteousness; which is to be discerned in the article of justification from the righteousness which God endueth us withal in justifying us, although inseparably they go together. And this we do, not for curiosity or contention sake, but for conscience sake that it might be quiet; which it can never be, if we confound distinction forgiveness of sins and Christ's justice imputed to us with regeneration and inherent righteousness.[99]

Bradford's definition of justification is brief, but a significant aspect of the formulation is that he links justification to faith. He explains that justification is totally the initiative of God, realised by means of Christ's work, which is the manifestation of God's mercy. Justification becomes effectual in the life of people, when appropriated by faith. Bradford does not provide an extensive definition of faith, but he underlines some key aspects which are relevant to justification. Thus, faith is not a view, a mere opinion, but a firm conviction which is the direct outcome of the work of the Holy Spirit. The appropriation of justification by means of faith transforms human intellect and emotions. The believer will subsequently submit himself to the will of God, so that he will acquire an inner righteousness. This inner righteousness of man, which is the result of the appropriation of justification by faith through the work of the Holy Spirit, must necessarily be distinguished from the righteousness with which God justifies us. In justification, God bestows upon us a righteousness which is not ours, but which belongs to Christ and is imputed to us. In conclusion, justification consists of two fundamental aspects: firstly, the forgiveness of sins and the imputation of Christ's righteousness and secondly, regeneration and inner righteousness.

---

98   *ibid.* 314.
99   *ibid.* 371-372.

2.3.2 John Foxe

The doctrine of salvation expressed primarily by means of justification by faith was an ongoing preoccupation for Foxe.[100] The first aspect of Foxe's doctrine of justification is the instrumental cause of justification, which resides in the fact that the merits of Christ are applied to us, as in Luther,[101] and made ours by means of faith. This statement is of great importance for Foxe's thought, because it sets the theological limits of his doctrine of justification. Thus, the only objective foundation of justification is the death of Christ. By his death, Christ acquired a certain merit to which Foxe evidently attaches a soteriological significance. This merit of Christ is firstly applied to us. Although he does not write explicitly who performs this application, Foxe undoubtedly infers that God is the one who applies the merits of Christ's death to us. This means that God considers Christ's merit to be ours, as if it really were ours. The second important fact is that the merit of Christ is not only applied to us or considered to be ours, but actually becomes ours, as God makes it ours. This necessarily involves the transformation of human nature. In his *Acts and Monuments*, just before discussing the doctrine of justification, John Foxe displays a list of what he calls "certain principles or general verities grounded upon the truth of God's Word." The essence of these principles is clearly soteriological and they are of great importance to the further assessment of justification. The soteriology of Foxe begins with a twofold statement of sin and righteousness. He explains that sin, with its direct result in death, has its origin in the first man and is generated to the rest of mankind by means of propagation through human nature. The scriptural text Foxe uses is Romans 5:17, from which it is clear that the man referred to is to Adam. Foxe then immediately announces that righteousness, with its direct outcome in life, has its origin in the obedience of another man. From the same text, Romans 5:17, it is obvious that this latter man is Christ. The means of propagation of righteousness and life is not by human nature, but by regeneration "of him by faith and baptism." Foxe underlines here a very important soteriological principle, which places the objective essence of

---

100 Fore more details see Glyn Parry, "John Foxe, 'Father of Lyes', and the Papists", in David Loades (ed.), *John Foxe and the English Reformation* (Scholar Press, 1997).

101 For Luther's application of the merits of Christ, see also the helpful discussion in Bernhard Lohse, *Martin Luther's Theology. Its Historical and Systematic Development* (Edinburgh: T&T Clark, 1999), 258.

regeneration in Christ, not in the believer. At the same time, regeneration deeply affects human nature through the faith of the believer. The link between faith and baptism has nothing to do with ascribing the same importance to both of them. Foxe always mentions faith first; baptism comes second, as a result of faith, which is certainly obvious in Foxe's first principle:

> As sin and death came originally by the disobedience of one to all men of his generation by nature: so righteousness and life come originally by the obedience of one to all men regenerated of him by faith and baptism.[102]

The means whereby God applies and then makes Christ's merit ours is faith. The entire work of God in justification is transferred upon the sinner by his faith in Christ. For Foxe, justification is mainly the remission of sins. This reality must be firmly established in the mind of the believer. The assurance of justification and salvation is given by its objective foundation in Christ. The second principle introduces the promise of God from Genesis 3:15, as seen from its formulation: "The promise of God was freely given to our first parents, without their deserving, that 'the seed of the woman should break the serpent's head'." Two things are important regarding the promise of God. Firstly, the content of the promise consists of the victory of woman's seed, of which it is said that it would break the serpent's head. The classical interpretation of this text is the victory of Christ over death, which secured our salvation from sin. Secondly, the means whereby the promise was uttered is significant. God gave his promise freely. The immediate logical conclusion is that salvation consists of Christ's victory over death and sin, a fact which had been decreed by God and given to humanity freely, without any merits. Accordingly, salvation is essentially the work of God, freely given to man, who cannot do anything to earn it. The third principle reinforces and clarifies the second, by introducing the person of Abraham and the promise God made specifically to him: "Promise was given freely to Abraham before he deserved anything, that in 'his seed all nations should be blessed'." Again, the promise of salvation has a twofold content: firstly, the origin of the promise of salvation is God himself, and secondly, God freely gave the promise of salvation to man, without requiring any merits from him.[103]

Against his Catholic opponents, Foxe makes a convincing point by saying that human works always destroy the assurance of salvation.

---

102 John Foxe, *The Acts and Monuments of John Foxe*, ed. George Townsend (London: Seeley, Burnside and Seeley, 1843), 71.
103 Foxe, *The Acts and Monuments*, 71.

The believer must be sure of the fact that his sins were forgiven, once he has exercised his faith in the atoning work death of Christ. Actually, this is the promise of God, which is based on faith, not on works:

> For whereas almighty God of mercy hath given us his Son to die for us, and with him hath given out his full promise, that whatsoever believeth upon him should be saved by their faith; and assigneth none other condition, either of the law, or any of works, but only of faith, to be the means between his Son and us [...] whereas the Christian reader of the Gospel, reading of the great grace and sweet promises of God given to mankind in Christ his son, might thereby take comfort of soul and be at rest and peace with the Lord his God.[104]

Foxe underlines the usefulness of works in justification, because human works will never be sufficient and they will never match the perfect requirements of God. The certainty and assurance of justification come by faith, which is apprehensive of God's free grace manifested in his promises. Faith is neither idle nor empty; it has a specific content, which is God's grace. Foxe has already admitted that God's grace is manifested in the atoning work of Christ, so true and justifying faith actually grasps Christ, who is its objective content. Faith is not a human enterprise, but it is a gift of God, given to us through the work of the Holy Spirit. Foxe is apparently convinced that faith is the "persuasion of the Holy Ghost", by which every believer is certain of his justification. Here, Foxe offers another brief definition of justification, which in his opinion consists of the forgiveness of sins and the bestowal of eternal life to the believer for the sake of Christ.[105]

Foxe is really concerned to ascribe salvation entirely to God. He realises that salvation is a broader concept than justification itself. Apparently, for Foxe, justification is only the beginning of salvation. The grace of God is active throughout the whole process of salvation, from the beginning of grace in justification to the consummation of grace in sanctification. Christ died for all our sins. He died for our original sin, as well as for our daily sins. At this point of his argument, Foxe needs to define justification once again. According to his definition, we are justified solely by the mercy of God through faith only, whereby we apprehend the merits of Christ.[106] Although he links faith directly to God, Foxe mentions contrition or repentance as prerequisite to faith. It is not clear whether contrition is a human action, but it appears to be something which is not the result of the free will, as for instance in Catholic theology. Because Foxe considers that in

---

104 *ibid.* 72-73.
105 *ibid.* 74.
106 *ibid.* 76.

Catholic theology contrition is the result of free will and not the Holy Spirit, it is logical to infer that, although a human sentiment, contrition is still the work of the Holy Spirit. Thus, for Foxe, contrition is "called in Scripture the sorrow of the heart, rising upon the consideration of sin committed and of the anger of God provoked, which sorrow driveth a man to Christ for succour; whereupon riseth faith."[107] Both contrition and faith are works of the Holy Spirit, who is the only one capable of radically transforming the sinful human nature in such a way that it display a new life, which Foxe terms – like Luther[108] – "new obedience". This new obedience causes the believer to perform good works, which are worthy of repentance. In the theology of Foxe, good works are of no use to justification, but they must not be excluded from Christian life. Actually, it is the duty of every believer, to whom justification was granted by faith, that he should live in accordance with the righteousness of Christ. Foxe confutes again the Catholic doctrine of justification and good works by writing that the efficient or formal cause of good works is faith, not free will or the *habitum virtutis*. He completely disagrees with Catholic doctrine, which ascribes to good works the so-called outcome of *justitia prima*. Good works do not function *ad integra naturalia*, but they are the result of faith, which is the gift of God. For a better explanation of the doctrine of good works, Foxe uses the well-known analogy of the fruitful tree. In his grace, God plants the gift of faith. Thus, faith is likened to a good root, which cannot stay idle but springs forth and bears fruit, which is obviously good works. For Foxe, it is clear that only faith justifies and produces good works. The works of the believer are good only to the extent that they spring from faith as an act of obedience.[109] Thus, obedience is an important concept in Foxe's theology and is rooted in Scripture, mainly in connection to the law.

The fourth principle affirms the reliability of Scripture or the Word of God, which needs no human adjustments: "To the Word of God neither must we add, nor take from it." The fifth and the sixth principle should be considered together as they introduce the concept of law. The fifth principle states the blessing ascribed to anybody who lives in accordance with the prescripts of the law: "He that doeth the works of the law shall live therein", while the sixth principle contains the curse attached to anybody to breaks the letter of the law: "Accursed is he which abideth not in everything that is written in the book of the law."

---

107 *ibid.* 77.
108 For a discussion on Luther's new obedience, see Althaus, *The Theology of Martin Luther*, 235-236.
109 Foxe, *The Acts and Monuments*, 75.

At this point, Foxe only introduces the concept of law, but as will be clear later on in the eleventh and the twelfth principle, the works of the law do not have any contribution to the righteousness which is required for salvation.[110]

In Foxe's theology, justification primarily consists of the remission of sins. He writes:

> In remission of sins therefore, these four things must concur together: first, the cause that worketh, which is the sacrifice of Christ's body; secondly, the promise that offereth; thirdly, faith that apprehendeth; fourthly, the repenting sinner that receiveth. And although sins daily do grow, which daily provoke us to crave remission, yet as touching the cause that worketh remission of our daily sins and the means which apprehend and apply the said cause unto us, they remain always one and perpetual; besides which the other cause nor means is to be sought of man. So that to them that be repenting sinner and be in Christ Jesus, there is no law to condemn them, though they have deserved condemnation: but they are under a perpetual kingdom and a heaven full of grace and remission to cover their sins and to impute their iniquities through the promise of God in Christ Jesus our Lord.[111]

This passage is important because it establishes the essentials of the work of God. The grace of God manifested in the atoning death of Christ is the objective basis of justification. Salvation from sin is a promise of God which has perpetual effectiveness, as Calvin clearly explains in his *Institutes*.[112] For this reason, God deserves to be worshipped. The seventh principle asserts the uniqueness of God's majesty: "God only is to be worshipped." As the broader discussion directly refers to salvation, it is fair enough to infer the uniqueness of God's majesty in salvation. The only artisan of salvation is God, who is able to forgive us in all the aspects of our lives.[113] This means that not only is our original sin forgiven, but also our daily sins are entirely pardoned. Faith is the factor which appropriates this soteriological reality to the life of the believer, so that he could continuously and unceasingly receive forgiveness of his sins by true repentance. One of the most important aspects of Foxe's definition of justification is the non-imputation of the believer's sins. Although Foxe does not explicitly mention here the concept of the imputation of righteousness, but uses the non-imputation of iniquity, the immediate logical corollary is that justification comes to accomplishment by the imputation of a certain righteousness to the believer.

---

110 *ibid.* 71.
111 *ibid.* 80.
112 Calvin, *Institutes*, 3.9.2.
113 Foxe, *The Acts and Monuments*, 71.

It should be mentioned here that the eighth principle scorns human righteousness: "All our righteousness is like the defiled cloth of a woman." Although not clearly stated, the righteousness Foxe infers is the righteousness which comes as a result of the works of law. The works of law offer a righteousness which is of no profit to salvation. The ninth and the tenth principle display the non-utility of sacrifices, as direct manifestations of the works of law. Sacrifices or the works of the law will not be needed for salvation is Foxe's ninth principle: "In all my holy hill they will not kill nor slay, saith the Lord."[114]

Returning to the question of the non-imputation of sins, it is clear that it presupposes the imputation of a sort of righteousness, which appears to be that of Christ, because Foxe explained from the very beginning that the instrumental cause of justification was the merit of Christ applied to us by means of faith. By his tenth principle, Foxe places salvation in the godly attitude of a regenerated human nature beyond the effect of sacrifices of legalistic works: "God loveth mercy and obedience more than sacrifice." Actually, Foxe wanted to say that faith will always result in obedience, an idea which is also found in Calvin.[115] As mentioned before, the eleventh and the twelfth principle affirm the inefficiency of the righteousness provided by the works of the law for salvation. The law, its works and righteousness, only reveal human sin, as stated in Foxe's eleventh principle: "The law worketh anger, condemneth and openeth sin." For salvation, humanity needs a new righteousness, which has its origin in Christ, and which is given to men by means of faith. This is the basic idea of Foxe's twelfth principle: "The end of the law is Christ, to righteousness, to every one that believeth." The thirteenth principle contains the starting point of salvation from human perspective. For man, salvation becomes effective to his own life by faith. Again, Foxe attaches baptism to faith, but only as a sign of faith: "Whosoever believeth and is baptized, shall be saved."[116]

Bearing all these things in mind, it must be highlighted that in his *Of Free Justification by Christ* Foxe explains what he means by justification:

> We should search for a righteousness, which is not moral human vertue, but which is a spiritual grace and gift of God, which is not ours, but which is proper to Christ, whence he only is called holy and just, and we are called justified in him, not upon the account of works, but faith, which God imputes for righteousness unto them that believe in his name. And hence it

114 *ibid.* 71.
115 Calvin, *Institutes*, 3.9.23.
116 Foxe, *The Acts and Monuments*, 71.

is rightly called the righteousness of faith and therefore faith it self is righteousness, whereby we are accounted righteous before God.[117]

Similarly, in his list of principles, it is only in his fourteenth principle that Foxe offers a brief statement of justification, which on man's part is by faith, and on God's part is freely given by grace. Justification has nothing to do with human works; it is completely the work of God: "A man is justified by faith without works, freely of grace, not of ourselves." For Foxe, his fifteenth principle offers a clear idea that justification is the remission of sins by the atoning death of Christ. Thus, the objective foundation of justification is the external work of Christ, not the internal human righteousness of legal works: "There is no remission of sins without blood." Foxe's next step is a basic description of sanctification. The life of any believer should prove justification by means of works which originate in faith, which is the only factor that confers validity and efficiency to human works, as in the sixteenth principle: "Whatsoever is not of faith is sin. Without faith it is impossible to please God."[118] This close connection between the remission of sins and the subsequent sanctification resembles Bucer's approach to justification as both the remission of sins and the impartation of righteousness.[119]

It is evident that, for Foxe, the righteousness of Christ imputed to the believer is the very content of justification. The seventeenth principle brings again to our attention the objective basis of salvation, which is Jesus Christ. Foxe mentions that Christ is the mediator between God and man, and the only one able to offer an atoning sacrifice for our sins: "One mediator between God and man, Christ Jesus. And he is the propitiation for our sins." Any human attempt to offer an effectual substitute of Christ's merit to God disregards God's gracious initiative in salvation, as Foxe writes in his eighteenth principle: "Whosoever seeketh by the law to be justified is fallen from grace." The last two principles, the nineteenth and the twentieth, deal with the matter of faithfulness. Firstly, Foxe states the faithfulness of God. Due to the faithfulness of God, humankind can be sure of salvation. If God promised he would grant us salvation, he would be faithful to his promise. For Foxe, the assurance of salvation should always be anchored in God: "In Christ be all the promises of God, *Est* and *Amen*." On the other hand, the justified man has a twofold duty in respect of his faithfulness. Every Christian must willingly and faithfully

---

117 John Foxe, *Of Free Justification by Christ*, 112, in V. Norskov Olsen, *John Foxe and the Elizabethan Church* (Berkeley: University of California Press, 1973), 124.

118 Foxe, *The Acts and Monuments*, 71.

119 For details, see Bucer, *Romans*, 12.51-56.

submit to the state authorities, and to God, his highest authority. Foxe shares a firm conviction that justification must necessarily be manifested outside the boundaries of the individual self. The immediate environment is society, with its members and people in charge. The ultimate level is divinity, as the justified man must constantly and faithfully live in reverence before God.[120] We are justified in Christ, not in ourselves or in our works. Should there be any righteousness counted for us in justification, this is the righteousness of Christ. For Foxe, the whole of salvation, including justification, is the initiative of God.

The next chapters are intended to present how all these ideas pertaining to the doctrine of salvation in the writings of the early English reformers were taken over and developed by Hooker in his sermons.

---

120 Foxe, *The Acts and Monuments*, 71.

3. The Necessity of Faith in the *Two Sermons upon St. Judes Epistle* (1582-1583)

The essence of Hooker's doctrine of salvation is the concept of faith, which is discussed from various perspectives in each of his sermons. To begin with, the two sermons on the Epistle of Jude are particularly important for Hooker's doctrine of salvation, because they display his view of the necessity of faith,[1] which is absolutely imperative to salvation.[2]

The *Two Sermons Upon S. Judes Epistle* appear to be Hooker's earliest writings on salvation. Although published only in 1614, by Joseph Barnes, it seems that they were delivered as early as 1582 or 1583.[3] The reason for choosing this date is a key statement of Hooker, according to which his congregation is asked "to consider how unkindly, and injuriously our owne countrimen and bretheren have dealt with us by the space of foure and twentie yeares".[4] The reference here is clearly to the English Catholics, who were in obvious religious growth by the time Hooker wrote these sermons. Two historical periods may be associated with the Catholic resurgence of the late sixteenth century England. Firstly, it might be the interval beginning with Elizabeth's accession, the 17th November 1558, or secondly with the promulgation of the Bull *Regnans in excelsis*, issued by Pius V on the 25th January 1570, whereby he excommunicated Elizabeth and absolved her subjects from their allegiance to her. Thus, the two possible dates for the delivery of these sermons are either 1582 or 1594. The earlier date is apparently closer to the historical events that marked the Catholic religious resurgence. It was early in the 1580s that the court plots took place, which were associated with Mary, Queen of Scots, who was a fervent

---

1   For Hooker's view of faith, see also Micks, "Richard Hooker as Theologian", 561; Faulkner, *Richard Hooker and the Politics of a Christian England*;

2   See also Milward, *Religious Controversies of the Elizabethan Age. A Survey of Printed Sources* (London: The Scholar Press, 1977), 105; Micks, "Richard Hooker as Theologian", 561.

3   For details, see Bauckham, "Hooker, Travers and the Church of Rome in the 1580s", *Journal of Ecclesiastical History* 29/1 (1978), 38-39.

4   Hooker, *Jude I* (*Works* V, 30.11-13).

Catholic. The plot of Francis Throckmorton was discovered, but the fear of a Catholic renewal was increased by the marriage negotiations between Elizabeth and the Duke of Anjou, who was a French Catholic. Moreover, Spain had recaptured some cities in the Low Countries, and formal Catholic representatives, the Jesuits and the seminary priests, began successful missions that threatened the English Reformation more than any other historical event associated with the last ten years of sixteenth century England. In this later period, and especially by 1594, Mary Stuart had already been executed, the Spanish Armada had been defeated, the Dutch insurgence for independence had proved fruitful to the detriment of Spain, and the English government had become more preoccupied with the Puritans than with the Catholics.[5]

3.1 The First Sermon on St. Jude

One of the first aspects that we grasp from Hooker's first sermon is that faith comes from God, so it is a must for salvation. Faith is delivered from God to the saints. Thus, the only people who have faith are the saints, who are called and sanctified by the work of God the Father.[6] He calls, sanctifies, and gives faith to those he ordained, and their duty is to maintain the faith.[7] Hooker does not write specifically that God ordains some in order that they should be called, sanctified, and given faith, but he does write that God ordained some to condemnation,[8] and an ungodly life; people who disregard the grace of God,[9] and deny the Lord Jesus Christ.[10] The immediate logical inference is that God ordains some people for salvation. After he ordains them, God calls them and

---

5   For more details on the date of writing and of publishing Hooker's sermons on Jude, see *Works* V, 2-4.

6   Lake, "Business as Usual? The Immediate Reception of Hooker's *Ecclesiastical Polity*", *The Journal of Ecclesiastical History* 52/3 (2001), 474.

7   Hooker, *Jude I* (*Works* V, 13.18-24).

8   Griffith Thomas (ed.), *The Principles of Theology*, 185.

9   For the importance of grace in Hooker see also Collinson, *Archbishop Grindal*, 41; Stevenson, *The Mystery of Baptism in the Anglican Tradition*, 42.

10 Hooker, *Jude I* (*Works* V, 13.16-18); for the centrality of Christ in Hooker, see also Schoeck, "From Erasmus to Hooker: An Overview", in McGrade (ed.), *Richard Hooker and the Construction of Christian Community*, 71.

then he gives them faith. But this work is done by the grace of God,[11] through the Lord Jesus Christ.[12]

3.1.1 Scripture and Salvation

The most important characteristic of these men is the fact that the Word of God had mentioned them through prophecies,[13] which are secretly inspired by God and uttered by the apostles of Christ.[14] The revelation of God in Scripture[15] is important because it is the means whereby we understand our salvation.[16] Salvation itself and the revelation of this salvation through the prophecies inspired by God is done by the work of the Holy Spirit[17] corroborated with the specific personalities of the human writers.[18] This whole discussion regarding prophecy is very important for Hooker, as it is directly linked to salvation. Prophecy is the means by which God promised our salvation: "The chiefe and principal matter of prophecie is the promise of righteousness, peace, holinesse, glory, victory, immortality *unto every soule which beleeveth, that Jesus is Christ, of the Jew first, and of the Gentile.*"[19]

---

11   Crerar, *Positive Negatives*, 175.
12   Then Hooker carefully describes those whom God ordained to condemnation, by means of his detailed exegesis of Jude 17-19.
13   Hooker, *Jude I* (*Works* V, 14.5-27).
14   *ibid.* 14.28-15.8.
15   For more details about Hooker's view of Scripture as the main source of revelation in matters of faith, see Higham, *Catholic and Reformed*, 27; Grislis, "The Hermeneutical Problem in Richard Hooker", 186; McAdoo, "Richard Hooker", Geoffrey Rowell (ed.), *The English Religious Tradition and the Genius of Anglicanism*, 115; Kaye, "Richard Hooker and Australian Anglicanism", *Sewanee Theological Review* 36/2 (1993), 227-245; Speed Hill, "Editing Richard Hooker: A Retrospective", *Sewanee Theological Review* 36/2 (1993), 187-199; Atkinson, *Richard Hooker and the Authority of Scripture, Tradition and Reason*, 129; Compier, "Hooker on the Authority of Scripture in Matters of Morality", in McGrade, *Richard Hooker and the Construction of Christian Community*, 251-259; Bartlett, "What Has Richard Hooker to Say to Modern Evangelical Anglicanism?", *Anvil* 15/3 (1998), 198.
16   Hooker, *Jude I* (*Works* V, 15.13-14). See also Hillerdal, *Reason and Revelation in Richard Hooker*, 75.
17   Hooker, *Jude I* (*Works* V, 17.8-9). See also Gane, "The Exegetical Methods of Some Sixteenth-Century Anglican Preachers: Latimer, Jewel, Hooker, and Andrews", *Andrews University Seminary Studies* XVII/1 (1979), 35. For the importance of the Holy Spirit, in Hooker, see also Shuger, "'Society Supernaturall': The Imagined Community of Hooker's *Laws*", in McGrade, *Richard Hooker and the Construction of Christian Community*, 307-330.
18   Hooker, *Jude I* (*Works* V, 17.20-24).
19   *ibid.* 18.1-4.

At least three important things can be seen in this short passage, which can also be seen in Foxe. Firslty, the initiative of our salvation belongs entirely to God.[20] It was God alone who promised humanity a means of salvation through his Word.[21] Secondly, our salvation consists of righteousness, holiness, glory, victory and immortality.[22] For the time being, Hooker does not fully explain what he means by each of these elements of salvation, but they at least point to the fact that they are essentially the work of God.[23] Thirdly, salvation comes by faith in Christ,[24] which is an obvious indication of Hooker's Protestant credentials.[25] Accordingly, faith for Hooker has an objective content, which is Christ himself. Thus, the constitutive elements of salvation, which are righteousness, peace, holiness, victory and immortality, although part of the believer's existence, are essentially part of Christ's own existence. For Hooker, faith grasps Christ and the benefits of his work of salvation.[26] By faith, the believer appropriates to his own life the most important characteristics of Christ. Thus, following Tyndale, Hooker writes that the righteousness, peace, holiness, glory, victory, and immortality of Christ become ours as part of our new existence in Christ.[27]

3.1.2 Salvation as the Work of Christ

Salvation comes only through the work of Christ at the cross,[28] which Frith names "the second purgatory" in the sense that it cleanses from sins,[29] and it actually becomes effectual to man's life by means of faith.[30]

---

20 Allison, *The Rise of Moralism*, 4; Booty, "Contrition in Anglican Spirituality: Hooker, Donne and Herbert", in William J. Wolf (ed.), *Anglican Spirituality* (Wilton: Morehouse-Barlow, 1982), 26; Kirby, "*Supremum Caput*: Richard Hooker's Theology of Ecclesiastical Dominion", *Dionysius* XII (1988), 96; Schwarz, "Dignified and Commodius: Richard Hooker's 'Mysticall Copulation' Metaphor", *Sewanee Theological Review* 43/1 (1999), 23.

21 Foxe, *The Acts and Monuments*, 71.

22 *ibid.* 71, and Morrel, "Richard Hooker, Theologian of the English Reformation", *Christianity Today* X/24 (1966), 10.

23 Foxe, *The Acts and Monuments*, 71.

24 Collinson, *Archbishop Grindal*, 41.

25 Voak, *Richard Hooker and Reformed Theology*, 173.

26 Morrel, "Richard Hooker, Theologian of the English Reformation", *Christianity Today* X/24 (1966), 9.

27 Tyndale, *Exposition of First John*, 117; Collinson, *Archbishop Grindal*, 41.

28 Crerar, *Positive Negatives*, 181.

29 Frith, *A Disputation of Purgatory*, 90.

For Hooker, as in Barnes, it is clear that salvation is by Christ only. He is the only objective foundation of our salvation.[31] It was only due to his mercy and love that we have been saved.[32] Hooker explains that there is a two way connection between Christ and humanity. Christ is linked to us by means of his grace, mercy and love.[33] On the other hand, we are linked to Christ by means of faith, as in Tyndale.[34]

Hooker describes this twofold connection within the context of salvation. Accordingly, faith is the only way whereby we have salvation worked out by Christ. Faith is the means by which we take Christ's salvation for ourselves; we appropriate salvation by faith.[35] Hooker is again careful to make a close and natural connection between salvation and God's revelation in Scripture.[36] We know of God's salvation because it is revealed in the Word of God,[37] and salvation is belief in the Word of God.[38] This idea is also supported by Frith, who dub the Word of God "the first purgatory".[39] Then, following Foxe, Hooker writes that salvation is not only a reality but it is a secure reality, because it was promised by God and revealed by him in his

---

30 Hooker, *Jude I* (*Works* V, 18.5-12). Before resuming his discussion of faith and salvation, Hooker firstly makes a thorough commentary on the characteristics of those who had been ordained by God to condemnation. The main feature of those who were ordained to condemnation is disobedience, as also suggested by Foxe, which is reflected in the fact that they always dispute against God, using the truth with the intention to distort the truth. The disobedience of the condemned is also reflected in the fact that they do not submit themselves to the righteousness of God, and that they do not have the Spirit of God within them. See *ibid.* 25.9-10.

31 Booty, "An Elizabethan Addresses Modern Anglicanism. Richard Hooker and Theological Issues at the End of the Twentieth Century", *Anglican Theological Review* LXXI/1 (1989), 8-24.

32 Barnes, *The Supplication of 1531*, lviii.b-lix.a.

33 Keble, *The Works*, vol. 2, 552.

34 Tyndale, *Prologue to Romans*, 123.

35 Archer, *Richard Hooker*, 33.

36 For the importance of God's revelation in Scripture, see also Bethell, *The Cultural Revolution of the Seventeenth Century*, 22; Atkinson, *Richard Hooker and the Authority of Scripture, Tradition and Reason*, 129; Bartlett, "What Has Richard Hooker to Say to Modern Evangelical Anglicanism?", *Anvil* 15/3 (1998), 198; the purpose of Scripture is to save, as noticed by Atkinson, "Hooker's Theological Method and Modern Anglicanism", *Churchman* 114/1 (2000), 54.

37 Jordan, *The Development of Religious Toleration*, 232; Grislis, "The Assurance of Faith according to Richard Hooker", in McGrade, *Richard Hooker and the Construction of Christian Community*, 240.

38 See also Barry, *Masters in English Theology*, 30, and Hill, *Society and Puritanism in Pre-Revolutionary England*, 31.

39 Frith, *A Disputation of Purgatory*, 90.

Word.[40] By faith, as also suggested by Tyndale, we appropriate this
salvation from Scripture[41] to our own lives, because we believe the
promise of God by faith.[42] Salvation does not affect the individual
believer only. Salvation must be seen outwardly, as every individual
believer manifests it externally through love for the rest of humanity. It
is of uttermost importance for Hooker that salvation should be
manifested through love both to fellow believers and to unbelievers:

> That which linketh Christ to us is his meere mercy and love towards us.
> That which tieth us to him is our faith in the promised salvation revealed in
> the Word of truth. That which uniteth and joyneth us amongst our selves,
> in such sort that wee are now as if we had but one heart and one soule, is
> our love. Who be inwardly in heart the lively members of this body, and
> the polished stones of this building, coupled and joined to Christ, as *flesh of
> his flesh and bones of his bones* by the mutuall bond of his unspeakable love
> towards them, and their unfained faith in him, thus linked and fastened
> each to other by a spirituall, sincere, and hartie affection of love without
> any manner of simulation, who be Jewes within, and what their names be,
> none can tell, save he whose eies doe behold the secret disposition of all
> mens hearts. He, whose eies are to dimme to behold the inward man, must
> leave the secret judgement of every servant to his owne Lord, accounting
> and using all men as brethren both neere and deare unto us, supposing
> Christ to love them tenderly, so as they keep the profession of the Gospell
> and joyne in the outward communion of Saints.[43]

The basis of his argument is again the love of Christ which is directed
towards all humanity. Our faith is apprehensive, as it is always
directed towards Christ. Christ is its content; faith actually grasps
Christ for the believer.

3.1.3 Salvation and Condemnation

A very important feature of Hooker's doctrine of salvation is the lack of
direct causality between God and those ordained to condemnation. It is
true that God ordained some to condemnation, but Hooker is far more
concerned to highlight the causality between those ordained to

---

40   Foxe, *The Acts and Monuments*, 71.
41   This means that, for Hooker, Scripture contains the knowledge of salvation. See also
     Pelikan, *The Christian Tradition*, vol. 4, 348; Bryan, "The Judicious Mr. Hooker and
     the Early Christians. The Relationship of Scripture and Reason in the First Century
     of the Christian Era", in Donald S. Armentrout (ed.), *This Sacred History. Anglican
     Reflections for John Booty*, 144. Kirby, "Richard Hooker's Theory of Natural Law in the
     Context of Reformation Theology", *Sixteenth Century Journal* XXX/3 (1999), 702.
42   Tyndale, *Prologue to Romans*, 124.
43   Hooker, *Jude I* (*Works* V, 25.21-26.7).

condemnation and their own inward self. It is clear from what he writes that Hooker believes in God's ordination of some to condemnation because of their sinful inward desires, not because of any cause which belongs to God's inner arbitrary decision. Thus, the ordination to condemnation is a rightful decision of God, because he punishes man's voluntary and sinful desire of not coming again to Christ,[44] and of not having any further fellowship with the rest of the believers.[45] Those ordained to condemnation have never been truly saved, although they might have been in the Church. Hooker is very eager to delineate the fact that they were in the Church, but they were not of the Church. Those who wilfully forsake the communion of saints have never had the spirit of God, which makes every believer aware of his sonship in relation to God the Father[46] and causes him to stand firm in the faith.[47] Actually, Hooker agrees with Tyndale that this is a proof that faith comes from the Spirit.[48]

Hooker is keenly aware of another possible problem which is directly linked to the doctrine of ordination to salvation or to condemnation. Within the community of the believers,[49] some might be tempted to judge the rest by subjectively assigning the members of a Church either to salvation or condemnation. Hooker firmly dismisses such an attempt, and urges each believer to judge himself in matters of personal salvation. This self-assessment is possible because of the inner testimony of the Holy Spirit in every believer, which is a sign of grace.[50] The Spirit of God confirms to every believer that he has been ordained to salvation,[51] because of his faith in Christ.[52] In Hooker, salvation has a twofold aspect: firstly, an objective aspect, according to which salvation is accomplished by God through the work of Christ[53] and secondly, a

---

44 See also Griffith Thomas (ed.), *The Principles of Theology*, 185.

45 Hooker, *Jude I* (*Works* V, 26.7-27.2); Wolf, Booty, and Thomas (eds), *The Spirit of Anglicanism*, 18; Booty, "An Elizabethan Addresses Modern Anglicanism. Richard Hooker and Theological Issues at the End of the Twentieth Century", 11.

46 See also Griffith Thomas (ed.), *The Principles of Theology*, 185.

47 Hooker, *Jude I* (*Works* V, 27.3-27.31).

48 Tyndale, *Prologue to Romans*, 123; Gane, "The Exegetical Methods of Some Sixteenth Century Anglican Preachers: Latimer, Jewel, Hooker, and Andrews", 35.

49 Kaye, "What Might Alasdair MacIntyre Learn from a Reading of Richard Hooker? Rivalry, Commonality, and Their Projects", *Sewanee Theological Review* 42/3 (1999), 347.

50 Keble, *The Works*, vol. 2, 552.

51 Gane, "The Exegetical Methods of Some Sixteenth Century Anglican Preachers: Latimer, Jewel, Hooker, and Andrews", 35.

52 Hooker, *Jude I* (*Works* V, 28.1-15); Collinson, *Archbishop Grindal*, 41.

53 Crerar, *Positive Negatives*, 181.

subjective aspect, according to which salvation is appropriated by the believer through faith.[54] One must, however, notice that this subjective aspect is worked out objectively. Our faith is in Christ,[55] and our salvation that we have through faith is inwardly confirmed within us by the work of the Holy Spirit.[56] Hooker mentions "our spirit", but he had previously written that the reprobate do not have the Spirit of Christ,[57] which leads to the logical inference that the saved do have the Spirit of Christ or God. In Hooker, the subjective aspect of salvation is always accompanied by this pneumatological dimension: "*I trust, beloved, wee knowe that wee are not reprobates*, because our spirit doth bear us record, that the faith of our Lord Jesus Christ is in us." This pneumatological dimension of the assurance of salvation[58] is reinforced when Hooker writes that God has initiated this process, as in Tyndale.[59] God sent his Spirit in order that we should know we are his sons.[60] The very fact that those who believe are sons of God is a warranty that salvation is objectively rooted in Christ.[61] Christ is the very content of the covenant between God himself and those who are saved. This teaching can also be seen in Tyndale, where justification is analysed within the doctrine of the covenant.[62] Following Frith,[63] Hooker explains that the Spirit of God acknowledges this and makes the believer sure of his salvation,[64] which was made possible by the atoning death of Christ on the cross:[65]

> But unto you, *because yee are sonnes, God hath sent forth the spirit of his sonne into your hearts*, to the end yee might knowe that Christ hath built you upon a rocke unmoveable, that he hath registered your *names in the booke of life*, that hee hath himselfe in a sure and everlasting covenant to be your God,

54 Secor, *Richard Hooker, Prophet of Anglicanism*, 185.
55 Collinson, *Archbishop Grindal*, 41.
56 Gane, "The Exegetical Methods of Some Sixteenth Century Anglican Preachers: Latimer, Jewel, Hooker, and Andrews", 35.
57 Hooker, *Jude I* (*Works* V, 27.7).
58 Griffith Thomas (ed.), *The Principles of Theology*, 186; see also Grislis, "The Assurance of Faith according to Richard Hooker", in McGrade, *Richard Hooker and the Construction of Christian Community*, 239.
59 Tyndale, *Exposition of Matthew*, 189.
60 Gane, "The Exegetical Methods of Some Sixteenth Century Anglican Preachers: Latimer, Jewel, Hooker, and Andrews", 35.
61 Collinson, *Archbishop Grindal*, 41.
62 Tyndale, *Prologue to Romans*, 125.
63 Frith, *A Disputation of Purgatory*, 90.
64 Gane, "The Exegetical Methods of Some Sixteenth Century Anglican Preachers: Latimer, Jewel, Hooker, and Andrews", 35.
65 For a discussion on the importance of Christ's death in Hooker, see Lake, *Anglicans and Puritans?*, 162.

and the God of your children after you, that hee hath suffered as much...
The Lord of his infinite mercy give us hearts plentifully fraught with the
treasure of this blessed assurance of faith unto the end.[66]

Before putting an end to his sermon, Hooker investigates the content of
salvation which he identifies from Scripture.

3.1.4 A Definition of Salvation

For his definition of salvation, Hooker uses the text from Colossians
1:22-23. Thus, salvation primarily consists of reconciliation with God[67]
as also suggested by Frith.[68] It was Christ alone who could accomplish
this reconciliation with God through his atoning death. Part of
reconciliation is the remission of sins by grace,[69] as in Cranmer,[70] and
sanctification in the sight of God, an idea which is also very dear to
Tyndale.[71] At this point, Hooker does not insist on this forensic aspect
of salvation,[72] according to which humans are considered without sin
and holy in the sight of God as a result of the death of Christ.[73] He
immediately links this forensic aspect to the much more practical level
of salvation, which should not exist only in the sight of God, but be
effectual in the life of the believer by faith. The duty of any saved
person is to exercise his faith in Christ and to stand fast in the promise
of salvation,[74] which is in line with Tyndale who wrote that we believe
the promise of God by faith.[75] Salvation has another dimension,
according to which those who are saved are also made alive in Christ.[76]

---

66   Hooker, *Jude I* (*Works* V, 29.28-30.9); Grislis, "The Assurance of Faith according to
     Richard Hooker", in McGrade, *Richard Hooker and the Construction of Christian
     Community*, 239.
67   See also Marshall, *Hooker and the Anglican Tradition*, 114; Griffith Thomas (ed.), *The
     Principles of Theology*, 186.
68   Frith, *A Disputation of Purgatory*, 90, and Cranmer, *The 1538 Articles*, 4.
69   See also Keble, *The Works*, vol. 2, 552; Secor, *Richard Hooker, Prophet of Anglicanism*,
     185.
70   Cranmer, *The 1538 Articles*, 4.
71   Tyndale, *Prologue to Romans*, 129.
72   Rupp, *Studies in the Making of the English Protestant Tradition*, 166.
73   Griffith Thomas (ed.), *The Principles of Theology*, 186; Lake, *Anglicans and Puritans?*,
     162.
74   Hooker, *Jude I* (*Works* V, 28.19-28.24). In Hooker, the promise of salvation is revealed
     in Scripture, see Speed Hill, "Editing Richard Hooker: A Retrospective", *Sewanee
     Theological Review* 36/2 (1993), 187-199.
75   Tyndale, *Prologue to Romans*, 124.
76   Collinson, *Archbishop Grindal*, 41.

Hooker again highlights the primacy of God in the work of salvation as does, for instance, Barnes.[77] It was only the mercy and the love of God that secured salvation for those who believe.[78] The remaining part of the sermon is not directly linked to the problem of faith and salvation, but it ends somewhat curiously in a doxological type of warning, which places Hooker, like Cranmer many years before,[79] in the position of asking his audience to acknowledge daily their allegiance and trust in God.[80]

3.2 The Second Sermon on St. Jude

The first major aspect of Hooker's doctrine of salvation in this sermon is the faithfulness of God. According to Hooker, God is very concerned with the situation of humankind. He can never forget humans, and if careful consideration shows any connection between God and humanity, Hooker believes that it was God himself who first established a direct link with humanity through his covenant.

3.2.1 Salvation and the Covenant of Grace

In Hooker, God's initiative in salvation is reflected primarily by means of his covenant. The righteousness of God, which is also very important to Tyndale,[81] is ultimately important within the broader context of salvation, because God only decided he should take action and get closely involved in the life of a humanity affected by sin due to his righteousness. At this point, Hooker agrees with Foxe that the result was God's covenant with humanity, a covenant whereby he promised them salvation, on the basis of his grace:[82]

---

77 Barnes, *The Supplication of 1531*, lviii.b-lix.a.
78 Hooker, *Jude I* (*Works* V, 28.29-31); Grislis, "The Assurance of Faith according to Richard Hooker", in McGrade, *Richard Hooker and the Construction of Christian Community*, 239.
79 Cranmer, *The 1538 Articles*, 4.
80 Hooker, *Jude I* (*Works* V, 34.25-35.11); Griffith Thomas (ed.), *The Principles of Theology*, 191; Sedgwick, "The New Shape of Anglican Identity", *Anglican Theological Review* LXXVII/2 (1995), 189.
81 Tyndale, *Exposition of First John*, 117.
82 Foxe, *The Acts and Monuments*, 71.

These sweet exhortations, which God putteth every where in the mouthes of the Prophets and Apostles of Jesus Christ, are evident tokens, that God sitteth not in heaven carelesse and unmindfull of our estate... Gods judgements shew plainly, that he cannot forget, the man whose heart hee hath framed and fashioned a new in simplicity and truth to serve and feare him. For the wickednesse of man was so great, and the earth so filled with crueltie, that it could not stand with the righteousness of God any longer to forbeare, wrathfull sentences brake out from him, *like wine from a vessel that hath no vent...*Yet then did *Noah finde grace in the eies of the Lord; I will establish my covenant with thee,* saith God, *thou shalt goe into the arke, thou, and thy sonnes, and thy wife, and thy sonnes wives with thee.*[83]

Thus, the first historical proof of God's desire to save some people from the sinful environment in which they lived was Noah. Hooker then takes another example, and describes the way Lot was saved, before God had judged and punished sin.[84] For Hooker it is clear that if God spared some in order that they should be saved, this is only because of his grace, and mercy.[85]

3.2.2 Salvation and Union with Christ

The next step in Hooker's argument is to direct the whole attention slightly towards the person of Christ. There is only one way for humanity to obtain eternal life, which is certainly a proof of salvation, namely the mercy of Christ. Again, Hooker is concerned to grant an objective foundation to salvation. Christ is the only firm basis for our salvation.[86]

Another element of salvation which Hooker tackles is faith, which makes God's salvation effectual for those who believe, thus establishing an intimate relationship between Christ and believers. The immediate result of God's salvation in human life is good works which, as also suggested by Frith and Cranmer, are necessary[87] in order that the life of

---

83 Hooker, *Jude II* (*Works* V, 37.25-38.10). For the proper attitude of man before God (fear and love), see also Booty, "Contrition in Anglican Spirituality: Hooker, Donne and Herbert", in William J. Wolf (ed.), *Anglican Spirituality* (Wilton: Morehouse-Barlow, 1982), 26.

84 Hooker, *Jude II* (*Works* V, 38.11-39.18).

85 *ibid.* 39.22; Crerar, *Positive Negatives,* 175.

86 Hooker, *Jude II* (*Works* V, 40.6-40.15); Booty, "An Elizabethan Addresses Modern Anglicanism. Richard Hooker and Theological Issues at the End of the Twentieth Century", 10.

87 See also Marot, "Aux origines de la théologie anglicane", *Irénikon* XXXIII (1960), 342; Collinson, *Archbishop Grindal,* 41; Gibbs, "Richard Hooker's *Via Media* Doctrine of Justification", 220.

the believer should be pleasing before God.[88] Thus the righteousness of good works is not a prerequisite to salvation – Tyndale is very careful to write that nobody is justified by the works of the law[89] – but is the result of applied faith, which makes God's salvation fruitful for the life of the believer.

> Put on righteousnesse as a garment: in steed of Civit have Faith, which may cause a *savour of life* to issue from you, and God shall be enamoured, he shal be ravished with your beauty. These are the ornaments, and bracelets, and jewels, which inflame the love of Christ, and set his hart on fire upon his spowse. We see, how he breaketh out in the Canticles at the beholding of this attire, *How faire art thou, and how pleasant art thou, O my love, in these pleasures!"*[90]

For Hooker, the righteousness of good works is the direct expression of the believer's sanctification, which necessarily flows from his faith,[91] a teaching which is common to Tyndale.[92] The believer is now set apart for God; he is the very place where God lives, he is the temple of God. Thus, for Hooker salvation infers a close relationship between God and the saved believer,[93] which is actually a union with God.[94] The believer's union with God is important because it is not the result of human efforts, but is the work of the Holy Spirit – another proof by which Hooker, like Tyndale,[95] underlines the objectivity of our salvation.[96] Hooker explains that union with God requires purity of life, because this union with God is also a union with Christ.[97] The theology of the union with Christ offers Hooker the possibility to introduce his Eucharistic theology, which basically sets forth two elements: faith and

---

88 Frith, *Patrick Places*, 31-34, and Cranmer, *The 1538 Articles*, 4.

89 Tyndale, *Prologue to Romans*, 123.

90 Hooker, *Jude II* (*Works* V, 40.25-41.1).

91 Collinson, *Archbishop Grindal*, 41; Gibbs, "Richard Hooker's *Via Media* Doctrine of Justification", 220.

92 Tyndale, *Exposition on First John*, 117.

93 Griffith Thomas (ed.), *The Principles of Theology*, 185.

94 McGrade, "Richard Hooker on the Lawful Ministry of Bishops and Kings", in W. J. Shiels and Diana Wood (eds), *The Ministry. Clerical and Lay* (Oxford: Blackwell, 1989), 184; Booty, "The Spirituality of Participation in Richard Hooker", *Sewanee Theological Review* 38/1 (1994), 11; Stevenson, *The Mystery of Baptism in the Anglican Tradition*, 42.

95 Tyndale, *Prologue to Romans*, 123.

96 Hooker, *Jude II* (*Works* V, 41.20-27).

97 *ibid.* 42.3; Booty, "The English Reformation: A Lively Faith and Sacramental Confession", 25; McGrade, "Richard Hooker on the Lawful Ministry of Bishops and Kings", in W. J. Shiels and Diana Wood (eds), *The Ministry. Clerical and Lay* (Oxford: Blackwell, 1989), 184; Kirby, *Richard Hooker's Doctrine of Royal Supremacy*, 46; Booty, "Anglican Identity: What is This Book of Common Prayer?", *Sewanee Theological Review* 40/2 (1997), 142.

repentance,[98] which are essential to Tyndale[99] and Foxe.[100] The Eucharist certifies our union with Christ by means of faith, and it must always be approached with repentance. For Hooker, repentance must be a constant factor in daily sanctification, because the believer is still influenced by his sinful human nature, which causes grief to God's Holy Spirit. The Eucharistic identification between the believer and the death of Christ functions in Hooker's theology as another objective proof of salvation.[101] Hooker resumes his discussion of faith and salvation by showing a practical result of faith, which consists of the defeat of evil. The outcome of applied faith is the overcoming of Satan, and consequently of sinful human desires. He again links this result to the objective foundation of salvation, which is Christ.[102] The proper knowledge of Christ[103] by faith is an effective means of putting off the sinful influences of our human nature.[104]

Hooker is convinced that salvation, which is the forgiveness of sins – we know this by faith, which is the forgiveness of sins in Tyndale's rendering[105] – is not effected because of any inward quality of human nature but – as is again highlighted by Tyndale[106] – for the sake of Christ's name.[107] Moreover, salvation is secured for all those who believe in Christ,[108] as Hooker writes – using the words of the apostle Peter – that believers are preserved in a state of grace,[109] so that they are *"heirs of the grace of life"*.[110] A very noteworthy aspect of Hooker's doctrine of faith is its ecclesiological dimension. To a remarkably great extent, Hooker analyses his doctrine of faith within the context of the Church.[111] God's special calling of believers is clearly directed towards the unity and the spiritual strength of the Church: "Having spoken thus

---

98   See also Gibbs, "Richard Hooker's *Via Media* Doctrine of Repentance", *Harvard Theological Review* 84/1 (1991), 59.

99   Tyndale, *The Answer to Sir Thomas More's Dialogue*, 369.

100 Foxe, *The Acts and Monuments*, 77.

101 Hooker, *Jude II* (*Works* V, 42.28-43.19).

102 Booty, "An Elizabethan Addresses Modern Anglicanism. Richard Hooker and Theological Issues at the End of the Twentieth Century", 10.

103 Booty, "Hooker's Understanding of the Presence of Christ in the Eucharist", 142.

104 Hooker, *Jude II* (*Works* V, 43.20-23).

105 Tyndale, *Prologue to Romans*, 125, and Bradford, *Writings*, 217-218.

106 Tyndale, *Prologue to Romans*, 129.

107 Hooker, *Jude II* (*Works* V, 43.25).

108 Collinson, *Archbishop Grindal*, 41.

109 Morrel, "Richard Hooker, Theologian of the English Reformation", 9.

110 Hooker, *Jude II* (*Works* V, 43.27).

111 Booty, "Contrition in Anglican Spirituality: Hooker, Donne and Herbert", in William J. Wolf (ed.), *Anglican Spirituality* (Wilton: Morehouse-Barlow, 1982), 26.

farre of the exhortation, as whereby we are called upon to *edifie and
build our selves*, it remaineth now, that wee consider the thing
prescribed, namely wherein we must bee built. This prescription
standeth also upon two points, the *thing* prescribed, and the *adjuncts* of
the *thing*. And that is our most pure, and *holy faith*."[112]

3.2.3 Salvation and Faith

The next passage is particularly important for Hooker's doctrine of
salvation. He begins his discussion with faith, which is the prerequisite
and an absolutely necessary element of salvation. Faith is the centre of
Hooker's doctrine of salvation, as it is the factor upon which everything
else depends. According to Hooker, even justification is performed by
God in view of faith in Christ, on the basis of God's calling. Actually,
should there be considered a blueprint of Hooker's *ordo salutis*, this
would contain the following stages:[113] God's calling in view of faith,
justification, and glorification. But this faith must necessarily be applied
practically in the Church with the specific purpose of spiritual
edification.[114] The welfare of the Church is granted by the faith of its
members, which is a warranty of God's salvation:

> The thing prescribed is *Faith*. For as in a chaine, which is made of many
> linkes, if you pull the first, you drawe the rest; and as in a ladder of many
> staves, if you take away the lowest, all hope of ascending to the highest
> will be removed, so because all the precepts and promises in the law and in
> the Gospell doe hang upon this, *Beleeve*; and because the last of the graces
> of God doth so follow the first, that he glorifieth none, but whom he hath
> justified, nor justifieth any, but whom he hath called to a true, effectual,
> and lively faith in Christ Jesus, therefore S. *Jude* exhorting us to *build our
> selves*, mentioneth here expresly only faith, as the thing wherein we must
> be edified, for that faith is the ground and the glorie of all the welfare of
> this building.[115]

At this point, Hooker takes a further step in defining faith. Faith is the
trust in God's mercy,[116] as in Cranmer.[117] Salvation infers also the

---

112 Hooker, *Jude II* (*Works* V, 44.4-9).
113 For Hooker's *ordo salutis*, see also Spinks, *Two Faces of Elizabethan Anglican Theology*,
     1999; Voak, *Richard Hooker and Reformed Theology*, 175.
114 Wolf, Booty, and Thomas (eds), *The Spirit of Anglicanism*, 29.
115 Hooker, *Jude II* (*Works* V, 44.10-44.21).
116 Griffith Thomas (ed.), *The Principles of Theology*, 191; Sedgwick, "The New Shape of
     Anglican Identity", *Anglican Theological Review* LXXVII/2 (1995), 189.
117 Cranmer, *The 1538 Articles*, 4. See also Louma, "Restitution and Reformation?
     Cartwright and Hooker on the Elizabethan Church", *Historical Magazine of the
     Protestant Episcopal Church* XLVI/1 (1977), 105.

granting of eternal life, but only to those who believe God. In order that anyone should receive God's deliverance from death and eternal life, Hooker writes in a manner similar to Bradford[118] that he or she must put their trust in the mercy of God, who began and continuously preserved his work of salvation. As the mercy of God was fully expressed in the death of Christ,[119] Hooker explains that the believer must put his entire trust[120] in the name of Christ, which is also the advice of Frith.[121] Again, faith is a direct reference to a grasping trust, because it actually apprehends Christ. The very content of faith is Christ, who guarantees life to anyone who trusts him: "It is the Lord that *delivereth mens soules from death*, but not except they put their trust in his mercy. It is God that hath given us eternall life, but not otherwise then thus, If wee believe in the name of the sonne of God; for *hee that hath not the sonne of God hath not life.*"[122] Because the faith of the believer is rooted in Christ,[123] it is the only thing that pleases God.[124]

Following the same line of thought, Hooker writes that any outcome of faith that must be practically manifested in good works,[125] as also suggested by Frith,[126] is acceptable to God because the content of faith is Christ.[127] Writing obviously against his Catholic opponents, Hooker contends that faith cannot be bought. Faith can be neither bought nor lent nor transferred to other subjects. Each must exercise his own faith, which grants him a right standing before God, and this concept is also vitally important to Barnes.[128] The forensic aspect of faith is clearly highlighted by Hooker,[129] when he asks whether a man

---

118 Bradford, *Writings*, 371-372.
119 Lake, *Anglicans and Puritans?*, 162.
120 Sedgwick, "The New Shape of Anglican Identity", *Anglican Theological Review* LXXVII/2 (1995), 189.
121 Frith, *The Revelation of Antichrist*, 461.
122 Hooker, *Jude II* (*Works* V, 46.13-17).
123 Collinson, *Archbishop Grindal*, 41.
124 Hooker, *Jude II* (*Works* V, 46.26-47.9).
125 Collinson, *Archbishop Grindal*, 41; Gibbs, "Richard Hooker's *Via Media* Doctrine of Justification", 220.
126 Frith, *Patrick Places*, 31-34.
127 Hooker, *Jude II* (*Works* V, 47.10-18).
128 Barnes, *The Supplication of 1531*.
129 Rupp, *Studies in the Making of the English Protestant Tradition*, 166. For a contrary opinion, see Williams, "Hooker: Philosopher, Anglican, Contemporary", in McGrade, *Richard Hooker and the Construction of Christian Community*, 372. See also Miller, "Seventeenth-Century Latin Translations of Two English Masterpieces: Hooker's *Polity* and Browne's *Religio Medici*", in Rhoda Schnur (ed.), *Acta Conventus Neo-Latini Abulensis. Proceedings of the Tenth International Congress of Neo-Latin Studies*, 59; Voak, *Richard Hooker and Reformed Theology*, 177.

who buys "the *overplus* of other mens merits, purchase[s] the fruits of other mens labours, and build[s] his soul by another mans faith" could have "his *heart right in the sight of God.*"[130] The problem of man's right standing before God can only be solved by faith. Faith is the means whereby salvation is given to man, and it is clear for Hooker that salvation, which essentially means eternal life, is only effective in those who believe, because he follows Scripture and writes that "*the just shall live by his owne faith*".[131]

3.2.4 Salvation and the Righteousness of Justification

At this point, Hooker makes a slight hint to the righteousness of Christ which is required for justification,[132] an idea which resembles that of Tyndale who said that Christ is our righteousness.[133] It is impossible for one man to justify another by means of his righteousness, mainly because human nature is sinful and it does not have an inherent spotless righteousness.[134] Only the Son of God is able to display the necessary righteousness for the justification of humankind, which is the beginning of salvation.[135]

> Our faith being such, is that indeed, which S. *Jude* doth here terme *Faith*, namely a thing most *holy*. The reason is this. We are *justified by Faith*. For *Abraham beleeved, and this was imputed unto him for righteousnesse*. Being justified, all our iniquities are covered, God beholdeth us in the righteousnesse which is imputed, and not in the sinnes which wee have committed.[136]

This passage is important for a variety of reasons. Firstly, it clearly asserts the doctrine of justification by faith.[137] Secondly, it displays the means by which justification is accomplished, namely by imputation of a certain righteousness,[138] as also suggested by Barnes.[139] Hooker does

---

130 Hooker, *Jude II* (*Works* V, 49.16-24).
131 *ibid.* 49.29.
132 Allison, *The Rise of Moralism*, 3.
133 Tyndale, *Exposition of First John*, 117.
134 Stanwood, "Of Prelacy and Polity in Milton and Hooker", in Margo Swiss and David Kent (eds), *Heirs of Fame. Milton and Writers of the English Renaissance*, 69.
135 Hooker, *Jude II* (*Works* V, 50.1-15).
136 *ibid.* 50.16-21.
137 Hooker's insistence on justification by faith is also noticed by Rowse, *The England of Elizabeth*, 487.
138 See also Keble, *The Works*, xcviii-xcix; Marshall, *Hooker and the Anglican Tradition*, 114; Morrel, "Richard Hooker, Theologian of the English Reformation", 9; Griffith Thomas (ed.), *The Principles of Theology*, 185; Hughes, *Faith and Works*, 41; Booty, "The

not say here what righteousness he had in mind, but it is clear that it is not the righteousness of the believer. From the previous passage, in which Hooker follows Foxe in writing that no man has the righteousness which is necessary for justification, and that only the Son of God can deliver man from death,[140] the obvious logical inference is that only Christ has the necessary righteousness for justification. Thirdly, justification has a twofold aspect: forensic[141] and actual. On the one hand, and his is similar to Barnes, we are justified before God,[142] because God looks at us through the righteousness of Christ,[143] as if it were ours; this is the source of justification both for Hooker and Cranmer.[144] This is the imputation of Christ's righteousness to us,[145] which is also clear in Bradford:[146] the righteousness of Christ is not ontologically ours, but it is ours functionally for the specific purpose of justification, as also explained by Foxe.[147] On the basis of the righteousness of Christ, God considers us righteous as if we truly were righteous. At this point, Hooker offers a brief definition of justification, according to which justification is the forgiveness of sins, very much in line with Tyndale's own definition.[148] In spite of the fact that we are sinners, God considers us without sin, as if we did not have any sin at all. The reality of forensic justification leads to the reality of actual justification, when the sinful man exercises his faith. By faith, forensic justification becomes effectual in his life. In Hooker, sin has a dual

---

English Reformation: A Lively Faith and Sacramental Confession", 25; Booty, "Anglican Identity: What is This Book of Common Prayer?", *Sewanee Theological Review* 40/2 (1997), 142.

139 Barnes, *The Supplication of 1531*, xliii.a.

140 Foxe, *The Acts and Monuments*, 71.

141 Rupp, *Studies in the Making of the English Protestant Tradition*, 166; Voak, *Richard Hooker and Reformed Theology*, 177.

142 Barnes, *The Supplication of 1531*, xliii.a. See also Booty, "The Spirituality of Participation in Richard Hooker", *Sewanee Theological Review* 38/1 (1994), 11.

143 Booty, "The Spirituality of Participation in Richard Hooker", *Sewanee Theological Review* 38/1 (1994), 11.

144 Cranmer, *Annotations on the King's Book*, 12.

145 Rupp, *Studies in the Making of the English Protestant Tradition*, 168, Morrel, "Richard Hooker, Theologian of the English Reformation", 9; Griffith Thomas (ed.), *The Principles of Theology*, 185; Booty, "Anglican Identity: What is This Book of Common Prayer?", *Sewanee Theological Review* 40/2 (1997), 142; Kirby, "The Paradigm of Chalcedonian Christology in Richard Hooker's Discourse on Grace and the Church", *Churchman* 114/1 (2000), 23-25.

146 Bradford, *Writings*, 371-372.

147 Foxe, *Of Free Justification by Christ*, 112.

148 Tyndale, *Prologue to Romans*, 125, and Bradford, *Writings*, 217-218.

quality: original and actual.[149] This brief definition of sin gives Hooker another chance to define more clearly what he means by justification. Justification is totally the work of God,[150] which is obvious in Foxe.[151] Hooker mentions again the imputation of righteousness[152] – see also Frith[153] – but he does not say to whom this righteousness belongs. Based on the previous arguments, it has been inferred that Hooker makes reference to the righteousness of Christ, although he does not clearly admit it. However, what he clearly states is that by justification through the imputation of righteousness all sins are forgiven in the case of those who believe.[154]

For Hooker, justification is both the forgiveness and the remission of all sins[155] by grace[156] – in line with Bradford's definition[157] – as if we had never been affected by sin, which is clear in the theology of Foxe.[158] In this respect, justification is effective, because it is done by God himself:

> But *imputation* or righteousness hath covered the sinnes of every soule which beleeveth; God by pardoning our sinne hath taken it away: so that now although our transgressions be multiplied above the haires of our head, yet being justified wee are as free, and as cleere, as if there were no one spot, or staine of any uncleanesse in us. For it is God that justifieth, and *who shall lay any thing to the charge of God chosen?* saith the Apostle in the 8. chapter to the Romans.[159]

Hooker continues to keep in balance the two aspects of justification: forensic and actual, but with particular stress on the actual aspect. Thus, Hooker writes that after our sins are forgiven and remitted, we are made the righteousness of God in Christ.[160] Tyndale, for instance, is

---

149 Hooker, *Jude II* (*Works* V, 50.22).
150 Rupp, *Studies in the Making of the English Protestant Tradition*, 167; Lake, "Business as Usual? The Immediate Reception of Hooker's *Ecclesiastical Polity*", *The Journal of Ecclesiastical History* 52/3 (2001), 474.
151 Foxe, *The Acts and Monuments*, 71.
152 Booty, "Anglican Identity: What is This Book of Common Prayer?", *Sewanee Theological Review* 40/2 (1997), 142.
153 Frith, *A Disputation of Purgatory*, 179; Booty, "The English Reformation: A Lively Faith and Sacramental Confession", 25.
154 Morrel, "Richard Hooker, Theologian of the English Reformation", 9; Griffith Thomas (ed.), *The Principles of Theology*, 185.
155 Rupp, *Studies in the Making of the English Protestant Tradition*, 166.
156 Keble, *The Works*, vol. 2, 552; Secor, *Richard Hooker, Prophet of Anglicanism*, 185.
157 Bradford, *Writings*, 217-218.
158 Foxe, *The Acts and Monuments*, 80.
159 Hooker, *Jude II* (*Works* V, 50.27-51.2).
160 Collinson, *Archbishop Grindal*, 41.

even more precise as he writes that Christ is our righteousness.[161] It is only the righteousness of God that grants us the blessing. Supposedly, Hooker means the grace of salvation because he mentions this within the context of the forgiveness of sins, which is his definition of salvation in agreement with Bradford.[162] Like Foxe, Hooker admits there is nothing intrinsic to man which might qualify him to have a right standing before God.[163] It is only the righteousness of God – that Hooker places in Christ – the one which assures the believer of his perfect condition in appearing before God correctly,[164] so belief in the righteousness of God is true justifying faith, as in Barnes:[165]

> Now sinne being taken away, wee are made *the righteousnesse of God in Christ.* For *David* speaking of this righteousnesse, saith, *Blessed is the man whose iniquities are forgiven.* No man is blessed but in the righteousnesse of God. Every man whose sinne is taken away is blessed. Therefore every man, whose sinne is covered, is made the righteousnesse of God in Christ. The righteousnesse doth make us to appear most holy, most pure, most unblamable before him.[166]

When Hooker introduces the concept of faith within his discussion, justification apparently loses its forensic aspect. Hooker reminds us that faith is the only element that justifies. He obviously makes direct reference to the fact that justification is appropriated by the believer to his own life through faith.[167] The result is that sin is actually remitted, and we are given the righteousness of God, which is utterly external to us.[168] It is clear that, by the appropriation through faith of the righteousness of God, in justification sinners are made holy: "This then is the sum of that which I say, faith doth justifie: justification washeth away sin: sin removed, we are cloathed with the righteousness which is of God: the righteousness of God maketh us most holy. Every of these I have proved by the testimony of Gods own mouth. Therefore I conclude, that faith is that which maketh us most holy, in consideration whereof it is called in this place, *Our most holy faith.*"[169]

---

161 Tyndale, *Exposition of First John*, 117.
162 Bradford, *Writings*, 217-218.
163 Foxe, *Of Free Justification by Christ*, 112.
164 Griffith Thomas (ed.), *The Principles of Theology*, 185.
165 Barnes, *The Supplication of 1531*, xciiii.b.
166 Hooker, *Jude II* (*Works* V, 51.3-9).
167 Secor, *Richard Hooker, Prophet of Anglicanism*, 185.
168 Schmidt, "Die Rechtfertigungslehre bei Richard Hooker", 388, and White, „Anglican Reflections on the Council of Trent in the Reign of Queen Elizabeth I", 290; Kirby, *Richard Hooker's Doctrine of Royal Supremacy*, 50.
169 Hooker, *Jude II* (*Works* V, 51.10-16).

The rest of the sermon is mainly concerned with the practical
results of justification and of faith, namely the edification of the Church
in faith, which is a recurrent theme in this sermon. One of the last important aspects concerning faith and justification in this sermon is the
pneumatological dimension that Hooker ascribes to applied faith.
Whatever happens in the community of the believers,[170] among those
who have been justified by faith, happens with the assistance of the
Holy Spirit.[171]

3.2.5 Salvation and the Holy Spirit

Salvation in general and calling, justification, and glorification in
particular are possible only by the work of the Holy Spirit, which is an
indication that salvation is by grace.[172] In Hooker's theology, the
pneumatological dimension of salvation and justification offers an
objective foundation for the doctrine. The Holy Spirit is active in the life
of every believer and is the only warranty that he can defeat sin, and
particularly the sinful impulsions of his nature. By the Spirit, God
dwells in the believer,[173] and the believer is intimately united to God,[174]
and the outcome of this is the defeat of sin. Hooker then explains that
the indwelling of God in the believer and the believer's union with God
is accomplished by faith alone,[175] which is indispensable to salvation.[176]
In this, Hooker is very close to Tyndale who writes that there is a direct
link between the Spirit and faith,[177] so it may be said that faith comes
from the Spirit.[178] Hooker again takes the opportunity to emphasise the
objectivity of salvation, by writing that faith must be built "upon the

---

170 Kaye, "What Might Alasdair MacIntyre Learn from a Reading of Richard Hooker?
    Rivalry, Commonality, and Their Projects", *Sewanee Theological Review* 42/3 (1999),
    347.
171 Gane, "The Exegetical Methods of Some Sixteenth Century Anglican Preachers:
    Latimer, Jewel, Hooker, and Andrews", 35.
172 Keble, *The Works*, vol. 2, 552; Secor, *Richard Hooker, Prophet of Anglicanism*, 185.
173 Rupp, *Studies in the Making of the English Protestant Tradition*, 168.
174 Stevenson, *The Mystery of Baptism in the Anglican Tradition*, 42.
175 *ibid.* 42.
176 Hooker, *Jude II* (*Works* V, 44.27-45.8); McGrade, "Richard Hooker on the Lawful
    Ministry of Bishops and Kings", in W. J. Shiels and Diana Wood (eds), *The Ministry.
    Clerical and Lay* (Oxford: Blackwell, 1989), 184; Booty, "The Spirituality of
    Participation in Richard Hooker", *Sewanee Theological Review* 38/1 (1994), 11.
177 Gane, "The Exegetical Methods of Some Sixteenth Century Anglican Preachers:
    Latimer, Jewel, Hooker, and Andrews", 35.
178 Tyndale, *Prologue to Romans*, 123.

rocke, which *rocke is Christ*".[179] Thus, in line with Foxe, salvation is primarily the work of God[180] in Christ,[181] and it consists of the deliverance of human souls from death.[182] This salvation, which is entirely the initiative and the work of God,[183] is not effectual in the life of men unless they exercise their faith in God through the work of the Holy Spirit.

Following the pattern of his first sermon, Hooker ends this sermon doxologically, by reminding his readers that work of God is actually the work of the Holy Trinity.[184]

---

179 Hooker, *Jude II* (*Works* V, 45.23-24); Archer, *Richard Hooker*, 22.

180 Rupp, *Studies in the Making of the English Protestant Tradition*, 167; Lake, "Business as Usual? The Immediate Reception of Hooker's *Ecclesiastical Polity*", *The Journal of Ecclesiastical History* 52/3 (2001), 474.

181 Collinson, *Archbishop Grindal*, 41.

182 Foxe, *The Acts and Monuments*, 71, and Morrel, "Richard Hooker, Theologian of the English Reformation", *Christianity Today* X/24 (1966), 9.

183 Allison, *The Rise of Moralism*, 4; Booty, "Contrition in Anglican Spirituality: Hooker, Donne and Herbert", in William J. Wolf (ed.), *Anglican Spirituality* (Wilton: Morehouse-Barlow, 1982), 26; Kirby, "*Supremum Caput*: Richard Hooker's Theology of Ecclesiastical Dominion", *Dionysius* XII (1988), 96; Schwarz, "Dignified and Commodius: Richard Hooker's 'Mysticall Copulation' Metaphor", *Sewanee Theological Review* 43/1 (1999), 23.

184 Hooker, *Jude II* (*Works* V, 57.10-13); Booty, "An Elizabethan Addresses Modern Anglicanism. Richard Hooker and Theological Issues at the End of the Twentieth Century", 10.

4. The Epistemology of Faith in the *A Learned and Comfortable Sermon of the Certaintie and Perpetuitie of Faith in the Elect* (1585)

The second aspect of Hooker's doctrine of salvation is the epistemology of faith or his understanding of faith as means of knowledge which is discussed primarily in his *A Learned and Comfortable Sermon of the Certaintie and Perpetuitie of Faith in the Elect*.

The sermon was published in 1612, but it seems to have been delivered in 1585, when Hooker began his theological controversy with Walter Travers. The text of the sermon, Habakkuk 1:4 ("Therefore the law is paralysed, and justice never prevails. The wicked hem in the righteous, so that justice is perverted."), proved to be the source of inspiration for other sermons. This particular sermon is of great importance because some of its theological themes are resumed by Hooker in other works, such as for instance *Master Hooker's Answer to Supplication that Master Travers Made to the [Privy] Counsell* and in the larger *A Learned Discourse of Justification, Workes and How the Foundation of faith is Overthrown*.

4.1 Faith and Knowledge

Hooker begins his sermon with a description of his epistemology. This is very important to his theology as it sets the boundaries within which humans exercise their natural abilities in order to know and explore their existence. Although Hooker's first thought is directed towards faith, and the likelihood that faith is normally weaker rather than stronger even in holy people, like for instance the prophets, he then axiomatically establishes his twofold epistemology. The starting point of Hooker's epistemology begins from the delineation of two realms: the spiritual realm, and the natural realm. Hooker does not discuss whether there is an ontological gap between the two, although this should be apparent from his entire theology. But at this point, what is really clear in Hooker's formulation is that there is an epistemological gap between the spiritual and the natural realm. Thus he infers that there are two kinds of people. There are firstly the natural men, and secondly, the spiritual men. Hooker's actual statement only consists of the inference that natural men cannot acknowledge the things of God, which obviously belong to the spiritual realm.

4.1.1 Spiritual Men

This being the case, Hooker consequently assumes the existence of spiritual men also, who have three characteristics. Firstly, spiritual men have the illumination of the grace of God,[1] which is also acknowledged by Bradford.[2] Secondly, they are directly led by God, and thirdly, they have faith. The most important point that concerns Hooker at this stage of his argument is the quality of faith. Based on his observation regarding the daily existence of spiritual men in the natural realm, Hooker notices that the quality of their faith is faulty. He states that the faith of these men is weak: something is hindering them from exercising and practicing a strong faith. The importance of Habakkuk 1:4, on which the entire sermon is based, proves to be relevant to Hooker's argument. In Habakkuk 1:4, the prophet wrote: "Therefore the law is paralysed, and justice never prevails. The wicked hem in the righteous, so that justice is perverted." But for Hooker, this particular text is important because it reveals the weakness of faith in relation to the law. This is in line with Tyndale, who writes that the faith of justification is separate from the law.[3] Apparently, spiritual men who have faith grow increasingly weaker in faith as they get gradually closer to the law. This is vital to Hooker's soteriology, because he understands that faith and the law as a means of apprehending salvation are utterly exclusive. The more that spiritual men cling to the law, the weaker their faith is. The logical outcome of this reasoning is that only faith can really and actually appropriate salvation. Although this is only an inference, Hooker however discusses the problem of the law within his epistemology. Thus the law and faith become a means of

---

1   For details about the importance of the Holy Spirit who enlightens reason see McAdoo, "The Influence of the Seventeenth Century on Contemporary Anglican Understanding of the Purpose and Function of Authority in the Church", in G. R. Evans (ed.), *Christian Authority. Essays in Honour of Henry Chadwick* (Oxford: Clarendon Press), 262-263.

2   Bradford, *Writings*, 371-372.

3   Tydale, *Prologue to the Romans*, 123.

knowledge.[4] This is not to say that epistemology is on the same level as soteriology, or that Hooker confuses them. Hooker is only assessing law and faith from the perspective of the created order, in which the existence of both spiritual and natural men is clearly mentioned, though delineated. Hooker's exegesis of Habakkuk 1:4 leads him to write that law and faith as means of knowledge are utterly and irreconcilably exclusive. This means that man cannot fulfill the demands of the law without faith, which is the gift of God[5] or without the external help from God,[6] as also suggested in Barnes.[7]

4.1.2 The Concept of Science

As his argument is further developed, Hooker gently changes his terminology, in such a way that the law, which so obviously fails as a means of knowledge, is suddenly replaced by the concept of science.[8] He consequently speaks of faith and science as means of knowledge. In this respect, Hooker displays his confidence in faith to the detriment of science:

> That meere naturall men do not nether know nor acknoledge the thinges of god, wee do not mervail, because they are spiritually to be discerned. But they in whose harts the light of grace doth shine, they that are taught of god, why are they so *weeake in fayth*? Why is their assenting to the law so scrupulous, so much mingled with feare and wavering? It seemeth strange that ever they should imagine the law to fail. It cannot seeme strange if wee waigh the reason. If the thinges which wee beleve be considered in them selves it may truly be sayd that fayth is more certain then any science.[9]

Thus, for Hooker, it is clear that faith is qualitatively stronger than science in connection with the degree of certainty that they provide to men in their enterprise of exploring their entire existence with the specific purpose of grasping knowledge of it. Hooker apparently believes that existence itself goes beyond the boundaries of the created order. He writes that there are some things that we believe, and for him it is clear that they exist, and we know of their existence by faith. Science, however, as another means of knowledge, should be able to

---

4   See also Bethell, *The Cultural Revolution of the Seventeenth Century*, 22.
5   See also Thornton, *Richard Hooker*, 56; Griffith Thomas (ed.), *The Principles of Theology*, 185; Collinson, *Archbishop Grindal*, 41.
6   Kirby, *Richard Hooker's Doctrine of Royal Supremacy*, 50.
7   Barnes, *The Supplication of 1531*, lxxxvii.a.
8   See also Harth, *Swift and Anglican Rationalism*, 41.
9   Hooker, *Certaintie* (*Works* V, 69.16-24).

explore them also. In this respect, Hooker is sceptical with regard to the capability of science to explore those things which transcend the created or natural realm. These things are spiritual, so it is only faith that can actually get an accurate knowledge of them. Science is weaker than faith should they both attempt to explore the spiritual things of the realm beyond the natural created order.

4.1.3 The Dual Concept of Certainty

Hooker's twofold epistemology becomes clearer when he introduces his dual concept of certainty. Strangely enough, Hooker does not attach his dual concept of certainty to science, but to faith, and more specifically to Christian faith. Hooker now abandons this discussion on science, because he considers that science is only concerned with the knowledge that we have through the senses. He seems to be convinced that any knowledge through the senses cannot but be associated with science, and science only offers fallible proofs and demonstrations. This is why he drops off his argument on science as a means of knowledge, and he begins to analyse the epistemology of the Christian faith, to which he attaches his dual concept of certainty. Thus, faith should be considered in relation to the certainty of evidence and the certainty of adherence: "That which we know either by sense or by most in fallible demonstration is not so certain as the principles articles and conclusions of Christian fayth concerning which wee must note that there is a certainty of evidence and a certainty of adherence".[10] The next step for Hooker is to consider both the certainty of evidence and the certainty of adherence in greater detail.

4.1.4 The Certainty of Evidence

Hooker defines the certainty of evidence by attaching two basic concepts to it. Firstly, the certainty of evidence is concerned with the human mind, and secondly it displays a manifestation of the truth. It is important to note that, for Hooker, the first aspect of faith is the assent of the mind in regard to the things to which faith is directed. When Hooker mentions the mind, it is clear that he is making reference to human reason.[11]

---

10   *ibid.* 69.24-70.1.
11   For the importance of reason in Hooker, see also Shirley, *Richard Hooker and Contemporary Political Ideas*, 88; Hillerdal, *Reason and Revelation in Richard Hooker*, 71-

Hooker's picture of the certainty of evidence, which is directly linked to reason, offers a clear explanation of how man should investigate the surrounding reality. By the certainty of evidence, faith triggers human reason in order that it should grasp the manifestation of the things that it explores. Hooker, however, makes a vital observation. The function of human reason is to assent to or to get hold of the manifestation of things approached, but it cannot explore the truth of these things. Faith is obviously concerned with spiritual things. When he discusses the methodology of reason as an essential faculty of faith,[12] Hooker has in mind spiritual, not natural things, which are explored by science. Consequently, human reason obviously has the capacity of exploring spiritual things,[13] but only to the extent that it assents to their truth. Human reason cannot fathom the truth of spiritual things; it can only acknowledge the truth of spiritual things. Hooker explains:

> Certainty of evidence wee call that, when the mind doth assent unto this or that; not because it is true in it selfe, but because the truth thereof is cleere, because it is manifest unto us. Of thinges in them selves most certain, except they be also most evident, our persuasion is not so assured as it is of thinges more evident although in themselves they be lesse certayn.[14]

In this respect, Hooker's analysis of the certainty of evidence is important, because he introduces his concept of revelation. Thus, man explores the realm of his existence because there are two means of revelation which help him. Hooker firstly mentions the light of grace, and secondly the light of nature. It is clear for Hooker that human epistemology is directly conditioned by an external factor, such as revelation, which consists of the light of grace, and the light of nature. But what is important to notice is that both grace and nature are external to man. Accordingly, when man explores the things of the

---

75; Hoopes, *Right Reason in the English Renaissance*, 127; Speed Hill, "The Evolution of Hooker's *Laws of the Ecclesiastical Polity*", 117-158; Orrù, "Anomy and Reason in the English Renaissance", *Journal of the History of Ideas* XLVII/2 (1986), 186; Sykes, "Richard Hooker and the Ordination of Women to the Priesthood", *Sewanee Theological Review* 36/2 (1993), 200-214 or Sykes, "Richard Hooker and the Ordination of Women to the Priesthood", in Janet M. Soskice (ed.), *After Eve* (Colins, 1990), 119-137; Davis, "'For Conformities Sake': How Richard Hooker Used Fuzzy Logic and Legal Rhetoric against Political Extremes", in McGrade, *Richard Hooker and the Construction of Christian Community*, 339.

12   For details about the faculty of reason in relationship to faith and grace, see Newey, "The Form of Reason: Participation in the Work of Richard Hooker, Benjamin Whichcote, Ralph Cudworth and Jeremy Taylor", *Modern Theology* 18/1 (2002), 7.

13   For the role of reason in exploring spiritual things, see Tebeaux, "Donne and Hooker on the Nature of Man: The Diverging 'Middle Way'", 31.

14   Hooker, *Certaintie* (*Works* V, 70.1-6).

spiritual realm, he uses both the light of grace, and the light of nature, which are themselves external means of revelation.[15]

The certainty of evidence, however, is more concerned with the light of nature, because it reveals the evidence of truth as far as spiritual things are concerned. Human reason, which results in the certainty of evidence, based on the natural light,[16] offers man the evidence or the clear manifestation of the truth of spiritual things. In spite of the fact that the light of grace should have a greater impact on human reason, Hooker is aware that human reason cannot but intellectually assent to spiritual things to the extent provided by the light of nature. In the spiritual realm itself, Hooker seems to have identified another epistemology, whereby the angels and the spirits of the righteous get their knowledge of spiritual things. Thus, following Cranmer,[17] Hooker speaks of the light of glory, which is available only to those beings which exist in the spiritual realm.

As far as the inhabitants of the natural realm are concerned, whenever they want to explore the things of the spiritual realm they should firstly exercise their faith according to the light of grace and consequently obtain a sure evidence of the truth of spiritual things. Hooker, however, carefully observes the world, and sees that this is not what really happens. It is the light of nature that offers a foundational certainty to man, when he exercises his faith. The first aspect of human nature that faith touches is reason, and the proofs that reason needs are only given to it by the light of nature. Accordingly, man first of all obtains a certainty of evidence in relation to the spiritual things he tries to explore by faith. Hooker writes:

> It is as sure if not surer that there be sprites as that there be men: but wee are more assured of these then of them because these are more evident. The trueth of somethinges is so evident, that not man which heareth them can doubt of them: As when wee heare, that *a part of anything is lesse then the whole*, the mind is constrayned to say this is true. If it were so in matters of fayth then as all men have equall certaintie of this, so no beleever should be more scripulous and doubtfull then another. But wee find the contrarie. The Angells and sprites of the righteous in heaven have certaintie most evident of thinges spirituall, but this they have by the light of glorie. That which wee see by the light of grace thought it be in deede more certain yeat

15 Sommerville, "Richard Hooker, Hadrian Saravia, and the Advent of the Divine Right of Kings", 231.

16 See also Hunt, *Religious Thought in England*, 60.

17 See also Cranmer's discussion about the image of glory, in Cranmer, *Annotations on the King's Book*, 12.

is it not to us so evidently certain as that which sense or the light of nature will not suffer a man to doubt of.[18]

Next, Hooker resumes the duality of his epistemology. He seems to be convinced of the essentially different nature of the spiritual realm and of the natural realm. The certainty of evidence should be used as a means of knowledge in the natural realm, because it is normal that solid and sensible proofs should offer certainty to the one who explores the natural realm. Hooker, however, cannot totally separate the certainty of evidence from the spiritual realm. The reason why he is actually compelled to use the certainty of evidence for at least partially fathoming the spiritual realm is only evident later, when Hooker begins to discuss the righteousness of Christ,[19] the very source of salvation,[20] which is similar to Cranmer's definition of salvation.[21]

At this point, it can only be inferred that faith needs the certainty of evidence due to the early existence of Christ. Although he is from the spiritual realm, Christ has lived in the natural realm. It is clear for Hooker that the certainty of evidence works better in the natural world. But the certainty of evidence is part of faith. In spite of the fact that the certainty of evidence primarily addresses the mind or human reason in respect to the things of the natural realm, it nevertheless acknowledges spiritual things. Christ, however, has lived in the natural realm; consequently, true faith[22] in Christ must necessarily consist of a mental or intellectual assent of his existence, but this is not the only aspect of true faith, as Tyndale correctly notices.[23] Faith offers to the believer the certainty of evidence in matters pertaining to the spiritual realm, such as the earthly existence of Christ, although it cannot explore its truth. True faith necessarily involves human reason, because Christ lived in the natural world, which is accessible to human reason. However, the truth of Christ's earthly existence cannot be explored by human reason, and cannot be endorsed by the certainty of evidence; by reason, the truth of Christ's earthly existence can only be admitted.

---

18   Hooker, *Certaintie* (*Works* V, 70.6-19).

19   Allison, *The Rise of Moralism*, 3; Booty, "The Spirituality of Participation in Richard Hooker", *Sewanee Theological Review* 38/1 (1994), 11.

20   Hooker, *Certaintie* (*Works* V, 71.28).

21   Cranmer, *Annotations on the King's Book*, 12.

22   Nothing is necessary for justification except for a true and lively faith. Collinson, *Archbishop Grindal*, 41.

23   Tyndale, *Exposition of First John*, 121.

4.1.5 The Certainty of Adherence

Hooker then introduces the second aspect of his doctrine of faith, by explaining the certainty of adherence. Faith does not consist only in the certainty of evidence, which is linked to human mind or human reason, but also in the certainty of adherence, which directly affects human heart. In fact, this is in line with Tyndale, who writes that the new heart comes from faith, which comes from the Spirit.[24] Hooker seems to be persuaded that in some instances the proofs of the spiritual realm are not so evident, but there is something in true faith that makes the believer wholeheartedly adhere to spiritual things, in spite of the lack of evident tokens. Thus, for Hooker, faith is not a mere intellectual assent of spiritual things by means of human reason, but also a firm trust in spiritual things[25] – as in Cranmer[26] – although the evident proofs are lacking.

> The other which wee call the certaintie of adherence is when the hart doth cleave and stick unto that which it doth believe. This certaintie is greater in us then the other. The reason is this: the fayth of a Christian man doth apprehend the wordes of the law, the promises of god, not only as true but also as good, and therefore even then when the evidence which he hath of the trueth is so small that it greaveth him to feele his weaknes in assenting thereunto, yeat is there in him such a sure adharence unto that which he doth but faintly and fearfully believe that his spirit *having once truly tasted the heavenly sweetnes* thereof all the world is not able quite and cleane to remove him from it but he striveth with him selfe to hope even against hope to believe even against all reason of believing, being settled with Job upon this unmoveable resolution, *thought God shall kill me I will not geve over trusting in him.* For why? This lesson remayneth for ever imprinted in his hart, *it is good for me to cleave unto god.*[27]

This passage is of particular importance because, by means of the certainty of adherence, Hooker attaches to faith a moral dimension.[28] He also explains the content of faith. Thus, faith appropriates to the believer not only the truth, but also the goodness of the promises of

---

24 Tyndale, *Prologue to Romans*, 123; Gane, "The Exegetical Methods of Some Sixteenth Century Anglican Preachers: Latimer, Jewel, Hooker, and Andrews", 35.

25 Griffith Thomas (ed.), *The Principles of Theology*, 191; Sedgwick, "The New Shape of Anglican Identity", *Anglican Theological Review* LXXVII/2 (1995), 189.

26 Cranmer, *The 1538 Articles*, 4.

27 Hooker, *Certaintie* (*Works* V, 70.31-71.15).

28 See also Sedgwick, "Revisioning Anglican Moral Theology", *Anglican Theological Review* LXIII/1 (1981), 10.

God,[29] and of the words of the law because, as Tyndale rightly notices, we believe the promises of God by faith.[30] Hooker clearly makes a direct reference to the law of God, which is closely linked to the promises of God. Both the law and the promises of God are spiritual things, which cannot be grasped by human reason.[31] The lack of sensible evidence is so frustrating in respect to the law and the promises of God, that human reason cannot be persuaded by them. However, following Cranmer,[32] Hooker writes that faith is not only the intellectual assent of spiritual things but also the heartfelt trust in spiritual things,[33] which involve the law and the promises of God, as underlined by Tyndale.[34]

Although he does not confer any other content to the law and promises of God, Hooker will later talk about Christ.[35] Thus, the law and the promises of God are closely related to Christ. As in the case of the certainty of evidence, the certainty of adherence must be approached and understood christologically. In this respect, Hooker is clear that faith is trust in Christ,[36] which is identical to Cranmer's definition.[37] The content of faith is Christ himself. Although faith has a twofold constitution, as it is formed both by the certainty of evidence and the certainty of adherence, Hooker writes that the certainty of adherence must prevail and be stronger. By the certainty of evidence and so by reason, faith can only assent to the truth of God's law and promises, revealed in the person of Christ.[38] Such a faith is not complete. It is only by the certainty of adherence that faith goes beyond its intellectual dimension and becomes complete by trust.[39] Thus, by trust, faith not only acknowledges, but also actually fathoms the truth

---

29 Malone, "The Doctrine of Predestination in the Thought of William Perkins and Richard Hooker", 107; Kirby, *Richard Hooker's Doctrine of Royal Supremacy*, 46.

30 Tyndale, *Prologue to Romans*, 124.

31 See also Hillerdal, *Reason and Revelation in Richard Hooker*, 75.

32 Cranmer, *The 1538 Articles*, 4.

33 Hooker, *Certaintie* (*Works* V, 71.1); Sedgwick, "The New Shape of Anglican Identity", *Anglican Theological Review* LXXVII/2 (1995), 189.

34 Tyndale, *Exposition of First John*, 121.

35 Hooker, *Certaintie* (*Works* V, 71.28).

36 Griffith Thomas (ed.), *The Principles of Theology*, 191; Collinson, *Archbishop Grindal*, 41; Sedgwick, "The New Shape of Anglican Identity", *Anglican Theological Review* LXXVII/2 (1995), 189.

37 Cranmer, *The 1538 Articles*, 4.

38 Kaye, "Authority and the Interpretation of Scripture in Hooker's *Of the Laws of Ecclesiastical Polity*", *The Journal of Religious History* 21/1 (1997), 97.

39 Griffith Thomas (ed.), *The Principles of Theology*, 191.

of God's law and promises revealed in Christ.[40] In spite of the lack of sensible proofs, which offer the certainty of evidence, true faith totally and wholeheartedly attaches itself to and scrutinizes the truth of spiritual things by the certainty of adherence. Actually, nothing should destroy the certainty of adherence, because by trust it is the only way to understand the law and the promises of God in Christ.[41] The logical reality is that there are no natural proofs that might contradict spiritual things, because there is both an ontological and an epistemological gap between the natural and the spiritual realm. In a final analysis, Hooker's twofold epistemology is closely linked to his dual doctrine of faith, which consists of the certainty of evidence and the certainty of adherence. Thus, the first component of faith is the intellectual assent to the earthly existence of Christ given by the certainty of evidence, but the most important aspect of faith is the firm trust in the law and promises of God revealed in Christ, given by the certainty of adherence.

4.2 Faith and Salvation

The next level of Hooker's sermon is his discussion of salvation in close connection to his understanding of faith. He begins by briefly describing sinful human nature, which is deeply affected by original sin.[42] Thus, from the perspective of salvation, humankind has lost the capacity of possessing and exercising a proper knowledge and love. This is a clear reference to the mere reality that human epistemology and morality are both fundamentally deficient. The faultiness of humanity is expressed by Hooker in contrast to salvation, which should ideally be characterized by firmness of conscience: "Now the minds of all men being so darkened as they are with the foggie damp of originall corruption, it cannot be that any mans hart living should be ether so enlightned in the knowledge or so established in the love of that wherein his salvation standeth as to be perfect, nether doubting

---

40   For the importance of God's revelation in Christ according to Hooker, see Booty, "Hooker and Anglicanism: Into the Future", *Sewanee Theological Review* 36/2 (1993), 220.

41   Collinson, *Archbishop Grindal*, 41.

42   See also Monahan, "Richard Hooker: Counter-Reformation Political Thinker", in McGrade, *Richard Hooker and the Construction of Christian Community*, 208; Voak, *Richard Hooker and Reformed Theology*, 140-141.

nor shrinking at all."[43] Hooker's approach to salvation and particularly to justification is interrogative. As a matter of fact he rhetorically asks a few questions that underline some basic aspects of his doctrine of salvation. Thus, from Hooker's interrogative approach, at least three main features of his soteriology should be singled out. Firstly, human inherent righteousness does not justify.[44] Secondly, true faith should necessarily be separated from inherent righteousness, as Bradford correctly notices.[45] Thirdly, Hooker infers the necessity of the righteousness of Christ for the effectiveness of justification.[46] It is obvious that Hooker asks his questions from the standpoint of a self-righteous person, who thinks that man should be justified by means of what he internally possesses in terms of pureness of life, which is supposedly translated into inherent righteousness.

4.2.1 The Firmness of Faith

In his earlier discussion on epistemology, Hooker has reached the conclusion that the second essential part of faith is the certainty of adherence, which touches the heart so that faith should be firm and full of confidence. In this respect, trust is the basic element of faith which clings to and intimately investigates the truth of spiritual things.[47] The result is a steadfast faith in those spiritual things.[48] Now, Hooker presents an alleged dilemma to the mind of the self-righteous person, who cannot understand the reason why any perfect human virtue does not quality to be like faith. In other words, the problem is why perfect human virtue cannot justify. Whether there is such a thing as perfect human virtue is not Hooker's concern to reveal. Nevertheless, from the way he formulates his questions, Hooker indirectly alleges that should anyone speak of anything perfect in human life this could only be faith, because faith comes from God. And it is only faith which justifies. It seems clear for Hooker, and also for Cranmer, that effective and true

---

43 Hooker, *Certaintie* (*Works* V, 71.16-20); for details about Hooker's view on corruption, see Kirby, *Richard Hooker's Doctrine of Royal Supremacy*, 46.

44 Gibbs, "Richard Hooker's *Via Media* Doctrine of Justification", 212; Booty, "The English Reformation: A Lively Faith and Sacramental Confession", 25.

45 Bradford, *Writings*, 371-372.

46 This is realised by imputation. See Rupp *Studies in the Making of the English Protestant Tradition*, 168; Hughes, *Faith and Works*, 41; Booty, "The Spirituality of Participation in Richard Hooker", *Sewanee Theological Review* 38/1 (1994), 11.

47 Griffith Thomas (ed.), *The Principles of Theology*, 191; Sedgwick, "The New Shape of Anglican Identity", *Anglican Theological Review* LXXVII/2 (1995), 189.

48 Hooker, *Certaintie* (*Works* V, 70.31-71.15).

justification is founded on the righteousness of Christ.[49] In contrast to the weakness of human nature with its imperfect virtues, the righteousness of Christ appears to be the objective foundation of justification.[50] Thus, the righteousness of Christ is the only component of justification, which offers firmness and certainty to faith. Hooker summarizes all these essentials in the following paragraph:

> If any such were, what doth let why that man should not be justified by his owne in herent righteousness? For righteousness inherent being perfect will justifie, and perfect fayth is apart of perfect righteousness in herent, yea a principall part, the root and the mother of all the rest, so that if the frute of every tree be such as the root is, fayth being perfect (as it is if it be not at all mingled with distrust and feare) what is there to exclud other Christian virtues from the like perfection? And then what need wee the righteousness of Christ? His garment is superfluous, wee may be honourably clothed with our owne robes if it be thus. But let them beware who challeng to them selves a strengh which they have not least they loose the comfortable support of that weakness which in deed they have.[51]

Then Hooker analyses the certainty of faith,[52] by offering a sort of psychological approach to the content of faith itself.[53] Hooker's conviction that faith is basically sure and certain reveals his exegesis of Genesis 15:6, where it is plainly stated that Abraham believed God, and this was reckoned unto him as righteousness, an observation noted by Barnes[54] and Tyndale.[55] Hooker contends firstly that the very fact that Abraham believed is an indication that he did not doubt. Hooker then smoothly changes the perspective, and focuses his discussion on us and the Holy Spirit that God gave us. Apparently, Hooker is convinced that God gives us his Holy Spirit at the same time as we exercise our faith.[56] Thus, one of the main features of Hooker's soteriology is the inseparability of faith from the Holy Spirit because, as also in Tyndale, faith is from the Spirit.[57] Following Tyndale, the pneumatology that

49 Cranmer, *Annotations on the King's Book*, 12.
50 Booty, "An Elizabethan Addresses Modern Anglicanism. Richard Hooker and Theological Issues at the End of the Twentieth Century", 10; Kirby, "The Paradigm of Chalcedonian Christology in Richard Hooker's Discourse on Grace and the Church", *Churchman* 114/1 (2000), 23-25.
51 Hooker, *Certaintie* (*Works* V, 71.20-72.1).
52 See also Milward, *Religious Controversies of the Elizabethan Age*, 105.
53 See also Hoopes, *Right Reason in the English Renaissance*, 131.
54 Barnes, *The Supplication of 1534*, and Cranmer, *Annotations on the King's Book*, 12.
55 Tyndale, *Prologue to Romans*, 128.
56 Gane, "The Exegetical Methods of Some Sixteenth Century Anglican Preachers: Latimer, Jewel, Hooker, and Andrews", 35.
57 Tyndale, *Prologue to Romans*, 123.

Hooker displays is obviously characterized by the assurance[58] granted by the Holy Spirit.[59] Should faith be firm, steadfast, and without doubt,[60] it is only because of the Holy Spirit, who assures us of our new existential status, namely to be sons of God. The father-son relationship that, by faith, actually exists between ourselves and God[61] has an epistemological purpose for us. We consequently understand spiritual things, because we actually and essentially comprehend their truth with our minds, which are illuminated by the Holy Spirit in justify-cation,[62] an idea also supported by Bradford.[63] Hooker immediately underlines the fact that this spiritual understanding is more powerful than a natural understanding of the things that exist in the created order. It is very important to note that Hooker promotes a view of faith which entails recognizing that the certainty of faith is given by the human mind being illuminated by the Holy Spirit so that it can fathom the truth of spiritual things.[64] Hooker writes:

> Some show, although no soundness of ground, ther is which maie be alleaged for defence of this supposed perfection in certaintie touching matters of our fayth. As first that *Abraham did beleeve* and doubted not, secondly that the spirit which God hath geven us to no other end but only to assure us that wee are the sonnes of God to enbolden us to call upon him as our Father, to open our eyes and make the trueth of thinges beleeved evident unto our mindes, is much mightier in operation then the common light of nature wherby wee discerne of sensible things.[65]

The clear delineation of natural things and spiritual things appears to be a constant feature of Hooker's epistemology and soteriology. According to Hooker, it is important and actually a real fact that every believer should have a stronger apprehension of spiritual things compared to whatever he perceives in the natural world. To this duality, Hooker attaches another one, which consists of the mercy of God in Christ,[66] also expressed in Barnes,[67] and the person of Christ

---

58   Griffith Thomas (ed.), *The Principles of Theology*, 186; Grislis, "The Assurance of Faith according to Richard Hooker", in McGrade, *Richard Hooker and the Construction of Christian Community*, 239.

59   Tyndale, *Exposition of Matthew*, 189.

60   Micks, "Richard Hooker as Theologian", 561.

61   Griffith Thomas (ed.), *The Principles of Theology*, 185.

62   Gane, "The Exegetical Methods of Some Sixteenth Century Anglican Preachers: Latimer, Jewel, Hooker, and Andrews", 35.

63   Bradford, *Writings*, 371-372.

64   Gane, "The Exegetical Methods of Some Sixteenth Century Anglican Preachers: Latimer, Jewel, Hooker, and Andrews", 35.

65   Hooker, *Certaintie* (*Works* V, 72.2-10).

66   Collinson, *Archbishop Grindal*, 41.

himself: "Wherefore wee must needs be much more sure of that wee beleev then of that wee see, wee must needs be more certain of the mercies of God in Christ Jesus then wee are of the light of the sonne when it shineth upon our faces."[68] This apparently could lead to the wrong conclusion that soteriology is more important than Christology,[69] but for Hooker, this is definitely not the case. Although Hooker did not further elaborate his explanation, it is fairly easy to infer its logical understanding. Christ lived in the natural world, so his earthly life is a solid proof to the human mind of his personal existence. To use Hooker's own formulations, the light of nature is sufficient for human reason to prove the existence of the person of Christ. The earthly existence of Christ is evident to reason, and it is easily believed, because the proofs that human reason actually needs lie in the historical person of Christ.

On the other hand, what is more difficult to prove is the aspect which lies beneath the historical person of Christ, namely salvation. It is clear that salvation is the manifestation of God's mercy,[70] but this is not obvious to human mind, because it does not pertain to the natural realm. For Hooker it is clear that the earthly and personal existence of Christ is part of the natural world, and consequently human mind can easily assess the truth of Christ's existence. But the mercy of God, the essence of justification[71] – which is in accordance with Bradford[72] – manifested by salvation in the work of the earthly person of Christ is not evident to human mind, because it belongs to the spiritual realm. Thus in accordance with Hooker's theory, it is only faith which can effectively search the truth of God's salvation in Christ.[73] Now, because faith is always present in the believer, together with the Holy Spirit, it is allegedly strong and doubt-free. What Hooker actually accomplishes in his argument is to attach "the thinges beleeved" to "the mercies of God in Christ Jesus", and "the common light of nature wherby wee discerne of sensible thinges" to "the light of the sonne when it shineth upon our faces." Thus, Hooker's comparison should not be understood soteriologically, but epistemologically. He does not infer that the mercy

---

67   Barnes, *The Supplication of 1531*, lviii.b-lix.a.

68   Hooker, *Certaintie* (*Works* V, 72.10-13).

69   For the importance of Christology in Hooker, see also Kirby, "*Supremum Caput*: Richard Hooker's Theology of Ecclesiastical Dominion", *Dionysius* XII (1988), 94.

70   Louma, "Restitution and Reformation?", 105.

71   Booty, "The Law of Proportion: William Meade and Richard Hooker", *St. Luke's Journal of Theology* XXXIV/2 (1991), 26.

72   Bradford, *Writings*, 371-372.

73   Collinson, *Archbishop Grindal*, 41.

of God in Christ, or God's salvation, is more important then the person of Christ, whereby salvation was accomplished. Hooker is only trying to state that, from the standpoint of what and how human beings know the surrounding reality, the mercy of God or the salvation of God in Christ should be stronger and more evident to faith than the earthly existence of Christ himself is to human reason.

4.2.2 The Reality of Doubt

In Hooker, faith has a certain degree of doubt:[74] "To that of Abraham, *He did not doubt*, I answere that this negation doth not exclude all fear all doubting, but only that which cannot stand with true fayth; it freeth Abraham from doubting through infidelity, not from doubting through infirmity; from the doubting of unbeleevers, not of weak beleevers."[75] This passage is particularly important because it shows Hooker's realistic perspective of redeemed human nature. The soteriology of Hooker consists of two fundamental aspects, which are realistically balanced: firstly, the existence of sin within human nature, and secondly, the existence of faith within redeemed human nature. It is clear to Hooker that the redeeming work of the Holy Spirit is accomplished within a sinful human nature. Consequently, although faith is doubt-free from the point of view that it is accompanied by the Holy Spirit, the same faith is doubtful from the perspective that it actually works within sinful human nature. But Hooker immediately feels obliged to explain what he means by doubt in relation to faith.[76] The only form of doubt which is present within true faith is what Hooker terms "doubt… by infirmity." It is logical to infer that Hooker makes a direct reference to human nature, which is far from being perfect. Although he does not specifically mention it, Hooker apparently makes a clear distinction between justified human nature and fallen human nature. As human nature is not perfect, true faith existing within such a nature will consequently be imperfect from the viewpoint of human nature only, but it will be perfect from the viewpoint of the Holy Spirit.

From the perspective of justified human nature, any doubt that is generated by the sinfulness of human nature can coexist with true faith,

---

74 Micks, "Richard Hooker as Theologian", 561.
75 Hooker, *Certaintie* (*Works* V, 72.13-18).
76 Micks, "Richard Hooker as Theologian", 561.

and the work of the Holy Spirit within the believer.[77] Nevertheless, Hooker warns that any other form of doubt, which is present in fallen human nature, is not characteristic of true faith. The "doubt... of infidelity" should then be associated with fallen human nature, in which faith and the work of the Holy Spirit are totally lacking.

It has been shown that the problem of epistemology in relation to soteriology was a real concern for Hooker. The way we know what we believe, and the amount of information we know about what we believe is clearly limited. Hooker seems to suggest that human understanding of salvation tends to be limited because of God's revelation.[78] This is not to be taken negatively, but again epistemologically. We know only some information regarding salvation, because God has chosen to reveal only that particular information to us.

> The reason which is taken from the power of the spirit were effectuall, yf God did worke like a naturall agent as the fier doth enflame and the sonne inlighten according to the uttermost of that abilitie which they have to bring forth there effectes, but the incomprehensible wisdome of God doth limit the effectes of his power to such a measure as seemeth best unto him selfe. Wherefore he worketh that certainty in all which sufficeth abundantly to their salvation in the life to come, but in none so great as attaineth in this lyfe unto perfection. Even so o Lord hath pleased thee, even so it is best and fittest for us, that feeling still our owne infirmity wee may no longer breath then pray *Adjuva Domine, help Lord our incrediliti*.[79]

In Hooker, it is only God's will that regulates the extent to which salvation is revealed to humanity. According to Hooker, God limited our knowledge of salvation thus allowing a certain degree of doubt in our faith with the specific purpose of making us totally dependent on himself.[80] Though redeemed, believers must always depend and rely upon God's guidance in matters pertaining to both the spiritual and the natural realm.

4.2.3 The Permanence of Faith

The next important aspect of Hooker's theology of salvation is that faith cannot be entirely lost, which means that faith is permanently present

---

77 Gane, "The Exegetical Methods of Some Sixteenth Century Anglican Preachers: Latimer, Jewel, Hooker, and Andrews", 35.

78 See also McAdoo, *The Spirit of Anglicanism*, 6-10.

79 Hooker, *Certaintie* (*Works* V, 72.24-73.3).

80 For he state of humanity being totally dependent upon God and his grace, see Neelands, "Hooker on Scripture, Reason and 'Tradition'", in McGrade (ed.), *Richard Hooker and the Construction of Christian Community*, 76-83.

in the life of the believer. It is possible that faith could grow weaker, but it never completely vanishes: "In this wee know wee are not deceyved nether can wee deceyve you when wee teach that the fayth wherby ye are sanctified cannot faile."[81] Hooker has previously linked faith to the Holy Spirit, so the strength of faith, which actually never leaves the believer, is entirely due to the Holy Spirit. As it is God who gives the Holy Spirit, whose work is closely linked to the faith of the believer, it is logically and theologically impossible that the work of God should fail. If faith is truly effective in connection with the work of the Holy Spirit, who comes from God himself, faith will forever remain in the believer because faith is from the Spirit, as Tyndale correctly points out.[82] It could be consequently inferred, by extension, that justification and salvation themselves remain forever in the believer, in such a way that they can never be lost.

Hooker further considers what happens to the believer. When God accomplishes the believer's union with Christ,[83] which is also discussed in Frith,[84] he bestows upon the believer what Hooker terms "the first grace", in accordance with 1 John 3:9, where the apostle writes that the seed of God remains in the believer.[85] This form of God's grace is utterly and essentially against the sin of human nature. It is the very nature of humanity to sin, but any sin committed by a believer will necessarily relate to a certain degree of doubt concerning spiritual things.[86] This being the case, the believer will always commit sins that cannot actually destroy his relationship to God.[87] Hooker explains that the believer cannot commit such a sin that could irremediably affect the grace of God, which therefore might be lost. It is impossible for genuine faith to fail. Should it be seriously accepted that God gives the grace of salvation, and that faith works closely in connection with the Holy Spirit, who is present within the believer, it is virtually and effectively impossible that faith, justification and salvation in general could ever be lost. Hooker explains:

---

81   *ibid.* 73.23-25.
82   Tyndale, *Prologue to Romans*, 123.
83   Morrel, "Richard Hooker, Theologian of the English Reformation", 10; Booty, "The English Reformation: A Lively Faith and Sacramental Confession", 25; McGrade, "Richard Hooker on the Lawful Ministry of Bishops and Kings", in W. J. Shiels and Diana Wood (eds), *The Ministry. Clerical and Lay* (Oxford: Blackwell, 1989), 184; Kirby, *Richard Hooker's Doctrine of Royal Supremacy*, 46; Booty, "Anglican Identity: What is This Book of Common Prayer?", *Sewanee Theological Review* 40/2 (1997), 142.
84   Frith, *Patrick Places*, 30.
85   See also Keble, *The Works*, vol. 2, 552.
86   Micks, "Richard Hooker as Theologian", 561.
87   Griffith Thomas (ed.), *The Principles of Theology*, 185.

> There was in Abakuk that which St John doth call the *seed of god,* meaning therby the first grace which God poureth into the harts of them that are incorporated into Christ. Which having received, if because it is an adversarie unto sinn, wee do therefore think wee sinn not both otherwise and also by a distrustfull and doubtfull apprehending of that which wee ought most stedfestly to beleeve, surely wee do but deceyve our selves. Yeat they which are borne of God do not sinne ether in this or in any other thing any such sinne as doth quit extinguish grace, clean cut them of from Christ Jesus, because the *seed of God* abideth in them and doth shield them from receyving any irremediable wound. Their fayth when it is at the strongest is but weake, yeat even then when it is at the weakest so strong that utterly it never faileth, it never perisheth altogeather no not in them who thinke it extinguished in them selves.[88]

Having established that faith can never be entirely lost by the believer, Hooker is then very preoccupied with the relationship between the inward essence of faith and its outward manifestation. Thus, he takes again a sort of psychological approach to faith, and asks whether deception is a sign of the lack of faith.[89] According to Hooker, some people do believe that sadness is a sign that something wrong has happened to faith. He, however, writes that joy should necessarily accompany faith, but only as "a separable accident." This phrase is of great importance, as it displays Hooker's philosophical approach to faith. Apparently Hooker is influenced by the Aristotelian philosophy of accidents and substance. In accordance with the philosophy of Aristotle, the accident should be fundamentally distinguished from the essence or substance of a certain thing. The essence can never change, but the accidents can and do change.[90]

Thus, as the essence of faith is concerned with salvation, and this cannot change, the accidents of faith, such as for instance the accompanying joy, can change or be totally lacking. The detachment of the accident of joy from the essence of faith does not infer that faith will cease to exist and still be manifested outwardly. It is clear to Hooker that what really counts is the essence of faith, whereby the believer is mindfully convinced by reason of the truth of salvation, and he is also heartily convinced by trust of the same truth of salvation.[91] Normally, the accident that accompanies the essence of faith is joy, but the natural

---

88   Hooker, *Certaintie* (*Works* V, 73.27-74.10).

89   *ibid.* 74.11-24.

90   For more details, see Jaroslav Pelikan, *Reformation of Church and Dogma, 1300-1700* (Chicago: The University of Chicago Press, 1985), 199; and G. R. Evans, *Problems of Authority in the Reformation Debates* (Cambridge: Cambridge University Press, 1992), 189.

91   Griffith Thomas (ed.), *The Principles of Theology,* 191; Sedgwick, "The New Shape of Anglican Identity", *Anglican Theological Review* LXXVII/2 (1995), 189.

realm is fundamentally affected by sin, and the believer will cones-
quently suffer from the sinful influence of natural things. Thus, he will
be grieved and disappointment will subsequently appear. Death and
other factors will cause some accidents of faith, like joy for instance, to
vanish but this does not imply that faith is also lost. Hooker is
convinced that "a greeved spirit is no argument of a faithless mind."[92]
In addition to the fact that disappointment and sorrow are not signs of
the lack of faith, which actually can never be lost entirely, this particular passage reveals the very essence of Hooker's soteriology, namely
the fundamental unity between reason and trust in matters of faith.

Hooker's epistemology is closely linked to his soteriology in such a
way that faith becomes a means of knowledge, with particular
reference to the knowledge of salvation,[93] and consequently to the
knowledge of God.[94] Reason and trust are constitutive to true faith.[95] In
the case of a genuine believer, faith will firstly impact his reason so that
he should get the certainty of evidence, whereby the believer gets a
certain conviction in view of the truth of spiritual things. But faith will
also appeal to the heart in order that it should acquire the certainty of
adherence, whereby the believer is fully convinced of the essence of the
truth of spiritual things. Thus, man should be certain of the truth of
spiritual things and reason plays an important role within Christian
epistemology.

4.2.4 From Unbelief to Faith

Up to this point, Hooker's argument reflected the theological reality
that deception is not a sign of the lack of faith. But now Hooker
changes his argument and he slightly moves his explanation towards
the conclusion that deception is a sign of faith. He takes the example of
a sorrowful man who, after performing a thorough introspection, is
fully convinced that he does not have faith at all. Hooker writes that
such a man is sorrowful because of his lack of faith. He then infers that

---

92   Hooker, *Certaintie* (*Works* V, 75.18-19).
93   Which is the goal of Scripture, as noticed by Haugaard, "Richard Hooker: Evidence
     of an Ecumenical Vision from a Twentieth Century Perspective", *Journal of
     Ecumenical Studies* XXIV/3 (1987), 434.
94   Kirby, "Richard Hooker's Theory of Natural Law in the Context of Reformation
     Theology", *Sixteenth Century Journal* XXX/3 (1999), 702.
95   See also McGrade, "Hooker's *Polity* and the Establishment of the English Church", in
     Richard Hooker, *Of the Laws of the Ecclesiastical Polity*, A. S. McGrade and Brian
     Vickers eds. (London: Sidgwick and Jackson, 1975), 21; Sedgwick, "The New Shape
     of Anglican Identity", *Anglican Theological Review* LXXVII/2 (1995), 189.

the sorrowful man would do anything to change the condition of his unbelief into a genuine belief:

> Tell this to a man that hath a mind decevid by too hard an opinion of him selfe and it doth but augment his griefe, he hath his answere ready: [...] I have throwly considered and exquisitely sifted all the corners of my hart, and I see what there is, never seeke to perswade me against my knowledg, I do not, I know I do not beleeve. Well, to favor them a litle in their weaknes, let the thing be graunted which they do imagine. Be it that they are faithles and without beliefe. But are they not greeved with ther unbeliefe? They are. Do they not wish it might and also strive that it may be otherwise? Wee know they do.[96]

The next step in the argument is that the man's willingness to change his unbelief into true faith originates in a "secret love" for spiritual things, or the things towards which faith is normally directed. Further on, Hooker links this willingness to believe in spiritual things to the very existence of these spiritual things. It appears that the logical conclusion is that nobody can love things which do not exist. The man who, in spite of his unbelief regarding spiritual things, still loves these things, necessarily believes or has faith in these things, although he is convinced he does not have any faith in them. Accordingly, if the sorrowful man, who is fully convinced he does not believe in spiritual things, visibly displays this secret love for spiritual things by the very fact that he wants to believe in them, it follows that faith actually exists within him. Hooker seems fairly convinced that lack of faith proves the nonexistence of spiritual things. Logically, faith itself proves the existence of spiritual things. It is true that this faith is not very strong, but it is still faith, and according to his previous theory, Hooker contends that faith will eventually recover from this weak state and will grow stronger. Hooker summarizes this analysis in the following paragraph:

> Whenc cometh this but from a secret love and liking which they have of those thinges that are beleeved? No man can love the thinges which in his own opinion are not. And if they thinke those thinges to be, which they show that they love when they desire to beleeve them, then must it needs be that by desiring to beleev they prove them selves to be true beleevers. For without faith, no man thinketh that thinges beleeved are. Which argument all the subtlety of infernall powres will never be able to dissolve. The faith therfore of true believers though it have many great and grevous dounfalls, yeat doth it still continew invincible, it conquereth and recovereth it selfe in the end. The dangerous conflictes whereunto it is

---

96   Hooker, *Certaintie* (*Works* V, 75.31-76.10).

subject are not able to prevail againste it. The prophet Abacuk remained faithfull in weaknes though weake in faith.[97]

However intriguing, Hooker's conclusion is generally consistent with his theory of the epistemological soteriology. It has been shown that his doctrine of faith consists of his twofold concept of certainty. Faith itself should always be discussed in terms of the certainty of evidence and the certainty of adherence. By the certainty of evidence, which appeals to human reason, faith acquires natural proofs in accordance to which the believer will subsequently be convinced of the truth of spiritual things. On the other hand, by the certainty of adherence, which appeals to the human heart, faith acquires spiritual proofs in accordance to which the believer will subsequently be convinced of the essence of the truth of spiritual things because, as Tyndale rightly contends, the new heart comes from faith.[98] Due to the application of this dual concept of certainty, which is fundamentally epistemological, to the doctrine of faith, which is essentially soteriological, Hooker reaches his theological conclusion by means of rational calculation, rather then by theological analysis.

There are, however, some inconsistencies in Hooker's theory. The flaw of Hooker's argument is the connection between the supposed love for spiritual things, and the actual or real existence of spiritual things. Such an inference is based on another faulty connection, this time between the alleged love for spiritual things and actual faith in spiritual things. It is true that faith should necessarily be manifested by love, and this would be consistent with Hooker's position, but there is not an actual guarantee that love should necessarily be manifested by faith. In other words, love is necessarily the result of faith, but faith is not necessarily the result of love. Moreover, the idea that love of spiritual things infers the actual existence of spiritual things is logically erroneous. This could mean that one's love for a goddess actually infers that this goddess really exists. As it has already been shown, another weak aspect of Hooker's argument is the connection between the supposed love and faith. This leads to the conclusion that there is the possibility that somebody could have faith or could be a Christian without being aware of this.

In this respect, it may be relevant to point out that Hooker's case is not singular within the history of theology. For instance, in the sixteenth century, Erasmus had promoted the view according to which salvation extends beyond the boundaries of historical Christianity into

---

97   *ibid.* 76.10-23.
98   Tyndale, *Prologue to Romans,* 123.

the virtuous morality of Antiquity. Thus, Erasmus believed that decent moral behaviour could be considered by God for salvation. Likewise, Zwingli displayed the same bias towards the broadening of salvation, in order that people who lived outside the chronological and geographical limits of Christianity could be saved. Zwingli, however, based his theory on God's election, not on the people's morality. Thus, godly pagans like Socrates and Scipio will be saved, because God must have elected them if they displayed a decent morality.[99] In addition to Erasmus and Zwingli, the most recent and notorious case is that of Karl Rahner. He based his concept of faith on his doctrine of revelation. By means of revelation, God does not offer mere information about an objective reality, but also a personal communion with man. Thus, revelation involves a response to faith, which is not only an intellectual assent, but also a complete and personal commitment to God. Rahner's problem is that he mixes transcendental revelation with general revelation, which leads to the inversion of the classical Christian view. Accordingly, special revelation, which alone is soteriological, is made available to people who have access only to general revelation, which is not soteriological. The result is obvious. All pagans, barbarians and philosophers included, could somehow have had access to a soteriological revelation, but they were not aware of this at the time. This led Rahner to formulate his famous theory of the "anonymous Christianity", which is very much in line with Erasmus, Zwingli and Hooker.[100]

At this point, the most serious flaw of Hooker's position is that he did not complete his view of faith with a pneumatological perspective, which could have offered an objective foundation to his theory. Thus the connection between love and faith could have become valid. If love were actually worked out by the Holy Spirit, Hooker's conclusion regarding the subsequent existence of faith would have been theologically sound because he would have considered an element of the spiritual realm such as faith as being from the Spirit, Tyndale writes,[101] and this grants the certainty of adherence to the sorrowful man. This means that should love have been the work of the Holy Spirit, the sorrowful man would have trusted in the existence of spiritual things. For Hooker, trust is essential to faith,[102] and this is also

99 See Timothy George, *Theology of the Reformers* (Leicester: Broadman Press, 1988), 146.

100 See J. A. di Noia, "Karl Rahner" in David F. Ford, *The Modern Theologians* (Oxford: Blackwell, 1997), 130.

101 Tyndale, *Prologue to Romans*, 123.

102 Griffith Thomas (ed.), *The Principles of Theology*, 191; Sedgwick, "The New Shape of Anglican Identity", *Anglican Theological Review* LXXVII/2 (1995), 189.

the case for Cranmer.[103] There is no faith without trust, which provides
the certainty of adherence. The next step would have followed
logically. Again, if love were worked out by the Holy Spirit, and if it
had already offered the certainty of adherence to the sorrowful man,
then this means that complete faith involves the certainty of evidence,
whereby the sorrowful man has been convinced of the truth of spiritual
things. There is a significant difference between mere intellectual assent
to spiritual things, given by the certainty of evidence, and the factual
trust in spiritual things, given by the certainty of adherence. The very
connection between them seems to have been a problem for Hooker.
He tried to link them using love, as an inherent element of human
nature, which is obviously part of the natural realm. Consideration of
the Holy Spirit, as part of the spiritual realm, would have been a more
useful solution, which would have kept the consistency of Hooker's
argument and would have offered an objective basis to his formulation.

4.2.5 The Permanence of Sin

Hooker's sermon continues with his concern regarding the weakness
and the sinfulness of human nature:

> It is trew; such is oure weake and waviringe nature that we have no soner
> received grace, but we ar redie to fall from it, we have no soner given oure
> assent to the law that it cannot faile, but the next conceipt which we ar
> redie to embrace is that it may that it dothe faile us. Thoug we find in oure
> selves a most willinge hart to cleave unceperble unto God even so far that
> we thincke unfanedlie with Peter *Lord I am redie to go with the into prisson
> and to death,* yeat how sone and how easelie, upon how smale occasion ar
> we changed if we be but a while lett alone, and left unto oure selves.[104]

In spite of the reality of faith in the life of the believer, human nature is
always prone to sin. However, if the believer does not fall into sin
again, it is apparently because something extrinsic to him supports him
and keeps him on the safe track. The frailty of human nature is
oftentimes seen in sheer enthusiasm, which almost immediately fades
away due to the inner sinful desires of man. Although they have faith,
people are not consistent in keeping to their good decisions, which they
had made as a result of faith, and very soon they relapse into sin, a
truth clearly expressed in Tyndale.[105] There is a way of preventing the
believer from reaching this situation, but it does not rest in the intrinsic

---

103 Cranmer, *The 1538 Articles*, 4.
104 Hooker, *Certaintie* (*Works* V, 76.23-31).
105 Tyndale, *Prologue to Romans*, 127.

qualities of the believer. The only way of preventing the believer from going back to his original sinful condition is the support of the Holy Spirit. The Christian can persevere in faith not by his own intrinsic powers, but by the extrinsic power of the Holy Spirit:

> The Galatians to day for theyre sakes that teache them the truth in chryest, content if hede weare, to *plucke oute there owne eyes* and the next day redie to plucke theirs which taught them. The love of *the aungell to the Church of Ephesus*, how greatly enflamed and how quicklie slacked. The hygher we flow the nerer we ar unto an ebb, yf men be respected as mere men accordinge to the wonted course of there alterable inclination with oute the heavenlie support of the spirytt.[106]

For Hooker, faith is weak, but the weakness of faith should always be assessed from the perspective of man and of his human nature, not from the perspective of God. Hooker seems to be convinced that if faith is weak, then it is only because faith works within a body, which is still affected by sin. Hooker describes carefully the methodology of sin in comparison to the existence of faith within the believer. The first level of faith that sin attacks is the certainty of evidence. Actually, Hooker notices that sin perverts firstly the mind. In the case of the believer, the sinful corruption[107] of the mind factually interrupts God's revelation. What Hooker has in mind here is the promise of God, which actually refers to salvation because, according to Tyndale, the promise is believed by faith.[108] The promise of God is not given in vain, but it corresponds with the reality of life.[109] Sin breaks this vital connection in such a way that the promise of God is not pictured in accordance with a given reality, so that the promise of God appears to be preposterous. Nevertheless, the promise of God for salvation in spite of sin is another objective aspect of Hooker's soteriology, and this very much resembles the definition of salvation promoted by Foxe.[110] From God's perspective, salvation has always been secure, but only for those who believe. Hooker is very careful to underline that the promise of God can only be appropriated by faith. Again, Hooker tries to root his doctrine objectively and mentions that faith should be directed towards Christ.[111] This being the case, the range of faith in terms of expectations

---

106 Hooker, *Certaintie* (*Works* V, 77.1-8).
107 Kirby, *Richard Hooker's Doctrine of Royal Supremacy*, 46; Bouwsma, "Hooker in the Context of European Cultural History", in Claire McEachern and Deborah Shuger (eds), *Religion and Culture in Renaissance England*, 149.
108 Tyndale, *Prologue to Romans*, 124.
109 Hooker, *Certaintie* (*Works* V, 77.17-21).
110 Foxe, *The Acts and Monuments*, 71.
111 Hooker, *Certaintie* (*Works* V, 77.16-17).

should transcend any given historical situation. Because the content of faith is objectively defined as being rooted in the person of Christ, faith should trigger its trust and expect that a certain promise of God will eventually have a correspondence in reality, in spite of any given historical impossibility. In this respect, the main feature of faith is lack of doubt. Hooker explains this reasoning in this passage:

> The simplicitie of faithe which is in Christe taketh the naked promyse of God his bare word and on that it resteth [...] The word of the promyse of God unto his people is *I will not leave the nor forsake the*, upon this the simplicitie of faith resteth, and it is not afrade of famine. Butt marcke how the subtiltie of Satan did corrupt the mindes of that *rebellious generation whose spiretes wear not faithfull unto god*. They beheld the desolate state of the desert in which they were, and by the wysdome of there sense concluded the promise of God to be but follie. *Can God prepare a table in the wildernes?* The word of promise unto Sara was *thow shalt beare a sonne*. Faith is simple and doubtethe not of it, but satan to corrupt this simplicitie of faith entangleth the minde of the woman with an argument drauen from common experience to the contrarie.[112]

Hooker is keenly aware that human nature is so biased towards sin that it can actually prevent man from being sensitive to the revelation of God.[113] This may be the reason why he displays a rather realistic view of salvation. The promise of God and human responsibility are intertwined in his soteriology. From the viewpoint of God, the promise of salvation[114] is not only virtually existent for the sake of humanity, as clearly contended by Frith,[115] but is actually made efficacious for those who believe in spite of any historical inadequacy. This, however, should not encourage anyone to live in total lack of responsibility in relation to the revealed promise of God. Hooker seems convinced that the paradox of salvation consists of this twofold response of God towards humanity: blessing for those who believe, and punishment for those who live irresponsibly.[116]

It should be stressed here that Hooker places the soteriological promise of God within the context of the sovereignty of God as did Bradford before him.[117] Thus God had known from the very beginning that humans would not be able to perform any actions effectively in order somehow to direct their lives towards any point beyond the

---

112 *ibid.* 77.16-17, 77.21-78.1.
113 *ibid.* 78.11-18.
114 Speed Hill, "Editing Richard Hooker: A Retrospective", *Sewanee Theological Review* 36/2 (1993), 187-199.
115 Frith, *Patrick Places*, 30, and Cranmer, *The 1538 Articles*, 4.
116 Hooker, *Certaintie* (*Works* V, 78.23-29).
117 Bradford, *The Writings of John Bradford*, 211.

boundaries of their own sinful human nature.[118] Hooker then explains the content of what he infers by the sovereignty of God in connection to soteriology. He apparently implies that despite difficult factual conditions, when even believers lead a miserable life of constant persecution, the sovereign will of God regarding salvation is still manifest in history.[119] So believers are preserved in faith,[120] and divinely supported by God in the midst of their troubled existence. Following Bradford,[121] Hooker writes that the mercy of God, which is soteriologically manifested in history, is the source of justification and a warranty of God's sovereignty displayed for the specific purpose that the believers should be preserved in view of the final completion of salvation.[122]

4.2.6 The Perseverance of Saints

Towards the end of his sermon, Hooker tries to find another objective foundation for his soteriology. In this respect, he mentions Luke 22:31, where Christ prayed for Peter's faith. The believer's preservation in faith, generally known as the perseverance of saints, and thus his personal abiding in salvation can be securely offered only by Christ. Hooker obviously makes reference to Christ as mediator between God and man,[123] an aspect which is vitally important for Frith.[124] Hooker is apparently convinced that the prayer of Christ the mediator is an essential part of Christian soteriology. The function of Christ's prayer is to strengthen the faith of the believer to such an extent that faith itself will never be completely lost. On the other hand, the prayer of Christ significantly diminishes the influence and the power of sin within the believer's human nature.[125] Up to this point, Hooker has always mentioned the faith of the believer. The preservation of the believer unto final salvation was assured by God on the basis of the faith of the

---

118 Hooker, *Certaintie* (*Works* V, 79.1-6).
119 d'Entrèves, *Riccardo Hooker*, 49; Haugaard, "The Scriptural Hermeneutics of Richard Hooker. Historical Contextualization and Teleology", in Donald S. Armentrout (ed.), *This Sacred History. Anglican Reflections for John Booty*, 167; Speed Hill, "Richard Hooker and the Rhetoric of History", *Churchman* 114/1 (2000), 13-14.
120 Morrel, "Richard Hooker, Theologian of the English Reformation", 9.
121 Bradford, *Writings*, 371-372.
122 Hooker, *Certaintie* (*Works* V, 79.29-80.19).
123 Thornton, *Richard Hooker*, 61.
124 Frith, *Patrick Places*, 30.
125 Hooker, *Certaintie* (*Works* V, 81.5-10).

believer. Now, Hooker suddenly mentions faith with reference to Christ. The faith that keeps us from relapsing into sin is the faith of Christ, as plainly stated by Tyndale.[126] The reality of Christ's faith as the objective foundation[127] of the believer's preservation unto salvation does not imply that the faith of the believer is futile. On the contrary, faith is required from the believer in order for salvation to be effectual for himself, but there must be a stronger element which warranties the objectivity and perpetuity of salvation. For Hooker, this is the faith of Christ, which actually preserves the faith of the believer. In this way, the faith of the believer is the means whereby divine adoption is worked out.[128] By faith, the believer becomes a child of God.[129]

Hooker advances a soteriology which is securely anchored in God, by means of the faith of the believer. In line with Cranmer, he writes that he main element of this faith is trust,[130] against which no historical factor could possibly act. Hooker ends his sermon by resuming the objectivity of God's salvation:

> I know in whom I have beleved, I am not ignorant whose precious blood haith bene sheed for me, I have a sheperd full of kindenes full of care and full of power: unto him I commit my self; his owne finger haith ingravened this sentense in the tables of my hart, *Satan haith desyred to wynnow the as wheate, butt I have praied that thy faith faile not.* Therefor the assurance of my hope I will labor to kepe as a jewell unto the end and by labor through the gratious mediation of his praier I shall kepe yt.[131]

This text contains the core of Hooker's doctrine of salvation. Thus, salvation firstly consists of an intellectual knowledge regarding its objective cause, which is also present in Tyndale.[132] The believer must have a rational understanding of the historical event whereby salvation was effected.[133] Hooker displays no hesitation when he singles out the soteriological event, which is Christ's atoning death on the cross, as contended by Frith.[134] It is important to note that Hooker clearly works

126 Tyndale, *Prologue to Romans*, 127.
127 Booty, "An Elizabethan Addresses Modern Anglicanism. Richard Hooker and Theological Issues at the End of the Twentieth Century", 10.
128 Wallace Jr., *Puritans and Predestination*, 77.
129 Hooker, *Certaintie* (*Works* V, 81.20-27).
130 Cranmer, *The 1538 Articles*, 4; Griffith Thomas (ed.), *The Principles of Theology*, 191; Sedgwick, "The New Shape of Anglican Identity", *Anglican Theological Review* LXXVII/2 (1995), 189.
131 Hooker, *Certaintie* (*Works* V, 82.11-18); for details about mediation in Hooker, see also Kirby, *Richard Hooker's Doctrine of Royal Supremacy*, 46.
132 Tyndale, *Exposition of First John*, 121.
133 Thornton, *Richard Hooker*, 26.
134 Frith, *A Disputation of Purgatory*, 90.

with a soteriological approach, which promotes the doctrine of a personal salvation. Christ died for every individual.[135] The image that Hooker attaches to God is that of a shepherd, which is a direct hint at the guided life of the believer.[136] Salvation is secure, because God guides the life of the believer in such a way that he follows the right direction towards the completion of salvation. Then salvation secondly consists of a committed trust in God,[137] which is identical to what Cranmer had said.[138] The intellectual awareness and knowledge is not sufficient, because it must necessarily be completed by this trust, which obviously transcends any natural evidence that might be offered by reason.[139] Trust is related to the work of Christ; Hooker actually makes a direct connection between trust and the prayer of Christ as mediator,[140] which Frith also discusses.[141] It is necessary that the believer should wholeheartedly trust in the work of Christ, as suggested by Cranmer,[142] be it either the atoning death or the mediatorial prayer. Both of them function as an objective foundation for salvation. Due to this objectivity of salvation, which is the warranty of salvation, the believer will never totally lose his faith. In this respect, the doctrine of faith should always be kept in tandem with the concept of assurance,[143] which proves to be essential to Tyndale.[144] There is no true salvation without genuine assurance. Like Frith, Hooker contends that the assurance of salvation[145] leaves no room for an idle life.[146] The position that Hooker presents in this text is essentially directed to God. Salva-

---

135 Booty, "Anglican Identity: What is This Book of Common Prayer?", *Sewanee Theological Review* 40/2 (1997), 142.

136 The believer is guided by the Spirit. See Bryan, "The Judicious Mr. Hooker and the Early Christians. The Relationship of Scripture and Reason in the First Century of the Christian Era", in Donald S. Armentrout (ed.), *This Sacred History. Anglican Reflections for John Booty*, 145-146.

137 Griffith Thomas (ed.), *The Principles of Theology*, 191.

138 Cranmer, *The 1538 Articles*, 4.

139 See also Lake, *Anglicans and Puritans?*, 152.

140 See also Thornton, *Richard Hooker*, 61; for details about mediation in Hooker, see also Kirby, *Richard Hooker's Doctrine of Royal Supremacy*, 46.

141 Frith, *Patrick Places*, 30.

142 Cranmer, *The 1538 Articles*, 4.

143 Grislis, "The Assurance of Faith according to Richard Hooker", in McGrade, *Richard Hooker and the Construction of Christian Community*, 239.

144 Tyndale, *Exposition of Matthew*, 189.

145 Griffith Thomas (ed.), *The Principles of Theology*, 186.

146 Frith, *An Epistle to the Christian Reader*, 466.

tion is not the work of man but the work of God,[147] as Foxe so powerfully explains.[148] Salvation is actually the gift of God.[149] The richness of salvation is so dear, that the believer should keep God's gift like a jewel.[150] In spite of the objectivity of salvation, Hooker does not lose his realism. Although salvation is the free gift of God for man, as in Barnes,[151] the believer will not be able to keep it on his own, even if he wanted to. The sinfulness of human nature hinders the believer[152] from keeping the God's gift of salvation by faith.[153] In this respect, the believer needs a stronger support, other than himself, and this is Christ.

Hooker ends his sermon by affirming once more the objective character of salvation. Christ knows that the believer finds himself in the impossibile situation of trying to keep salvation on his own, so he offers to support him in prayer. The prayer of Christ is the warranty that the gift of salvation will stay with the believer forever.

---

147 See also Rupp, *Studies in the Making of the English Protestant Tradition*, 167; Lake, "Business as Usual? The Immediate Reception of Hooker's *Ecclesiastical Polity*", *The Journal of Ecclesiastical History* 52/3 (2001), 474.

148 Foxe, *The Acts and Monuments*, 71.

149 Griffith Thomas (ed.), *The Principles of Theology*, 185.

150 Booty, "An Elizabethan Addresses Modern Anglicanism. Richard Hooker and Theological Issues at the End of the Twentieth Century", 19.

151 Barnes, *The Supplication of 1531*, xliii.a.

152 Orr, *Reason and Authority*, 180.

153 Thornton, *Richard Hooker*, 56; Collinson, *Archbishop Grindal*, 41; Archer, *Richard Hooker*, 33.

5. The Foundation of Faith in the *A Learned Discourse of Justification, Workes and How the Foundation of Faith is Overthrown* (1586)

Hooker's view of the foundation of faith is the third aspect of his doctrine of salvation and is laid out in the *A Learned Discourse of Justification, Workes, and How the Foundation of Faith is Overthrown*.[1] His *Discourse of Justification* was published in 1612 and contains several sermons delivered before March 1586.[2] It was then that Hooker, already in his first year at the Temple, had spoken out against the doctrines of his fellow-lecturer, Walter Travers. The speech originally consisted of three separate sermons which comprised of the extent of the differences between Hooker and Travers. Habakkuk 1:4 again inspired the sermon, but this time, Hooker chose only to use its second part: "Therefore the law is paralysed, and justice never prevails. The wicked hem in the righteous, so that justice is perverted." Theologically, the discourse seeks to understand the foundation of faith from the perspective of justification and sanctification, both of which contain a special kind of righteousness.

5.1 The Righteousness of Justification

Hooker begins his discourse by tackling the subject of the righteousness of justification. Thus, he uses the second part of Habakkuk 1:4, slightly altering the language so as to highlight the conclusion: "ABAK. 1.4. *the*

---

1   The information that this chapter is based on can also be found in Corneliu C. Simuţ, "Continuing the Protestant Tradition in the Church of England: The Influence of the Continental Magisterial Reformation on the Doctrine of Justification in the Early Theology of Richard Hooker as Reflected in his *A Learned Discourse of Justification, Workes, and How the Foundation of Faith is Overthrown* (1586)", PhD thesis, Aberdeen (2003), 78-187, or Corneliu C. Simuţ, *Richard Hooker and his Early Doctrine of Justification. A Study of his* Discourse of Justification (Aldershot:Ashgate, 2005), 49-142

2   For a competent discussion of justification, see also Voak, *Richard Hooker and Reformed Theology*, 167-216.

wicked doth compasse aboute the rightuous: therefore perverse judgment doth proceed." These alterations may seem insignificant, however the entire introduction of the discourse depends on what Hooker does here. A mere observation of the text that Hooker uses helps establish from the beginning the order of the problems that he intends to analyse. Three major points arise. First, he will briefly discuss the wicked. Then, he will approach the righteous. Finally, he will use the end of the verse as the beginning of his discussion about the prevalence of wrong judgment.

5.1.1 The Imperfect Righteousness of Man

Hooker does not spend much time with the first issue, which is the discussion about the wicked. In his mind, only two kinds of wicked men exist: those inside the Church versus those outside the Church. He states that those within the Church may be judged by the Church, but those outside the Church will be judged by God. The Church exercises its judgment role for its wicked members by separating the righteous from the wicked[3] that refuse to repent. Hooker does not identify the wicked "outside the Church," yet he does offer the explanation that in Habakkuk's time, the verse would have referred to the Babylonians and thus would have fallen under God's legal jurisdiction.[4]

Hooker moves on to discussing the righteous and begins with a rather pessimistic assessment of human nature, exhibiting his classic distrust in men's righteousness. Even if some people could be considered "righteous," this righteousness is not the same as "perfection." An important observation is that Hooker mentions this imperfect righteousness only when he is speaking of what he calls "the natural man."[5] Clearly, the natural man cannot possibly possess total righteousness in or by himself. In fact, he has no inherent qualities which could even lead to the development of righteousness in this life.[6] This absence of righteousness, for Hooker, is the equivalent of sin.[7] All men have inherited sin, as part of the natural realm. No one in the natural world can be sin-free displaying a perfect and complete righteousness. This brings Hooker to the issue regarding the Virgin Mary, the mother of Christ. Since Mary was born in the natural world,

3 Griffith Thomas (ed.), *The Principles of Theology*, 185.
4 Hooker, *Justification* (*Works* V, 105.1-23).
5 *ibid.* 105.23-24.
6 Booty, "The English Reformation: A Lively Faith and Sacramental Confession", 25.
7 Hooker, *Justification* (*Works* V, 106.1).

she is not exempt from the rest of humanity that is intrinsically affected by sin. The sin that affects humanity, including Mary, is titled by Hooker as "the ancient sin," a clear reference to original sin[8] that is passed down to every human being by birth.

5.1.2 The Perfect Righteousness of Christ

Hooker speaks soteriologically early on in his sermon, linking the foundation of faith to the work of Christ. He believes that the work of Christ should apply to all human beings, including Mary. Since original sin affects every human being, it is not possible for a human to avoid the state of total unrighteousness:

> A peccati enim veteris nexu per se non est immunis, nec ipsa genetrix redemptoris. *The mother of the Redeemer her self otherwise then by redemption, is not loosed from the bande of that anciente synne.* If Christ have paide a ransom for all, even for her, it followeth that all without exception were captives. *If one have died for all, all were deade,* dead in synne, all synfull therfore none absolutely rightuous in them selves.[9]

Hooker then contrasts the unrighteous human nature with the perfect righteousness of Christ,[10] resembling Tyndale, who had written that Christ is our righteousness.[11] The contrast continues on, this time seen between the natural man (totally affected by sin and unrighteousness) and the Christian (possessing a perfect righteousness that comes through Christ[12] who paid our ransom), as is also pointed out by Cranmer.[13] The only possible way that a human being can live in a state of complete and total righteousness is in connection to Christ. There is no perfect righteousness without Him.[14] Hooker does explain a reason for Christ being inseparably linked to the possibility of us being perfectly righteous:

---

8   Voak, *Richard Hooker and Reformed Theology*, 141.

9   Hooker, *Justification* (*Works* V, 106.13-19). For details about the death of Christ for all men in Hooker's view, see also Lake, "Calvinism and the English Church 1570-1635", in Margo Todd (ed.), *Reformation to Revolution. Politics and Religion in Early Modern England*, 186.

10   The righteousness of Christ, which is external to man, is imputed to the believer. See also Rupp, *Studies in the Making of the English Protestant Tradition*, 168, and Allison, *The Rise of Moralism*, 3; Booty, "The Spirituality of Participation in Richard Hooker", *Sewanee Theological Review* 38/1 (1994), 11.

11   Tyndale, *Exposition of First John*, 117.

12   Collinson, *Archbishop Grindal*, 41.

13   Cranmer, Works II, 130.

14   Hooker, *Justification* (*Works* V, 106.19-21).

> Christe is made unto us wisdome, Justice, sanctification, and Redempcion;
> Wisdome, becawse he hath revealed his Fathers will: Justice, becawse he
> hath offred hym self a sacrifice for Synne: Sanctification, becawse he hath
> geven us of his spirit: Redempcion, becawse he hath appointed a daie to
> vindicate his Children out of the handes of corrupcion into libertie which is
> glorious. Howe Christ is made Wisdome, and howe Redempcion, it may be
> declared   when   occasion   serveth,   but   howe   Christ   is   made   the
> righteousness of men, we are now to declare.[15]

This quote is important because it lays out Hooker's overall view of
salvation. First, he desires to build a firm foundation for his soteriology.
That is why he, like Cranmer, mentions God's will, the first aspect of
this foundation.[16] By mentioning the will of God, Hooker clearly
indicates that salvation has its ultimate origin in God Himself. It is not
a work of man, but a work of God,[17] an important truth stated by
others, including Foxe.[18] Furthermore, salvation is not only the work of
God, but it was initiated by God as well. Salvation's source belongs
totally to God. Second, salvation could only be accomplished in Christ.
Several elements appear here that help illustrate Hooker's doctrine of
salvation. The first element is wisdom (Christ as wisdom and
incarnation of the wisdom of God), as in Bradford.[19] Even though it
may be a soteriological concept, Hooker sees wisdom as the element
that describes the origin of salvation. The epistemological indicator is
Christ as wisdom, thus describing God's initiating salvation[20] because
this discloses His will. Salvation's content is then first explained
through the relationship between justice and Christ's sacrifice for sin,[21]
imagery also found in Frith.[22] Hooker refers to the justice of God, which

---

15   *ibid.* 108.21-109.5.

16   Cranmer, *The 1538 Articles*, 4.

17   Rupp, *Studies in the Making of the English Protestant Tradition*, 167; Lake, "Business as
     Usual? The Immediate Reception of Hooker's *Ecclesiastical Polity*", *The Journal of
     Ecclesiastical History* 52/3 (2001), 474.

18   Foxe, *The Acts and Monuments*, 71.

19   Bradford, *The Writings of John Bradford*, 211.

20   Allison, *The Rise of Moralism*, 4; Booty, "Contrition in Anglican Spirituality: Hooker,
     Donne and Herbert", in William J. Wolf (ed.), *Anglican Spirituality* (Wilton:
     Morehouse-Barlow, 1982), 26; Kirby, "*Supremum Caput*: Richard Hooker's Theology
     of Ecclesiastical Dominion", *Dionysius* XII (1988), 96; Schwarz, "Dignified and
     Commodius: Richard Hooker's 'Mysticall Copulation' Metaphor", *Sewanee
     Theological Review* 43/1 (1999), 23.

21   See also Keble, *The Works*, vol. 2, 552, and Morrel, "Richard Hooker, Theologian of
     the English Reformation", *Christianity Today* X/24 (1966), 9.

22   Frith, *The Revelation of Antichrist*, 460.

required a sacrifice for the forgiveness of sins, as explained by Cranmer.[23]

Next, salvation's content is seen in redemption, here associated with the concept of freedom from corruption or sin.[24] Here, Christ's sacrifice is seen as having two different functions: first, it solves the tension of God's justice, and secondly, it resolves the problem of human sin. Through Christ's sacrifice, sin is forgiven because God's justice has been satisfied[25] – here, Hooker is following Frith[26] – and then that sin is remitted because of the freedom from corruption that comes to man through the faith which forgives sins, as pointed out by Tyndale.[27] Finally, salvation's content is described by sanctification, connected, according to Hooker, to the Holy Spirit's work. Salvation begins with God (both the initiative[28] and the inception) and then finds its means through the sacrifice of Christ (bringing both forgiveness and remission for sin),[29] which is our justification,[30] an idea backed up by Cranmer,[31] Bradford,[32] and Foxe.[33] The continuation of salvation is seen in the act of sanctification. Yet, even this aspect, though closely related to the daily existence of human beings, has no objective support within human nature. The Holy Spirit remains the one who completes sanctification, not the believer, as Tyndale also pointed out.[34]

5.1.3 The Concept of Righteousness

Later in his sermon, Hooker briefly summarizes the way he sees righteousness:

---

23   Cranmer, Works II, 130.
24   Kirby, *Richard Hooker's Doctrine of Royal Supremacy*, 46; Bouwsma, "Hooker in the Context of European Cultural History", in Claire McEachern and Deborah Shuger (eds), *Religion and Culture in Renaissance England*, 149.
25   Morrel, "Richard Hooker, Theologian of the English Reformation", 9; Gibbs, "Richard Hooker and Lancelot Andrew on Priestly Absolution", in McGrade, *Richard Hooker and the Construction of Christian Community*, 272.
26   Frith, *A Disputation of Purgatory*, 90.
27   Tyndale, *Prologue to Romans*, 125.
28   Schwarz, "Dignified and Commodius: Richard Hooker's 'Mysticall Copulation' Metaphor", *Sewanee Theological Review* 43/1 (1999), 23.
29   Keble, *The Works*, vol. 2, 552.
30   Rupp, *Studies in the Making of the English Protestant Tradition*, 166.
31   Cranmer, *The 1538 Articles*, 4.
32   Bradford, *Writings*, 217-218.
33   Foxe, *The Acts and Monuments*, 80.
34   Tyndale, *Prologue to Romans*, 123.

There is a glorifyinge righteousnes of men in the Worlde to comme, and
there is a justefying and a sanctefyinge righteousnes here. *The righteousnes
wherewith we shalbe clothed* in the world to comme, is both perfecte and
inherente: that whereby here we are justified is perfecte but not inherente,
that whereby we are sanctified, inherent but not perfecte. This openeth a
way to the plaine understandinge of that graund question, which hangeth
yet in controversie betwene us and the Churche of *Rome*, aboute the matter
of justefying righteousnes."[35]

The description of the extent of salvation makes this text particularly
important. Elsewhere, salvation has been described as originating in
the spiritual world, since this salvation is entirely God's initiative.[36]
Still, however spiritual may be its origin, salvation is intended for
mankind (or the natural world). Thus, salvation begins with God, is
bequeathed to mankind and then continues on in the spiritual world,
where it finds completion. The essential element for Hooker's theology
of salvation is the concept of righteousness, for it is through righteousness that salvation is fulfilled. Hooker's clarity on this subject brings
him to connect righteousness to both the natural and supernatural
(spiritual) realms.

5.1.4 The Three Types of Righteousness

Hooker uses this section of his argument to address the quality of
righteousness as well as the specific realm in which each type finds its
manifestation. Therefore, he details three types of righteousness.[37] He
begins with the righteousness of glorification (obviously part of
righteousness on the spiritual level), which represents the final stage of
God's work of salvation. The righteousness of glorification is complete
in quality and location. Hooker sees the righteousness of glorification
as perfect since it comes from the spiritual realm. The righteousness of
glorification's location is the human being, because Hooker believes it

---

35 Hooker, *Justification* (*Works* V, 109.6-14).

36 Booty, "Contrition in Anglican Spirituality: Hooker, Donne and Herbert", in William
    J. Wolf (ed.), *Anglican Spirituality* (Wilton: Morehouse-Barlow, 1982), 26; Kirby,
    "*Supremum Caput*: Richard Hooker's Theology of Ecclesiastical Dominion", *Dionysius*
    XII (1988), 96. Schwarz, "Dignified and Commodius: Richard Hooker's 'Mysticall
    Copulation' Metaphor", *Sewanee Theological Review* 43/1 (1999), 23.

37 Gibbs, "Richard Hooker's *Via Media* Doctrine of Justification", 216; Haugaard,
    "Richard Hooker: Evidences of an Ecumenical Vision from a Twentieth Century
    Perspective", *Journal of Ecumenical Studies*, XXIV/3 (1987), 434; Fitzsimmons Allison,
    "The Pastoral and Political Implications of Trent on Justification: a Response to the
    ARCIC Agreed Statement *Salvation and the Church*", *The Saint Luke's Journal of
    Theology* XXXI/3 (1988), 213.

to be inherent. Earlier he showed that human nature as it stands has no intrinsic or inherent quality[38] that could allow it to qualify as perfect. Still, since in glorification human nature becomes part of the spiritual realm, every aspect of its essence (including righteousness) is perfect. Hooker clearly believes that this is valid only in the final stage of salvation, and he is well aware that all that takes place in glorification does not occur in the spiritual realm, but in the natural. It is in the natural realm that Hooker distinguishes between the second and third types of righteousness.

The second type of righteousness that Hooker describes actually occurs first chronologically: the righteousness of justification, perfect in quality, yet extrinsic to man in its location.[39] Man is not active in justification; Hooker infers that the righteousness of justification is a gift[40] that man receives passively. This type of righteousness has nothing to do with mankind's natural qualities and is in fact totally alien to human nature. Hooker saves the bulk of his discussion on this type of righteousness for later on in his argument. For now, he quickly mentions the third type of righteousness, that of sanctification[41], which flows from justification, as in Bradford.[42] It seems that Hooker places the righteousness of sanctification within human beings, so it is inherent, in terms of its location. Hooker concludes that the righteousness of sanctification is incomplete in quality as long as man is living within the natural realm.

Hooker's discourse now turns to the laying out of several ways to look at justification, some of which come from the Church of Rome,[43] and others from the Protestant Church. The sinlessness of Mary, Christ's mother, is the only aspect that Hooker considers salient in Catholic theology (the Catholic view sees Mary as being preserved by Christ and thus clean from all sin).[44]

---

38 Stanwood, "Of Prelacy and Polity in Milton and Hooker", in Margo Swiss and David Kent (eds), *Heirs of Fame. Milton and Writers of the English Renaissance*, 69.

39 See also Schmidt, "Die Rechtfertigungslehre bei Richard Hooker", 388; Kirby, *Richard Hooker's Doctrine of Royal Supremacy*, 46; Stanwood, "Of Prelacy and Polity in Milton and Hooker", in Margo Swiss and David Kent (eds), *Heirs of Fame. Milton and Writers of the English Renaissance*, 69.

40 Kirby, "Richard Hooker as an Apologist of the Magisterial Reformation in England", in McGrade, *Richard Hooker and the Construction of Christian Community*, 226.

41 Kirby, *Richard Hooker's Doctrine of Royal Supremacy*, 50.

42 Bradford, *Writings*, 218.

43 See also Milward, *Religious Controversies of the Elizabethan Age*, 105.

44 Hooker, *Justification* (*Works* V, 109.15-17).

5.1.5 Doctrines Common to Catholics and Protestants

Hooker begins by introducing four doctrines found both in Catholic and Protestant theology. First, he mentions the sinfulness of human nature that affects every human being. Hooker believes sin is inherited by birth and does not come from the offence. Every single human being inherits a nature, defiled by sin even from biological inception. This of course means that man cannot meet the requirements of God's justice and thus completely alienates him from God.[45] Secondly, he points out that Catholics and Protestants agree that only God can be the one to accomplish justification, should it be considered at all. Hooker agrees with Foxe[46] that justification remains the work of God alone.[47] Human nature holds nothing inherent[48] that could bring justification. Only God actually justifies the human soul. Justification's necessity derives from God's absolute justice, and this is a sufficient cause that the work of God in justification[49] needs absolutely no collateral support in order that justification should be incepted, and then properly effected.[50] Third, following Tyndale,[51] Hooker believes that justification is realised solely on the basis of Christ's merits.[52] He also agrees with Foxe that Christ's merits[53] leave no room for human achievements in the act of justification.[54] Although the atoning death of Christ[55] is not explicitly mentioned at this stage, Hooker supposedly has this in mind as the event which achieved the merits necessary for the realisation of

45   *ibid.* 109.17-20, and Morrel, "Richard Hooker, Theologian of the English Reformation", 9; Griffith Thomas (ed.), *The Principles of Theology*, 186.
46   Foxe, *The Acts and Monuments*, 71.
47   Rupp, *Studies in the Making of the English Protestant Tradition*, 167; Lake, "Business as Usual? The Immediate Reception of Hooker's *Ecclesiastical Polity*", *The Journal of Ecclesiastical History* 52/3 (2001), 474.
48   Stanwood, "Of Prelacy and Polity in Milton and Hooker", in Margo Swiss and David Kent (eds), *Heirs of Fame. Milton and Writers of the English Renaissance*, 69.
49   Lake, "Business as Usual? The Immediate Reception of Hooker's *Ecclesiastical Polity*", *The Journal of Ecclesiastical History* 52/3 (2001), 474.
50   Hooker, *Justification* (*Works* V, 109.20-23).
51   Tyndale, *Prologue to Romans*, 125.
52   Rupp, *Studies in the Making of the English Protestant Tradition*, 167; Booty, "The English Reformation: A Lively Faith and Sacramental Confession", 25.
53   Stanwood, "Of Prelacy and Polity in Milton and Hooker", in Margo Swiss and David Kent (eds), *Heirs of Fame. Milton and Writers of the English Renaissance*, 69.
54   Foxe, *The Acts and Monuments*, 76.
55   Lake, *Anglicans and Puritans?*, 162.

justification.[56] Finally, Hooker distinguishes between the efficient and the meritorious causes of justification.[57] The efficient cause is Christ as God, [58] since justification would have been impossible had it not been for Christ's divinity. The meritorious cause of justification is Christ as man.[59] Mankind had to have a certain degree of merit in order to satisfy God's justice[60], but human nature, being inherently sinful, could not be the source of this merit; Tyndale, for instance, also wrote that justification is not from man.[61] Even so, God claimed the merit from man. Only Christ as man could provide the necessary merit, for his human nature had not been defiled by sin.[62] Furthermore, since he was also God, he had the effectual power to accomplish justification through the merit he obtained at the cross (also discussed by Frith)[63] by the atoning death of his sinless human nature (as described by Cranmer).[64] Hooker clarifies that although justification is totally the work of God[65], there is something required from mankind. It is here that Hooker first introduces the concept of the application of justification. Hooker paints a picture of justification as being a medicine provided by God. The medicine cannot take effect, however, until it is applied to human nature. Christ's merit must be applied to human life[66] in order to put justification into effect, as also suggested by Cranmer.[67] Hooker sees each of these four major points as being common to both Catholic and Protestant theology.[68]

---

56   Hooker, *Justification* (*Works* V, 109.23-24).

57   Toon, *Foundations for Faith*, 94; Voak, *Richard Hooker and Reformed Theology*, 178.

58   Toon, *Foundations for Faith*, 94; Voak, *Richard Hooker and Reformed Theology*, 178.

59   See also Walton, *The Lives*, 217. Toon, *Foundations for Faith*, 94; Voak, *Richard Hooker and Reformed Theology*, 178.

60   Gibbs, "Richard Hooker and Lancelot Andrew on Priestly Absolution", in McGrade, *Richard Hooker and the Construction of Christian Community*, 272.

61   Tydale, *Prologue to Romans*, 123.

62   Kirby, *Richard Hooker's Doctrine of Royal Supremacy*, 46.

63   Frith, *A Disputation of Purgatory*, 90.

64   Cranmer, *The 1538 Articles*, 4.

65   Rupp, *Studies in the Making of the English Protestant Tradition*, 167; Lake, "Business as Usual? The Immediate Reception of Hooker's *Ecclesiastical Polity*", *The Journal of Ecclesiastical History* 52/3 (2001), 474.

66   See also Rupp, *Studies in the Making of the English Protestant Tradition*, 167; Booty, "The English Reformation: A Lively Faith and Sacramental Confession", 25.

67   Cranmer, *Works* II, 133.

68   Hooker, *Justification* (*Works* V, 109.24-110.6).

5.1.6 Points of Disagreement between Catholics and Protestants

Hooker lays out three major disagreements between Catholics and
Protestants: "Wherein then do we disagree? We disagree aboute the
nature of the very essence of the medicine whereby Christe cureth our
disseas, aboute the manner of applyinge it, aboute the nomber and the
power of means which God requireth in us for the effectual applyinge
thereof to our soules comforte."[69] The three soteriological doctrines that
divided Protestants and Catholics in the sixteenth century are the
nature of justification, the application of justification and the proper
human condition required of God after the application of justification.
Though short, this analysis of sixteenth century theology becomes the
foundation of an expanded description of the Catholic view of justification. Hooker believes this clarification to be necessary before he can set
his own doctrine of justification within a broader Protestant soteriology. Hooker manages to capture in one single sophisticated sentence
the essence of the Catholic doctrine of justification. The starting point is
the recognition that a person must have a certain righteousness in order
to be justified. The righteousness of justification is external to human
nature,[70] because it is both divine and spiritual.[71] In order to become
effectual, this righteousness must be received into the soul of man. Justifying righteousness within the human soul has two main implications. First, Hooker looks at the ecclesiological implication, resulting in
the justified person being included in the body of Christ, the Church.[72]
Second, like Frith,[73] Hooker describes the moral implication,[74] resulting
in the human being's becoming able to perform good works[75] that
accord with God's nature and exist out of love for Christ.

---

69   *ibid.* 110.7-11.
70   Schmidt, "Die Rechtfertigungslehre bei Richard Hooker", 388; Kirby, *Richard
     Hooker's Doctrine of Royal Supremacy*, 50.
71   Kirby, *Richard Hooker's Doctrine of Royal Supremacy*, 46; Stanwood, "Of Prelacy and
     Polity in Milton and Hooker", in Margo Swiss and David Kent (eds), *Heirs of Fame.
     Milton and Writers of the English Renaissance*, 69.
72   Booty, "The English Reformation: A Lively Faith and Sacramental Confession", 26;
     Lake, "Calvinism and the English Church 1570-1635", in Margo Todd (ed.),
     Reformation to Revolution. Politics and Religion in Early Modern England, 186.
73   Frith, *Patrick Places*, 31-34.
74   Sedgwick, "Revisioning Anglican Moral Theology", *Anglican Theological Review*
     LXIII/1 (1981), 10.
75   Collinson, *Archbishop Grindal*, 41; Gibbs, "Richard Hooker's *Via Media* Doctrine of
     Justification", 220.

5.1.7 The Catholic Understanding of Justification

Hooker sees the Catholic doctrine of justification as encompassing the entire human being. Justification in this sense has implications for both body and soul. There is also a forensic element to justification in Catholic theology, so that, through the act of justification, the human soul is made acceptable before God. Hooker claims here that Catholic theology quietly changes its theological language to make justification become grace. Grace's chief function is to bring about forgiveness and more importantly the remission of sins.[76] Hooker totally agrees with Cranmer,[77] Bradford[78] and Foxe[79] on this vital aspect of Christian theology. The work of grace is founded solidly on the merit of Christ,[80] as described also by Cranmer.[81] Hooker very fairly assesses the strengths and weaknesses of Catholic theology. He does not lose sight of the objective grounds of justification, and he is clear on what results from justification based on Christ's merit: total deliverance from sin and eternal death[82], and in this he follows the example of Foxe.[83]

Going further, Hooker approaches the delicate issue of how justification is applied, accomplished in Catholic theology by the infusion of grace. Hooker sees this as a major problem, but he does not criticise the position here; at this point, he only lays out the Catholic point of view. The infusion of grace makes grace inherent to human nature. This means that this inherent grace (now proper to human nature) can grow gradually, until justification becomes enhanced, but on the basis of merit.[84] Hooker points out that the concept of merit then becomes inherent to human nature. This implies that the merit necessary for enhancing inherent grace and justification no longer belongs

---

76 Rupp, *Studies in the Making of the English Protestant Tradition*, 166.
77 Cranmer, *The 1538 Articles*, 4.
78 Bradford, *Writings*, 217-218.
79 Foxe, *The Acts and Monuments*, 80.
80 Hughes, *Theology of the English Reformers*, 47; Booty, "The English Reformation: A Lively Faith and Sacramental Confession", 24; Booty, "An Elizabethan Addresses Modern Anglicanism. Richard Hooker and Theological Issues at the End of the Twentieth Century", 10; Stanwood, "Of Prelacy and Polity in Milton and Hooker", in Margo Swiss and David Kent (eds), *Heirs of Fame. Milton and Writers of the English Renaissance*, 69.
81 Cranmer, Works II, 133.
82 Morrel, "Richard Hooker, Theologian of the English Reformation", 9.
83 Foxe, *The Acts and Monuments*, 71.
84 Bauckham, "Hooker, Travers and the Church of Rome in the 1580s", 47.

to Christ, but to the Christian who performs good works.[85] Justification and grace can increase in the Christian only by means of merit, which is seen in good works. We know this by faith because, as clearly pointed out by Tyndale, it is only by faith that we may be sure that we can increase in our salvation.[86] Finally, Hooker describes a double concept of justification within Catholic thinking. Justification is described as a twofold process: the first justification is the infusion of grace by the merits of Christ into the sinner,[87] who then becomes a Christian, and the second justification is the increase of grace by the merits of good works.[88] Hooker deals with these soteriological issues in detail in the following passage:

> When they [the Catholics] are required to shewe, what the rightouosnes is whereby a christian man is justefied, they aunswer... but in fact something prior to and more important than the infused virtues, such as faith, hope and love; it is the very condition which is supposed to be in these virtues, just like it is their origin and root) a devyne spirituall qualitie, which qualitye receyved into the soule, doth firste make it to be one of them who are borne of god, and secondly endue it with power to bringe forth suche workes as they do that are borne of him, even as the soule of man beinge joyned unto his bodie, doth firste make him to be in the number of reasonable creature, and secondly inhable him to performe the naturall functions which are proper to his kynde, that it maketh the soule gratious and amiable in the sighte of god, in regarde whereof it is termed grace, that it purgeth, purefieth, washeth owt all the staines and pollutions of synne, so from eternall death and condempnacion the rewarde of synne: This grace they will have to be applied by infusion, to thende that as the bodye is warme by the heate which is in the bodye, so the soule mighte be rigtuous by inherente grace, which grace they make capable of increase: as the body maie be more warme, so the soule more and more justified, accordinge as grace shalbe augmented, the augmentacion whereof is merited by good workes, as good workes are make meritorious by it, wherefore the firste receipte of grace is in theire divinitye the firste justification, the increase whereof the seconde justification.[89]

Hooker believes that the Catholic doctrine of justification is both flawed and subjective, because it is based solidly on the merits of good works. Taking the Catholic position at face value means that logically, grace will decrease if good works are not performed by the Christian. Hooker

---

85 Collinson, *Archbishop Grindal*, 41; Gibbs, "Richard Hooker's *Via Media* Doctrine of Justification", 220.

86 Tyndale, *Prologue to Romans*, 125.

87 Stanwood, "Of Prelacy and Polity in Milton and Hooker", in Margo Swiss and David Kent (eds), *Heirs of Fame. Milton and Writers of the English Renaissance*, 69.

88 See also Macek, *The Loyal Opposition. Tudor Traditional Polemics, 1535-1558*, 181.

89 Hooker, *Justification* (*Works* V,110.11-111.7).

observes that sins committed daily may eventually weaken the Christian's inherent merit to the point that his salvation is annulled because of the existence of mortal sin.[90]

Aware that the Catholic theologians have noticed this possibility, Hooker points out their dogmatic solution which centres on the mode in which the Christian is infused by grace.[91] The most important method by which grace is infused in a person is through baptism. Hooker believes this is the primary flaw of the Catholic view of grace. This infusion of grace through baptism does not require either faith or works. Baptism results in the infusion of grace that in its turn results in the forgiveness and remission of original sin[92] as well as its punishment.[93] This infusion of grace through baptism applies to infidels and wicked people, with the specific purpose that their original and actual sins should be forgiven and remitted. Temporal and eternal punishment is also annulled.[94] Baptism for infants and adults from a pagan context thus forms the first justification and the infusion of grace. The Catholic understanding of grace has thus clearly sought to safeguard the objectivity of justification through linking it to conditions that lie outside the human. From this point, the Catholic doctrine of grace moves forward to see the virtual increase or decrease of grace in the Christian based on merits (acquired by good works) or demerits (from evil deeds). Hooker believes that this is what the Catholic position is of the second justification.[95] Still, he knows that Catholic theology does not restrict grace to the merits of good works alone. There are many ecclesiastical ordinations (one example is the recitation of *Ave Maria*; another would be the papal decrees or the sacrament of penance) that supposedly convey grace. However, the kind of grace conferred by these ordinations is weaker than the grace obtained by infusion at the time of the first justification. This grace, of the weaker variety, needs human cooperation in the sense of pilgrimages and fasts. Hooker knows that this cooperation is only possible if certain conditions of the created realm (such as time) do not hinder the sinner

---

90   *ibid.* 111.8-10.

91   See also Marshall, *Hooker and the Anglican Tradition*, 114.

92   By contrast, see Foxe's discussion about the forgiveness and remission of original sin in Foxe, *The Acts and Monuments*, 80. See also Voak, *Richard Hooker and Reformed Theology*, 141, for information about original sin in Hooker.

93   Hooker, *Justification* (*Works* V, 111.10-16).

94   *ibid.* 111.16-20.

95   *ibid.* 111.20-23.

172   The Foundation of Faith

from performing the good works necessary in view of their accumu-
lated merits for the remission of sin and eternal punishment.[96]

5.1.8 The Protestant Understanding of Justification

Hooker turns from his assessment of the Catholic doctrines of grace
and justification to his own analysis of Protestant doctrine, which he
claims is Scriptural and in agreement with the Apostle Paul's
writings.[97] Once again, Hooker sees a threefold sense of the concept of
righteousness: the righteousness of justification, the righteousness of
sanctification and the righteousness of glorification.[98] The time has
come for Hooker briefly to discuss his view of the righteousness of
justification.[99] He begins by clearly stating that this righteousness is
totally external to the human being,[100] and not in any way inherent in
human nature. Human beings have nothing that could possibly be
labelled a quality worthy of meriting justification. Through this
definition, Hooker separates justification's inception (as well as
justification itself) from the domain of human relationships. The act of
justification is not performed on the basis of human nature or human
action. Hooker links justification to Christ, as the objective foundation
of justification,[101] the very essence of justification,[102] and the only One
through whom justification can be effected. Justification both begins
with Christ and continues to apply to Christians because of Christ
alone.[103] What does belong to Christians, however, is faith. Hooker
closely connects faith with the believer's union with Christ.[104] If the

96   *ibid.* 111.23-112.6.
97   *ibid.* 112.8-13.
98   See also Schmidt, "Die Rechtfertigungslehre bei Richard Hooker", 388.
99   Kirby, *Richard Hooker's Doctrine of Royal Supremacy*, 46.
100 *ibid.* 50.
101 Booty, "An Elizabethan Addresses Modern Anglicanism. Richard Hooker and
     Theological Issues at the End of the Twentieth Century", 10; Kirby, "The Paradigm
     of Chalcedonian Christology in Richard Hooker's Discourse on Grace and the
     Church", *Churchman* 114/1 (2000), 23-25.
102 Booty, "The Law of Proportion: William Meade and Richard Hooker", *St. Luke's
     Journal of Theology* XXXIV/2 (1991), 26.
103 Kirby, *Richard Hooker's Doctrine of Royal Supremacy*, 46.
104 Booty, "The English Reformation: A Lively Faith and Sacramental Confession", 25;
     McGrade, "Richard Hooker on the Lawful Ministry of Bishops and Kings", in W. J.
     Shiels and Diana Wood (eds), *The Ministry. Clerical and Lay* (Oxford: Blackwell, 1989),
     184; Kirby, *Richard Hooker's Doctrine of Royal Supremacy*, 46; Booty, "Anglican
     Identity: What is This Book of Common Prayer?", *Sewanee Theological Review* 40/2
     (1997), 142.

believer is in Christ, justification is then effectual.[105] In fact, faith is what accomplishes the union of faith, making it almost impossible to delineate faith clearly when discussing the process of justification.

Hooker sees faith as the necessary condition for justification to take place. This quality of faith falls somewhere between the sinlessness of Christ and the sinfulness of human beings. Hooker reiterates his pessimistic view of human nature, the essence of which he sees as sinful and resulting in unrighteous behaviour. With human nature being what it is, it is almost impossible to conceive that such a nature could merit or especially accomplish something to effect the act of justification. God, however, makes justification possible through Christ. Even though man lacks all righteousness, God finds man in Christ through faith.[106] Thus, Hooker lies down a forensic aspect for his doctrine of justification,[107] since before justification was made effectual in man, God considered man as being in Christ through faith,[108] a doctrine which is essential to Tyndale's theology.[109] This is another way to say that man is justified. Being in Christ essentially means being justified.[110] Justification is always rooted in Christ himself, and the justified man is in Christ. This act is the work of God,[111] as in Foxe.[112] There does exist, however, the element of faith, which connects man to the work of God. Still, Hooker does not mean that man can somehow influence the very essence of justification, but it does condition the effectiveness of justification to a quality of man. Thus, in terms of location, faith belongs to man. Hooker describes the forensic aspect of justification, but now links it to the outcome of justification. Faith is the key concept, standing between God and the sinner. Following Frith, Hooker believes that God manifests his grace towards sinners and forgives sin by non-imputation.[113] The result of this is that God does not

105 Collinson, *Archbishop Grindal*, 41.
106 Secor, *Richard Hooker, Prophet of Anglicanism*, 185.
107 Rupp, *Studies in the Making of the English Protestant Tradition*, 166; Voak, *Richard Hooker and Reformed Theology*, 177.
108 Collinson, *Archbishop Grindal*, 41.
109 Tyndale, *Prologue to Romans*, 128.
110 Collinson, *Archbishop Grindal*, 41.
111 Rupp, *Studies in the Making of the English Protestant Tradition*, 167; Lake, "Business as Usual? The Immediate Reception of Hooker's *Ecclesiastical Polity*", *The Journal of Ecclesiastical History* 52/3 (2001), 474.
112 Foxe, *The Acts and Monuments*, 71.
113 Frith, *A Disputation of Purgatory*, 179, and Morrel, "Richard Hooker, Theologian of the English Reformation", 10. See also Hughes, *Faith and Works*, 44; Booty, "Anglican Identity: What is This Book of Common Prayer?", *Sewanee Theological Review* 40/2 (1997), 142.

impute humanity's sins to its members, an aspect which is seen clearly in Tyndale.[114]

Furthermore, as a result of his incorporation in Christ, God forgives sin, annuls punishment and accepts the individual as being united with Christ.[115] God considers each person as having perfect righteousness, as if the person had kept the Law in its entirety. Hooker infers the forensic aspect of justification, but he never separates it from its application of effectiveness.[116] Faith stands as the link between justification's forensic aspect, its practical application and effectiveness. God can consider the believer as totally righteous and united with Christ only through faith,[117] located within the believer. It was mentioned above briefly that God considers the believer to be righteous, as if he had performed all the requirements of the Law, even though he cannot, as stated by Barnes.[118] Had the law been obeyed in its entirety, then the law could have offered perfect human righteousness to the fully obedient. But Hooker states that the righteousness that comes from justification supersedes that of the perfect human,[119] the reason being that in origin and essence, the righteousness of justification is not human, but divine.[120] The righteousness that comes from justification originates and finds its essence in Christ,[121] the only objective foundation of justification.[122] Therefore, even if man could fully obey the law's requirements and obtain a perfect human righteousness, justification's righteousness still remains superior because it is the divine righteousness of Christ,[123] as set out in Cranmer.[124] Hooker describes more fully these issues regarding justification:

---

114 Tyndale, *Prologue to Romans*, 129.
115 Morrel, "Richard Hooker, Theologian of the English Reformation", 10; Collinson, *Archbishop Grindal*, 41.
116 Voak, *Richard Hooker and Reformed Theology*, 177.
117 Secor, *Richard Hooker, Prophet of Anglicanism*, 185.
118 Barnes, *The Supplication of 1531*, lxxxvii.a.
119 Kirby, *Richard Hooker's Doctrine of Royal Supremacy*, 46.
120 Stanwood, "Of Prelacy and Polity in Milton and Hooker", in Margo Swiss and David Kent (eds), *Heirs of Fame. Milton and Writers of the English Renaissance*, 69.
121 Collinson, *Archbishop Grindal*, 41; Booty, "The Law of Proportion: William Meade and Richard Hooker", *St. Luke's Journal of Theology* XXXIV/2 (1991), 26.
122 Booty, "The English Reformation: A Lively Faith and Sacramental Confession", 24; Booty, "An Elizabethan Addresses Modern Anglicanism. Richard Hooker and Theological Issues at the End of the Twentieth Century", 10; Kirby, "The Paradigm of Chalcedonian Christology in Richard Hooker's Discourse on Grace and the Church", *Churchman* 114/1 (2000), 23-25.
123 Rupp, *Studies in the Making of the English Protestant Tradition*, 168, and Allison, *The Rise of Moralism*, 3; Booty, "The Spirituality of Participation in Richard Hooker", *Sewanee Theological Review* 38/1 (1994), 11.

But the righteousnes wherein we muste be found if we wilbe justified, is not our owne, therefore we cannot be justefied by any inherente qualitie. Christe hath merited rightuousnes for asmany as are *found in hym*. In him God findeth us if we be faithfull for by faith we are incorporated into hym. Then alghough in ourselves we be altogether synfull and unrightuous, yett even the man which in him self is ympious, full of inequity, full of synne, him beinge found in Christe through faith, and having his synne in hatred through repentaunce, hym God beholdeth with a gratious eye, putteth awaie his syn by not ymputing it, taketh quite awaie the ponishemente due thereunto by pardoninge it, and accepteth him in Jesus Christe as perfectly righteous as if he had fulfilled all that is comaunded hym in the lawe, shall I saie more perfectly righteous then if him self had fulfilled the whole lawe?[125]

The forensic aspect of justification reveals God's plan, conceived before the creation of the world.[126] Christ's atoning death displays this plan's application in the world.[127] Hooker underlines briefly the application of justification within history.[128] He does not deny the reality of God's plan, but he does stress that the effectual foundation of justification is God's plan being applied in the created world. The death of Christ made the perfect plan of justification effectual.[129] Christ's death obviously took place as a historical event, so Hooker believes that something actually took place when Christ was dying on the cross, something which accounts for the real and objective character of this event,[130] also competently analysed by Frith.[131] Following Frith's teaching,[132] Hooker states that an actual exchange took place between Christ and humanity at that moment. The sinless Christ accepted the sins of the world, and his righteousness was considered to be humanity's, even though humanity had none. It came as no surprise to

---

124 Cranmer, *Annotations on King's Book*, 12.

125 Hooker, *Justification* (*Works* V, 112.22-123.4).

126 For more details on Hooker's doctrine of creation, see Kirk, "The Meaning and Application of Reason in the Works of Richard Hooker", *The Saint Luke's Journal* IV/1 (1961), 26.

127 Morrel, "Richard Hooker, Theologian of the English Reformation", 10.

128 d'Entrèves, *Riccardo Hooker*, 49; Haugaard, "The Scriptural Hermeneutics of Richard Hooker. Historical Contextualization and Teleology", in Donald S. Armentrout (ed.), *This Sacred History. Anglican Reflections for John Booty*, 167; Speed Hill, "Richard Hooker and the Rhetoric of History", *Churchman* 114/1 (2000), 13-14.

129 Lake, *Anglicans and Puritans?*, 162.

130 For Hooker's sense of history, see Louma, "Who Owns the Fathers? Hooker and Cartwright on the Authority of the Primitive Church", *The Sixteenth Century Journal* VIII/3 (1977), 58; Gregg, "Sacramental Theology in Hooker's *Laws*: A Structural Perspective", *Anglican Theological Review* 73/2 (1991), 161.

131 Frith, *A Disputation of Purgatory*, 90.

132 Frith, *Patrick Places*, 30.

Hooker that this idea could present an epistemological barrier to human reason. But he was not concerned with whether or not the doctrine could be considered foolish. The true Christian finds comfort and wisdom in the fact that this exchange of sin and righteousness between humanity and Christ took place with the death of Christ on the cross.

Hooker sees the historical reality being narrowed down to two basic, but distinct events. First, man sinned and God suffered. These two are brought together in Christ, who was made sin, even though he was sinless, so that humanity could be made righteous, even though sinful. Hooker concludes by tearing down the Catholic doctrine that sees justification as inherent grace. Hooker does not accept that grace could somehow be inherent to human nature.[133] Grace is always seen as being external to humans,[134] which is an indication of the necessity of grace.[135] Any other doctrine risks perverting the Gospel truth:[136]

> I muste take heed what I saie, but the Apostle saith, God *made hym which knewe no synne, to be synne for us, that we mighte be made the righteousnes of God in hym.* Suche we are in the sighte of God the Father, as in the very sonne of God him self: Lett it be compted follye or frensye or furye, or whatsoever. It is our wisdome and our comforte, we care for no knowledge in the worlde but this, that man hath synned and God *hat suffred*, that God hath made hym self the synne of menne, and that men are made *the righteousnes of god.* Youe see therfore that the Churche of Rome in teaching justification by inherente grace, doth perverte the truth of Christe, and that by the handes of his Apostles we have receyved otherwise that shee teacheth.[137]

Justification, therefore, comes from God, not from within human beings, and justification is solely dependent on God's grace. Once the righteousness that comes from justification becomes ours, salvation displays the next step, sanctification and its righteousness.

---

133 Booty, "The English Reformation: A Lively Faith and Sacramental Confession", 25.

134 Kirby, *Richard Hooker's Doctrine of Royal Supremacy*, 50.

135 Porter, *Reformation and Reaction in Tudor Cambridge*, 334; Davis, "'For Conformities Sake': How Richard Hooker Used Fuzzy Logic and Legal Rhetoric against Political Extremes", in McGrade, *Richard Hooker and the Construction of Christian Community*, 339.

136 For the importance of the Church's loyalty to the Gospel in Hooker, see Haugaard, "Towards an Anglican Doctrine of Ministry: Richard Hooker and the Elizabethan Church", *Anglican and Episcopal History* LVI/3 (1987), 279.

137 Hooker, *Justification* (*Works* V, 113.4-15).

5.2 The Righteousness of Sanctification

Now that he has dealt with the righteousness of justification, Hooker turns to the righteousness of sanctification.[138] From the outset, he distinguishes three important aspects. First, unlike justification's righteousness, the righteousness of sanctification is inherent, actually belonging to or being located within human nature.[139] Second, in contrast with justification's righteousness (received freely from God in Christ[140] by faith, as explained by Cranmer[141] and Tyndale[142]), the righteousness of sanctification comes from human effort. Third, the righteousness of justification and righteousness of sanctification are distinct in their nature.

5.2.1 The Unity between Justification and Sanctification

Even if Hooker separates the righteousness of justification from the righteousness of sanctification, he continues to see the two as complementary. Justification's righteousness must exist before sanctification's righteousness can begin. Without the righteousness of justification, there is no righteousness of sanctification. This is a truth which Hooker believes strongly suggests the chronological priority that justification holds over sanctification.[143] Linking justification to sanctification indicates that faith is proved by good works:[144]

> Nowe concerninge that rightuousnes of sanctification, we denye it not to be inherente, we graunte that without we work we have it not, onely we distinguishe it as a thinge in nature differente from the rightuousness of justification. We are righteous the one waie by the faith of Abraham; the

---

138 Kirby, *Richard Hooker's Doctrine of Royal Supremacy*, 50.
139 Stanwood, "Of Prelacy and Polity in Milton and Hooker", in Margo Swiss and David Kent (eds), *Heirs of Fame. Milton and Writers of the English Renaissance*, 69.
140 Collinson, *Archbishop Grindal*, 41.
141 Cranmer, *Works* II, 130.
142 Tyndale, *Prologue to Romans*, 123.
143 This is also a proof of the absolute priority of faith in justification. See also George, *The Protestant Mind of the English Reformation*, 45.
144 See also Keble, *The Works*, xcviii-xcix; Booty, "The English Reformation: A Lively Faith and Sacramental Confession", 24; Sykes, *The Study of Anglicanism*, 67; Booty, "An Elizabethan Addresses Modern Anglicanism. Richard Hooker and Theological Issues at the End of the Twentieth Century", 14-15.

other waie excepte we do the workes of Abraham we are not righteous. Of
the one Ste Paule. *To hym that worketh not, but beleeveth faith is compted for
rightuousnes.* Of the other Ste John, *Qui facit justitiam Justus est. He is
righteous which worketh rightuousnes.* Of the one Ste Paule doth prove by
Abrahams example, that we have it of faith without workes. Of the other
Ste James by Abrahams example, that by *workes we have it and not onely by
faith.* Ste Paule doth playnly sever theis two partes of Christian
rightuousnes one from the other for in the vi th to the Romaynes thus he
wryteth *Being freed from synne and made servaunts unto god, youe have your
fruite in holynes and the end everlasting lyfe.* Yee are made free from synne,
and made servauntes unto god, this is the rightuousnes of justification, *yee
have your fruite in holynes,* this is the righuousnes of sanctification; by the
one we are interested in the righte of inheritinge, by the other we are
broughte to the actuall possessinge of eternall blisse, and so thend of both
is everlasting life.[145]

Hooker believes that the forensic aspect of justification (God's work)
should always be connected to the practical aspect of sanctification (our
work).[146] Sanctification depends on justification. God's consideration
that a human being is righteous must be reflected in the daily life of the
justified person, through good works,[147] as Frith also notes.[148] Although
Hooker makes a theological distinction between justification and
sanctification,[149] he nowhere indicates that the unity between them
should be denied.[150] The passage above reveals one of the strongest
points of Hooker's view of salvation, the synthesis between justification
and sanctification. This actually points to another equally important
synthesis: Paul's soteriology and James soteriology.[151] Justification is
indeed God's action, through which he considers a sinner righteous,
but this act does not guarantee the sanctification of the sinner. Still,
Hooker understands that the work of God in justification[152] should
somehow be made effective to the sinner, and he sees this taking place

145 Hooker, *Justification* (*Works* V, 113.16-114.6).
146 Rupp, *Studies in the Making of the English Protestant Tradition*, 166; Voak, *Richard
    Hooker and Reformed Theology*, 177.
147 Collinson, *Archbishop Grindal*, 41; Gibbs, "Richard Hooker's *Via Media* Doctrine of
    Justification", 220.
148 Frith, *Patrick Places*, 31-34.
149 Voak, *Richard Hooker and Reformed Theology*, 169.
150 Booty, "The English Reformation: A Lively Faith and Sacramental Confession", 24;
    Sykes, *The Study of Anglicanism*, 67; Booty, "An Elizabethan Addresses Modern
    Anglicanism. Richard Hooker and Theological Issues at the End of the Twentieth
    Century", 14-15.
151 See also Keble, *The Works*, xcviii-xcix; Gibbs, "Richard Hooker's *Via Media* Doctrine
    of Justification", 216.
152 Lake, "Business as Usual? The Immediate Reception of Hooker's *Ecclesiastical Polity*",
    The Journal of Ecclesiastical History 52/3 (2001), 474.

through faith. When the believer exercises faith, something takes place within him. The sinner, previously without righteousness, is changed inwardly in order to display a righteousness of his own (which Hooker calls the righteousness of sanctification). This proves that justification and sanctification can be separated for didactic purposes, while they are still united by faith in the theological reality.

Sanctification, however, cannot exist on its own. In terms of its righteousness, sanctification's existence is conditional to the righteousness of justification. The righteousness of sanctification belongs to man (and is therefore inherent to man), but its origin lies in the righteousness of justification which is brought through Christ's righteousness (and is thus inherent to Christ).[153] Both acts form part of God's plan of salvation,[154] and salvation does not come about because of man's initiative or power. God has always initiated and sustained salvation for sinful humanity. Hooker is keenly aware of this fact, due to his understanding of justification as being the forgiveness and the remission of sins[155] based on God's grace[156], which is similar to the definition of justification in Cranmer[157] and Foxe.[158] Thus, according to Hooker, justification as a work rests entirely in the hands of God,[159] as emphatically underlined by Bradford.[160] Salvation, however, does not end with the simple forgiving of sins but with eternal life. Therefore, the synthesis between justification and sanctification must encompass a third element of salvation, namely glorification. Hooker believes that glorification is another element that shines light on the objectivity of God's salvation. Justification (manifested in sanctification) has been conceived with glorification in mind, through which the justified and sanctified people of God will one day receive eternal life. Particularly important for this understanding of the unity of salvation and the ultimate proof of God's grace is the concept of inheritance. Salvation

---

153 Stanwood, "Of Prelacy and Polity in Milton and Hooker", in Margo Swiss and David Kent (eds), *Heirs of Fame. Milton and Writers of the English Renaissance*, 69.
154 Booty, "The English Reformation: A Lively Faith and Sacramental Confession", 24; Sykes, *The Study of Anglicanism*, 67; Booty, "An Elizabethan Addresses Modern Anglicanism. Richard Hooker and Theological Issues at the End of the Twentieth Century", 14-15.
155 Rupp, *Studies in the Making of the English Protestant Tradition*, 166.
156 Keble, *The Works*, vol. 2, 552.
157 Cranmer, *The 1538 Articles*, 4.
158 Foxe, *The Acts and Monuments*, 80.
159 Rupp, *Studies in the Making of the English Protestant Tradition*, 167; Lake, "Business as Usual? The Immediate Reception of Hooker's *Ecclesiastical Polity*", *The Journal of Ecclesiastical History* 52/3 (2001), 474.
160 Bradford, *Writings*, 217-218.

does not only provide freedom from sin, but also life with God. Justification and the sanctification which follows were never intended to offer human beings a new type of existence to be lived on their own, but an all new existence lived together with God. Believers do not only enjoy the forgiveness and remission of sins; they inherit eternal life and consequently all the blessings of living in God's presence.[161]

5.2.2 Good Works as the Content of Sanctification

Hooker's discourse next turns to sanctification's content. Again, he stresses the necessity of evident tokens, such as good works,[162] that exist to prove that justification has taken place, as pointed out in Barnes.[163] This plays an important role in Hooker's theology, for it refers especially to the Jews.[164] In this way, for Hooker, it seems that God's plan for salvation is the same for both Christians and Jews. This infers a uniformity of soteriology for all humankind. Consequently, God has always had the same plan of salvation, applied indiscriminately to every member of the human race. There was never a different methodology of salvation, one for Jews and another one (distinct in its essence) for Christians. Hooker appears to be fairly convinced that God has always had a single intention regarding the content and methodology of salvation. Two implications arise from this principle. First, it implies that God did not change salvation's blueprint because of historical conditions like the emergence of Christianity within Judaism. Second, Christianity's emergence as a result of Christ's work within history[165] did not signal some sort of divine change in God's plan for salvation.

A real danger is posed to the person who understands the righteousness of sanctification as inherent to the believer, because, though justified, he remains a sinner the rest of his life.[166] Hooker understands

---

161 Kaye, "What Might Alasdair MacIntyre Learn from a Reading of Richard Hooker? Rivalry, Commonality, and Their Projects", *Sewanee Theological Review* 42/3 (1999), 347.

162 Collinson, *Archbishop Grindal*, 41; Gibbs, "Richard Hooker's *Via Media* Doctrine of Justification", 220.

163 Barnes, *The Supplication of 1531*, l.b.

164 Hooker, *Justification* (*Works* V, 114.5-7).

165 Speed Hill, "Richard Hooker and the Rhetoric of History", *Churchman* 114/1 (2000), 13-14.

166 Kirby, *Richard Hooker's Doctrine of Royal Supremacy*, 50.

the potential for pride to develop within the believer,[167] even to the point that he could falsely conclude that his inherent righteousness might be the basis upon which God considered him righteous in the first place.[168] But Hooker states firmly that only Christ's righteousness can offer the foundation of justification.[169] God considers a person righteous on the basis of Christ's righteousness[170] also confirmed by Cranmer.[171] Therefore, Christ's righteousness is indeed intrinsic to Christ, but completely alien to the believer. Here, Hooker clarifies an important detail regarding the righteousness of sanctification, normally associated with the righteousness that comes from good deeds. For example, Hooker continues the theological argument put forth by Bradford, who wrote that we were "quickened to labour with the Lord in sanctification."[172] These good works, however, do not constitute the only external works we perform, but they should also include our internal thoughts. Thus, the righteousness of sanctification derives from both external good deeds, as explained by Barnes,[173] and internal pure thoughts. Hooker understands the possibility of a believer displaying his external good works so as to please others, even while his thoughts do not line up with the goodness and purity of the Spirit.[174] Hooker warns that it is ultimately God who judges all and who considers the righteousness or unrighteousness of our deeds and thoughts.[175] Furthermore, if the righteousness of sanctification is indeed inherent to man, it logically follows that this righteousness is imperfect, which means the Christian cannot put his confidence in it. He must put all of his trust in Christ's righteousness,[176] as advocated by Cranmer[177],

---

167 Booty, "The Spirituality of Participation in Richard Hooker", *Sewanee Theological Review* 38/1 (1994), 11.
168 Hooker, *Justification* (*Works* V, 114.24-29). See also Booty, "Elizabethan Religion: Disorder Ordered", *Anglican Theological Review* 73/2 (1991), 130.
169 Booty, "The English Reformation: A Lively Faith and Sacramental Confession", 24; Booty, "An Elizabethan Addresses Modern Anglicanism. Richard Hooker and Theological Issues at the End of the Twentieth Century", 10; Booty, "The Spirituality of Participation in Richard Hooker", *Sewanee Theological Review* 38/1 (1994), 11.
170 See also Rupp, *Studies in the Making of the English Protestant Tradition*, 168, and Allison, *The Rise of Moralism*, 3.
171 Cranmer, *Annotations on the King's Book*, 12.
172 Bradford, *Writings*, 218.
173 Barnes, *The Supplication of 1531*, l.b.
174 Malone, "The Doctrine of Predestination in the Thought of William Perkins and Richard Hooker", 107; Kirby, *Richard Hooker's Doctrine of Royal Supremacy*, 46.
175 Hooker, *Justification* (*Works* V, 114.29-115.16).
176 Griffith Thomas (ed.), *The Principles of Theology*, 191; Booty, "The Spirituality of Participation in Richard Hooker", *Sewanee Theological Review* 38/1 (1994), 11;

for it is only that righteousness that makes justification possible and also satisfies the righteous requirements of the law.[178] Man's righteousness is nothing but sin, and his essence is wickedness[179] manifested in external deeds and internal thoughts. After all, this is what is confirmed in Habakkuk 1:4, the verse that inspired Hooker's whole discourse on the topic of justification.[180]

5.2.3 The Schism between Catholics and Protestants

The following section of Hooker's argument is extremely important, being that it holds the ideas that triggered controversy with Walter Travers. First, Hooker claimed that a study on the *Epistle to the Hebrews* had led him to conclude that God's revelation through the work of Christ had resulted in the setting up of the visible Church.[181] Hooker believed the visible Church is formed of sanctified people. It is interesting to note that he links their sanctification to the proclamation of the Gospel, even though he immediately explains that obedience makes up the essence of sanctification, as affirmed by Foxe.[182] Hooker sees the Gospel as having a didactic purpose, for God delivered many lessons to sinful humanity through the work of Christ. The visible Church's specific task is to preach this truth[183] while bringing comfort to the rest of humanity, which is affected by sin. Second, Hooker clearly indicated that the Church of Rome had not brought comfort to the lives of the people sitting under its preaching. The conclusion that Hooker draws is that the Protestant Church was justified in departing from the Catholic Church:

> When we had laste the epistle of Ste Paule to the hebrewes in our handes, and of that epistle theis wordes *In theis laste daies he hath spoken unto us by his sonne*, after we had thence collected the nature of the visible Church of Christe and had defyned it to be a Comunitye of men [by sanctification I

Sedgwick, "The New Shape of Anglican Identity", *Anglican Theological Review* LXXVII/2 (1995), 189.

177 Cranmer, *The 1538 Articles*, 4.

178 Hooker, *Justification* (*Works* V, 115.16-116.17).

179 Thus, "salvation is nothing else than the bridging of the gulf between man's infinite wickedness and God's infinite goodness." See Kirby, *Richard Hooker's Doctrine of Royal Supremacy*, 46.

180 Hooker, *Justification* (*Works* V, 116.18-117.9).

181 Booty, "The Quest for the Historical Hooker", *Churchman* 80/3 (1966), 190.

182 Foxe, *The Acts and Monuments*, 75.

183 For details about the importance of preaching in Hooker, see Lake, *Anglicans and Puritans?*, 162-163.

meane a separation from others not professinge as they do: For true holines do not consiste in true professing but in obeing the truth of Christ] sanctefied through the profession of that truth which God hath taughte the worlde by his sonne and had declared that the scope of christian doctrine is the comforte of them whose hartes are overcharged with the burden of synne, and had proved that the doctrine professed in the Church of Rome doth bereve men of comforte both in theire lyves and att theire deathes, the conclusion whereunto in thend we came of all was this. The Church of Rome beinge in faith so corrupted as she is and refusing to be reformed as shee doth we are to sever our selves from her.[184]

In spite of the English Protestants' decision to separate themselves from the Catholic Church, the Church of England continued to practice many Roman Church traditions not found in Scripture. From this point of view and according to the Gospel of Christ, although not to Church doctrine and tradition, the word "presbyter" was more relevant than the word "priest." The episcopacy is a Church established custom,[185] changeable[186] if proved not to work.[187] Nonetheless, these are matters of "indifference," not affecting the salvation of human souls, as Christianity's essential doctrines do. According to Hooker, one could follow these traditions "indifferently," due to Church tradition, authority, and reason.[188] The Puritans disagreed with Hooker's opinion on this matter, so Hooker sought to offer a basic response. First, Christians should not rely solely on Scripture,[189] for there are, after all, other ways of obtaining knowledge and discovering God's law and will,[190] even if Scripture remains the final authority for Christians[191] and that

---

184 Hooker, *Justification* (*Works* V, 117.17-118.1).

185 See also Hunt, *Religious Thought in England*, 58. For more details on episcopacy, see Sommerville, "Richard Hooker and his Contemporaries on Episcopacy: An Elizabethan Consensus", *The Journal of Ecclesiastical Studies* 35 (1984), 177-187; Crowley, "Erastianism in England to 1640", *Journal of Church and State* 32/3 (1990), 562; Atkinson, *Richard Hooker and the Authority of Scripture, Tradition and Reason*, 129.

186 As it is the result of a natural process. See Munz, *The Place of Hooker in the History of Thought*, 60, and Allen, *A History of Political Thought in the Sixteenth Century*, 216.

187 For an opposite view, see Keble, *The Works*, lxxv, and Cargill Thompson, "The Philosopher of the 'Politic Society'. Richard Hooker as a Political Thinker", 50.

188 Barry, *Masters in English Theology*, 50.

189 Davies, *Episcopacy and the Royal Supremacy*, 42.

190 See also Jordan, *The Development of Religious Tolerance*, 227.

191 John Walton, "Tradition of the Middle Way: The Anglican Contribution to the American Character", *Historical Magazine of the Protestant Episcopal Church* XLIV/5 (1975), 31; Haugaard, "The Bible in the Anglican Reformation", in Frederick H. Borsch (ed.), *Anglicanism and the Bible*, 73; Owen, "Is There an Anglican Theology?", in Darrol M. Bryant (ed.), *The Future of Anglican Theology*, 4; Kaye, "Authority and the Interpretation of Scripture in Hooker's *Of the Laws of Ecclesiastical Polity*", *The Journal of Religious History* 21/1 (1997), 88, 91.

which supplements the limited religious knowledge available to reason.[192] Unless these means of knowledge contradict reason, they should be used in the theological enterprise.[193] Reason was given by God to help reach a better understanding of his revelation.[194] This is why many Church practices have remained throughout history, because they conformed to reason.[195]

5.2.4 The Salvation of Catholics

Going further, Hooker delivered the text that brought about the controversy with Travers. Contending that the Protestant decision to separate from the Catholic Church was a good one, Hooker brings up a few issues he believes he must clarify regarding some practising Catholics. Because he believes that God has a unitary soteriology, not affected by historical matters, Hooker asserts that God had worked to save many individual Catholics despite the flawed ecclesiastical practice of their Church. To back up his position, Hooker states that Catholic believers who may have done wrong by following the Catholic Church's teaching have committed sins out of ignorance.[196] God's salvation plan for humanity does not fail, even if history is full of errant ecclesiastical practices.

Throughout this debate, Hooker has clearly aligned himself with the early English reformers and their general view of salvation and justification. He agrees, for example with Foxe,[197] that salvation and especially justification remain entirely God's work[198] and not dependent upon human actions. The objective foundation of salvation

---

192 Hudson, "Three Steps to Perfection: *Rasselas* and the Philosophy of Richard Hooker", *Eighteenth Century Life* 14/3 (1990), 35.

193 See also Locke, "Equal Ministries: Richard Hooker and Non-episcopal Ordinations", *Anvil* 14/3 (1997), 176.

194 Hoopes, *Right Reason in the English Renaissance*, 127; Brockwell, "Answering to 'Known Men': Bishop Reginal Pecock and Mr. Richard Hooker", 142.

195 For further details, see Hooker, *Of the Laws of the Ecclesiastical Polity*, vol. I-II (Books I-IV), Introduction by Christopher Morris (London: J. M. Dent & Sons LTD, 1907), viii ff.

196 Hunt, *Religious Thought in England*, 62, and Peter McGrath, *Papists and Puritans under Elizabeth I*, 320.

197 Foxe, *The Acts and Monuments*, 71.

198 Rupp, *Studies in the Making of the English Protestant Tradition*, 167; Lake, "Business as Usual? The Immediate Reception of Hooker's *Ecclesiastical Polity*", *The Journal of Ecclesiastical History* 52/3 (2001), 474.

is established by the forensic aspect of justification[199] by which God considers anyone justified and righteous[200] on the basis of the merits of Christ through faith,[201] also a vital aspect in Foxe.[202] Hooker does not restrict genuine faith to Protestant Churches. Once it is understood that God applies justification to humanity because of the faith of its individual members, it is preposterous to claim that at least some Catholic Church members did not have genuine faith. It then follows that if certain Catholics did actually profess true and genuine faith in God, then God considered them righteous based on the merits of Christ through their faith. The most important aspect of Hooker's soteriology at this point is the mercy of God, which is the origin of salvation both in Barnes[203] and Bradford.[204] Had there been no mercy involved in God's plan, all of humanity would have face condemnation. Hooker, though, believes that humanity has been shown God's mercy and that this mercy has been applied to human beings on the grounds of their faith, not because of their ecclesiastical affiliation. Hooker, accordingly, concludes by recognising the possibility that some members of the Catholic Church are indeed saved:

The example of our fathers maie not reteyne us in Comunion and fellowshipp with that Churche under hope that we so contynewinge mighte be saved aswell as they. God I double not was mercifull to save thouwsandes of them though they lyved in popish supersticions in asmuche as they synned ingorauntly: But the truth is nowe laid open before our eyes. The former parte of th is laste sentence, namely theis wordes *I doubte not but God was mercyfull to save thowsandes of our fathers lyvinge in popishe supersticions in asumuche as they synned ignorauntly* this sentence I beseech youe to mark and to sifte it with the stricte severitie of austere judgemente that if it be found as gold it maie stande suteable to the pretious foundacion whereupon it was then laide, for I proteste that if it prove to be *haie or stuble* myne owne hand shall sett fire to it. Two questions have risen by occasion of the speech before alledged, the one whether our fathers infected with popishe errours and

---

199 Rupp, *Studies in the Making of the English Protestant Tradition*, 166; Voak, *Richard Hooker and Reformed Theology*, 177.

200 Griffith Thomas (ed.), *The Principles of Theology*, 185.

201 See also Rupp, *Studies in the Making of the English Protestant Tradition*, 167, and Booty, "The English Reformation: A Lively Faith and Sacramental Confession", 24; Stanwood, "Of Prelacy and Polity in Milton and Hooker", in Margo Swiss and David Kent (eds), *Heirs of Fame. Milton and Writers of the English Renaissance*, 69; Secor, *Richard Hooker, Prophet of Anglicanism*, 185.

202 Foxe, *The Acts and Monuments*, 76.

203 Barnes, *The Supplication of 1531*, lviii.b-lix.a.

204 Bradford, *Writings*, 371-372.

supersticions mighte be saved, the other whether thire ignoraunce be a
resonnable inducemente to make us thinck that they mighte.[205]
Here, Hooker advances his belief that it is probable that some Catholic
Church members were saved[206] by equating the Church of Rome with
Babylon in Revelation 18:4.[207] Hooker is totally convinced that this
identification is indeed the only proper way to interpret this verse, and
he uses two more apocalyptic symbols to support his theory: Matthew
24:16 and Genesis 19:15. Hooker claims that both these texts are
warnings to Catholics that unless they forsake their Churches they will
be punished by God.[208]

Still, Hooker is keenly aware that historically speaking, many
Catholics deepened the ties with their Church instead of cutting the
ties. The problem that arises concerns *how* and in what way God was
able to save some Catholics, who continued to defend their Church
despite God's command to abandon it.[209] Hooker, again, pleads in
favour of ignorance,[210] mainly because he believes that the Church's
heretical practices (belief in non-scriptural tradition, the supremacy of
the pope, the Eucharistic transubstantiation, sacrificial masses for the
dead, intercessory powers of the saints) were enforced within the
Church hierarchy, leaving simple Christians with no way to combat
these ideas. Due to theological ignorance, many Catholics accepted
wholeheartedly these errant practices, adhering to them with pure
motives and a clear conscience. Repentance, accompanied by faith,[211]
must exist for the accomplishment of salvation, for these as well as
anyone else, also pointed out by Foxe.[212] Repentance must also exist on
behalf of those who have become aware of the heresy in many Catholic
practices, even if they still hold them to be true. Hooker concludes that
the Catholics not aware of the Church's heretical teaching due to their
ignorance along with the Catholics who were aware and afterward

---

205 Hooker, *Justification* (*Works* V, 118.2-18).
206 See also Knox, *Walter Travers*, 76; Archer, *Richard Hooker*, 23-25; Milton, *Catholic and
     Reformed*, 106.
207 Hooker, *Justification* (*Works* V, 118.21-26).
208 *ibid.* 118.26-119.5.
209 *ibid.* 119.5-11.
210 See also Walton, *The Lives*, 218, and Peter McGrath, *Papists and Puritans under
     Elizabeth I*, 320.
211 Gibbs, "Richard Hooker's *Via Media* Doctrine of Repentance", *Harvard Theological
     Review* 84/1 (1991), 59.
212 Foxe, *The Acts and Monuments*, 77.

repented of that teaching were indeed saved by God.[213] Devout Catholics may not have denied Christ directly, but they have denied him indirectly because of their ignorance.[214] Even with that said, they must still be considered members of the Christian Church, for they thirsted after righteousness. They will taste salvation in spite of the heresies they unintentionally upheld, which is an idea also developed by Barnes.[215] God will surely have mercy[216] on these people because they are part of God's elect.[217]

Hooker understands that the main point of contention that Protestants have with Catholics is the addition of works as being necessary for salvation. He believes the Catholic soteriology teaches that Christ and good works are the foundation of Christian faith. In defence of God's elect found within the Church of Rome, Hooker writes that adding good works to Christ as the foundation of Christianity does not necessarily change the essence of salvation.[218] He further states that salvation includes both justification and sanctification.[219] Moreover, both of these are accomplished by God through Christ and the Holy Spirit.[220] This stands as additional evidence, as also in Frith,[221] that election is based on God's grace,[222] and should be seen as God's benevolent attitude towards human beings.[223] It should be noted here that defining grace in this manner places Hooker in line with the crucial arguments of Barnes[224] and Bradford.[225] Hooker further

---

213 Hooker, *Justification* (*Works* V, 119.12-120.20). See also Milton, "The Church of England, Rome, and the True Church: The Demise of a Jacobean Consensus", in Fincham Kenneth (ed.), *The Early Stuart Church, 1603-1642*, 192-193.

214 See Walton, *The Lives*, 218, and Peter McGrath, *Papists and Puritans under Elizabeth I*, 320; Milton, *Catholic and Reformed*, 146.

215 Barnes, *The Supplication of 1531*, lviii.b-lix.a.

216 Hunt, *Religious Thought in England*, 62.

217 Hooker, *Justification* (*Works* V, 146.25-148.2).

218 Booty, "The Law of Proportion: William Meade and Richard Hooker", *St. Luke's Journal of Theology* XXXIV/2 (1991), 26.

219 Hooker, *Justification* (*Works* V, 149.29); Booty, "The English Reformation: A Lively Faith and Sacramental Confession", 24; Sykes, *The Study of Anglicanism*, 67; Booty, "An Elizabethan Addresses Modern Anglicanism. Richard Hooker and Theological Issues at the End of the Twentieth Century", 14-15.

220 Hooker, *Justification* (*Works* V, 150.1).

221 Frith, *Patrick Places*, 29.

222 See also Rowse, *The England of Elizabeth*, 487; Collinson, *Archbishop Grindal*, 41; Wallace Jr., *Puritans and Predestination*, 77; Grislis, "The Assurance of Faith according to Richard Hooker", in McGrade, *Richard Hooker and the Construction of Christian Community*, 240.

223 Hooker, *Justification* (*Works* V, 150.6-10).

224 Barnes, *The Supplication of 1531*, xliii.a.

makes clear that the addition of good works to salvation is not the same debate described in the New Testament regarding circumcision. The requirement of circumcision for salvation is denounced explicitly in the New Testament, whereas good works are implicitly required.[226] Arguing that good works and circumcision are essentially the same debate also implies a dichotomy within the concept of righteousness. The righteousness of circumcision is the righteousness of the scribes and Pharisees, explicitly rebuked in Matthew 5:20. Nevertheless, following Frith,[227] Hooker is convinced that the righteousness of good works actually confirms the righteousness of justification and in fact must exist in the life of someone who has experienced the new birth in Christ.[228]

Hooker makes an important distinction between the laity (innocent of the alleged heresies of the Roman Church) and the clergy, popes and councils (guilty of the wrongdoings).[229] Hooker urges the Protestant Church to have compassion on the average Catholic Church members, for they are not responsible for the heresies of the Church as a whole.[230]

Hooker explains that the true way of salvation is applied by God to everyone. For those who as a part of the Catholic Church followed its practices in ignorance, the only way to salvation is to escape the judgment of God.[231] To escape God's judgment, one must appeal to the seat of God's mercy.[232] Here, Hooker condemns Origen, who extended salvation to even the devil and his angels.[233] God's salvation is not given to all of humanity. Following Barnes,[234] Hooker writes that God's

---

225 Bradford, *Writings*, 312.

226 Hooker, *Justification* (*Works* V, 150.11-151.4). Actually, good works are inevitably a necessary part of a justified person's life. Gibbs, "Richard Hooker's *Via Media* Doctrine of Justification", 220.

227 Frith, *Patrick Places*, 31-34.

228 Hooker, *Justification* (*Works* V, 151.4-8); Collinson, *Archbishop Grindal*, 41; Gibbs, "Richard Hooker's *Via Media* Doctrine of Justification", 220; Lake, "Business as Usual? The Immediate Reception of Hooker's *Ecclesiastical Polity*", *The Journal of Ecclesiastical History* 52/3 (2001), 474.

229 Hooker, *Justification* (*Works* V, 120.21-121.1).

230 *ibid.* 121.1-121.16.

231 *ibid.* 121.28-29. This means that the Catholic Church may be a true Church of God. See also Patterson, "Hooker on Ecumenical Relations: Conciliarism in the English Reformation", in McGrade, *Richard Hooker and the Construction of Christian Community*, 296.

232 Hooker, *Justification* (*Works* V, 121.29-30). See also Louma, "Restitution and Reformation?", 105.

233 Hooker, *Justification* (*Works* V, 121.30-31).

234 Barnes, *The Supplication of 1531*, lviii.b-lix.a.

mercy has been manifested[235] as the essence of justification to only a part of humanity. God's mercy applies only to those who put their faith in the finished work of Christ. In agreement with Foxe,[236] Hooker believes that faith and repentance are absolutely essential for someone to receive salvation through Christ.[237]

Hooker believes it important to offer doctrinal reasons that favour the Catholic Church, so as to prove that Catholic theology does not explicitly deny[238] that salvation is by Christ alone,[239] seen as Lord and Saviour, an image of Christ also used by Cranmer.[240] Because there are several common doctrines between the Protestants and Catholics, Hooker believes it necessary to mention them. He begins with Christ's atoning death[241] that results in the forgiveness of sins and grants the remission of all sins,[242] also advocated by Bradford[243], that eventually brings heavenly rewards for the faithful life of the believer as a proof of his grace.[244] He continues by pointing out that the atoning death of Christ is seen as sufficient for everyone but it is effectual only for those who, in faith, personally apply it to themselves. Then, in line with Cranmer,[245] Hooker claims that the atoning death of Christ was made effectual for our justification, in order that God did not require any merits from us before granting us salvation,[246] instead requiring the merits of Christ[247] which is also important to Foxe.[248] Finally, good works performed after the initial act of justification have no value in themselves, but they do become meritorious only because of the atoning death of Christ.[249]

---

235 Booty, "The Law of Proportion: William Meade and Richard Hooker", *St. Luke's Journal of Theology* XXXIV/2 (1991), 26.

236 Foxe, *The Acts and Monuments*, 77.

237 Hooker, *Justification* (*Works* V, 121.31-122.13).

238 Milton, *Catholic and Reformed*, 146.

239 Kirby, *Richard Hooker's Doctrine of Royal Supremacy*, 46.

240 Cranmer, *Annotations on the King's Book*, 12.

241 For an informative analysis of the death of Christ in Hooker, see Lake, *Anglicans and Puritans?*, 162.

242 Rupp, *Studies in the Making of the English Protestant Tradition*, 166.

243 Bradford, *Writings*, 217-218.

244 Keble, *The Works*, vol. 2, 552.

245 Cranmer, Works II, 130.

246 Marshall, *Hooker and the Anglican Tradition*, 113.

247 Rupp, *Studies in the Making of the English Protestant Tradition*, 167; Stanwood, "Of Prelacy and Polity in Milton and Hooker", in Margo Swiss and David Kent (eds), *Heirs of Fame. Milton and Writers of the English Renaissance*, 69.

248 Foxe, *The Acts and Monuments*, 76.

249 Hooker, *Justification* (*Works* V, 157.10-22). See also Hughes, *Faith and Works*, 40-41.

5.2.5 Christ as the Foundation of Faith

Hooker believes that as long as the foundation of faith is upheld salvation is secure.[250] In order to be saved, one must firmly hold to the foundation of faith.[251] Hooker then goes on to say that faith's foundation is found in the writings of the evangelists and apostles, which together form Scripture.[252] Still, the person of Christ and his work of salvation stand as the very essence of Scripture.[253] Thus, Scripture must be read christologically.[254] Inner faith and the external affirmation of Christ's salvific work make up the objective foundation of salvation.[255] That means that anyone who denies Christ and his work is hopelessly lost.[256] Concerning the length of the human life and the dedication to Christ required for salvation, Hooker believes that one's life must end with that person confessing Christ as Saviour and Redeemer,[257] a requirement also supported by Frith.[258] Christ alone is the means by which God effected his salvation:[259]

> But howe many millions of them are knowne so to have ended theire mortall lyves that the drawing of theire breath hath ceased with the uttering of this faith: *Christ my savyor my Redeemer Jesus*? and shall we saie that suche did not hold the foundacion of Christian faith? Aunswere is made that this they mighte unfeynedly confesse and yett be farre enough

---

250 See also Crofts, "The Defense of the Elizabethan Church: Jewel, Hooker and James I", *Anglican Theological Review* LIV/1 (1972), 23, and Bauckham, "Hooker, Travers and the Church of Rome in the 1580s", 43. See also Booty, "The English Reformation: A Lively Faith and Sacramental Confession", 24; Archer, *Richard Hooker*, 23.

251 Hooker, *Justification* (*Works* V, 122.14-27).

252 *ibid.* 122.28-30.

253 Kaye, "Authority and the Interpretation of Scripture in Hooker's *Of the Laws of Ecclesiastical Polity*", *The Journal of Religious History* 21/1 (1997), 97.

254 Atkinson, *Richard Hooker and the Authority of Scripture, Tradition and Reason*, 129.

255 Booty, "The English Reformation: A Lively Faith and Sacramental Confession", 24; Booty, "An Elizabethan Addresses Modern Anglicanism. Richard Hooker and Theological Issues at the End of the Twentieth Century", 10; Kirby, "The Paradigm of Chalcedonian Christology in Richard Hooker's Discourse on Grace and the Church", *Churchman* 114/1 (2000), 23-25.

256 Hooker, *Justification* (*Works* V, 123.3-23).

257 Bartlett, "What Has Richard Hooker to Say to Modern Evangelical Anglicanism?", *Anvil* 15/3 (1998), 198.

258 Frith, *The Revelation of Antichrist*, 461, and Cranmer, *Annotations on the King's Book*, 12.

259 See also White, "Anglican Reflections to the Council of Trent in the Reign of Queen Elizabeth I", 283; Kirby, *Richard Hooker's Doctrine of Royal Supremacy*, 46.

from salvacion: for *behold* saith the apostle *I Paul saie unto youe that if youe be circumcised Christ shall proffytt youe nothing*. Christ in the worke of mans salvation is alone.[260]

Hooker sees salvation as consisting of two fundamental aspects. The first is objective salvation, or the every essence of salvation, which describes Christ's work at the cross[261], as also in accordance with Frith.[262] The second aspect is subjective salvation, or the application of salvation, through which Christ's work becomes effectual to the believer. It is here that Hooker clearly affirms that the concept of objective salvation is identical both in Catholic and Protestant theology. Catholics agree with Protestants that the very essence of salvation lies in Christ's work on the cross. The crucial difference between Catholics and Protestants lies in the application of salvation. Catholics add something to salvation's application, although Hooker does not elaborate more at this point. The only example he offers is the Galatians, those who believed that circumcision had to be added to their belief in Christ in order for salvation to be effectual. Hooker holds together this parallel between the Galatians and the Catholics, all the while inferring that both groups must wholeheartedly put their trust in the mercy of God to be saved. He concludes that many Catholics have experienced God's mercy, but only because they truly embraced the Gospel of Christ.[263] Hooker follows the teaching of Cranmer[264] by writing that salvation becomes effectual only when the believer clearly acknowledges Christianity's foundation, which is Jesus Christ as Lord and Saviour.[265] People can be justified and thereby saved only if they believe that their salvation comes from faith in Christ.[266] Hooker adds an important detail here, claiming that salvation comes from faith in Christ *alone*.[267] There can be no other foundation to Christian faith apart

---

260 Hooker, *Justification* (*Works* V, 123.24-124.5).

261 Booty, "The Law of Proportion: William Meade and Richard Hooker", *St. Luke's Journal of Theology* XXXIV/2 (1991), 26.

262 Frith, *A Disputation of Purgatory*, 90.

263 Hooker, *Justification* (*Works* V, 124.7-125.11).

264 Cranmer, *Annotations on the King's Book*, 12.

265 Hooker, *Justification* (*Works* V, 145.1-10); Booty, "An Elizabethan Addresses Modern Anglicanism. Richard Hooker and Theological Issues at the End of the Twentieth Century", 10.

266 Hooker, *Justification* (*Works* V, 145.20); Collinson, *Archbishop Grindal*, 41.

267 Hughes, *Theology of the English Reformers*, 47; Kirby, *Richard Hooker's Doctrine of Royal Supremacy*, 46.

from Christ.[268] Hooker believes that this is the reason the apostle Paul warned the Galatians that putting circumcision next to Christ as the foundation of faith was totally wrong. There, the problem is even more serious, for the reference to circumcision implies all of the Mosaic law, including all its human works and efforts,[269] which are opposed to the grace of God manifested in Christ alone.[270] Hooker affirms Cranmer's view[271] that Christ alone is the foundation of Christianity.[272] Should anyone desire to be justified and saved[273] he must put all of his faith in Christ,[274] not in human efforts designed to accomplish the law's strict requirements.[275]

5.2.6 The Necessity of Repentance

The paragraph that follows is very important for a clear understanding of Hooker's soteriology. It is here that he contrasts sin with repentance.[276] Like Foxe,[277] Hooker believes firmly that salvation cannot come without repentance. There has been no exception to this rule, even from the very beginning. Nobody is exempted from displaying his repentance in view of salvation. This results in Hooker inferring that any Catholic who never showed true repentance for his sins certainly did not taste God's salvation. Hooker sees repentance as a daily practice, not just a once-and-for-all event. Even the most insignificant sin must be brought before God in repentance for one to be justified, also seen in Barnes[278] and Foxe.[279] Hooker remains a realist

268 Booty, "The English Reformation: A Lively Faith and Sacramental Confession", 24; Booty, "An Elizabethan Addresses Modern Anglicanism. Richard Hooker and Theological Issues at the End of the Twentieth Century", 10.
269 Marot, "Aux origines de la théologie anglicane", 342.
270 Collinson, *Archbishop Grindal*, 41.
271 Cranmer, *The 1538 Articles*, 4.
272 Booty, "An Elizabethan Addresses Modern Anglicanism. Richard Hooker and Theological Issues at the End of the Twentieth Century", 10.
273 Neelands, "Hooker on Scripture, Reason and 'Tradition'", in McGrade (ed.), *Richard Hooker and the Construction of Christian Community*, 76-83.
274 Griffith Thomas (ed.), *The Principles of Theology*, 191; Booty, "The Spirituality of Participation in Richard Hooker", *Sewanee Theological Review* 38/1 (1994), 11; Sedgwick, "The New Shape of Anglican Identity", *Anglican Theological Review* LXXVII/2 (1995), 189.
275 Hooker, *Justification* (*Works* V, 145.2-146.22).
276 Gibbs, "Richard Hooker's *Via Media* Doctrine of Repentance", *Harvard Theological Review* 84/1 (1991), 59.
277 Foxe, *The Acts and Monuments*, 77.
278 Barnes, *The Supplication of 1531*.

though, understanding that people sin daily without being aware of it. This becomes part of Hooker's argument for why repentance must always be a daily process, by which the sinner asks God to forgive his sins, even if the sinner does not know for sure how many he has committed or what they are. Every Christian must be alert and aware of his actions. He must learn to identify sins from his good actions, and then he must repent for each sin specifically. Even then, Hooker believes that some people will not realise the existence of all of their sins, no matter how attentive they might be. The sins to which the believer is oblivious will be taken care of by Christ. Following Bradford, Hooker writes that the grace of God in the forgiveness and remission[280] of unknown sins[281] is manifested through the mediatorial work of Christ[282] (also pointed out by Frith)[283] with the sole condition being that the believer must live in a continual state and with a genuine attitude of repentance:

> What although they repented not of theire errours? God forbid that I should open my mouth to gainsaie that which Christe him self hath spoken *Excepte ye repent ye shall all perish*. And if they did not repente they perished. But with all note that we have the benefite of a double repentaunce; The leaste synne which we comytt in deed word or thoughte is death without repentaunce. Yett howe many thinges do escape us in every of theis which we do not knowe, howe many which we do not observe to be synnes. And without the knowledge without the observacion of syn there is no actuall repentaunce. It cannot then be chosen but that foreasmany as hold the foundacion and have all knowne synne and errour in hatred, the blessing of repentaunce for unknowne synnes and errours is obteyned att the handes of God through the gracious mediation of Christe Jesus for such suters as crye with the prophett David *purg me o Lord from my secret synnes*.[284]

This text is important because it underlines the centrality of repentance for salvation's application. Hooker knows that his discourse is now focusing on salvation's subjective aspect, for repentance must originate within the believer. He still does not lose sight of salvation being the

---

279 Foxe, *Of Free Justification by Christ*, 112.
280 Keble, *The Works*, vol. 2, 552. See also Rupp, *Studies in the Making of the English Protestant Tradition*, 166.
281 Bradford, *Writings*, 217-218.
282 See also Thornton, *Richard Hooker*, 61.
283 Frith, *Patrick Places*, 30.
284 Hooker, *Justification* (*Works* V, 125.13-126.6); for details about mediation in Hooker, see also Kirby, *Richard Hooker's Doctrine of Royal Supremacy*, 46.

work of God,[285] as highlighted in Foxe.[286] Again he stresses the objective
character of salvation. Hooker believes that even the subjective aspect
of salvation, which is our duty, is totally dependent on the objective
foundation of salvation, which is God's duty,[287] and God accomplishes
this salvation solely by means of the mediatorial work of Christ.[288]

Hooker's discussion on repentance continues[289] with his introduce-
tion of repentance as a twofold concept: general and particular. In line
with Barnes,[290] Hooker refers to general repentance as the recognition
that man is a sinner who must seek God's mercy through faith[291] in
Christ's love and then turn away from sin.[292] Particular repentance is
the acknowledgement that particular works were not good, but mere
sins, which is a vital concept for Frith.[293] Particular repentance is what
actually brings God's mercy into the life of the sinner.[294]

Hooker believes that this is, in fact, what happened to some Catholics.[295] He summarises here by pointing out four reasons why some
Catholics were truly saved, even though they had lived according to
the faulty doctrine of their Church. First, some Catholics experienced
salvation because they adhered to the foundation of Christianity,
namely to the belief in the Christ's atoning death[296] as the objective reason for salvation, and because they also practiced particular repentance
of the sins they were aware of.[297] Second, some Catholics were saved
because they were ignorant of the mistaken doctrines of the Church,

---

285 Rupp, *Studies in the Making of the English Protestant Tradition*, 167; Lake, "Business as
   Usual? The Immediate Reception of Hooker's *Ecclesiastical Polity*", *The Journal of
   Ecclesiastical History* 52/3 (2001), 474.

286 Foxe, *The Acts and Monuments*, 71.

287 For man's dependence upon God, see Neelands, "Hooker on Scripture, Reason and
   'Tradition'", in McGrade (ed.), *Richard Hooker and the Construction of Christian
   Community*, 76-83.

288 Booty, "The English Reformation: A Lively Faith and Sacramental Confession", 24;
   Booty, "An Elizabethan Addresses Modern Anglicanism. Richard Hooker and
   Theological Issues at the End of the Twentieth Century", 10; for details about
   mediation in Hooker, see also Kirby, *Richard Hooker's Doctrine of Royal Supremacy*, 46.

289 Gibbs, "Richard Hooker's *Via Media* Doctrine of Repentance", *Harvard Theological
   Review* 84/1 (1991), 59.

290 See also Barnes, *The Supplication of 1531*, lviii.b-lix.a.

291 Secor, *Richard Hooker, Prophet of Anglicanism*, 185.

292 Hooker, *Justification* (*Works* V, 127.6-14).

293 Frith, *The Revelation of Antichrist*, 462.

294 Louma, "Restitution and Reformation?", 105.

295 For details, see also Jordan, *The Development of Religious Toleration*, 227.

296 Lake, *Anglicans and Puritans?*, 162.

297 Hooker, *Justification* (*Works* V, 127.15-27).

and thus they believed them wholeheartedly, but out of ignorance.[298] Third, some Catholics tasted salvation because, even if they were ignorant regarding some wrong doctrines, they still opposed some of the more gruesomely mistaken doctrines of the pope.[299] Finally, some Catholics were saved because they believed in the content of divine truth, which was wrongly worded in Catholic doctrine, but expressed correctly in Protestant theology. Hooker uses justification as an example, which could imply sanctification. Thus, he sees the problem of someone being justified by works as having a proper theological answer. If one defines justification as including sanctification, then that believer is indeed justified both by faith and works.[300] On the other hand, if one defines justification and does not include sanctification in the definition, the outcome is that the believer is justified by faith alone.[301]

In summary, Hooker believes that general repentance, based on the foundation of Christ alone,[302] is saving repentance and Hooker clearly states that some Catholics have experienced it. However, since no one is fully sanctified, it is impossible for someone to be aware of every particular sin. Even though a man should repent of every transgression that he knows he has committed, because of his innate weakness, he is unable to repent of all of his sins. Surely this is a powerful application of Luther's *simul justus et peccator* principle to the Catholic question. Here, Hooker is actually implying very cleverly that Travers and the Puritans are holding to a kind of works righteousness, which demands the "enumeration" of particular sins as being a condition for obtaining forgiveness, a belief the Lutheran *Angsburg Confession* criticises.[303]

5.2.7 The Salvation of Godly Pagans

One of the aspects that makes Hooker's doctrine of salvation so fascinating is his belief that some pagans will have their sins forgiven, an idea already alluded to in his *A Learned and Comfortable Sermon of the Certaintie and Perpetuitie of Faith in the Elect.*[304] It was there that Hooker had written about the existence of a secret love within some people for

298 *ibid.* 127.27-128.2, and Peter McGrath, *Papists and Puritans under Elizabeth I*, 320.
299 Hooker, *Justification* (*Works* V, 128.2-5).
300 See also Sykes, *The Study of Anglicanism*, 67.
301 Hooker, *Justification* (*Works* V, 128.5-18).
302 Booty, "An Elizabethan Addresses Modern Anglicanism. Richard Hooker and Theological Issues at the End of the Twentieth Century", 10.
303 See the *Augsburg Confession* in Schaff, *The Creeds*, vol. 3, 14.
304 For details, see also Jordan, *The Development of Religious Toleration*, 227.

the things believed. He had decided that if that secret love were within
a person and if that person did want to believe in spiritual things, then
the faith in those spiritual things already did exist. Now, Hooker
promotes his view that even heathens that are truly preoccupied with
what is proper conduct prove that they too wish to receive God's
mercy. That, in turn, points to their wish to have their sins forgiven.
Hooker does admit that for these pagans, repentance is not a
requirement, for they have no way of knowing that repentance is
necessary for the forgiveness of their sins:

> But we washe a wall of lome, we labour in vayne, all this is nothinge, it
> doth not prove it cannott justefie that which we goe about to mainteyne:
> Infidells and heathen men are not so godless, but that they maie not doubt
> crie gode mercye and desire in generall to have thire synnes forgiven them.
> To suche as deny the foundacion of faith ther can be no salvation according
> to the ordynarye course which God doth use in saving men without a
> particuler repentaunce of that errour.[305]

Here, Hooker once again makes use of a psychological approach to
salvation, an approach that involves the conscience's full participation.
Salvation is thus granted to the person who is fundamentally
convinced of the rightness of his own actions. This firm conviction in
another way of salvation may very well grant salvation, because this
powerful belief lies at the heart of the matter. Hooker reaffirms that
only one foundation of faith – belief in Christ alone – counts for our
salvation.[306] Still, the Catholic Church throughout history has taught its
followers that salvation is also by works and not only by Christ. This
understanding is of course fundamentally flawed, for it does not line
up with God's prescription. However, Hooker believes that if Catholics
believed with all their hearts, being totally convinced that Christ and
works together provided the way to salvation, they erred, but the error
was out of ignorance,[307] and not an error worthy of them being refused
salvation. Hooker himself remains convinced that salvation is refused
specifically to those who on purpose, and knowing the truth, promoted
the flawed Catholic doctrines.[308] Therefore, God's punishment comes
upon only those who directly and wilfully deny Christ as the foundation of faith.

---

305 Hooker, *Justification* (*Works* V, 126.7-17).
306 Booty, "The English Reformation: A Lively Faith and Sacramental Confession", 24;
   Kirby, *Richard Hooker's Doctrine of Royal Supremacy*, 46.
307 See also Walton, *The Lives*, 218.
308 Hooker, *Justification* (*Works* V, 126.29-127.5).

Hooker has followed Cranmer[309] in establishing that salvation includes the indirect, unwilling denial of Christ as Lord and Saviour.[310] He now turns to his explanation of the significance of holding the foundation of faith. For this task, he begins by summarising a previous idea that he had promoted, namely that some pagans were saved before Christ's death, even though they knew nothing of his teaching and existence. In the past, others have seen Hooker in light of his resemblance to Erasmus, Zwingli, and more recently Karl Rahner. Still, one must not miss Hooker's attempt to link salvation to firm and objective reality, generally known as the providence of God.[311] Hooker agrees with Bradford[312] in his promotion of a single, integrated theology of providence which he sees as manifested to all of God's creation.[313] In this line of thought, salvation can be understood not only by means of spiritual devices, but also by means of natural abilities. Hooker seems to place human nature within the framework of God's active providence.

This means that God's providence is manifested in human nature with a soteriological purpose, for man, though unaware, has the natural ability to hold the foundation of Christian faith:

> There are which defend that many of the gentiles who never heard the name of Christe held the foundacion of christianitye. And whie? They acknowledged many of them the providence of god, his infynite wisdome strength and power, his goodnes and his mercie towards the children of men, that God had judgemente in store for the wicked, but for the righteous that seekes him rewardes etcetera. In this which they confessed, that lyeth covered which we beleeve. In the rudyments of thire knowledge concerninge god, the foundacion of our faith concerning Christe lieth secretly wrapped up and is virtually contayned. Therfore they held the foundacion of faith though they never hearde it.[314]

---

309 Cranmer, *Annotations on the King's Book*, 12.

310 Booty, "The English Reformation: A Lively Faith and Sacramental Confession", 24; Booty, "An Elizabethan Addresses Modern Anglicanism. Richard Hooker and Theological Issues at the End of the Twentieth Century", 10.

311 The authority of providence is essential to Hooker. See Kaye, "Authority and the Interpretation of Scripture in Hooker's *Of the Laws of Ecclesiastical Polity*", *The Journal of Religious History* 21/1 (1997), 88; Grislis, "The Assurance of Faith according to Richard Hooker", in McGrade, *Richard Hooker and the Construction of Christian Community*, 239. Speed Hill, "Richard Hooker and the Rhetoric of History", *Churchman* 114/1 (2000), 13-14.

312 Bradford, *Writings*, 213-214.

313 For the importance of creation in Hooker, see Booty, "The Judicious Mr. Hooker and the Authority in the Elizabethan Church", in Stephen W. Sykes (ed.), *Authority in the Anglican Communion*, 101.

314 Hooker, *Justification* (*Works* V, 135.1-11).

Here, Hooker's view is filled with philosophical inconsistencies and overly optimistic theology.[315] Philosophically speaking, one can hardly accept the view that lack of knowledge can serve the same function as conviction, especially since Christian salvation demands conviction. Faith, the concept necessary to salvation, clearly expresses that conviction. To his credit, Hooker tries to root soteriology in God, but his view loses sight of the reality of human nature. Hooker seeks salvation as being totally linked to God, which at first sight seems to bring a certain soteriological security, but he does nothing to link human nature to salvation apart from the general belief in God's providence. If Hooker is correct, then a human being is completely powerless to express in any way his decision concerning salvation. Furthermore, Hooker's view leads to the acceptance of a man being saved without even being aware of this reality. Hooker does not distinguish clearly between awareness and knowledge. Missing from his soteriological schema is an expressed knowledge of Christ, and in its stead is a simple awareness of one's life facts or of one's righteous life. What logically follows such reasoning is that faith becomes superfluous, no longer representing a condition for salvation.

It is important to point out, however, that this particular belief does not permeate all of Hooker's soteriological doctrine. It seems to be more of an appendix to his broader doctrine of salvation, an attempt to explain the fate of the righteous who lived before the time of Christ. Hooker always asserts the necessity of Christ for human salvation. Salvation is granted only when one affirms the foundation of faith – Christ as Lord and Saviour.[316] The other side of the coin infers that salvation is refused once one denies that foundation. Hooker believes that both denial and affirmation come from humans who have a certain knowledge of the Christ they are denying or affirming. Moreover, Hooker believes that a true knowledge of Christ[317] will manifest itself through a clear affirmation of Christ's death and resurrection[318] for human salvation.[319] Hooker has a two-fold concept of denial, one that helps distinguish between Christian and non-Christian belief. The

---

315 See also Shirley, *Richard Hooker and Contemporary Political Ideas*, 88; Lurbe, "Political Power and Ecclesiastical Power in Richard Hooker's *Laws of Ecclesiastical Polity*", *Cahiers Elisabéthains* 49 (1996), 21.

316 Booty, "The English Reformation: A Lively Faith and Sacramental Confession", 24; Booty, "An Elizabethan Addresses Modern Anglicanism. Richard Hooker and Theological Issues at the End of the Twentieth Century", 10.

317 Booty, "Hooker's Understanding of the Presence of Christ in the Eucharist", 142.

318 See also Morrel, "Richard Hooker, Theologian of the English Reformation", *Christianity Today*, X/10 (1966), 9.

319 Hooker, *Justification* (*Works* V, 135.27-136.3).

direct denial is normally ascribed to pagans. The indirect denial refers clearly to Catholics, those who believed the erroneous teachings of Christian Churches. This double concept of denial serves to separate those whom Hooker believes to be saved or unsaved. Hooker claims that only those who directly deny Christ (the pagans) are lost.[320] Those who deny Christ indirectly are still saved, because their error is out of ignorance.[321]

5.2.8 The Theological Unity between Paul and James

Hooker goes on to clarify that Paul speaks of justification apart from its link to sanctification, while James teaches that justification implies sanctification. Hooker must introduce again the concept of righteousness so as to make this distinction clear. The righteousness that comes from justification is different than that of sanctification.[322] Hooker follows Bradford[323] in writing that the righteousness of justification is imputed to the believer,[324] making it something that is completely alien to the human.[325] Yet, the righteousness of sanctification does indeed reside internally in the human. Hooker returns again to his synthesis between justification and sanctification,[326] stating that genuine sanctification cannot exist apart from justification. In Abraham's case, the righteousness that God imputed to him was closely connected to his willingness to offer his Son as a sacrifice.[327] The strong point in Hooker's view of salvation is his offering of an integrative and holistic view that links justification to sanctification. He

---

320 Bauckham, "Hooker, Travers and the Church of Rome in the 1580s", 43; Milton, *Catholic and Reformed*, 146.

321 Hooker, *Justification* (*Works* V, 136.3-23).

322 For details, see Stanwood, "Of Prelacy and Polity in Milton and Hooker", in Margo Swiss and David Kent (eds), *Heirs of Fame. Milton and Writers of the English Renaissance*, 69.

323 Bradford, *Writings*, 371-372.

324 Booty, "The English Reformation: A Lively Faith and Sacramental Confession", 25; Booty, "The Spirituality of Participation in Richard Hooker", *Sewanee Theological Review* 38/1 (1994), 9-20; Kirby, "Richard Hooker as an Apologist of the Magisterial Reformation in England", in McGrade, *Richard Hooker and the Construction of Christian Community*, 226; Stevenson, *The Mystery of Baptism in the Anglican Tradition*, 42.

325 Kirby, *Richard Hooker's Doctrine of Royal Supremacy*, 50.

326 Booty, "The English Reformation: A Lively Faith and Sacramental Confession", 24; Sykes, *The Study of Anglicanism*, 67; Booty, "An Elizabethan Addresses Modern Anglicanism. Richard Hooker and Theological Issues at the End of the Twentieth Century", 14-15.

327 Morrel, "Richard Hooker, Theologian of the English Reformation", 9.

argues that both justification and sanctification are bestowed upon the
believer through grace.[328] He also agrees with Cranmer[329] and Foxe[330]
that God bestows justifies us because of Christ and then grants us
sanctification through the working of proper righteousness within us:

> For excepte ther be an ambiguity in some terme, Ste Paule and Ste James
> do contradicte eche other which cannot be: nowe, there is no ambiguity in
> the name either of faith or of workes both beinge mente by them, both in
> one and the same sence. Fynding therefore that justification is spoken of by
> Ste Paule without ymplying sanctification, when he proveth that a man is
> justefied by faith without workes, finding likewise that justificacion doth
> sometymes implye sanctificacion also with it I suppose nothing more
> sound then so to interprett Ste James as speaking not in that sence but in
> this we have alredy shewed, that there are two kindes of Christian
> rightuousnes the one without us which we have by imputacion, the other
> in us which consisteth of faith hope charitie and other Christian virtues.
> And Ste James doth prove that Abraham had not onely the one becawse
> the thing he beleved *was imputed unto him for rightuousnes* but also the other
> becawse *he offred up his sonne.* God gyveth us both the one Justice and the
> other, the one by accepting us for righteous in Christe, the other by
> workinge Christian rightuousnes in us.[331]

One should take note of how Hooker does not ascribe sanctification
completely to man alone. Bradford also writes that in sanctification we
labour with the Lord.[332] Thus, sanctification is not in its entirety a work
of man, but demands the support of God. In sanctification, God is
helping and directly supporting the believer, and the logical inference
that follows this is that without God's help, man would be unable to
sanctify himself.

Next, Hooker launches into an explanation that indicates that
sanctification is triggered by the spirit of adoption, or according to
Bradford, the spirit of sanctification.[333] This spirit of adoption is the
means by which God directly supports the believer in the process of
sanctification.[334] The believer receives the spirit of adoption from God;
it is in not a state that is inherent to human nature.[335] Hooker falls back
on this explanation to display again what he believes to be the objective

---

328 Keble, *The Works*, vol. 2, 552.
329 Cranmer, *The 1538 Articles*, 4.
330 Foxe, *The Acts and Monuments*, 74.
331 Hooker, *Justification* (*Works* V, 128.19-129.10).
332 Bradford, *Writings*, 218.
333 Bradford, *Writings*, 218.
334 Booty, "The Spirituality of Participation in Richard Hooker", *Sewanee Theological Review* 38/1 (1994), 11.
335 Stanwood, "Of Prelacy and Polity in Milton and Hooker", in Margo Swiss and David Kent (eds), *Heirs of Fame. Milton and Writers of the English Renaissance*, 69.

foundation of salvation. At every stage, salvation remains initiated and primarily worked out by God[336] and not by man, as powerfully defended by Foxe.[337] It makes no difference whether the topic at hand is justification or sanctification, for both of them are seen as being initiated by God[338] and simultaneously supported by God on behalf of the believer.[339] The spirit of adoption (alien to human nature, but nevertheless received by the believer) has practical results in the believer's life, and these are good works,[340] as taught by Frith.[341] Because sanctification relates to both God and the believer, the process contains two kinds of righteousness. Hooker describes the righteousness of sanctification as being habitual and actual.[342] When he speaks of the habitual righteousness of sanctification,[343] Hooker is referring to that righteousness that is produced within the believer at the moment he first exercises faith and becomes indwelled by the Holy Spirit. The habitual righteousness of sanctification is marked out by the indwelling of the Holy Spirit.

Hooker considers the actual righteousness of sanctification as being the result of good works.[344] Still, he does not offer a chronological scheme for justification and sanctification[345] or their respective types of righteousness. Sanctification cannot be separated from justification. Likewise, the righteousness of sanctification cannot be separated from the righteousness of justification. Separating these aspects would theologically be separating the very works of God. Hooker sees God's

---

336 Rupp, *Studies in the Making of the English Protestant Tradition*, 167; Lake, "Business as Usual? The Immediate Reception of Hooker's *Ecclesiastical Polity*", *The Journal of Ecclesiastical History* 52/3 (2001), 474.

337 Foxe, *The Acts and Monuments*, 71.

338 Allison, *The Rise of Moralism*, 4; Booty, "Contrition in Anglican Spirituality: Hooker, Donne and Herbert", in William J. Wolf (ed.), *Anglican Spirituality* (Wilton: Morehouse-Barlow, 1982), 26; Kirby, "*Supremum Caput*: Richard Hooker's Theology of Ecclesiastical Dominion", *Dionysius* XII (1988), 96; Schwarz, "Dignified and Commodius: Richard Hooker's 'Mysticall Copulation' Metaphor", *Sewanee Theological Review* 43/1 (1999), 23.

339 Morrel, "Richard Hooker, Theologian of the English Reformation", 9.

340 Collinson, *Archbishop Grindal*, 41; Gibbs, "Richard Hooker's *Via Media* Doctrine of Justification", 220.

341 Frith, *Patrick Places*, 31-34.

342 Voak, *Richard Hooker and Reformed Theology*, 175.

343 See also Gibbs, "Richard Hooker's *Via Media* Doctrine of Justification", 220; Booty, "The English Reformation: A Lively Faith and Sacramental Confession", 25.

344 Booty, "The English Reformation: A Lively Faith and Sacramental Confession", 25.

345 Sykes, *The Study of Anglicanism*, 67; Booty, "An Elizabethan Addresses Modern Anglicanism. Richard Hooker and Theological Issues at the End of the Twentieth Century", 14-15.

salvific work as being unified and not able to be broken and scattered. At the moment of justification, sanctification is also received.[346] Hooker summarizes these ideas in the following paragraph:

> The proper and moste ymediate efficiente cawse in us of this latter is the *spirite of adoption* which we have receyved into our hartes: that whereof it consisteth whereof it is really and formally made are those infused virtues proper and particular unto saintes, which the spirite in that very momente when firste it is given of God bringeth with it. The effected thereof are suche accions, as the apostle doth call *the fruites the workes the operacions* of the spirit: the difference of which operacions from the roote whereof they springe maketh it nedfull to putt ii kindes likewise of sanctifying rightuousnes *habituall and actuall*. *Habituall* that holynes wherewith our soules are inwardly indued the same instante when firste we begyn to be the temples of the holy goste: *Actuall* that holynes which afterward bewtefieth all the partes and actions of our life, the holynes for which *Enoch Job Zachery Elizabeth* and other saintes are in Scripture so highly comended. If here it be demaunded which of theis we do firste receyve? I aunswere that the spirite, the virtues of the spirite, the habituall justice which is ingrafted, the externall justice of Christe Jesus which is ymputed, theis we receive all att one and the same tyme. Whensoever have any of theis we have all, they goe together.[347]

It is here that Hooker goes deeper in explaining his concept of faith. Until now, he has described faith as being a hinge between justification and sanctification,[348] and subsequently between the work of God and the work of man. But he has just argued that ultimately even sanctification is a work of God because of the spirit of adoption, the Holy Spirit, that is given to the believer. Hooker seems convinced that sanctification is primarily God's work, even if man is responsible for the righteousness of sanctification. Still, until now, faith has been viewed as simply an element that connected justification to sanctify-cation. Now, Hooker promotes the idea that this faith, even though required from man, is also the work of God because its inception depends upon the granting of the spirit of adoption.[349] Put another way, God first bestows the Holy Spirit on the sinner, and it is the Holy Spirit himself who initiates faith within the believer. Faith is the aspect that

---

346 See also Keble, *The Works*, xcviii-xcix.

347 Hooker, *Justification* (*Works* V, 129.10-29); Kirby, *Richard Hooker's Doctrine of Royal Supremacy*, 50.

348 Booty, "The English Reformation: A Lively Faith and Sacramental Confession", 24; Sykes, *The Study of Anglicanism*, 67; Booty, "An Elizabethan Addresses Modern Anglicanism. Richard Hooker and Theological Issues at the End of the Twentieth Century", 14-15.

349 Gane, "The Exegetical Methods of Some Sixteenth Century Anglican Preachers: Latimer, Jewel, Hooker, and Andrews", 35.

confers unity to Hooker soteriology, because it is the link between justification and sanctification. Furthermore, faith makes God's salvation objective, because it is accomplished by the Holy Spirit, through whom the believer is adopted by God.

Hooker then points out that if faith is required for salvation, then it must be necessary for justification and sanctification. The flow of logic then makes faith belong both to justification and sanctification. When faith is considered independently, it falls to justification. But when it is linked to hope and love, it becomes an integral part of sanctification. Hooker's line of thinking in this regard secures the objective aspect of salvation while keeping the theological concepts united, and thus answers the question regarding the salvation of some Catholics. Since faith is a vital part of both justification and sanctification, if one were to believe that salvation is granted by faith *and* works, he would not be entirely off base.[350] Hooker sees good works as completing justification, meaning that they make possible salvation's continuation, they prove that justification has taken place[351] and show we love Christ,[352] as also explained by Frith.[353] In the same way, good works cannot be made effective without faith. So, from justification's perspective, it is true that salvation is by faith alone.

On the other hand, when looking at salvation from the perspective of both justification and sanctification, salvation is indeed by faith and by works, which is the doctrine taught and held to by Catholics. Going further, one can assume that there is no true justification without the presence of good works, since justification is essentially and vitally linked to sanctification, both realised through faith.[354] Hooker states:

> Yett sith no man is justefied excepte he beleeve and no man beleeveth except he hath faith and no man hath faith unles hee *have receyved the spirit of adoption* for asmuche as theis do necessarily inferred justification, but justification doth of necessity presuppose them, we muste nedes holde that ymputed rightuousnes in dignitye being the chefeste is notwithstandinge in order the laste of all theis, but actuall rightuousnes which is the rightuousnes of good works succedeth all followeth after all both in order and in tyme, which thing being attentively marked sheweth plainly howe

---

350 Sykes, *The Study of Anglicanism*, 67; Booty, "An Elizabethan Addresses Modern Anglicanism. Richard Hooker and Theological Issues at the End of the Twentieth Century", 14-15.

351 Collinson, *Archbishop Grindal*, 41.

352 Marot, "Aux origines de la théologie anglicane", 342.

353 Frith, *Patrick Places*, 31-34.

354 Sykes, *The Study of Anglicanism*, 67; Booty, "An Elizabethan Addresses Modern Anglicanism. Richard Hooker and Theological Issues at the End of the Twentieth Century", 14-15.

the faith of true belevers cannot be divorsed from hope and love, howe faith is a parte of sanctification and yet unto justificacion necessary, howe faith is perfected by good wourkes and yet no worke of ours good without faith finally howe our fathers mighte hold we are justefied by faith alone and yett hold truly that without good workes we are not justefied.[355]

Seeking to defend his position that some Catholics are truly saved, Hooker links the concept of merit,[356] (obviously including the doing of good works) to the reality of the heavenly reward. Through this, Hooker denies the Protestant doctrine that sees good works as futile, since that doctrine allegedly leads to a view of salvation that confers no importance to good deeds. Hooker believes that good works are very important, so much so that they will eventually bring a proper reward. But he does not lose sight of the fact that placing too much emphasis on good works in regards to salvation could lead to errant theory that good works are the basis of salvation, as explained by Barnes.[357] This is the error that had taken root in Catholicism. Hooker heads in another direction at this point, offering a vivid illustration of how, in light of death, the importance of good works wanes considerably, a doctrine that was vital to Foxe.[358] Hooker is convinced that the reality of death diminishes the importance of good works. Agreeing with Cranmer,[359] Hooker states that death blows away any possible illusion that good works could be the basis of salvation. Instead, death brings forth a pure faith, a genuine trust in Christ[360] alone as the objective cause of salvation.[361]

5.2.9 The Concept of Law

It is here that Hooker introduces his thoughts on the concept of law.[362] Hooker sees the law in two ways: a civil law and a spiritual law.[363] At

355 Hooker, *Justification* (*Works* V, 129.29-130.12).

356 See also Walton, *The Lives*, 219.

357 Barnes, *The Supplication of 1531*, l.b.

358 Foxe, *The Acts and Monuments*, 71.

359 Cranmer, *The 1538 Articles*, 4.

360 Collinson, *Archbishop Grindal*, 41; Booty, "The Spirituality of Participation in Richard Hooker", *Sewanee Theological Review* 38/1 (1994), 11; Sedgwick, "The New Shape of Anglican Identity", *Anglican Theological Review* LXXVII/2 (1995), 189.

361 Hooker, *Justification* (*Works* V, 130.12-131.8); Griffith Thomas (ed.), *The Principles of Theology*, 191. See also Kirby, "The Paradigm of Chalcedonian Christology in Richard Hooker's Discourse on Grace and the Church", *Churchman* 114/1 (2000), 23-25.

362 See also Sommerville, "Richard Hooker, Hadrian Saravia, and the Advent of the Divine Right of Kings", 231; Orrù, "Anomy and Reason in the English Renaissance",

this point in the discourse, he presents briefly his political theory regarding the status and function of civil law. It is conceived and enforced by public authorities in order that the common good should be preserved in society. The basis for initiating and enforcing civil law is social plurality, the belief that a political society is formed from a large group of individuals. Civil law serves to determine the best way by which the entire group of individuals should live and behave as a single social corpus. Civil law is therefore meant to secure order within society. It is founded on the principle of non-violence, the basic norm that directs society. Hooker believes that once a society lacks this fundamental principle of non-violence, what inevitably takes place is the destruction of the common wealth of that society.

> This worlde foundacion being figuratyvely used hath alwais reference to somewhat which resembleth a materiall buyldinge as both the doctrine of Christianity and the comunitye of Christians do. By the masters of the civill pollecye nothing is so muche inculcated as that comon wealthes are founded upon laws for that a multitude cannot be compacted into one bodye otherwise then by a comon acceptacion of lawes whereby they are to be kepte in order. The grownd of all civill lawes is this, *No man ought to be hurte or injured by annother.* Take awaie this perswasion and youe take awaie all lawes, take awaie lawes and what shall become of comon wealthes?[364]

Clearly, Hooker is seeking to describe the laws of the civil community, which are political in nature, in such a way that later he can explain the laws of the Christian community, which are spiritual in nature.[365] Hooker states firmly that he does not wish to speak much of the invisible Church, which he considers to be the mystical body of Christ,[366] and not existent in history. He intends to discuss the laws of the visible Church, those laws that come from the Christian doctrines of

---

Journal of the History of Ideas XLVII/2 (1986), 186. See also Lockwood O'Donovan, *Theology of Law and Authority in the English Reformation*, 137; Moore, "Recycling Aristotle: The Sovereignty Theory of Richard Hooker", *History of Political Thought* XIV/3 (1993), 345-359.

363 For details about Hooker's concept of law, see Forte, "Richard Hooker's Theory of Law", *The Journal of Medieval and Renaissance Studies* 12 (1982), 157.

364 Hooker, *Justification* (*Works* V, 132.2-11).

365 Kaye, "What Might Alasdair MacIntyre Learn from a Reading of Richard Hooker? Rivalry, Commonality, and Their Projects", *Sewanee Theological Review* 42/3 (1999), 347.

366 See also Lecler, *Toleration and the Reformation*, vol. 2, 401; Archer, "Hooker on Apostolic Succession: The Two Voices", *Sixteenth Century Journal* XXIV/1 (1993), 72; Lurbe, "Political Power and Ecclesiastical Power in Richard Hooker's *Laws of Ecclesiastical Polity*", *Cahiers Elisabéthains* 49 (1996), 19.

Scripture.[367] This means that Hooker's ecclesiology depends principally upon his doctrine of Scripture. His purpose in bringing these two doctrines together is eventually to point to the doctrine of salvation. Hooker sees Scripture as containing Christian doctrine, which is the foundation of the laws of the Christian spiritual community.[368] But since Christian doctrine is the teaching of salvation,[369] this clearly shows the way by which a sinner can be saved and incorporated[370] into the visible Church of God.

5.2.10 The Importance of Scripture

One can safely assume that for Hooker, both soteriology and ecclesiology are linked inextricably to his doctrine of Scripture. Hooker takes great care when he speaks of his methodology in interpreting Scripture. Christians are not to look to Scripture for answers that belong to reason, and what is discovered by reason (if it does not contradict Scripture) can and must be trusted.[371]

> So it is in our spirituall Christian communitye, I do not nowe meane that body misticall whereof Christe is the onely hed, that buyldinge undiscernable by morall eyes wherein *Christe is the cheif corner stone*, but I speake of the visible Church, *the foundacion* whereof is the doctryne *of the prophettes and Apostles* profeste. The marke whereunto theire doctrine tendeth is pointed att in those wordes of Paul unto Christe *thou haste the wordes of eternall life*. In those of Paule to Tymothye. *Scripture are able to make thee wise unto salvation*.[372]

---

367 For the role of the Church in making laws, see also Stanwood, "Stobaeus and Classical Borrowing in the Renaissance, with Special Reference to Richard Hooker and Jeremy Taylor", *Neophilologus* 59 (1975), 141.

368 See also Hunt, *Religious Thought in England*, 60, and Davies, *Episcopacy and the Royal Supremacy*, 45; Bryan, "The Judicious Mr. Hooker and the Early Christians. The Relationship of Scripture and Reason in the First Century of the Christian Era", in Donald S. Armentrout (ed.), *This Sacred History. Anglican Reflections for John Booty*, 144.

369 Kirby, "Richard Hooker's Theory of Natural Law in the Context of Reformation Theology", *Sixteenth Century Journal* XXX/3 (1999), 702.

370 Morrel, "Richard Hooker, Theologian of the English Reformation", 9.

371 For details on Hooker's view of reason, see also Jordan, *The Development of Religious Toleration*, 228; Brockwell, "Answering to 'Known Men': Bishop Reginald Pecock and Mr. Richard Hooker", 142.

372 Hooker, *Justification* (*Works* V, 132.12-19).

Thus, Hooker follows Bradford[373] in claiming that Scripture contains the teaching of salvation,[374] the way by which man can obtain eternal life in Christ.[375]

5.2.11 The Desire for Salvation

Hooker now pauses for a few moments from the main part of his argument in order to state that human nature fundamentally desires to obtain eternal life.[376] Hooker believes that mankind has always had an innate desire for immortality. Because this desire is inherent in every human being, mankind has often resorted to what Hooker calls superstitions in order to obtain this eternal life. The emergence of world religions is a direct result of humanity's attempts to gain eternal life in other ways. But since humans are powerless in the face of death, they are helpless in bringing about eternal life, an idea also found in Foxe.[377] Death proves that man is unable to obtain eternal life or salvation on his own. Because all humanity finds itself in this predicament, Hooker believes that salvation must fundamentally be an action devised, incepted, and accomplished by God alone. True salvation from death comes only as a result of the work of God, not man.[378] All human life has an end. Hooker believes that the end of human life leads to two different situations. Human life may end in death (as the world religions or superstitions claim) or it may end in eternal life (as upheld by the doctrine of the Gospel). Eternal life is in its essence salvation. Hooker, as usual, describes the content of salvation by emphasising its objective nature. Salvation is not brought about by man, but is the work of God in Christ,[379] as shown by Barnes[380] and Foxe.[381] This belief does not, however, cheapen salvation at all. God's grace, through which salvation is possible, is manifested in the riches of His mercy. For

---

373 Bradford, *Writings*, 314.
374 Kirby, "Richard Hooker's Theory of Natural Law in the Context of Reformation Theology", *Sixteenth Century Journal* XXX/3 (1999), 702; Atkinson, "Hooker's Theological Method and Modern Anglicanism", *Churchman* 114/1 (2000), 54.
375 Atkinson, *Richard Hooker and the Authority of Scripture, Tradition and Reason*, 129.
376 See also Marshall, *Hooker and the Anglican Tradition*, 111; Neelands, "Hooker on Scripture, Reason and 'Tradition'", in McGrade (ed.), *Richard Hooker and the Construction of Christian Community*, 76-83.
377 Foxe, *The Acts and Monuments*, 71.
378 Rupp, *Studies in the Making of the English Protestant Tradition*, 167.
379 Collinson, *Archbishop Grindal*, 41.
380 Barnes, *The Supplication of 1534*.
381 Foxe, *The Acts and Monuments*, 71.

Hooker, the mercy of God is the beginning of salvation, a belief that
lines up quite well with the theology of Barnes[382] and Bradford.[383]

5.2.12 A Unique Foundation of Faith for the
Old and the New Testament

The paragraph below taken from Hooker's discourse describes
salvation's content in terms of the foundation of faith.[384] Hooker
explains that the foundation of faith, the essential component to
salvation, has been purchased and a price has been paid for it, namely,
the death of Christ:[385]

> The desire of ymortalitye and of the knowledge of that whereby it maie be
> atteyned is so natural unto all men that even they which are not perswaded
> what they shall do notwithstanding wishe that they mighte knowe a waie
> howe to see no end of life. And becawse naturall meanes are not able still
> to resiste the force of death there is *no people in the earthe so savage* which
> hath no devised some supernaturall helpe or other to flye unto for ayde
> and succour in the extremities againste the enemyes of theire lyves. A
> longing therefore to be saved without understanding the trewe waie howe
> hath byn the cawse of all the supersticions in the world. O that the
> miserable estate of others which wander in darknes and wotte not whether
> they goe could gyve us understanding hartes worthily to esteeme the
> riches of the mercies of God towards us before whose eyes *the dores of the*
> *kingdome of heaven* are sett wide open [...] The doctryne of the Gospel
> proposeth salvacion as the end. And doth it not teache the waie of
> atteyning thereunto? Yes, the *damsel possessed with a spirite of devynation*
> spake the truth, *Theis men are the servauntes of the moste high God which shewe*
> *unto us the waie of salvation. A newe and lyving waie which Christe hath prepared*
> *for us through the vayle that is his fleshe,* salvation purchased by the death of
> Christ.[386]

Hooker is convinced that the objective foundation of salvation[387] is the
death of Christ.[388] Here, he stresses again his belief in the consistency of

382 Barnes, *The Supplication of 1531*, lviii.b-lix.a.

383 Bradford, *Writings*, 371-372.

384 Hooker, *Justification* (*Works* V, 131.22-132.1); Booty, "The English Reformation: A
     Lively Faith and Sacramental Confession", 24; Booty, "An Elizabethan Addresses
     Modern Anglicanism. Richard Hooker and Theological Issues at the End of the
     Twentieth Century", 10.

385 Lake, *Anglicans and Puritans?*, 162.

386 Hooker, *Justification* (*Works* V, 132.21-133.22).

387 Kirby, "The Paradigm of Chalcedonian Christology in Richard Hooker's Discourse
     on Grace and the Church", *Churchman* 114/1 (2000), 23-25.

388 Lake, *Anglicans and Puritans?*, 162.

salvation, by which the means of salvation has been the same for all people. Hooker believes that the person and work of Christ secured salvation for all human beings. In the Old Testament, described by Hooker as the time of the law, is a genuine proof of a salvation that has always been valid due to Christ's death alone. Beginning with the New Testament period, named by Hooker the time of grace, the same salvation through Christ's death has become effective, through its taking place within humanity. Salvation remains secure, not because it was put into effect by Christ, who could have been a merely human Messiah, but because it was accomplished by Christ Jesus, the divine Messiah and Son of God.

5.2.13 The Role of the Holy Spirit in the Incarnation of Christ

Even though Hooker does not put too much emphasis on pneumatology, it is clear that he sees it as playing an important role within salvation, because it accomplishes the whole process of incarnation.[389] Hooker understands that incarnation is an essential part of salvation,[390] as highlighted by Frith.[391] Likewise, salvation is not the work of man but the work of God, which is a fundamental belief of Foxe.[392] Jesus Christ, who became flesh in order to accomplish our salvation,[393] received constant assistance from the Holy Spirit. In seeking to offer a clear understanding of salvation, Hooker construes the classical image of Jesus Christ, traditionally described as being both truly human and truly God. Therefore, Hooker finds importance in tracing Christ's human lineage, while associating Christ closely with God by pointing out the relationship Christ had with God His Father through the Holy Spirit. Thus, Christ as the Son of God, who died for

---

389 See also Barry, *Masters in English Theology*, 43, and Marshall, *Hooker and the Anglican Tradition*, 112; Booty, "An Elizabethan Addresses Modern Anglicanism. Richard Hooker and Theological Issues at the End of the Twentieth Century", 11; Kaye, "What Might Alasdair MacIntyre Learn from a Reading of Richard Hooker? Rivalry, Commonality, and Their Projects", *Sewanee Theological Review* 42/3 (1999), 347.

390 Thornton, *Richard Hooker*, 54; Booty, "An Elizabethan Addresses Modern Anglicanism. Richard Hooker and Theological Issues at the End of the Twentieth Century", 10; Kaye, "Authority and the Interpretation of Scripture in Hooker's *Of the Laws of Ecclesiastical Polity*", *The Journal of Religious History* 21/1 (1997), 88; Gibbs, "Richard Hooker and Lancelot Andrew on Priestly Absolution", in McGrade, *Richard Hooker and the Construction of Christian Community*, 271.

391 Frith, *Patrick Places*, 30.

392 Foxe, *The Acts and Monuments*, 71.

393 Hillerdal, *Reason and Revelation in Richard Hooker*, 75.

humanity's sins, is the ultimate core of salvation and the only foundation of Christian faith by the work of the Spirit:[394]

> By this foundation the children of God before the tyme of the written lawe were distinguished from the sonnes of men, the reverend patriarkes both profeste it lyvinge and spake expresly of it att the hower of theire death. It comforted Job in the middeste of greif. It was afterwards likewise the anckrehold of all the righteous in Israell from the wryting of the lawe to the tyme of grace. Every prophett maketh mencion of it. It was so famously spoken of aboute the tyme when the coming of Christe to accomplishe the promises which were made longe before drewe nere that the sound thereof was heard even amoungste the gentiles. When he was come as many as were his acknowledged that he was theire salvation. He, that longe expected hope of Israel, he, that *seed in whome all the nations of the world should be bleste*. So that nowe his name is a name of ruyne, a name of death and condempnacion unto suche as dreame of a newe *messias*, to asmany as look for salvation by any other then by him. *For amongste men there is given no other name under heaven whereby we muste be saved*. Thus muche Ste Marke doth intymate by that which he putteth in the very fronte of his boke making his entraunce with theis wordes *the begyning of the Gospell of Jesus Christe the sonne of God*, his doctrine he termeth the Gospel becawse it teacheth salvation, the Gospell of Jesus Christ the sonne of God becawse it teacheth salvation by him. This is then the foundacion whereupon the frame of the Gospell is erected. That verye Jesus whome the *virgen conceyved of the holy goste*, whom Simeon *imbraced in his armes* whom Pilate condemned whome the Jewes crucefied whome the Apostles preached, *he is christe the Lord* the onely Saviour of the world: *Other foundacion can no man laie*.[395]

Hooker's doctrine of salvation is centred in Christology, deeply rooted in his doctrine of God and the Holy Spirit. The reason he approaches soteriology in this manner is so that he can lay a firm and objective foundation to everything covered by salvation, which can be understood only through the work of the Spirit. Hooker only brings theological reasons in his Christological analysis of salvation. Still, his Christological soteriology lines up with his epistemology of the twofold concept of faith, which he describes with an equally double concept of certainty: of evidence and of adherence. No evidence exists that could possibly convince and satisfy the mind regarding salvation. Salvation must be seen as a result of the Spirit's work.

Hooker views salvation as being entirely a spiritual reality that pertains to the spiritual realm, which means that the Holy Spirit must

---

394 Booty, "The English Reformation: A Lively Faith and Sacramental Confession", 24; Booty, "An Elizabethan Addresses Modern Anglicanism. Richard Hooker and Theological Issues at the End of the Twentieth Century", 10.

395 Hooker, *Justification* (*Works* V, 133.22-134.22).

play a crucial part in bringing about an adequate understanding of salvation. Therefore, salvation must be investigated by trust,[396] appealing primarily to the heart and only secondarily to the mind, although the latter aspect must also be present. Even though salvation is in its essence spiritual, it is also a historical reality, consisting of an objective aspect: the atoning death of Christ.[397] Hooker's purpose in offering a Christological argumentation is to describe an objective foundation to the Christian doctrine of salvation which would be epistemologically and theologically satisfying.

5.2.14 Salvation and Election

Now Hooker turns again to the issue of salvation from the standpoint of election, the truth that proves God's active involvement in salvation. This is an issue that Barnes is also preoccupied with.[398] For Hooker, salvation may be equated with the acquisition or the obtaining of the glory of Christ, as explained by Cranmer.[399] However, individuals can obtain Christ's glory only if they have been chosen by God. This means that election is the first step in the process of salvation as well as a clear manifestation of God's grace,[400] similar, for instance, to Frith.[401] Still, God continues to be directly and actively involved in human salvation by effectively calling every single individual to salvation. Hooker's soteriological picture of objective salvation, which is initiated by God, who works out the foundation of human redemption, is completed by the doctrine of effectual calling. The third element of God's direct involvement in salvation, behind election and effectual calling, is justification. Hooker clearly states that justification is by faith, and it seems that this is the only stage in the salvation process wherein the individual has a certain level of personal involvement. Even though

---

396 Booty, "The Spirituality of Participation in Richard Hooker", *Sewanee Theological Review* 38/1 (1994), 11; Sedgwick, "The New Shape of Anglican Identity", *Anglican Theological Review* LXXVII/2 (1995), 189.

397 Lake, *Anglicans and Puritans?*, 162.

398 Barnes, *The Supplication of 1531*, xliii.a.

399 Cranmer, *Annotations on the King's Book*, 12.

400 See also Rowse, *The England of Elizabeth*, 487; Hillerdal, *Reason and Revelation in Richard Hooker*, 66-67; Collinson, *Archbishop Grindal*, 41; Wallace Jr., *Puritans and Predestination*, 77; Grislis, "The Assurance of Faith according to Richard Hooker", in McGrade, *Richard Hooker and the Construction of Christian Community*, 240.

401 Frith, *Patrick Places*, 29, and Bradford, *Writings*, 215-216.

God is the One who justifies and is active in this process, faith is a soteriological component that pertains to human beings.[402]

Hooker relegates man's role in justification to a passive state. God is still the one who works out justification and gives faith through the spirit of adoption, clearly a sign of grace.[403] It is the spirit of adoption, who is in fact the Holy Spirit, who produces saving faith. We can ultimately say that God is the one who produces faith in the individual. Hooker understands that from the anthropological perspective, it is impossible for a human being to obtain salvation. The highest level to which one can ascend is the general knowledge of God.[404] Whether or not knowledge of God comes from direct and special revelation from God, this knowledge is not sufficient for salvation. The missing link that is necessary is the work of the spirit of adoption. Therefore, the individual needs to be persuaded and then to believe. This is what is ultimately important for salvation.[405]

Hooker's soteriology follows closely the Reformed[406] blueprint of *ordo salutis*: election, effectual calling, justification, sanctification, and glorification.[407] From the standpoint of sanctification, salvation is seen as having four aspects: soteriological, moral, psychological and relational. The soteriological aspect refers to the forgiveness and remission of sins[408] through the grace of God,[409] which is the very essence of salvation and justification according to Cranmer,[410] Bradford,[411] and Foxe.[412] Even though the beginning of the salvation process begins with justification, it continues through the daily increase of faith.[413] The second aspect of Hooker's soteriology is moral,[414] from his understanding of the final outcome of salvation as being essentially

---

402 Hooker, *Justification* (*Works* V, 136.23-137.3).
403 Keble, *The Works*, vol. 2, 552.
404 Kirby, "Richard Hooker's Theory of Natural Law in the Context of Reformation Theology", *Sixteenth Century Journal* XXX/3 (1999), 702.
405 Hooker, *Justification* (*Works* V, 136.30-137.3).
406 For Hooker's Reformed credentials, see also Avis, "Richard Hooker and John Calvin", *The Journal of Ecclesiastical History* 32 (1981), 27; Lake, *Anglicans and Puritans?*, 162.
407 See also Voak, *Richard Hooker and Reformed Theology*, 175.
408 Rupp, *Studies in the Making of the English Protestant Tradition*, 166.
409 Keble, *The Works*, vol. 2, 552.
410 Cranmer, *The 1538 Articles*, 4.
411 Bradford, *Writings*, 217-218.
412 Foxe, *The Acts and Monuments*, 80.
413 Hooker, *Justification* (*Works* V, 137.8).
414 Sedgwick, "Revisioning Anglican Moral Theology", *Anglican Theological Review* LXIII/1 (1981), 10.

good for humanity both corporately and individually. Third, salvation is psychological, since the believer becomes all the more joyous and secure of his purpose and position in existing.[415] Finally, salvation is relational, because the believer has a relationship with God,[416] to whom he is expected to display a wholehearted reverence.[417]

Hooker recognizes that the best way to formulate the doctrine of soteriology is to say that salvation comes through Christ alone.[418] Still, this formula comprises aspects that pertain to human action, such as the faith needed for justification, and the good works that further the process of sanctification. When Protestants claim that justification is by Christ alone, they are implying that good works, the visible mark of Christian hope and love, will take place in the process of sanctification that follows.[419] Faith, hope and love cannot be separated within the salvation process[420] involving both justification and sanctification[421] because these qualities are signs of grace.[422] God gives justification to believers, however, as a sign that this gift is for the benefit of his elect,[423] for through justification God considers us perfect in all respects as if we were truly perfect, despite the reality of our sheer imperfection:[424]

> But we saie our salvation is by Christ alone therefore howsoever or whatsoever we add unto Christe in the matter of salvation we overthrowe Christe. Our case were very hard if this argumente so universally ment as it is proposed were sound and good. We our selves do not teach Christe alone excluding our owne faith unto justeficacion, Christe alone excluding our owne workes unto sanctification, Christe alone excluding the one or the other as unnecessary unto salvation. It is a childishe cavil wherewith in the matter of justificacion our adversaryes do so greatly please them selves exclaiming that we tread all Christian virtues under feete and require

---

415 Hooker, *Justification* (*Works* V, 137.9).
416 Griffith Thomas (ed.), *The Principles of Theology*, 185.
417 Hooker, *Justification* (*Works* V, 137.10).
418 Kirby, *Richard Hooker's Doctrine of Royal Supremacy*, 46.
419 Collinson, *Archbishop Grindal*, 41; Gibbs, "Richard Hooker's *Via Media* Doctrine of Justification", 220.
420 Booty, "The English Reformation: A Lively Faith and Sacramental Confession", 25; Gibbs, "Richard Hooker and Lancelot Andrew on Priestly Absolution", in McGrade, *Richard Hooker and the Construction of Christian Community*, 272.
421 Sykes, *The Study of Anglicanism*, 67; Booty, "An Elizabethan Addresses Modern Anglicanism. Richard Hooker and Theological Issues at the End of the Twentieth Century", 14-15.
422 Keble, *The Works*, vol. 2, 552, and Marshall, *Hooker and the Anglican Tradition*, 113.
423 See also Hillerdal, *Reason and Revelation in Richard Hooker*, 75, and Morrel, "Richard Hooker, Theologian of the English Reformation", 9.
424 See also Booty, "Understanding the Church in Sixteenth-Century England", *Sewanee Theological Review* 42/3 (1999), 279.

nothing in Christians but faith because we teache that faith alone justefieth, whereas we by this speech never mente to exclude either hope and charitye from beinge always joined as inseparable mates with faith in the man that is justified, or workes from being added as necessarye duties required att the handes of every justefied man; but to shew that faith is the onely hand which putteth on Christ unto Justeficacion and Christ the onely garmente which being so putt on covereth the shame of our defiled natures, hideth the imperfections of our workes, preserveth us blameless in the sighte of God before whome otherwise the very weaknes of our faith were cawse sufficiente to make us culpable, yea to shutt us out from the kingdome of heaven where nothing that is not absolute can enter."[425]

Hooker is only offering a general statement about justification here, but it is one that he will develop in detail. The Protestant belief in salvation by Christ alone means that Christ did not need human help in accomplishing salvation.[426] Again, Hooker goes over the order of the events of salvation, beginning his *ordo salutis* with election,[427] as in Bradford,[428] continuing with effectual calling, justification and sanctification, and then concluding the list with glorification. It is necessary, however, to remember that Hooker believes that each of these stages in the salvation process have been accomplished by Christ alone, who needed no assistance in working out our salvation.[429] Furthermore, the plan of salvation had always been designed by God, so Christ was only acting in accordance with the blueprint that God had already designed. Christ's historical work was absolutely necessary for God's plan to be fulfilled and for justification to be enforced. Therefore, believers were accepted in the sight of God even before creation, but only because of Christ's work in history.[430] Each event in Hooker's *ordo salutis* was accomplished in Christ,[431] and what's more, the whole design stands as a proof of God's magnificent love and grace – manifested towards

---

425   Hooker, *Justification* (*Works* V, 151.9-152.3).

426   Kirby, *Richard Hooker's Doctrine of Royal Supremacy*, 46.

427   See also Rowse, *The England of Elizabeth*, 487; Grislis, "The Assurance of Faith according to Richard Hooker", in McGrade, *Richard Hooker and the Construction of Christian Community*, 240.

428   Bradford, *Writings*, 215-216.

429   Wallace Jr., *Puritans and Predestination*, 77.

430   See also d'Entrèves, *Riccardo Hooker*, 49; Griffith Thomas (ed.), *The Principles of Theology*, 186. For the relationship between creation and redemption, see also Haugaard, "The Scriptural Hermeneutics of Richard Hooker. Historical Contextualization and Teleology", in Donald S. Armentrout (ed.), *This Sacred History. Anglican Reflections for John Booty*, 167; Speed Hill, "Richard Hooker and the Rhetoric of History", *Churchman* 114/1 (2000), 13-14.

431   Collinson, *Archbishop Grindal*, 41.

humankind even before God created the world. God's work of grace,[432] particularly justification and election, was done entirely in Christ[433] – the strongest foundation,[434] according to Bradford[435] – as a powerful statement that shows salvation is objectively the work of God in Christ,[436] not the accomplishment of human works.

> As we have receyved so we teache that besides the bare and naked worke wherein Christe without any other associated finished all the partes of our redemption and purchased salvation him self alone, for conveyance of this emmynente blessing unto us many thinges are of necessitie required, as to be knowne and chose of God before the foundacions of the world, in the world to be called justefyed, sanctified after we have lefte the world to be receyved into glory. Christe in every of theis hath somewhat which he worketh alone. Through him *according to the eternall purpose of God* before the foundacion of the world, borne crucified buryed raised etcetera we were in a gratious aceptacion knowne unto God longe before we were seene of men. God knew us loved us was *kinde towardes us in Christe Jesus.* In him we were elected to be heires of life.[437]

Hooker agrees with Barnes[438] that man's role in salvation is passive, while God actively works out salvation. Following Cranmer[439] and Foxe[440], Hooker states that the effectual results of justification are redemption and the remission of sins[441] based on Christ's atoning death at the cross, a doctrine also fundamental for Frith,[442] so that justice be restored[443] and the offence of sin fully paid for.[444] Concerning sanctification, Christ alone sanctifies believers both individually, as born again people, and corporately, as members of his Church, in view of the final glorification. The doctrine of justification refers to the way

---

432 Rupp, *Studies in the Making of the English Protestant Tradition*, 167.

433 Collinson, *Archbishop Grindal*, 41; Wallace Jr., *Puritans and Predestination*, 77.

434 Booty, "An Elizabethan Addresses Modern Anglicanism. Richard Hooker and Theological Issues at the End of the Twentieth Century", 10.

435 Bradford, *Writings*, 312-313.

436 Collinson, *Archbishop Grindal*, 41; Booty, "The English Reformation: A Lively Faith and Sacramental Confession", 24; Kirby, "The Paradigm of Chalcedonian Christology in Richard Hooker's Discourse on Grace and the Church", *Churchman* 114/1 (2000), 23-25.

437 Hooker, *Justification* (*Works* V, 152.15-27).

438 Barnes, *The Supplication of 1531*, xliii.a.

439 Cramer, *The 1538 Articles*, 4.

440 Foxe, *The Acts and Monuments*, 80.

441 Rupp, *Studies in the Making of the English Protestant Tradition*, 166.

442 Frith, *A Disputation of Purgatory*, 90.

443 Griffith Thomas (ed.), *The Principles of Theology*, 185.

444 Cranmer, Works II, 130.

that God sees Christ's accomplishment as being in each believer, as if it had been done by them.

> Thus farre God through Christe hath wroughte in suche sorte alone that our selves are mere patients working no more then dead and senceles matter, wood or stone or iron in the artificers hand, no more then the claye when the potter appointeth it to be framed for the honorable use, naie not so muche, for the matter whereupon the craftes man worketh he chooseth being moved with the fitnes which is in it to serve his turne: in us no such thing. Towching the reste, that which is laid for the foundacion of our faith importeth further that by him wee are called, that *we have redemption remission of synnes through his blood* health by his strypes Justice by him, that he doth *sanctefie his Church and make it glorious to him self,* that *entraunce into joye* shalbe gyven us by him, yea all thinges by him alone. Howebeit not so by him alone as if in us to our vocation the hering of the Gospell, to our justificacion faith, to our sanctification the fruites of the spirite, to our entraunce into reste perseveraunce in hope in faith in holynes weare not necessarye.[445]

Despite our imperfection, we were expected to hear the Gospel as a result of election and effectual calling, but only God made these possible in Christ.[446] Likewise, the faith needed for justification and the good works required for sanctification were expected from imperfect people,[447] but even before creation God considered these qualities to be perfect in us due to the work of Christ.[448] Furthermore, perseverance in faith,[449] hope and holiness was also expected from faulty human beings, but again, God considered these qualities to be complete in Christ on our behalf.

5.2.15 Faith, Reason and Revelation

Hooker defines faith as fundamentally consisting of the belief that "Jesus Christ is the only Saviour of the world."[450] Continuing his argument, Hooker returns to his twofold epistemology, this time applying it to human existence. Thus, man's life is both natural and spiritual. Here, though, Hooker does not spend much time investigating the natural

---

445 Hooker, *Justification* (*Works* V, 152.27-153.15).

446 Collinson, *Archbishop Grindal*, 41.

447 *ibid.* 41; Gibbs, "Richard Hooker's *Via Media* Doctrine of Justification", 220.

448 This connection between redemption and creation is essential to Hooker. See Haugaard, "The Scriptural Hermeneutics of Richard Hooker. Historical Contextualization and Teleology", in Donald S. Armentrout (ed.), *This Sacred History. Anglican Reflections for John Booty*, 167.

449 Morrel, "Richard Hooker, Theologian of the English Reformation", 9.

450 *ibid.* 137.27.

life, deciding instead to tend to the spiritual life. Hooker's view of spiritual life is corporate, meaning that Christ encompasses the whole of human existence. Spiritual life assumes the actual presence of Christ within the believer,[451] to the effect that Christ should actually dwell in his soul.[452] When the believer lives spiritually, his soul and mind are possessed by Christ. Spiritual truths may be discerned by the use of reason, but this only takes place with the help of divine revelation through the Holy Spirit's work.[453] Simply put, the Holy Spirit is the cause of spiritual life while Jesus Christ is its content. By connecting every aspect of salvation to God, Hooker reiterates his objective basis of salvation. At this point in his argument, it is sanctification – as part of salvation – that is rooted in God's active involvement in the believer's life through the Holy Spirit's work on the basis of Christ's work, an observation that Barnes makes as well.[454] It must be pointed out, however, that sanctification is not only the work of God. The work is primarily carried out by God, but sanctification requires that the believer be involved, specifically that he should listen to the teaching of the Gospel. Even though reason and revelation are extremely important in sanctification, Hooker ascribes the ultimate significance to revelation,[455] brought about by the Holy Spirit:[456]

> The cawse of life spirituall in us is christ, not carnally nor corporally inhabitinge but dwelling in the soule of man as a thinge, which when the minde apprehendeth it is said to inhabit and posses the mynde. The mind conceyveth Christe by hering the doctryne of christianitye. As the lighte of nature doth cawse the mind to apprehend those truthes which are meerely rationall so that saving truth which is far above the reache of humanitye be conceyved. All theis are ymplied wheresoever any one of them in mencioned as the cawse of spirituall life.[457]

---

451 Stone, *A History of the Doctrine of the Holy Eucharist*, 240. See also George, *The Protestant Mind of the English Reformation*, 348; "Hooker et la doctrine eucharistique de l'Eglise anglicane", *Revue des Sciences Philosophiques et Théologiques"* 58/2 (1974), 236; Booty, "Contrition in Anglican Spirituality: Hooker, Donne and Herbert", in William J. Wolf (ed.), *Anglican Spirituality* (Wilton: Morehouse-Barlow, 1982), 26.

452 For details about the presence of Christ in Hooker's theology, see Barry, *Masters in English Theology*, 46 and Rupp, *Studies in the Making of the English Protestant Tradition*, 168.

453 Hoopes, *Right Reason in the English Renaissance*, 127.

454 Barnes, *The Supplication of 1531*, xliii.a.

455 Bartlett, "What Has Richard Hooker to Say to Modern Evangelical Anglicanism?", *Anvil* 15/3 (1998), 198.

456 It should be noted here that, according to Ernst Troeltsch, Hooker was unable to reconcile reason with revelation, so he finally ended up in "a kind of mysticism". For details, see Troeltsch, *The Social Teaching of the Christian Churches* (London, 1931).

457 Hooker, *Justification* (*Works* V, 137.27-138.5).

Utilising his wealth of biblical knowledge, particularly Romans 8:10, Philippians 2:16 and Colossians 3:4, Hooker briefly sums up his doctrine of salvation, as indicated below.

5.2.16 Christ, the Gospel and the Holy Spirit

Three important elements come together to form Hooker's doctrine of salvation: Christ, the Gospel, and the Holy Spirit. Christ is the foundation, the essence of salvation,[458] without whom salvation would not have been possible. The Gospel is the means by which Christ is connected to humanity. Hooker has a keen awareness of the historical and geographical gap between the historical Jesus and contemporary generations. It is this historical sensitivity that causes him to include the Gospel within the broader plan of salvation. The last element in Hooker's brief summary of salvation is the Holy Spirit, who guarantees the accomplishment of salvation. Through the Holy Spirit's work, man is convinced of the truth of the Gospel and this leads him to believe in the historicity and effectiveness of Christ's work, whose image as Saviour is essential also to Cranmer.[459] Thus, Hooker wrote that "wherfore when we read that *the spirite is our lyfe* or *the word our lyfe* or *Christe our lyfe* we are in everye of theis to understand that our life is Christe by the hearing of the Gospell apprehended as a Saviour and assented unto through the power of the holy goste."[460]

Hooker begins to develop further the content of salvation through the extensive use of Scriptural texts. What Hooker wishes to make clear from the beginning is that salvation is intellectually comprehensive, able to be grasped by human reason.[461] For him, salvation is a new birth.[462] He follows Foxe in contending that human existence has radically changed from death and condemnation to life, as a direct result of salvation.[463] Hooker understands that this fundamental change

---

458 Booty, "The English Reformation: A Lively Faith and Sacramental Confession", 24; Booty, "An Elizabethan Addresses Modern Anglicanism. Richard Hooker and Theological Issues at the End of the Twentieth Century", 10; Booty, "The Law of Proportion: William Meade and Richard Hooker", St. Luke's Journal of Theology XXXIV/2 (1991), 26.

459 Cranmer, Annotations on the King's Book, 12.

460 Hooker, Justification (Works V, 138.5-9).

461 See also Jordan, The Development of Religious Toleration, 228, and Booty, "Hooker and Anglicanism", 233.

462 Lake, "Business as Usual? The Immediate Reception of Hooker's Ecclesiastical Polity", The Journal of Ecclesiastical History 52/3 (2001), 474.

463 Foxe, The Acts and Monuments, 71.

can be measured only in terms of results, but at the same time, these results depend totally on a spiritual reality, which he describes as possession. The individual must possess Christ in order to have life. This language of possession reveals that between Christ and the believer there must exist an intimate relationship.[464] From this truth, it is clear that life, the result of salvation, flows from Christ and ultimately from God, since Hooker believes Christ to be the Son of God, in accordance with the Scriptures.[465] He logically concludes that the origin of salvation is in God.[466]

The life that salvation offers is not ordinary, but everlasting, and this life is again a spiritual reality that flows from Christ. Hooker, like Bradford,[467] explains that Christ's work was primarily to bring to pass forgiveness and remission of sin,[468] which in itself is a sign of grace,[469] and that this is the reason why he had to die and then be raised again. For Hooker sin clearly results in death, a truth that Foxe also believed,[470] so the work of Christ not only forgot and remitted human sins, but also dealt death its blow of defeat forever. Here, Hooker again writes of salvation in terms of justification, the element that offers the believer the opportunity to be given a new status. The man who is justified has life, or better said, everlasting life, even as he lives on earth.[471] Possessing everlasting life is what proves that a believer can enjoy his new status in position before God. It would seem impossible for one to taste eternal life while continuing to live on finite earth. One would assume that eternal life begins when earthly life ends, but as far as God is concerned, the justified believer possesses eternal life while still living in history.[472] Although when seen in the lens of forensic justification God considers the justified believer to have eternal life even now in actual history, this still remains a factual reality. Man

---

464 Griffith Thomas (ed.), *The Principles of Theology*, 185.
465 Atkinson, *Richard Hooker and the Authority of Scripture, Tradition and Reason*, 129.
466 Hooker, *Justification* (Works V, 138.9-14).
467 Bradford, *Writings*, 217-218.
468 Rupp, *Studies in the Making of the English Protestant Tradition*, 166.
469 Keble, *The Works*, vol. 2, 552.
470 Foxe, *The Acts and Monuments*, 71.
471 For the importance of history in Hooker, see d'Entrèves, *Riccardo Hooker*, 49; Davis, "'For Conformities Sake': How Richard Hooker Used Fuzzy Logic and Legal Rhetoric against Political Extremes", in McGrade, *Richard Hooker and the Construction of Christian Community*, 339; Speed Hill, "Richard Hooker and the Rhetoric of History", *Churchman* 114/1 (2000), 13-14.
472 For Hooker's sense of history, see also Munz, *The Place of Hooker in the History of Thought*, 36.

possesses eternal life, only when this life is rooted in Christ.[473] Hooker takes great care in preserving the uttmost importance of the person of Christ when relating his doctrine of justification, for this aspect is what makes Hooker's entire line of reasoning secure and objective.[474]

In the same way, Hooker's soteriology has a strong pneumatological aspect, as he proclaims that eternal life can be preserved within human beings when the Holy Spirit is living within us, together with Christ the Lord, an important truth acknowledged also by Bradford.[475] Next, Hooker tackles the important issue of whether or not one can lose one's salvation. His conclusion follows the typical Reformed stance:[476] salvation can never be lost once one has truly experienced the new birth of God:[477]

> Whereupon I conclude that although in the first kinde no man lyveth that synneth not, and in the second as perfecte as any do lyve maie syn, yet sith *the man which is borne of god*, hath a promise that in him *the seed of God shall abide*, which seed is a sure preservatyve againste the synes of the third sute, greater and clerer assurance we cannot have of any thing then of this, that from such syns God shall preserve the righteous *as the aple of his eye* forever.[478]

Because Hooker's view manages to balance the work of God and sinful human nature, he is preoccupied with the presence of sin.

5.2.17 The Presence of Sin

Hooker's view of the presence of sin in man is fairly realistic,[479] yet he admits that God's work cannot be annulled. Once Christ's presence[480] and the Holy Spirit have been established within the believer,[481] the

---

473 Collinson, *Archbishop Grindal*, 41.

474 Hooker, *Justification* (*Works* V, 138.16-139.2).

475 Bradford, *Writings*, 314.

476 See also Jordan, *The Development of Religious Toleration*, 226.

477 Lake, "Business as Usual? The Immediate Reception of Hooker's *Ecclesiastical Polity*", *The Journal of Ecclesiastical History* 52/3 (2001), 474.

478 Hooker, *Justification* (*Works* V, 141.4-11). For details about assurance in Hooker, see also Grislis, "The Assurance of Faith according to Richard Hooker", in McGrade, *Richard Hooker and the Construction of Christian Community*, 239.

479 Grislis "The Assurance of Faith according to Richard Hooker", in McGrade, *Richard Hooker and the Construction of Christian Community*, 242.

480 See also George, *The Protestant Mind of the English Reformation*, 348.

481 Stone, *A History of the Doctrine of the Holy Eucharist*, 240.

new birth is secure and true.[482] It is unimaginable that Christ and the Spirit could dwell within a person who would later in life commit such a grave sin that he would lose his salvation. Since Christ is stronger than sin, the believer is preserved in the state of grace, even though it is true that everyone sins. Hooker closely follows the opinion of Foxe[483] in having a soteriology that is theocentric through and through, for Christ and the Spirit are portrayed as dwelling within the believer[484] and preventing him from committing sins that could break his relationship with God. This relationship between God and the believer[485] is based on a love too strong for God to allow his beloved to face sin alone. Every believer[486] can rest assured that the power of God which lives in him and the consequent existence in a perpetual state of grace maintains the firm foundation of salvation in the person and work of Christ,[487] a belief fundamental to Frith[488] and Bradford also.[489] Hooker argued earlier that directly denying Christ his rightful place as the foundation of faith led to condemnation.[490] According to his doctrine of salvation, Hooker now argues that it is impossible for a true believer to deny Christ directly, because the very fact that Christ and Spirit live within him prevents him for committing such a terrible sin.[491]

When speaking of salvation, Hooker constantly focuses on sinful human nature, which he believes continues to influence everyone that God has justified. To explain how it is possible for a justified believer to be forgiven the sins that take place after rebirth, Hooker returns to his twofold concept of repentance.[492] When a believer sins out of ignorance, he is saved through general repentance. In the same way, if a believer holds to a heretical teaching, God will grant him forgiveness through actual repentance. Concerning the sin of directly denying Christ, God

---

482 Lake, "Business as Usual? The Immediate Reception of Hooker's *Ecclesiastical Polity*", *The Journal of Ecclesiastical History* 52/3 (2001), 474.

483 Foxe, *The Acts and Monuments*, 71.

484 Rupp, *Studies in the Making of the English Protestant Tradition*, 168.

485 Griffith Thomas (ed.), *The Principles of Theology*, 185.

486 *ibid.* 186; Grislis, "The Assurance of Faith according to Richard Hooker", in McGrade, *Richard Hooker and the Construction of Christian Community*, 239.

487 Booty, "The English Reformation: A Lively Faith and Sacramental Confession", 24; Booty, "An Elizabethan Addresses Modern Anglicanism. Richard Hooker and Theological Issues at the End of the Twentieth Century", 10.

488 Frith, *Patrick Places*, 31-34.

489 Bradford, *The Works of John Bradford*, 312.

490 Griffith Thomas (ed.), *The Principles of Theology*, 185.

491 Hooker, *Justification* (*Works* V, 141.11-14).

492 Gibbs, "Richard Hooker's *Via Media* Doctrine of Repentance", *Harvard Theological Review* 84/1 (1991), 59.

will surely preserve the justified believer from ever committing such a sin.[493] Some might criticise Hooker's view as being overly optimistic, for it makes our salvation depend totally on God's will and subsequent action. But Hooker believes that human will and action is extremely important. He notes that there is a major difference between those who support a theological heresy but want to know the truth and those who stubbornly and persistently remain with errant doctrine without any desire for truth.[494]

Another important aspect to note when exploring Hooker's understanding of salvation is his belief that God will give the believer heavenly rewards in spite of man's sinful condition. God gives his rewards to the believer, not because the believer has done a series of good works, for even the good works he has done are affected by sin. The believer is rewarded because he has faith, which is the foundation and starting point for all good works.[495] Thus, God's rewards flow from his grace, not the merit assumed by the believer's good deeds. The believer is justified by God on the basis of faith, not works. Furthermore, the believer is justified by God, not only because of his faith, but because of Christ in whom he believes.[496] Hooker sees salvation as being totally by grace,[497] and diametrically opposed to the meritorious view of salvation. He defends this understanding of salvation by grace[498] by claiming that it is the only soteriology mentioned in Scripture.[499] Hooker's major preoccupation is to leave soteriology in the hands of God alone. Thus, his approach intends to ascribe all salvation to God, lest man have something about which he can boast. Hooker's theology is influenced by Barnes, especially in his view of grace as a gift[500] that has nothing to do with human efforts but has everything to do against human sin. Salvation comes from God, or as Tyndale put it, justification is also from God,[501] because of his mercy, as in Barnes,[502] and this salvation consists of the total remission of our sins,[503] as

493 Hooker, *Justification* (*Works* V, 142.1-7).
494 *ibid.* 142.20-143.1.
495 Collinson, *Archbishop Grindal*, 41.
496 Hooker, *Justification* (*Works* V, 159.25-160.4).
497 Secor, *Richard Hooker, Prophet of Anglicanism*, 185.
498 Malone, "The Doctrine of Predestination in the Thought of William Perkins and Richard Hooker", 112.
499 Atkinson, *Richard Hooker and the Authority of Scripture, Tradition and Reason*, 129.
500 Barnes, *A Supplication of 1531*, xliii.a; Griffith Thomas (ed.), *The Principles of Theology*, 185.
501 Tyndale, *Prologue to Romans*, 123.
502 Barnes, *The Supplication of 1531*, lviii.b-lix.a.
503 Keble, *The Works*, vol. 2, 552.

advocated by Foxe,[504] through the new birth[505] and the renewing of our hearts through the Holy Spirit's inner work in sanctification.[506] It seems that for Hooker, the mercy of God is the essence of salvation,[507] which is also stated by Bradford.[508] Therefore, God stands willing to forgive all those who sin out of ignorance, including Catholics.[509]

As he approaches the end of his discourse, Hooker resumes his former argument that devout Catholics who sin out of ignorance will be saved. Hooker does not see all sins as being equal; thus, he can picture God forgiving those who sin out of ignorance[510] but who had had an intense desire to know more truth about God.[511] Hooker defends his view by pointing to 1 Timothy 1:13, where Paul writes that he obtained God's mercy because he had sinned out of ignorance in unbelief.[512] The final paragraphs in the discourse serve as a plea against presumptuous sins and against those who persist in stubbornness and maliciousness by continuing to believe wrong doctrines and commit evil deeds. Even in this context, Hooker describes God as merciful, as also noted by Barnes,[513] but here he urges everyone to take great care in avoiding such conscious sins.[514] Lastly, Hooker challenges the believers to live out their justification, forgiving all who sin against them. The true believer must be willing to accord others forgiveness with a humble and peaceful mind[515] for peace is the essence of the believer's new relationship to God,[516] a truth also established by Foxe.[517]

---

504 Foxe, *The Acts and Monuments*, 80.
505 Lake, "Business as Usual? The Immediate Reception of Hooker's *Ecclesiastical Polity*", *The Journal of Ecclesiastical History* 52/3 (2001), 474.
506 Hooker, *Justification* (*Works* V, 160.23-161.11).
507 Booty, "The Law of Proportion: William Meade and Richard Hooker", *St. Luke's Journal of Theology* XXXIV/2 (1991), 26.
508 Bradford, *Writings*, 371-372.
509 Hooker, *Justification* (*Works* V, 162.18-19).
510 See also Walton, *The Lives*, 218, and Peter McGrath, *Papists and Puritans under Elizabeth I*, 320.
511 Hunt, *Religious Thought in England*, 62.
512 Hooker, *Justification* (*Works* V, 165.27-28).
513 Barnes, *The Supplication of 1531*, xciiii.b.
514 Hooker, *Justification* (*Works* V, 167.19-28).
515 *ibid.* 168.3-169.20.
516 Griffith Thomas (ed.), *The Principles of Theology*, 185.
517 Foxe, *The Acts and Monuments*, 72-73.

6. The Apology of Faith in *Master Hooker's Answer to the Supplication that Master Travers Made to the [Privy] Counsell* (1586)

Hooker's *A Learned and Comfortable Sermon of the Certaintie and Perpetuitie of Faith in the Elect* and his *A Learned Discourse of Justification, Workes and How the Foundation of faith is Overthrown* triggered the response of Walter Travers, who publicly criticised Hooker's doctrine of salvation. As a consequence, in 1586 Travers was no longer allowed to perform his preaching duties at the Temple Church "orelswhere", as he complains in his defence, *A Supplication made to the Privy Counsell*, in which he asks that his ministry should be restored on the virtue of the fact that he was not invited to explain personally the accusations forwarded against him.[1]

6.1 Travers' Accusations

In his *Supplication*, Travers lists the main points of Hooker's doctrine of justification, which stay at the core of his public criticism.

---

1   *Works* V, 171. See also Travers, *A Supplication to the Privy Counsel*, in *Works* V (190.18-191.21). It appears that John Whitgift, the Archbishop of Canterbury, who favoured Hooker, accused Travers of not being "laufully called to the function of the ministerie, nor allowed to preach, according to the lawes of this Church of England" (192.25-27) and for preaching "without lycence" (195.17). Travers' answer fosters proofs for the dismissal of both accusations. Firstly, he wrote he had been ordained by the "nationall Sinodes of the low countries, for the dyrection and guidaunce of their Churches" (193.2-3). Travers explained that his ordination was valid for the Church of England, as it also functioned in "all the french and Scottishe Churches" (193.4-5). In addition to this, he secondly mentioned that had had permission to preach from the bishop of London (195.21-22), who obviously acknowledged the validity of his ordination. Thirdly, Travers explained that he had never wanted to take Hooker's place as master of the Temple, although he should have been appointed to this position (195.29-197.30). Travers insists that the main reason for his public criticism of Hooker was the fact that he had discovered "sondrie unsound matters in his doctrine" (198.1).

6.1.1 Wrong Authority for the Doctrine of Predestination

Firstly, Hooker reportedly told Travers that, concerning the doctrine of predestination,[2] his best author was his own reason, when the latter urged him to seek the advice of other Church leaders in matters pertaining to doctrine.[3]

6.1.2 Wrong Doctrine of Assurance

Secondly, Travers wrote that Hooker preached that the assurance of what we believe by the Word of God was not so certain as the things we perceive by sense.[4] Travers immediately explains that this dogmatic statement should be reversed so that the things we believe by the Word of God be more certain than the things we perceive by sense or reason.[5]

6.1.3 Wrong Doctrine of Salvation

Thirdly, Travers approaches the very sensitive matter of the salvation of Catholic believers, which, for Hooker, proved to be of importance. Accordingly, Travers explains that Hooker held that the Catholic Church was a true Church of Christ.[6] Moreover, Travers wrote that, for Hooker, the Catholic Church is a holy Church by virtue of the fact that it has professed the revelation of God by his son, Jesus Christ. Travers admits Hooker has never said that the Catholic Church were pure and perfect, but Hooker nevertheless expressed his doubt regarding the impossibility that at least some Catholic believers could be saved. Hooker actually insisted that some Catholics could be granted salvation

---

2   For Hooker's understanding of predestination, see also Micks, "Richard Hooker as Theologian", 561.

3   Travers, *A Supplication*, in *Works* V (198.21-24). See also Gibbs, "Theology, Logic and Rhetoric in the Temple Controversy between Richard Hooker and Walter Travers", *Anglican Theological Review* LXV/2 (1983), 185.

4   Travers, *A Supplication*, in *Works* V (200.6-7).

5   *ibid.* 200.7-11.

6   Patterson, "Hooker on Ecumenical Relations: Conciliarism in the English Reformation", in McGrade, *Richard Hooker and the Construction of Christian Community*, 296; Secor, *Richard Hooker, Prophet of Anglicanism*, 185; Lake, "Business as Usual? The Immediate Reception of Hooker's *Ecclesiastical Polity*", *The Journal of Ecclesiastical History* 52/3 (2001), 465.

by God because they were unwillingly ignorant in doctrinal matters.[7] In Travers' opinion, such a teaching is contrary to Scripture, causes prejudice to the faith of Christ, and encourages sinners to continue in their wrong way of life to the destruction of their souls.[8] As such, Travers answered that, according to Scripture, those Catholic believers, who were dogmatically ignorant because they had been taught that faith was in part by works, were not saved. However, lest he should be accused of professing a very narrow understanding of salvation, Travers is prepared to admit that, should any Catholics be saved, this is not due to their ignorance,[9] but to their knowledge of and faith in the truth.[10]

6.1.4 Wrong Doctrine of Scripture

Fourthly, Hooker is believed to have said that Scripture did not ultimately judge whether a man who died within the Catholic Church could be saved or not. According to what Travers said of Hooker's doctrine, Catholics do have "a faith of Christ" and a "general repentaunce of all their errours", despite their understanding of justification as being partly by works and merits.[11] In the end, according to Travers, Hooker's understanding of Scripture is not adequate because it does not solve the problem of the salvation of Catholics.

6.1.5 Wrong Understanding of Protestant Doctrines

Fifthly, Travers explained that Hooker had tried to convince his audience that there were only small differences between the doctrine of the Church of Rome and the doctrine of the English Church, which for Travers is a faulty understanding of Protestant doctrines.[12] Likewise, according to Hooker, Catholics acknowledged all men as sinners, "even the blessed virgen", although some still hold she is free from sin. Furthermore, Catholic teaching has at its core the idea that the

---

7   Travers, *A Supplication*, in *Works* V (200.12-18).
8   *ibid.* 200.20-25.
9   See also Knox, *Walter Travers*, 70-88.
10 Travers, *A Supplication*, in *Works* V (200.26-201.6).
11 *ibid.* 201.20-202.4.
12 Milton, *Catholic and Reformed*, 211.

righteousness of Christ is the only meritorious cause[13] for the remission of sins and the realisation of justification.[14] Hooker, however, plainly admitted that the methodology of applying the righteousness of Christ is different in Catholic and English protestant theology.[15]

6.1.6 Wrong Understanding of the Catholic Doctrine of Justification

Sixthly, Hooker asserted that the Church of Rome did not directly overthrow the foundation of justification by Christ alone, in other words Catholics did not profess a wrong doctrine willingly, but only because of the teachings of their Church leaders.[16] Such a reality drew Hooker closer to the conclusion that salvation was available to Catholic believers.[17] Travers strongly rejected Hooker's assessment of the Catholic doctrine of justification and wrote that Catholic theology directly denies the salvation of humankind by Christ or by faith alone, without works of the law.[18]

6.1.7 Wrong Doctrine of Good Works

Seventhly, as the last theological argument against his opponent, Travers wrote that Hooker considered the works added to justification by Catholics to be works commanded by God and, therefore, accepted by him. Hooker then reportedly said that anybody who professed Christ and possibly justification by works should be cheerful as God is not a "captious sophister" but "a mercifull God", who will not condemn the ignorance[19] of those who wholeheartedly confess at least Christ.[20] It should be said here that Tyndale spoke of a certain

---

13   Toon, *Foundations for Faith*, 94. See also Booty, "The Spirituality of Participation in Richard Hooker", *Sewanee Theological Review* 38/1 (1994), 11; Voak, *Richard Hooker and Reformed Theology*, 178.

14   See also Rupp, *Studies in the Making of the English Protestant Tradition*, 168, and Allison, *The Rise of Moralism*, 3.

15   Travers, *A Supplication*, in *Works* V (203.14-21).

16   For details about how the Church of Rome distorted the doctrine of justification by faith alone, see Bauckham, "Hooker, Travers and the Church of Rome in the 1580s", 40; Milton, *Catholic and Reformed*, 146.

17   Travers, *A Supplication*, in *Works* V (203.29-204.3).

18   *ibid.* 204.10-14.

19   See Hunt, *Religious Thought in England*, 62, and Peter McGrath, *Papists and Puritans under Elizabeth I*, 320.

20   Travers, *A Supplication*, in *Works* V (206.22-208.5).

justification by works, which seems to be the process of sanctification, only after stating the main tenets of justification by faith.[21] For Travers, however, this theory is so preposterous that it does not even deserve to be analysed: "the absurditie of which speech I need not to stand uppon."[22]

6.2 Hooker's Defence

It should be said that Travers' *Supplication* had a wide circulation due to the reasonable character of his theological arguments. Such being the case, Hooker was put in the position of replying in order to clarify the differences between himself and Travers. It is a known fact that Travers addressed his letter to the Privy Council, where he had some supporters. As he was keenly aware of the large acceptance of Travers' theology, Hooker was forced to defend his doctrine of salvation and his understanding of faith, so he wrote his *Answer* to the *Supplication* in March or April 1586. The *Answer* was cleverly addressed to his own supporter, John Whitgift, the Archbishop of Canterbury.[23]

6.2.1 The Authority for the Doctrine of Predestination

In order to offer a clear explanation of the theological differences between his theology and that of Travers, Hooker chose to deal separately with all the points discovered to be false by his opponent. Thus, he begins with the doctrine of predestination,[24] in respect to which Travers accused Hooker to have used his own reason for its assessment rather than the Word of God. It seems that Hooker was not interested in presenting a clear theological argument in his favour at this point but rather used an obvious ecclesiastical support for whatever he had said in general. So, he mentions that he taught his doctrine publicly to an audience, a Church, which could have refuted his arguments, should they be false or contrary to Scripture. In

---

21 Tyndale, *Prologue upon James*, 161-162, and Tyndale, *Prologue to the Book of Numbers*, 69. See also Booty, "The Spirituality of Participation in Richard Hooker", *Sewanee Theological Review* 38/1 (1994), 11.

22 Travers, *A Supplication*, in *Works* V (208.6-7).

23 *Works* V, 211.

24 For details, see Cromartie, "Theology and Politics in Richard Hooker's Thought", *History of Political Thought* XXI/1 (2000), 48.

addition, Hooker resorts to the ecclesiastical authority of the Bishop of London, who apparently was in the auditorium when Hooker had preached his views on predestination. Consequently, it seems clear for Hooker that Travers had a different hermeneutic, which led him towards his own private interpretation of the doctrine of predestination. Hooker displays here quite a stern attitude towards Travers, accusing him of being somehow theologically narrow-minded as he alleges that only Travers and his supporters understood the predestination lecture differently and, according to Hooker, this happened because they had read only a limited number of books on the subject at stake:

> This matter was not broched in a blynde alley or uttered where none was to heare it, that had skill with auchtoritye to controll, or covertly insynuated by some glydinge sentence. That which I taughte was att Paules crosse. It was not hudled in amonges other matteres in suche sorte that it could passe without notynge, it was opened, it was proved, it was some reasonable tyme stood uppon. I see not which way my Lord of London who was presente and heard it can excuse so greate a faulte, as paciently without rebuke or controlmente afterwards to heare any man there teache *otherwise then the Word of God doth,* not as it is understood by the private interpretacion of somme one or two men, or by a speciall construccion receyved in some fewe bookes but *as it is understood by all the Churches professinge the Gospell,* by them all and therefore even by our owne also amonges others.[25]

To conclude, Hooker was convinced the authority for his doctrine of predestination is the ecclesiastical See of the bishop of London and the Churches which proclaim the Gospel (a hint at Protestant Churches). The final authority, however, in matters concerning the doctrine of predestination is the Word of God.

6.2.2 The Doctrine of Assurance

The second point of controversy between Hooker and Travers is the assurance of faith,[26] which is also fundamental to Tyndale.[27] In Hooker's theology, faith is closely connected to, and actually refers to, the spiritual realm or spiritual things. The theological problem that emerged was whether human beings were assured of spiritual things

---

25 Hooker, *Answer to the Supplication* (*Works* V, 236.5-18).
26 See also Wallace Jr., *Puritans and Predestination,* 77; Grislis, "The Assurance of Faith according to Richard Hooker", in McGrade, *Richard Hooker and the Construction of Christian Community,* 239.
27 Tyndale, *Exposition of Matthew,* 189.

by means of God's Word or by means of the senses. Travers accused Hooker of saying that the assurance concerning spiritual things which man acquires by his senses is stronger than the assurance of spiritual things which man obtains by the Word of God.[28] Hooker does not deny this affirmation but explains that a certain misunderstanding has caused Travers to launch the accusation because the entire problem lies within the realm of theological interpretation and methodology. Thus, should spiritual things be considered, it is an objective reality that they exist regardless of whether people are aware of them or not. Hooker includes the Word of God and its promises within the wider realm of spiritual things, as in Foxe.[29] He is ready to admit that even faith is an objective reality pertaining to them because, in the end, we believe God's promises by faith, as also suggested by Tyndale.[30] However, man is not a perfect creature and consequently the assurance that he acquires concerning spiritual things is not perfect at all. Hooker actually explains that the teaching of the Word of God and his own explanation of its theology is fully theological in methodology. Thus, he admits the promises of God's Word are sure, but the assurance which man has concerning these promises and the entire realm of spiritual things is not perfectly certain. Hooker states that God himself uses arguments taken from human experience in order to prove the reality of spiritual things. If spiritual things are not fully clear to man, then man himself is to blame, not God who is always willing to disclose the reality of spiritual things to humanity. In the end, the entire controversy is a matter of hermeneutics, as Travers approached the assurance of faith theologically, from God's perspective, while Hooker tackled it anthropologically, from man's perspective. Thus, from God's perspective, the assurance of faith should be certain as the objectivity of spiritual things is theologically beyond doubt, but from man's perspective the assurance of faith or of spiritual things is less certain. Hooker writes:

> The nexte thinge discovered is an opinion aboute the assuraunce of mens perswasyon in matters of faith: I have taughte he saith *That the assurance of thinges which we beleeve by the word is not so certeyne as of that we perceyve by sense.* And is it as certayne? Yea I taughte as he hym self I truste woulde not denye that the thinges which God doth promys in his worde are surer unto us then any thinge we touche handle or see, but are we so sure and certeyne of them? if we be, why doth God so often prove his promises unto

---

28 Grislis, "The Assurance of Faith according to Richard Hooker", in McGrade, *Richard Hooker and the Construction of Christian Community*, 246.

29 Foxe, *The Acts and Monuments*, 71.

30 Tyndale, *Prologue to Romans*, 124.

us as he doth by arguments taken from our sensible experiences? We must
be surer of the profe then of the thinge proved, otherwise it is no profe.[31]

According to Hooker's understanding of the doctrine of justification,
the assurance of faith is part of the spiritual life of the justified person,[32]
as in Frith.[33] Nevertheless, the justified person continues to live within a
body which is still affected by sin; thus, the assurance of the justified
person concerning faith and spiritual things will be far from perfect.

6.2.3 The Doctrine of Good Works

At this point, Hooker discusses the importance of Scripture and of
spiritual discipline in the life of justified people, which also discloses
his view of good works. The steadfastness and power of faith depend
on the spiritual life of whoever has been justified by God. Spiritual
discipline entails daily prayer and striving in order that the assurance
of faith should increase because, in Tyndale for instance, it is by faith
that we know we may increase in salvation and in good works.[34] It is
clear from Hooker's argument that this entire process, which is directed
towards the augmentation of the assurance of faith, is part of
sanctification, which follows justification.

> Howe is it that if tenne men do all looke upon the moone, every one of
> them knoweth it as certenly to be the moone as another: But many
> beleevinge one and the same promis all have not one and the same fulnesse
> of perswasion? Howe falleth it out that men beinge assured of any thinge
> by sense can be no surer of it then they are, whereas the strongest in faith
> that lyveth uppon the earth hath always neede to labor and stryve, and
> praie that his assuraunce concerninge heavenly and spirituall thinges maie
> growe increasse and be augmented?[35]

Thus, the good works which are done by the justified man, such as
prayer and the study of the Word of God,[36] are not a condition for

---

31   Hooker, *Answer to the Supplication* (*Works* V, 236.20-30); Grislis, "The Assurance of
     Faith according to Richard Hooker", in McGrade, *Richard Hooker and the Construction
     of Christian Community*, 239.

32   Griffith Thomas (ed.), *The Principles of Theology*, 186.

33   Frith, *Patrick Places*, 31-34.

34   Tyndale, *Prologue to Romans*, 125.

35   Hooker, *Answer to the Supplication* (*Works* V, 236.30-237.7); Grislis, "The Assurance of
     Faith according to Richard Hooker", in McGrade, *Richard Hooker and the Construction
     of Christian Community*, 239.

36   McGrade, "Richard Hooker: Apologist for All Seasons", *St. Mark's Review* 141 (1990),
     16; Wall, "Hooker's 'Faire Speeche': Rhetorical Strategies in the *Laws of Ecclesiastical
     Polity*", in Donald S. Armentrout (ed.), *This Sacred History. Anglican Reflections for*

receiving justification, but a necessity of sanctification for the empo-
wering of the assurance of faith.[37]

6.2.4 The Doctrine of Salvation

When it came to identifying the very core of the whole controversy,
Hooker himself admitted it was about the doctrine of salvation with
special reference to justification. In his *Supplication*, Travers accused
Hooker of being too biased towards conceding that there were only
small matters of difference between Catholics and Protestants in regard
to justification. Hooker's answer is again an exposition of theological
methodology, as he wants to make sure that distinctions between the
two types of theology are better understood. This is why he shows the
points of agreement first, and only then discloses the affirmations in
which they are different. Hooker explains that he uses this method in
order to sort out the points of agreement and disagreement between
Catholics and English Protestants concerning the doctrine of justification, and consequently, the doctrine of grace:

> In settinge the question betwene the Churche of Rome and us aboute Grace
> and justificacion, least I shoulde gyve them occasion to saie (as comonly
> they do) that when we cannot refute theire opinions we propose to our
> selves suche insted of theirs as we can refute I tooke it for the beste and
> most perspicuous waie of teaching to declare first howe farre we do agree,
> and then to shewe our dysagreament, not generally (as master Travers his
> wordes would cary it, for the easyer fasenynge of that uppon me, where
> with (savinge onely by hym) I was never in my lyfe touched), but aboute
> the matter of Justificacion onely, for farther I had not cawse to medle at
> that tyme.[38]

The next step Hooker takes after the clarification of this theological
methodology is to identify the very words of Travers' accusation
regarding the doctrinal differences between Catholics and English
Protestants. So, he draws attention to the formulation of Travers, who
wrote in his *Supplication* that Hooker had said that, between Catholic
and English Protestant theology, there was consent in the most
important dogmatic issues and disagreement in things which lack
theological weight. Hooker, however, refutes Travers' formulation and
immediately fosters a counterargument as he informs his readers that

---

John Booty, 133; Haigh, *English Reformations*, 283; Schoeck, "From Erasmus to Hooker:
An Overview", in McGrade (ed.), *Richard Hooker and the Construction of Christian
Community*, 71.

37   Griffith Thomas (ed.), *The Principles of Theology*, 186.

38   Hooker, *Answer to the Supplication* (*Works* V, 238.3-13).

Catholics and Protestants do not agree in respect to the essence of the remedy for sin. Both theologies agree that there is a remedy for sin, and this medicine, as Hooker calls it, is used by Christ himself to cure human sinful nature. Consequently, both Catholics and Protestants do have a Christological oriented soteriology, by virtue of their acknowledgement of the importance of the work of Christ and of the efficiency of the remedy for sin. Nevertheless, for Hooker, this is not enough to make a complete theological unification between Catholics and Protestants in soteriological matters. He explains that the main difference between the two theologies is the essence of the remedy for sin and, by inference, the very way of its application to people's lives:

> What was then my offence in this case? *I did* (as he sayth) *so sett it out as if we hadd consented in the greatest and weightiest pointes and differed onely in smaller matters*: It will not be found when it cometh to the ballaunce a lighte difference where *we dissagree* as I did acknowledge that we do *aboute the very essence of the medicine, whereby Christ cureth our disseaze.*[39]

So, there are differences between Catholics and Protestants concerning the doctrine of salvation. For Hooker, two such differences are very important: the essence of salvation (with reference to justification), and the way to apply salvation.

6.2.5 Hooker's Understanding of the Catholic Doctrine of Justification

In direct connection to the doctrine of justification, Hooker discusses the doctrine of original sin, especially from the perspective of Catholic Mariology. Hooker's assessment of the Catholic dogma concerning "the blessed virgen" should be understood within the wider condition of sinful humanity. Thus, despite her privileged place in the theology of the Church of Rome, Hooker seems to draw the conclusion that, for Catholics, Mary's human-spiritual condition is similar to the state of the rest of humanity. This infers that her nature is affected by sin to the same extent to which the rest of humankind has been exposed. Hooker, however, is aware of the fact that this doctrine had not gained a unanimous appreciation within Catholic Christianity. Accordingly, there were then some Catholic theologians who still shared the theory that Mary was free from sin, in regard to both her conception and life. In attempting to prove that the dominant Catholic view is that Mary was affected by sin like the rest of man and women, Hooker chooses to launch an audacious explanation, which is far from being thoroughly

---

39   *ibid.* 238.13-18.

persuasive. Hooker uses the writings of Bonaventure to explain that all human beings have fallen into sin so that all of them are deeply affected by sin. The English divine seems to have been fully convinced by Bonaventure's theology regarding original sin, although the former Catholic cardinal and Franciscan monk is far from being *the* most representative theologian of medieval Catholicism.[40] Clinging to this particular argument which he had found in Bonaventure, Hooker expresses his conviction that, since Bonaventure's time (he died in 1274), the number of theologians who had been in favour of Mary's sinfulness was larger that the number of theologians who supported her innocence:

> The one is I said *they acknowledge all men synners even the blessed virgen though some of them free her from synne.* Put the case I had affirmed that onely some of them free her from synne and had delyvered it as the most curraunt opinione amonges them that she was conceaved in synne, doth not *Bonaventure* saie playnely *omnes fere* In a manner all men do holde this? doth he not bringe many reasons wherefore all men should hold it, were their voice synce that tyme ever counted, and theire number found smaller which hold it, then theires that hold the contrary?[41]

The only conclusion is that, at least for Hooker, medieval and early modern Catholicism has generally held the pervasive character of sin, which should be applied to everybody, including the famous exception so oftentimes represented by the Virgin Mary, especially towards the end of the Middle Ages.[42] Hooker has a very clear mind about justification in Catholic and Protestant theology and he is far to good a theologian to let his entire argumentation be lost by Travers' accusation. This is why he always quotes Travers and the affirmations

---

40 J.C.H. Aveling believes Hooker was sympathetic to moderate Catholicism. For details, see Aveling, "The English Clergy in the 16th and 17th Centuries", in J.C.H. Aveling, D.M. Loades, and H.R. McAdoo (eds), *Rome and the Anglicans. Historical and Doctrinal Aspects of Anglican-Roman Catholic Relations* (Berlin: W. de Gruyter, 1982), 94-95.

41 Hooker, *Answer to the Supplication* (*Works* V, 239.6-14).

42 Although Bonaventure is not *the* most representative figure of medieval Catholicism, Hooker does make a point by using his arguments. Bonaventure died in 1274, which is the year when death claimed the life of another famous Catholic theologian, Thomas Aquinas. Both Aquinas and Bonaventure were "maculists", or promoters of Mary's sinfulness. For them, Mary was a woman who shared the common condition of sinful humanity, she was affected by sin, like every human being. This view did not represent the dominant interpretation of Catholic Mariology as it was countered by the theology of the "immaculists", who claimed that Christ somehow managed to keep Mary free from sin. The theory of the maculists was promoted especially by Duns Scotus, and it prevailed in the Late Middle Ages. For more details, see Alister McGrath, *Historical Theology. An Introduction to the History of Christian Thought* (Oxford: Blackwell, 1998), 115, 121.

uttered against him, including the opinions reached at the Council of
Trent, which, overall, do not appear to be of any help for Hooker's
argument. For his part, Travers used the doctrine issued at the Council
of Trent as normative for the entire Catholic theology, or at least for the
Catholic theology of his time. Hooker is well aware of the reality of
Tridentine Catholicism, which is contrary to the teaching of its masters,
Aquinas and Bonaventure, in matters pertaining to the doctrine of
original sin and especially to the most disputed Mariology. Catholic
theologians gathered at the Council of Trent agreed with the doctrine of
the immaculate conception, at least by inference or mere utterance
though not by an elaborate theological exposition:

> This same holy Sinod doth nevertheless declare, that it is not its intention
> to include in this decree, where original sin is treated of, the blessed and
> immaculate Virgin Mary, the mother of God; but that the constitutions of
> Pope Sixtus IV., of happy memory, are to be observed, under the pains
> contained in the said constitutions, which it renews.[43]

It is clear that for Post-Reformation Catholicism, Mariology was
somehow separated from the doctrine of original sin. The entire human
race was indeed affected by original sin, but in the case of the Virgin
Mary, things seemed to have suffered a slight alteration, as if she had
been granted a special favour by God in respect to her own human
nature. Such a theory of original sin cannot but exert a particular
influence on the doctrine of justification, which thus becomes schizo-
phrenic in the sense that it is now dual: there is a type of justification
which applies to humanity in general and another type of justification
which is valid only in the case of Mary. The matter at stake is utterly
important, because the justified person will continue to commit sins as
a result of the fact that he or she lives in a body which is affected by
original sin. This is what both Catholics and Protestants have declared
– and Hooker knows this very well indeed – but for Catholics,
Mariology seems to be an exception to the general rule of justification,
especially from the perspective of original sin, which is the very source
of daily transgression. The formulation issued by the theologians at
Trent is revelatory:

> If any one saith, that a man once justified can sin no more, nor lose grace,
> and that therefore he that falls and sins was never truly justified; or, on the
> other hand, that he is able, during his whole life, to avoid all sins, even

---

43 "The Canons and Decrees of the Council of Trent", Decree concerning Original Sin,
    Session V, the 17th of June 1546, in Philip Schaff, *The Creeds of Christendom*, vol. 2
    (Grand Rapids: Baker Books, 1996), 88.

those that are venial – except by a special privilege from God, as the Church holds in regard of the Blessed Virgen: let him be anathema.[44]

Catholic Mariology established at Trent did not help Hooker's argument on justification and original sin. Travers realised the situation and used it against him. Hooker was aware of it but he could not give up so easily when it came to a theological debate. So Hooker explained that Tridentine Catholicism, although up to date in those days, did not and could not be representative for the entire Catholic tradition. This is why he resorts to the theology of Bonaventure, as it has been already shown, and he must have known that Aquinas shared the same view regarding original sin and justification.[45] Actually, Hooker openly admits that the decisions taken at Trent are contrary to the general Catholic view of original sin as applied to the case of the Virgin Mary. The theology of the Council of Trent seemed to be to the detriment of Hooker's argument but he used it in such a way as to turn it to his favour and concluded that the general Catholic perception in matters of original sin was similar to the Protestant ideology, regardless of whether the Virgin Mary comes into the issue or not, because she shares the sinful nature of the whole humanity:

> Lett the question then be whether I might saye, the moste of the *acknowledge all men synners even the blessed virgen her self*; to shewe thet theire generall receyved opinion is the contrary the Tridentine Counsell is alledged peradventur not altogether so consideratly, for if that Councell have by resolute determynacion freed her, if it hold as master Travers saith it doth *that she was free from synne*, then must the Churche of Rome needes condemne them that holde the contrary.[46]

Hooker sensed the tension between his view of historical Catholicism and his apprehension of Tridentine Catholicism. Although throughout the history of Catholicism he had detected a lack of consensus regarding the doctrine of original sin with reference to Mary, the case was evidently different with Catholic doctrine of the Council of Trent, which asserted that Mary was preserved without sin. Hooker is aware that this doctrine is contrary to the teaching of leading Catholic figures like Aquinas and Bonaventure,[47] but at this point it seems that he is not interested in continuing his lecture on the evolution of Catholic doctrine before Trent and neither is he willing to let Travers draw him

---

44   "Canons and Decrees of the Council of Trent", Decree on Justification, Session VI, the 13th of January 1547, Chapter XVI, Canon XXIII, in Philip Schaff, *The Creeds of Christendom*, vol. 2 (Grand Rapids: Baker Books, 1996), 115.

45   See Hooker, *Answer to the Supplication* (*Works* V, 240.3-5).

46   *ibid.* 239.14-21.

47   *ibid.* 240.2-5.

near to Catholicism of any sort. The master of the Temple also perceives with accuracy the claims which Travers has set against him. As
such, Hooker knew that Travers wanted to make him a promoter of a
mild attitude towards Catholic theology, which in those days was
surely not the best goal to aim at. Such a position, if proved, would
certainly have attracted the notice of both lay and religious authorities
of England, like the Queen, Parliament and the Archbishop of
Canterbury.

Hooker, however, is not intimidated by Travers' claims, and he
cautiously sets up to work out a theological dismissal of all accusations
which had been presented against his religious view. Thus, he begins
with an accurate description of the Catholic doctrine of original sin in
matters of Mariology, as perceived by the Council of Trent. In his
opinion, the Council of Trent was not preoccupied to give a normative
definition regarding Mary's situation, which was supposedly left
within the reality of theological obscurity. In contrast to the attitude of
Catholic divines at Trent, Hooker explains his own position concerning
the theology of the council, as he claims that his description of
Tridentine Catholic doctrine is clear and precise. Mary is free from sin
due to Christ, but the rest of humanity is not exempted from the presence of sin, which is shared by every human being:[48]

> Fynally that the fathers of Trente have not sett downe any certenty aboute
> this question, but left it doubtfull and indifferente, nowe whereas my
> wordes, which I had sett downe in writinge before I uttered them were
> indede thies *Although they imagin that the mother of our Lord Jesus Christ were*
> *for his honor and by his speciall protection preserved cleane from all synne, yet*
> *concerninge the rest they teach as we do that all have synned.*[49]

At this particular point of his discourse, Hooker not only defend
himself but also launches a counterattack against Travers, whom he
accuses of misreading his manuscripts. This is very important as it
shows that Hooker did not have the slightest intention of getting close
to Catholicism for the sake of an easy religious reconciliation, but
actually identifies the core of the theological disagreement between
Catholicism and Protestant dogma. Hooker discloses the fact that
Travers was not in the possession of the most accurate version of his
theological affirmations. Thus, following Travers' version, in his desire
to draw Catholicism closer to Protestantism, Hooker would supposedly
have asserted that Catholic theology upheld the pervasiveness of
original sin, which affected everybody including Mary. This could have

---

48   Grislis, "The Assurance of Faith according to Richard Hooker", in McGrade, *Richard*
      Hooker and the Construction of Christian Community, 242.
49   Hooker, *Answer to the Supplication* (*Works* V, 241.6-12).

been a pertinent accusation but Hooker is not willing to assume it. He rather corrects Travers and writes that his statement was slightly though significantly different. According to Hooker, the Catholic theology of the late sixteenth century was not in line with Catholicism in general in promoting the sinfulness of Mary but it allowed for her innocence while the rest of humanity was affected by sin. In he following paragraph, Hooker presents the difference between the statement which Travers ascribed to him and the formulation which he had actually written:

> Against my wordes they mighte with more pretence take excepcion because so many of them thincke shee had synne, which exception notwithstandinge the proposicion beinge indefynite and the matter contingent, they cannot take becawse they graunt that many whome they counte grave and devout among them thincke shee was cleere from all synne, but whether master Travers did note my wordes hym self or take them uppon the credit of someother mens notynge, the tables were faulty where in it was noted. *All men synners even the blessed virgen,* when my speeche was rather *All men excepte the blessed virgen.*[50]

Hooker continues to come forward with proofs of Travers' misreading of his texts. The next such example is directly linked to the doctrine of justification.

6.2.6 Hooker's Understanding of Protestant Doctrines

Travers wrote that Hooker had said of the Catholics that they held the righteousness of Christ[51] as the only meritorious cause[52] of the remission of sins.[53] There is, however, a distinction between Catholics and Protestants, and this refers to the way of applying the righteousness of Christ to people: "To leave this, another fault he fyndeth, that I sayde *They teache Christs righteousnes to be the onely meritorious cause of takinge awaye synne and differ from us onely in applying of it.*"[54] This seems to be a very straightforward theological statement but Hooker was apparently disturbed by it. It is clear that Travers attempted to draw Hooker closer to the Catholic position once more by

---

50 *ibid.* 241.12-21.
51 See also Tyndale, *Exposition of First John*, 117. See also Booty, "The Spirituality of Participation in Richard Hooker", *Sewanee Theological Review* 38/1 (1994), 11.
52 Toon, *Foundations for Faith*, 94; Voak, *Richard Hooker and Reformed Theology*, 178.
53 See also Cranmer, *The 1538 Articles*, 4, and Allison, *The Rise of Moralism*, 3.
54 Hooker, *Answer to the Supplication* (*Works* V, 241.21-24).

the concision of the argument. Hooker's reply was longer and not entirely revelatory at a first glance:

> I did saie and do, *they teache as we doe; That althoughe Christ be the onelye meritorious cause of our Justice, yet as a medicyne whiche is made for helth doth not heale by beinge made but by beinge applied, so by the merits of Christ there canne be no life or Justification without the application of his merits. But aboute the manner of applyinge Christ aboute the number and power of means whereby he is applyed, we dissent from them.* This of our dissentinge from them is acknowledged.[55]

The hermeneutical key of interpreting this text is not primarily theological but rather literary. When he wrote this passage, Hooker did not use only his theology. He seems to have successfully worked with a literary device which brought the whole argument to his benefit: "*they teache as we do.*" The importance of Hooker's explanation lies in these five words. Travers' brief statement unwillingly inferred that Hooker's alleged words were firstly a direct affirmation of the Catholic doctrine. It is very obvious that Hooker was dissatisfied with such a possible hint, and he refuted Travers by writing that the Catholics "*teache as we do*" before explaining the doctrine. Unlike Travers, Hooker's intention is to focus the attention on the Protestant approach of justification, not on the Catholic understanding of it. When reading the words of Travers, it is as if one had read a Catholic phrase. With Hooker, however, things are different, and his entire paragraph seems primarily Protestant. He acknowledges that Catholics say the same, but what he wrote was intended to be Protestant.

Thus, Hooker's explanation contains a number of theological points. Firstly, his entire reply is Protestant. The fact that Catholics profess the same interpretation of justification is incidental rather than a matter of express notification, as it seems to have been for Travers. Secondly, the meritorious cause of justification is Christ only.[56] This means that the foundation of justification is objective, as it lies in Christ[57] not in humanity. In other words, justification is a theological reality which was initiated and supported by God in Christ. Thirdly, justification is likened to a medicine – obviously with reference to sin. The remission of sin appears to be the result of justification,[58] as in

55   *ibid.* 241.24-242.2.

56   Toon, *Foundations for Faith*, 94; Voak, *Richard Hooker and Reformed Theology*, 178.

57   Collinson, *Archbishop Grindal*, 41; Booty, "The English Reformation: A Lively Faith and Sacramental Confession", 24; Booty, "An Elizabethan Addresses Modern Anglicanism. Richard Hooker and Theological Issues at the End of the Twentieth Century", 10; Kirby, "The Paradigm of Chalcedonian Christology in Richard Hooker's Discourse on Grace and the Church", *Churchman* 114/1 (2000), 23-25.

58   Rupp, *Studies in the Making of the English Protestant Tradition*, 166.

Foxe,[59] which is a sign of grace.[60] However, justification and the remission of sins are closely related, which is evident in Cranmer.[61] Hooker writes about the merits of Christ,[62] also important to Foxe,[63] which are the very heart of justification[64] and which seem to point to the atoning death of Christ,[65] as also advocated by Tyndale.[66] Fourthly, justification is not a mystical medicine but an active reality which transforms human life, which is also the convinction of Barnes.[67] Justification is effective only if applied to people. Hooker does not explain here how the application of justification should be performed. Nevertheless, he makes an interesting connection between justification and life. One cannot say for sure whether Hooker did this on purpose, but the link between justification and life speaks clearly of what Hooker had in mind when he considered justification. The purpose of justification is the remission of sins and obviously the subsequent gift of life. Fifthly, there is a difference between Protestants and Catholics when it comes to the method of applying justification.

Hooker may have disliked Travers trying to make him a protector of Catholicism but, in the end, he could not but be fair. Assuming the risk of dull repetition, he mentions some Protestant fundamental doctrines, which are identical to Catholic teachings. As far as justification is concerned, sin hinders people from sharing the blessings of God. It is only Christ, or the merits of Christ, which restore the path to God's blessings.[68] The essence of salvation, and implicitly of justification, is the death of Christ,[69] which must be applied in order that justification be effective.[70] The purpose of justification is the glory of God, which seems to be fundamental to Cranmer,[71] and the happiness of man. The

---

59 Foxe, *The Acts and Monuments*, 80.

60 Keble, *The Works*, vol. 2, 552.

61 Cranmer, *The 1538 Articles*, 4.

62 Stanwood, "Of Prelacy and Polity in Milton and Hooker", in Margo Swiss and David Kent (eds), *Heirs of Fame. Milton and Writers of the English Renaissance*, 69.

63 Foxe, *The Acts and Monuments*, 76.

64 Rupp, *Studies in the Making of the English Protestant Tradition*, 167.

65 Lake, *Anglicans and Puritans?*, 162.

66 Tyndale, *Prologue to Romans*, 125.

67 Barnes, *The Supplication of 1531*, xliii.a.

68 Griffith Thomas (ed.), *The Principles of Theology*, 185; Stanwood, "Of Prelacy and Polity in Milton and Hooker", in Margo Swiss and David Kent (eds), *Heirs of Fame. Milton and Writers of the English Renaissance*, 69.

69 Booty, "The Law of Proportion: William Meade and Richard Hooker", *St. Luke's Journal of Theology* XXXIV/2 (1991), 26.

70 Lake, *Anglicans and Puritans?*, 162.

71 Cranmer, *Annotations on the King's Book*, 12.

efficient cause of justification is the mercy of God,[72] as in Barnes.[73] This is a clear affirmation of God's primacy in salvation, also acknowledged by Bradford.[74] The instrumental cause of justification is baptism[75] and the meritorious cause is Christ.[76] There is a close connection between Christ, or the work of Christ, and the result of justification, which is the remission of sins,[77] very much in line with Cranmer.[78] Justification is not possible without Christ, whose passion is the only foundation of a life which lacks the guilt of sin,[79] original and actual.[80]

Although the doctrine of justification in Protestant thought is similar to Catholic teaching in such a considerable number of points, Hooker has to disclose the utter difference between the two theological traditions. The formal cause of justification is, for Catholics, the inherent righteousness of man.[81] This interpretation allows for a significant role of man in the process of justification, which means that it is no longer entirely the work of God.[82] God may have the primacy in justification, but he does not have full control over its realisation in or application to humanity.[83]

Another major point of debate between Travers and Hooker was the salvation of the Catholics. Travers alleged that Hooker's doctrine caused prejudice to the faith of Christ and encouraged lost people to continue with a life of sin. Hooker does not foster an elaborate theological reply but the mentions that such a claim would actually

---

72 The mercy of God is manifested in Christ, so the efficient cause is Christ as God, see Voak, *Richard Hooker and Reformed Theology*, 178. Toon, *Foundations for Faith*, 94.

73 Barnes, *The Supplication of 1531*, lviii.b-lix.a.

74 Bradford, *Writings*, 371-372.

75 Voak, *Richard Hooker and Reformed Theology*, 178.

76 Toon, *Foundations for Faith*, 94; Voak, *Richard Hooker and Reformed Theology*, 178.

77 Rupp, *Studies in the Making of the English Protestant Tradition*, 166.

78 Cranmer, *The 1538 Articles*, 4.

79 Morrel, "Richard Hooker, Theologian of the English Reformation", 9; Griffith Thomas (ed.), *The Principles of Theology*, 185.

80 Hooker, *Answer to the Supplication* (*Works* V, 242.3-24).

81 It is interesting to notice that Hooker does not say which is the formal cause of justification in his theology or in Protestant theology in general. However, if the formal cause of justification in Catholic theology is the inherent righteousness of man, which was criticised by all Protestant reformers, it is logical to suppose that the formal cause of justification in Protestant theology is the imputed righteousness of Christ. Toon, *Foundations for Faith*, 94. See also Allison, *The Rise of Moralism*, 3, and Voak, *Richard Hooker and Reformed Theology*, 178.

82 Gibbs, "Richard Hooker's *Via Media* Doctrine of Justification", 212.

83 Hooker, *Answer to the Supplication* (*Works* V, 242.24-245.1).

accuse him of denying the divinity of Christ,[84] which he did not do.[85] What he did do was to introduce the concept of mercy within his doctrine of justification, following the example of Barnes.[86] This enabled him to bring forth a sympathetic approach to the plight of Catholics. Thus, Hooker wrote that Catholics were saved due to the mercy of God but only to the extent that they had sinned out of ignorance[87]: "*I doubte not but God was mercifull to save thowsandes of our fathers lyvinge heretofore in popishe supersticions in asmuche as they synned ingoraunlly.*"[88] He explains that this particular text should be interpreted within its wider context, because it had been written as part of a larger exposition against the pope.[89]

Alongside mercy, election and reprobation cannot be avoided in Hooker's discussion of justification,[90] which is also true of Frith[91] and Bradford.[92] At this point, Hooker makes an essential distinction between the permissive cause and the positive cause of reprobation. He explains that God is only the permissive cause of reprobation, not the positive cause. Such an answer discharges God of the alluded guilt of choosing some people for eternal damnation. Hooker indirectly says that the positive cause of reprobation lies in the reprobate themselves and particularly in their sin. Accordingly, God must not be blamed for the final state of the reprobate: "I had termed God a permissive and no positive cawse of the evell which the schoolmen do call *malum culpae.*"[93] But the question of whether God *wants* to choose some particular individuals for eternal happiness and other for eternal damnation is still in need of an answer. Hooker introduces another distinction between the absolute and the conditional will of God in matters of

---

84   For the importance of the union between humanity and divinity in the person of Christ, see Thornton, *Richard Hooker*, 61. See also Wolf, Booty, and Thomas (eds), *The Spirit of Anglicanism*, 36-41; and Gareth, Bennett, "The Church of England and the Royal Supremacy", *One in Christ*, XXII/4 (1986), 308; Kirby, "*Supremum Caput*: Richard Hooker's Theology of Ecclesiastical Dominion", *Dionysius* XII (1988), 109; Crerar, *Positive Negatives*, 181-182.

85   Hooker, *Answer to the Supplication* (*Works* V, 251.10-20).

86   Barnes, *The Supplication of 1531*, lviii.b-lix.a.

87   See also Walton, *The Lives*, 218; Peter McGrath, *Papists and Puritans under Elizabeth I*, 320; McGrade, "The Public and the Religious in Hooker's *Polity*", 404; and Bauckham, "Hooker, Travers and the Church of Rome in the 1580s", 46.

88   Hooker, *Answer to the Supplication* (*Works* V, 251.21-23).

89   *ibid.* 251.24-25.

90   See also Rowse, *The England of Elizabeth*, 487; Collinson, *Archbishop Grindal*, 41.

91   Frith, *Patrick Places*, 29.

92   Bradford, *Writings*, 215-216.

93   Hooker, *Answer to the Supplication* (*Works* V, 252.31-253.2).

election and reprobation.[94] The will of God manifested in the work of election is conditional, not absolute. Thus, God grants salvation to the elect, namely to those believers who revere, obey, and serve him: "Secondly that to their objection who saie *If I be elected do what I will I shalbe saved* I had aunswered that the will of God in this thinge is not absolute but conditionall to save his elected beleving fearing and obedientlye servinge him."[95]

It seems that Hooker was indeed very preoccupied to give a thorough answer to the teaching of election, because he must have sensed its importance for the whole discussion of justification.[96] Despite the complex character of the issue, Hooker is convinced that God must not be blamed for the reprobation of the lost. He nevertheless admits that reprobation is the result of a decision taken by God but this should be connected to the worthiness of every human being. Hooker knows that such an approach involves a certain reflection on temporality, history and metaphysics. The way individual faith relates to history and eternity is equally important.[97] In Hooker's thought, the problem has reached a final verdict as he writes that election and reprobation are – at least to some extent – conditioned to the inner quality of man. God is aware of the worthiness of every human being but this truth should not be assessed in terms of history. For Hooker, the judgement of whether man is worthy to be elected or reprobate lies is the reality of God beyond history. Consequently, it is the sovereignty of God which has the final decision on the decision of election or reprobation, also defended by Frith.[98] Hooker explains:

> Thirdly that to stop the mouthes of suche as grudge and repine againste God for rejectinge castawaies I had taughte that they are not rejected no not in the purpose and cousell of God without a forseen worthynes of rejection goinge though not in tyme yett in order before.[99]

This theological argument is not satisfactory to Hooker. Left alone, such a conclusion would lead to the idea that God does not take into account the historical existence of man. As humanity exists within time and history, Hooker attempts to formulate a teaching which includes God's

---

94 See also Knox, *Walter Travers*, 75.

95 Hooker, *Answer to the Supplication* (*Works* V, 253.2-5).

96 Collinson, *Archbishop Grindal*, 41.

97 d'Entrèves, *Riccardo Hooker*, 49; Speed Hill, "Richard Hooker and the Rhetoric of History", *Churchman* 114/1 (2000), 13-14.

98 Frith, *A Mirror to Know Thyself*, in Trueman, *Luther's Legacy*, 146, and Bradford, *The Writings of John Bradford*, 211.

99 Hooker, *Answer to the Supplication* (*Works* V, 253.5-9).

sovereign perspective over the life of his creation.[100] Thus, election infers two distinct theological realities: firstly, God's foreknowledge of the elect, and secondly, God's permissiveness of misery in the life of the elect. The first point is an evident link between the world of God and the world of creation. In Hooker's thought, God virtually knows in advance the life and the worthiness of the elect, before they actually *exist* as human beings. This is another acknowledgement of God's sovereignty over his creation, but Hooker is again extremely cautious with his words. The second point at issue presupposes God's active involvement in the life of his elect. Although the elect go through tremendous difficulty and misery in their historical existence, they are never lost from God's sight. In his sovereignty, God secretly works out his plan and freely[101] extends his compassion towards the elect by means of a divine utterance, as also underlined by Cranmer.[102] At this point, it is impossible to know the way God supervises his entire plan of election. Hooker can only state that God decided that some people shall have life and they will not die. Although he knows the life of the elect before the existence of time and history, God is in total control over their lives within the flow of historical events.[103] According to Hooker, God can never be rightfully accused of a deliberate partisanship, on the one hand, in favour of his elect,[104] and on the other hand, to the detriment of the reprobate. Although God knows in advance the life of every single human being, he nevertheless offers his mercy towards them when they commit sins and undergo terrible conditions:

> For if godes electinge do in order (as needes it muste) presuppose the foresighte of theire beinge that are elected, though they be elected before they be, nor onely the posityve foresighte of theire beinge, but also the permissive of theire being miserable, becawse election is through mercie and mercie doth alwaie presuppose miserye it followeth that the very chose of God acknowledge to the praise of the riches of his exceeding free compassion that when he is his secrett determinacion sett it downe *those shall lyve and not dye*, they laie as ouglye spectacles before his as leapers

---

100 Haugaard, "The Scriptural Hermeneutics of Richard Hooker. Historical Contextualization and Teleology", in Donald S. Armentrout (ed.), *This Sacred History. Anglican Reflections for John Booty*, 167.

101 Lake, *Anglicans and Puritans?*, 162.

102 Cranmer, Works II, 130.

103 Speed Hill, "Richard Hooker and the Rhetoric of History", *Churchman* 114/1 (2000), 13-14.

104 See also Tyndale about God's favour or grace in Tyndale, *Prologue to Romans*, 128. For this favour, which is the grace of God, see Booty, "The Spirituality of Participation in Richard Hooker", *Sewanee Theological Review* 38/1 (1994), 12.

covered with dounge and mire as ulcers putrefied in theire fathers loines miserable worthy to be had in detestation.[105]

One should never loose sight of this intricate mixture of time, history, foreknowledge and eternity. There is always something in humanity which sentences it to death, for instance, the disobedience of man, which is also tackled by Foxe.[106] Therefore, the theology of election must hold in balance the action of God before history and the life of man within it.[107] The will of God in election is entirely sovereign[108] but God is always full of grace and fair in his judgments,[109] also admitted by Bradford.[110] Should there be any actual effective cause of reprobation, this is the sin of men and women. It is relevant to notice that Hooker promotes a theology of suffering when he explains the doctrine of election. Historically, the elect are never left without the possibility of living by themselves in accordance with the laws of God. They may live as they please but Hooker plainly affirms that misery will follow. Suffering, however, is not always the result of sin but secretly blends with the will of God to save his elect.[111] God's sovereignty should always be sought in the misery of the elect's historical existence because God works out his plan by means of suffering:

> And shall any forsaken creature be able to saie unto God *Thou dideste plounge me in the deepes* and assigned me unto the endlesse tormentes onely to satisfie thine owne will, findinge nothinge in me for which I could seeme in thy sighte so well worthy to feele everlasting flames?[112]

Ultimately, it is the concept of mercy which explains election,[113] which is also the case in Barnes.[114] In spite of man's sinfulness, God has mercy on his elect and graciously saves them.

---

105 Hooker, *Answer to the Supplication (Works* V, 253.9-20).

106 Foxe, *The Acts and Monuments*, 71.

107 Speed Hill, "Richard Hooker and the Rhetoric of History", *Churchman* 114/1 (2000), 13-14.

108 Wallace Jr., *Puritans and Predestination*, 77.

109 Collinson, *Archbishop Grindal*, 41.

110 Bradford, *Writings*, 211.

111 Lake, *Anglicans and Puritans?*, 162.

112 Hooker, *Answer to the Supplication (Works* V, 253.20-24).

113 Collinson, *Archbishop Grindal*, 41.

114 Barnes, *The Supplication of 1531*, lviii.b-lix.a.

6.2.7 The Doctrine of Scripture

The last point that Hooker wants to clarify in his disputation with Travers is the question of authority which reflects his view of Scripture. Travers had accused Hooker of having his own human reason as authoritative in matters of theology with disregard to the teaching of Scripture. Hooker completely rejects this evaluation and plainly affirms that the only reason he used was not human reason but the reason of God.[115] He then makes a direct connection between divine reason[116] and the divine Word. Hooker admits he had used the arguments of the apostle Paul, but his words are part of Scripture and they express the divine reason of God. Nothing of God's reality can be known by the reason of man. Now Hooker links revelation with salvation and explains that the things of God can only be known by the reason of God. This is the only reason that may be used in theology and this is the only kind of authority Hooker had always had in mind:

> I alleged therefore that which mighte under no pretence in the worlde be dissalowed namely a reson not meaninge thereby *myne owne reason* as nowe it is reported, but true sounde divyne reason, reson whereby those conclusions mighte be out of Ste Paule demonstrated and not probably discoursed of onely, reson proper to that science whereby the thinges of God are knowne, theologicall reason which out of principles in scripture that are playne soundly deduceth more doubtfull inference, in suche sorte that being herd they neither can be denied nor any thing repugnaunte unto them receyved, but whatsoever was before otherwise by miscollecting gathered out of darker places is therby forced to yeld it self and the true consonaunte meaning of sentences not understood is broughte to lighte. This is the reson which I entended.[117]

Hooker is well aware that all these statements may seem theoretical. Towards the end of his *Answer*, he tries to apply his teaching of salvation (with its various aspects) to the life of the Church. One cannot say for sure whether or to what extent Hooker was disturbed by Travers' accusations, but Hooker's concluding words are an invitation towards the spiritual unity of the Church. The doctrine and the life of the Church must be kept united by the bond of God. One God, one

---

115 Booty, "The Judicious Mr. Hooker and the Authority in the Elizabethan Church", in Stephen W. Sykes (ed.), *Authority in the Anglican Communion*, 98.

116 For the use of divine reason in Hooker, see also Knox, *Walter Travers*, 84.

117 Hooker, *Answer to the Supplication* (*Works* V, 255.3-16).

Lord, one faith, one Spirit and one baptism are the living realities which must safeguard both the teaching and the unity of the Church.[118]

---

118 For further details, see Hooker, *Answer to the Supplication* (*Works* V, 256.17-257.16). For the connection between the Spirit and the teaching of the Church, see also Gane, "The Exegetical Methods of Some Sixteenth Century Anglican Preachers: Latimer, Jewel, Hooker, and Andrews", 35; Booty, "Understanding the Church in Sixteenth-Century England", *Sewanee Theological Review* 42/3 (1999), 279.

7. The Anthropology of Faith in the *A Learned Sermon of the Nature of Pride* (1586)

The last aspect of Hooker's doctrine of salvation is the anthropology of faith which describes how faith functions within the human being. Hooker debated this problem in his *A Learned Sermon of the Nature of Pride*. Unfortunately, the date of the delivery of the sermon is unknown, so whether the sermon pertains to Hooker's controversy with Travers or not is a matter of historiography which has not been entirely clarified. There is, however, a clue that might set a date for its utterance: the fact that the scriptural text for the sermon is Habakkuk 2:4 might place it next to the *A Learned and Comfortable Sermon on the Certaintie and Perpetuitie of Faith in the Elect* and the *A Learned Discourse of Justification, Workes and How the Foundation of faith is Overthrown,* which are both constructed on biblical information from Habakkuk 1:4. A historical argument for a possible chronology of the sermon cannot be fostered in any way, which makes it unsure whether it was indeed preached before or after *A Learned and Comfortable Sermon on the Certaintie and Perpetuitie of Faith in the Elect,* or even before or after the *A Learned Discourse of Justification, Workes and How the Foundation of faith is Overthrown.* Making use of a mere logical inference, it could be argued that should Hooker have preached sequentially from the book of Habakkuk in accordance with the flow of chapters, *A Learned and Comfortable Sermon on the Certaintie and Perpetuitie of Faith in the Elect* and *A Learned Discourse of Justification, Workes and How the Foundation of faith is Overthrown,* which are based on Habakkuk 1:4, would have to have been followed by *A Learned Sermon of the Nature of Pride,* for which the starting point was Habakkuk 2:4. In any case, it is not unreasonable to suppose that it could have been delivered in the same year as the other two sermons, namely between March 1585 and March 1586.[1]

---

1   *Works* V, 299.

7.1 Nature and Grace

In this sermon, Hooker starts his soteriological discussion with the plight of humanity. Using a theological method which very much resembles that of Calvin in his *Institutes of the Christian Religion*,[2] the sorrowful estate in which man stands as part of the fallen created order is a pretext and a reality as well for Hooker's analysis of salvation. The dichotomy of sin and its remedy, death and life, misery and happiness, unrighteousness and righteousness is encompassed by the then already well established scholastic terminology of nature and grace.[3] Although, at this point, Hooker has not yet begun his discussion on salvation, the influence of his overall Reformed theology may easily be discerned.[4] Thus, he brings to the discussion the idea that God could not leave his creation in a sinful state without acting towards its recovery. Hooker chose to express this particular thought interrogatively but such an approach does not by any means diminish its powerful inference, namely that God initiated the work of purifying his creation from the defilement of sin. At the same time, Hooker acknowledges that the reality of sin is present historically, whereas the reality of salvation is given intentionally. Man is to be found righteous, which is a clear affirmation of a work that had been done by an external agent. Following Foxe,[5] Hooker's intention is straightforward and it attempts to establish God as the initiator of man's salvation:

> By which reason all being wrapped up in sinne and made therby the children of death, the mindes of all men being plainly convicted not to be right: shall wee think that God hath endued them with so manie excellencies moe not only then any but then all the creatures in the world besides to leave them all in such estate that they had bene happier if they

---

2 It is a known fact that Calvin begins his *Institutes* with what he called "the knowledge of God the Creator", which is actually his First Book of the *corpus*, and which debates the problem of the created order, sin, and impiety. The Second Book is "the knowledge of God the Redeemer", which although begins with the matter of original sin, is still primarily concerned with the remedy of sin. Jean Calvin, *Institutes of the Christian Religion* (Grand Rapids: Eerdmans, 1997), 31-32.

3 The complementarity and interdependence of nature and grace is also noticed by Lake, *Anglicans and Puritans?*, 152; Neelands, "Hooker on Scripture, Reason and 'Tradition'", in McGrade (ed.), *Richard Hooker and the Construction of Christian Community*, 76-83.

4 See also Jordan, *The Development of Religious Toleration*, 226.

5 Foxe, *The Acts and Monuments*, 71.

had never been? Heere cometh necessarily in a nue waie unto salvation so that they which were in the other perverse maie in this be found straight and righteous. That the waie of nature, this the waie of grace.[6]

Hooker continues by drawing a sharp distinction between the two ways. Thus, the way of nature, which is obviously associated with the Catholic theology of the scholastic heritage, has three major characteristics.

7.1.1 The Way of Nature

In order to describe the first, Hooker clearly alludes to the natural realm which strengthens his idea concerning the way of nature. For him, the soteriology of the Catholic scholastic tradition is primarily based on anthropology,[7] which is specifically expressed in the importance of works. Man is important as he performs works that acquire a supposedly necessary righteousness in the eyes of God. According to this view, salvation is based on man's merit and is accordingly given to him by God.

The second characteristic of the way of nature is again the focus on the importance of man in the scheme of salvation. Catholic scholastic theology argues that man has a natural ability to fulfil the necessary righteousness of salvation. In this context, it is relevant to notice that righteousness not only belongs to man, namely it is inherent to him, but it also lies within the naturally given strengths of human nature to fulfil it. This duality supports the anthropological aspect of the scholastic doctrine of salvation, which Hooker will strongly refute.

As far as the third characteristic of nature's way is concerned, it should be noticed that Catholic thought ultimately makes a direct connection between the doctrine of salvation and the doctrine of creation.[8] Thus, man's capacity to fulfil the righteousness of salvation

---

6   Hooker, *Pride* (*Works* V, 312.30-313.7).

7   For details about Hooker's anthropology, see Loyer, "Contract social et consentment chez Richard Hooker", *Revue des Sciences Philosophiques et Théologiques* 59/3 (1975), 386; Booty, "The Law of Proportion: William Meade and Richard Hooker", *St. Luke's Journal of Theology* XXXIV/2 (1991), 26; Lurbe, "Political Power and Ecclesiastical Power in Richard Hooker's *Laws of Ecclesiastical Polity*", *Cahiers Elisabéthains* 49 (1996), 21; Neelands, "Hooker on Scripture, Reason and 'Tradition'", in McGrade (ed.), *Richard Hooker and the Construction of Christian Community*, 76-83; Percy, *Introducing Richard Hooker and the Laws of the Ecclesiastical Polity*, 24.

8   Haugaard, "The Scriptural Hermeneutics of Richard Hooker. Historical Contextualization and Teleology", in Donald S. Armentrout (ed.), *This Sacred History. Anglican Reflections for John Booty*, 167.

through works is only due to the goodness of God who created him in a state of perfection.[9] Basically, man's goodness manifested in all good works, which acquire the righteousness of salvation, is said to have its origins in the eternal goodness of God's perfection. To quote Hooker:

> The end of that way salvation merited presupposing the righteousness of mens wourkes, their righteousness a naturall hability to do them, that hability the goodnes of God which created them in such perfection.[10]

In an evident contrasting position stands the other way, which Hooker termed the way of grace.

7.1.2 The Way of Grace

The entire approach is theological, although the human being remains the starting point of the argument. Man, however, is a passive receptor only. By contrast, God is the active agent, who bestows salvation by grace.[11] Accordingly, salvation is given by God to man; it is a gift[12] which has absolutely nothing to do with man's inner righteousness,[13] which is also acknowledged by Barnes.[14] It is utterly impossible for man to produce the righteousness which could be necessary for his salvation. The possibility of such an achievement lies beyond the capacity of human nature. Man passively receives the righteousness of salvation, but Hooker is more confident in a different way of expressing this positive truth. He does not explicitly say that the gift of salvation consists of God's righteousness which is given to man, but rather uses a more negative statement. As such, salvation is the forgiveness of man's unrighteousness and this is equalled to justification itself, identical to what Bradford has to say about justification and salvation.[15] For Hooker, this is justification proper: the forgiveness of sins, also valid in Tyndale.[16] Thus, justification is an

---

9   Malone, "The Doctrine of Predestination in the Thought of William Perkins and Richard Hooker", 107; Kirby, *Richard Hooker's Doctrine of Royal Supremacy*, 46.

10 Hooker, *Pride* (*Works* V, 313.7-10).

11 Keble, *The Works*, vol. 2, 552, and Malone, "The Doctrine of Predestination in the Thought of William Perkins and Richard Hooker", 109; Secor, *Richard Hooker, Prophet of Anglicanism*, 185.

12 Griffith Thomas (ed.), *The Principles of Theology*, 185.

13 This is realised by faith, as noticed by Thornton, *Richard Hooker*, 56.

14 Barnes, *The Supplication of 1531*, xliii.a.

15 Bradford, *Writings*, 217-218.

16 Tyndale, *Prologue to Romans*, 125.

external act, realised by God and given to man.[17] Justification is not part
of human nature, and nor is it part of the created order, as it is beyond
the natural ability of man to fulfil its required righteousness. Justification is not inherent in humanity either ontologically or functionally:[18]

> But the end of this waie salvation bestowed upon men as a guift
> presupposing not theire righteousnes but the forgivenes of their
> unrighteousness, justification; their justification not their naturall hability
> to doe good…[19]

Hooker writes that the only thing man can do is to be sorry for his
sinful life. At this point, the element of faith becomes vital.

7.1.3 Faith and Christ

In Hooker, faith though present in sinful human beings must be
anchored in Christ.[20] Christ should be the aim of faith, as faith itself has
no existence of its own apart from Christ. By extension, there is no
justification and renewal of life for anybody apart from Christ. Hooker
is clear about the necessity of faith and about the quality of faith, of
which he writes that it should be firm. Christ incorporates the entire
range of possibilities on the grounds of which salvation is possible in
reality. Following Tyndale,[21] Hooker acknowledges that salvation was
given to men for Christ's sake and it is only because of Christ that
sinful men are accepted by God. Thus, salvation is not only the
forgiveness of sins but also God's acceptance, as also described by
Cranmer.[22] As such, salvation is not only declarative but also relational.
God forgives sins, so that forgiven men might have a new relationship
with him.[23] This is man's vocation, as Hooker subsequently explains,
and this vocation is directly linked to God's election as, for instance, in
Bradford.[24] Consequently, salvation and election cannot be separated,
which is also true in Frith.[25]

---

17   Kirby, *Richard Hooker's Doctrine of Royal Supremacy*, 50.
18   Booty, "The English Reformation: A Lively Faith and Sacramental Confession", 25.
19   Hooker, *Pride* (*Works* V, 313.10-13).
20   Collinson, *Archbishop Grindal*, 41.
21   Tyndale, *Prologue to Romans*, 129.
22   Cranmer, *The 1538 Articles*, 4.
23   Griffith Thomas (ed.), *The Principles of Theology*, 185.
24   Bradford, *Writings*, 215-216.
25   Frith, *Patrick Places*, 29.

7.1.4 Election and Christ the Mediator

Election is the act whereby God chose to select a number of people from all those who have sinned and, in Hooker's thinking, it has a double theological foundation. Firstly, election is the act of God,[26] who expressed his sovereign will in selecting some from the many. Secondly, election is real only in Christ.[27] Within salvation in general, election has no existence of its own apart from Christ.[28] Within the process of salvation, election is totally dependent on the mercy of God[29] – as plainly acknowledged by Barnes[30] and Bradford.[31] Thus, the relationship between God's election and mercy[32] is a theological mystery. Such a term attached to both election in particular and salvation in general makes them even less approachable by men. Not only that man is without the possibility of achieving his own salvation but he is totally unable to think of it as the solution of his sinful condition. In this context, the foundation of salvation, which is Christ,[33] is introduced by Hooker in his office of mediator,[34] which is also of great importance to Frith.[35] As man is totally incapable of either achieving or even considering salvation, it is Christ who both makes it possible and available to humanity. Christ is the mediator between God's mystery of salvation and man's inability to find the remedy for his misery. This whole reality is part of a divine plan, which underlines the forensic aspect of salvation (and of justification as part of the salvific process).[36] God himself had decided that Christ should be the mediator between God and man. This is to say that God himself had decided that salvation should be performed by Christ for the sake of

---

26 Wallace Jr., *Puritans and Predestination*, 77.
27 Collinson, *Archbishop Grindal*, 41; Wallace Jr., *Puritans and Predestination*, 77.
28 Wallace Jr., *Puritans and Predestination*, 77.
29 Collinson, *Archbishop Grindal*, 41.
30 Barnes, *The Supplication of 1531*, lviii.b-lix.a.
31 Bradford, *Writings*, 371-372.
32 Collinson, *Archbishop Grindal*, 41.
33 Booty, "The English Reformation: A Lively Faith and Sacramental Confession", 24; Booty, "An Elizabethan Addresses Modern Anglicanism. Richard Hooker and Theological Issues at the End of the Twentieth Century", 10.
34 See also Thornton, *Richard Hooker*, 61; for details about mediation in Hooker, see also Kirby, *Richard Hooker's Doctrine of Royal Supremacy*, 46.
35 Frith, *Patrick Places*, 30.
36 Rupp, *Studies in the Making of the English Protestant Tradition*, 166.

humans as, for instance, in Frith.[37] Again, Hooker's explanation is theologically oriented, as he wrote that God had appointed Christ in his office as mediator, and consequently as achiever of man's salvation. This is how Hooker put it:

> ...but their hartie sorrow for not doing and unfained beliefe in him for whose sake not doers are accepted, which is their vocation; their vocation thelection of God taking them out from the number of lost children; their election a mediatour in whom to be elect; this mediation inexplicable mercy, his mercy their mistrie for whome he voutchafed to make him selfe a mediatour.[38]

Hooker displays a very realistic picture of what salvation actually is for human life. It has been shown that the justified man enters a new range of relationships, of which the most important is that with God but this does not mean that corruption[39] is totally eradicated from his earthly body.

7.2 The Concept of Pride

Hooker now introduces his concept of pride.[40] Sin continues to affect man's life and pride is only the pretext for Hooker to transfer his discussion from salvation as God's act to salvation as part of man's life. Pride may be a good example of the sinful persistence of bad habits throughout one's life. Pride is obviously a sin and, as such, continues to manifest itself even in the life of the justified person.

7.2.1 Natural and Spiritual Pride

Hooker is not very concerned with what might be called "natural pride", which is thought to affect the unsaved. This is pride which man takes in "bewtie strength riches power knowledge"[41] and it is

---

37 Frith, *Patrick Places*, 30.

38 Hooker, *Pride* (*Works* V, 313.14-19); for details about mediation in Hooker, see also Kirby, *Richard Hooker's Doctrine of Royal Supremacy*, 46.

39 Bouwsma, "Hooker in the Context of European Cultural History", in Claire McEachern and Deborah Shuger (eds), *Religion and Culture in Renaissance England*, 149.

40 Booty, "Elizabethan Religion: Disorder Ordered", *Anglican Theological Review* 73/2 (1991), 130; Booty, "The Spirituality of Participation in Richard Hooker", *Sewanee Theological Review* 38/1 (1994), 11.

41 Hooker, *Pride* (*Works* V, 317.2).

manifested "as acknowledgments of some mens excellencie above others."[42] Hooker, however, has focused his attention upon "spiritual pride", which affects the saved. The best example for this type of pride is the behaviour of Christ's disciples, who although they had been in the presence of Christ[43] for quite some time, were still under the deceitful influence of pride. This is Hooker's way of illustrating Luther's *simul/semper justus et peccator*, which is a clear affirmation of man's spiritual bivalency as a saved being:

> But his disciples feeding them selves with a vain imagination for the time that the Messias of the world should in Jerusalem erect his throne and exercise dominion with great pomp and outward stateliness, advanced in honour and terrene power above all the princes of the earth, began to think how with their Lords condition their own would also rise: that *having left and forsaken all to follow him*, their place about him should not be mean: and because they were many it troubled them much *which of them should be the greatest man.* When sute was made for two by name that of them *one might sit at this right hand and the other at his left,* the rest began to stomack, ech taking it grievously that any should have what all did affect.[44]

There is, however, a remedy for pride and, generally, for sinful influences in the life of the believer. As salvation is grounded in Christ[45] by faith, the saved person should correct his or her attitude in accordance with the example of Christ. Hooker explains that salvation totally changes one's life, which also implies that salvation turns values upside down. Things which seem normal to the unsaved will seem to be totally abnormal to the saved. Only the saved is able to discern spiritually that pride is deceitful and that his entire life must be closely connected to Christ's. By extension, only the saved is able to see his sin and perceive it accordingly, and only the justified has the God-given capacity to overcome sin.[46]

7.2.2 The Mechanism of Pride

In order to explain better how salvation works, Hooker starts with the investigation of the mechanism of pride. In his understanding, pride is the result of the malfunction of mind's faculty of evaluation. Although it is not clear whether he refers to the unsaved or to the saved, Hooker

---

42 *ibid.* 317.7-8.

43 Booty, "Contrition in Anglican Spirituality: Hooker, Donne and Herbert", in William J. Wolf (ed.), *Anglican Spirituality* (Wilton: Morehouse-Barlow, 1982), 26.

44 Hooker, *Pride* (*Works* V, 317.14-25).

45 Collinson, *Archbishop Grindal*, 41.

46 For more details see Hooker, *Pride* (*Works* V, 317.25-318.15).

in convinced that a proud man is incapable of properly assessing a wrong idea. In fact, the mind of a proud man does not have the ability to overcome the error of evaluating an idea which is not in accordance with real truth. This will immediately cause a behavioural pattern, by which the proud man will see himself as better than others so that the result of his own reasoning fails to match the truthfulness of reality. Such a distorted mechanism of the mind is the very cause of pride, and a man who is affected by it will always think of himself in terms which are higher than those he applies to everybody around him. Hooker explains:

> There is in the hart of every proud man first an errour of understanding a vain opinion wherby he thinketh his own excellency and by reason thereof his wourthines of estimation regard and honour to be greater then in truth it is. This maketh him in all his affections accordingly to raise up him selfe, and by this inward affections his outward acts are fashioned.[47]

This is an excellent description of human nature. It appears that Hooker's doctrine of salvation is built upon the basis of a very serious anthropological evaluation of humanity. Hooker is working at this particular argument in view of his later analysis of justification. He is a fine observer of man's life and is sometimes quite willing to waste a substantial amount of ink on a detailed description of how pride affects human existence. Here is an example:

> ...how they bear their heades over others, how they browbeath all men which do not receyve their sentences as oracles with mervelous applause and approbation, how they looke upon no man but with an indirect countenance nor here any thing saving their own praises with patience, nor speak without scornfulnes and disdain; how they use their servants as if they were beasts, their inferiours as servants, their equals as inferiours, and as for superiours acknowledg none; how they admire them selves as venerable puissant wise circumspect provident every way great, taking all men besides them selves for ciphers poore inglorious silly creatures, needles burthens of the earth, ofscowringes, no nothing: in a wourd for him which marketh how irregular and exorbitant they are in all thinges it can be no hard thing heerby to gather that pride is nothing but an inordinate elation of the mind proceeding from a false conceipt of mens excellency in things honoured which accordingly frameth also their deeds and behaviour unlesse there be cunning to conceal it. For a foul scar may be coverd with a fair cloth. And as proud as Lucifer may be in outward appearance lowly.[48]

Pride is sin, and the attempt to cover it is a common feature of man, as it has just been shown. Humanly speaking, Hooker is keenly aware that

---

47   ibid. 318.17-23.
48   ibid. 319.24-320.10.

nothing can be done against pride, which is the cause of all troubles in the world:[49]

> No man expecteth grapes of thissles: nor from a thing of so bad a nature can other then sutable frutes be looked for. What harm soever in private families there groweth by disobedience of children, stubbornes of servants, untractablenes in them who although they otherwise may rule yeat should in consideration of the imparitie of their sex be also subject: whatsoever harm by strife amongst men combined in the fellowship of greater societies, by tyrannie of potentates ambition of nobles rebellion of subjects in civil states, by heresies schisms divisions in the Church, naming pride we name the mother which brought them foorth and the only nurce that feedeth them. Give me the hartes of all men humbled and what is there that can overthrow or disturb the peach of the world? Wherein many things are cause of much evell but pride of all.[50]

Such an enterprise, however, serves an established purpose: that of providing an accurate doctrine of salvation, which – for Hooker – contains the very medicine against the sinfulness of pride.

7.2.3 Salvation as Remedy for Pride

This may be easy to say but it proves to be a difficult task when dealt with by personal involvement in the matter. Hooker knows this and he expresses his rather unrealistic wish (of which he is aware) to have a precise cure for pride. There is no such thing as an easy treatment for a sick mind but still Hooker is convinced that the first thing to do is to deal with the error of the mind. A proud man must be confronted with his own misjudgements. When he realises the error of his assessment of himself and others, pride should virtually disappear:

> To declaime of the swarmes of evels issuing out of pride is an easie labour. I rather wish that I could exactly prescribe and perswade effectuallie the remedies wherby a soar so grievous might be cured, the meanes how the pride of swelling mindes might be taken down. Whereunto so much we have alredy gained that the evidence of the cause which breedeth it pointeth directly unto the likeliest and fittest help to take it away. Diseases that come of fullness emptines must remove. Pride is not cured but by abaiting the errour which causeth the mind to swell. Then seing that they swell by misconcept of their own excellency, for this cause oall which tendeth to the beating down of their pride whether it be advertisement from men or from God him selfe chastisement, it then maketh them case to

---

49   See also Walton, The Lives, 220.
50   Hooker, Pride (Works V, 320.11-23).

be proud when it causeth them to see their errour in overesteeming the think they were proud of.[51]

Again, this seems to be a rather easy theoretical dismissal but such an approach is all man can do to repair the disastrous outcome of pride. The only problem of the recipe is that the most important ingredient is still missing and Hooker is not unaware of it. Man might try to implement this remedy but it will show absolutely no results if the firm foundation of salvation is overlooked. In and by himself, man is left totally helpless in his attempt to overcome the sinfulness of pride. This is why he needs an external agent for the remedy to work, and this is divine intervention by Christ. Pride is sin, and sin has affected the whole world. Only Christ is able to restore this plight,[52] and only Christ is the Redeemer[53] of humanity from either pride or any other sin. Invariably, the medicine for pride is humility, which should be followed in accordance with Christ's example – as in Frith[54] – but this is acquired only by saving faith. In this context, faith is what makes the proud man aware of his fall; it is the awareness that his recovery resides in God. Man has nothing of his own because whatever he has in his possession, including faith, is a gift from God.[55] Tyndale, for instance, writes that the same is true about salvation which is from God.[56] This is why pride is vanity; it is mere delusion. It has always been that the work of God through Christ cured man of his pride and helped him live in full self-awareness. At this point, Hooker resorts to the classical Protestant method of argumentation: firstly, he displays the truth of Scripture as proof of his doctrine, then he supplies various texts from the ecclesiastical tradition in support of the same view. From Scripture, Hooker chose Job and Paul to explain that salvation as the remedy for sinful pride is entirely a gift of God,[57] and man has nothing to produce to his own benefit apart from the divine intervention of God:

> At this mark Job in his apologie unto his eloquent frendes aimeth. For percyving how much they delighted to heer them selves talk as if they had

---

51   ibid. 320.24-321.6.
52   Griffith Thomas (ed.), *The Principles of Theology*, 185.
53   Bartlett, "What Has Richard Hooker to Say to Modern Evangelical Anglicanism?", *Anvil* 15/3 (1998), 198.
54   Frith, *Patrick Places*, 30.
55   Thornton, *Richard Hooker*, 56; Griffith Thomas (ed.), *The Principles of Theology*, 185; Collinson, *Archbishop Grindal*, 41.
56   Tyndale, *Prologue to Romans*, 123.
57   Booty, "An Elizabethan Addresses Modern Anglicanism. Richard Hooker and Theological Issues at the End of the Twentieth Century", 19.

given their poore afflicted familiar a schooling of mervelous deepe and rare
instruction, as if they had taught him more then all the world besides could
acqaint him with, his answere was to this effect: Yee swell as though ye
had conceyved some great matter but as for that which ye are delivered of
who knoweth it not? Is any man ignorant of these thinges? At the same
mark the blessed apostle driveth, *Ye abound in all things ye are rich ye raign
and would to Christ wee did raign with you*. But boast not. For what have ye or
are ye of your selves? To this mark all those humble confessions are referd
which have bene alwais frequent in the mouths of Saincts trulie wading in
the triall of them selves: as that of the prophet, *Wee are nothing but soarnes
and festered corruption*; our verie light is darkness and our righteousness it
selfe unrighteous...[58]

That the world of man is evidently contrasted with that of God, and
that the deeds of man are in the sheerest opposition to the deeds of God
is a reality which Hooker explains with quotations from the theological
tradition of the early Middle Ages.

7.3 Hooker and Medieval Catholicism

The first theologian quoted by Hooker is Gregory I. The immense
difference between man and God is evident:

...that of Gregorie, *Let no man ever put confidence in his own deserts; sordet in
conspectus judicis quod fulget in conspectus operantis, In the sight of that dread-
full judg it is noisome which in the doers judgment maketh a bewtifull show...*[59]

Likewise, the words of Anselm that Hooker quotes as second proof
from the Church's scholastic tradition are, in fact, a wholehearted
doxology addressed to a sovereign and benevolent God,[60] an image of
God which is basic to Tyndale.[61] The idea of man's merit is rejected and
the essential soteriological aspect of the argument is the underlining of
God's goodwill towards sinful humanity:

...that of Anselm, *I adore the I blesse the Lord God of heaven and Redeemer of the
world with all the power habilitie and strength of my hart and soul for thy*

---

58   Hooker, *Pride* (*Works* V, 321.6-16); Kirby, *Richard Hooker's Doctrine of Royal Supremacy*,
     46.
59   Hooker, *Pride* (*Works* V, 321.20-27). See also Gregory I, *Expositio* 5.7, in *Opera Omnia*
     (Paris: Apud Corolam Guilard & Guilielmum Desboys, 1551).
60   Targoff, "Performing Prayer in Hooker's *Laws*: The Efficacy of Set Forms", in
     McGrade, *Richard Hooker and the Construction of Christian Community*, 275-282.
61   Tyndale, *Prologue to Romans*, 128.

goodness so unmeasurablie extended not in regard of my merits whereunto only torments were due but of thy mere unprocured benignitie.[62]

When using these two testimonies from the Catholic theology of the early Middle Ages, Hooker apparently had another purpose in mind, which served to clarify further the distinction between the way of nature and the way of grace.[63]

7.3.1 Early Medieval Catholicism and Late Medieval Catholicism

As has been shown previously, Hooker identifies the way of nature with the Catholic theology of his day, while the way of grace is evidently the Protestant theology which he himself professed. Hooker was always a careful historian and he proved to be extremely careful not to dismiss the entire Catholic tradition as contrary to Scripture.[64] Nevertheless, the theology of the English Catholics in the last two decades of the 16th century was the successor of Late Medieval Scholasticism, which – it is generally accepted – was strongly opposed by the Protestant Reformation. At this point, Hooker felt that a distinction should be made between Catholic theology in general (as, for instance, the theology of the Early Middle Ages) and Catholic theology of later ecclesiastical tradition (as, for example, the theology of the Late Middle Ages), which was reflected in the Rhemist translation of the New Testament.

7.3.2 The Soteriological Implications of the Rhemist Translation

Hooker was dissatisfied with this English translation, as it was made from Latin. For a scholar of his stature, such an enterprise is academically unacceptable and theologically unsound. The Rhemist Catholics also published some additional commentary notes, which openly teach that the value of human works should be taken into higher consideration when dealing with salvation. Hooker was disturbed by this argument mainly because, for him, the underscoring of the merit of works is nothing other than mere pride. Even worse,

---

62 The text from Anselm's works has not been identified. For details, see "Commentary", in *Works* V, 809.

63 See also Kirby, "Richard Hooker's Theory of Natural Law in the Context of Reformation Theology", *Sixteenth Century Journal* XXX/3 (1999), 701.

64 For the validity of tradition in relationship to Scripture, see also Barry, *Masters in English Theology*, 30.

such teaching actually encourages people to take pride in their own works and consequently leads them to the false impression that they might be in the position of earning their salvation. Hooker is convinced that Christian humility will never profess works as counting for one's salvation but rather Christ as the only foundation of our salvation.[65] Hooker wrote that the early Catholic scholastics would certainly disapprove of the theology which was produced by his contemporary opponents, the Rhemist Catholics:

> If these fathers should be raised again from the dust and have the books layd open before them wherein such sentences are found as this *wourks no other then the value desert price and wourth of the joyes of the kingdome of heaven; Heaven in relation to our wourks as the very stipend which the hired labourer covenanteth to have of him whose wourk he doth, a thing equally and justly answering unto the time and waight of his travails rather then a voluntarie or bountifull guift. Annot. Rhem. In 1. Cor. 3.* If I say those reverend fore rehersed fathers whose bookes are so full of sentences witnessing their Christian humilitie should be raised from the dead and behold with their eyes such things written would they not plainlie pronounce of the authours of such writ that they were fuller of Lucifer then of Christ, that they were proud harted men and carried more swelling mindes then sincerely and feelingly known Christianitie can tolerate?[66]

Hooker's question is rhetorical and the answer is obvious. Salvation is a gift,[67] as in Barnes, for instance,[68] and it is not given to man as a result of his merits, because it is impossible for man to produce works of righteousness in the eyes of God without divine assistance.

7.4 The Constant Influence of Sin

The theme of the persisting influence of sin in the life of the saved is resumed by Hooker when he prepares the introduction of a short analysis of God's sovereignty over man's plans.

---

65   Booty, "The English Reformation: A Lively Faith and Sacramental Confession", 24; Booty, "An Elizabethan Addresses Modern Anglicanism. Richard Hooker and Theological Issues at the End of the Twentieth Century", 10.

66   Hooker, Pride (*Works* V, 321.27-322.10). See also *The new testament of Jesus Christ, translated faithfully into English, out of the authentical Latin,...In the English College of Rhemes* (Rheims: John Fogny, 1582), 430.

67   Griffith Thomas (ed.), *The Principles of Theology*, 185.

68   Barnes, *The Supplication of 1531*, xliii.a.

7.4.1 The Mercy and Sovereignty of God

Hooker admits that the influence of sin is so powerful that, in many instances, man reaches the point of totally losing his right judgement. When this happens, Hooker imitates Barnes[69] in saying that it is only the mercy of God and his divine correction which prove to function as the last resort for man's awakening, a concept which is also approached by Bradford.[70] For example, Hooker uses David's words to acknowledge that God's punishment acted as a means of salvation:

> If therefore the prophet David instructed by good experience have acknowledged, Lord I was even at the point of clean forgetting my selfe and of straying from my right mind: but thy rod hath bene my reformer, *it hath bene good for me* even as much as my soul is wourth *that I have bene with sorrow troubled.*[71]

Hooker seems convinced that the sovereignty of God is the ultimate element of salvation. This is why man should not be proud but should rather display a humble attitude to life, because all our actions are under God's close scrutiny. Pride is sin, and sin is not favoured by God. On the other hand, humility is a Christian virtue, which pleases God. This lesson might sound simplistic but this is what Hooker actually discovered, and his formulation of the truth involved is simply straightforward: "My strength hath bene my ruine and my fall my stay."[72]

7.4.2 Justification, Sanctification, and the Reality of Pride

Hooker's choice of Habakkuk 2:4 to support his views on salvation is remarkable both in content and intention. The content of the verse: "...*the just by his faith shall live*"[73] makes an evident connection between the status and the life of the justified person. As far as the intention of the verse is concerned, the sanctification of the justified seems to be the essence of the assertion. With these two combined, it is clear that, theologically speaking, justification and sanctification should not be

---

69   *ibid.* lviii.b-lix.a.
70   Bradford, *Writings*, 371-372.
71   Hooker, *Pride* (*Works* V, 322.15-19).
72   *ibid.* 324.14.
73   *ibid.* 325.7.

separated.[74] The status of the justified, which is regulated by justification itself, is a matter that must be seen practically, so that the life of the justified should reflect the work of God in justification. Habakkuk was concerned with the wealth of proud and sinful people, which seemed to increase to the detriment of their humble and just fellow men, whose possessions grew smaller. Hooker, however, has a rather optimistic exegesis of the text at hand and suggests that God's plans are different from what men usually consider. Thus, the reality according to which the justified are persecuted by their sinful enemies should actually be translated into a teaching with a double meaning. As has been the case throughout this sermon, the key to deciphering the prophet's text is the notion of pride, which is an epithet for sin and a reality of everyday life. In Hooker's words:

> As that complaint which heretofore the prophet Abacuk hath made unto God in the person of thafflicted people of God had two principall respects, the one to the fourishing estate of impious and cruel persecutours, the other to the wofull and hard condition of saincts persecuted by their crueltie: So this short abridgment of answere thereunto made hath likewise a doble relation. It threatneth the one sort that their swelling pride doth prognosticate their spedy ruine; the other which counted them selves the children of death it reviveth and with the hope of life laid up in store for them it causeth their brused harts to rejoyce.[75]

Taking into account these considerations, Hooker's conclusion is fairly easy to reach: pride leads to destruction, while humility is the source of joyful life.

7.4.3 Pride and Faith

The opposite of pride is faith. The contrast in Habakkuk's text and consequently in Hooker's explanation is unfolded at two main levels. The first is the reality of practical existence, in which one could trace the dichotomy of justice and injustice. The second level though is the reality of theological truth, which Hooker decrypted by his use of pride and faith. As the very essence of salvation in general and justification in particular, faith has a threefold function. Firstly, faith is an eschatological reality as it gives the life promised by God. Actually, as Tyndale

---

74   Booty, "The English Reformation: A Lively Faith and Sacramental Confession", 24; Sykes, *The Study of Anglicanism*, 67; Booty, "An Elizabethan Addresses Modern Anglicanism. Richard Hooker and Theological Issues at the End of the Twentieth Century", 14-15.
75   Hooker, *Pride* (*Works* V, 324.16-25).

also says, we believe God's promise by faith.[76] Secondly, faith is the indicator of one's salvation, or of one's justification and sanctification.[77] Thirdly, faith should always be linked to the guarantee of life itself. The spiritual life of man in history[78] cannot be pictured without faith.[79] Likewise, there is absolutely no chance for anyone to have a life beyond history apart from faith. In other words, faith spiritually secures both this life and the life to come, and is the sign of both. Hooker's explanation is revealing:

...for *the just by his faith shall live.* For explication whereof the woordes them selves do offer occasion to speak first of the promise of life; secondly of their qualitie to whome life is promised; and in the last place of that dependency wherby the life of the just is heere said to hang on their faith.[80]

Hooker continues his argument with the question of whether faith should have a foundation of itself or not. In order that his readers understand better, he makes a brief comparison between animal life and human life. Following the well-known scholastic argument in accordance with which a living creature is considered alive by virtue of movement,[81] Hooker writes that such a movement is the result of divine creation. Life itself is natural according to creation, but divine according to its fundamental origin. At this point, Hooker applies the distinction between the life of animals and that of human beings, insisting on the fact that man is the most important creature of God. Thus, man has a natural life according to the fact that it is a created being, and he also has a spiritual life according to the reality of divine intervention. Though not sufficiently underlined here, the idea of divine sustenance of life is present: the spiritual life of man cannot exist apart from the special and external work of God.[82]

---

76 Tyndale, *Prologue to Romans,* 124.
77 Sykes, *The Study of Anglicanism,* 67; Booty, "An Elizabethan Addresses Modern Anglicanism. Richard Hooker and Theological Issues at the End of the Twentieth Century", 14-15.
78 Speed Hill, "Richard Hooker and the Rhetoric of History", *Churchman* 114/1 (2000), 13-14.
79 See also d'Entrèves, *Riccardo Hooker,* 49.
80 Hooker, *Pride (Works* V, 325.7-11).
81 For more details on the scholastic theory of movement, see Etienne Gilson, *La philosophie au Moyen Age. Des origins patristiques à la fin du XIVe siècle* (Paris: Editions Payot, 1986), 490.
82 Hooker, *Pride (Works* V, 325.12-21).

7.5 Spiritual Life and the Presence of Christ

Hooker's use of the scholastic argument of movement is only a pretext to the introduction of his views on life, which are based on the information in Scripture. Following an entire line of biblical texts, Hooker begins his investigation into the depths of spiritual life, which is part of his larger doctrine of salvation. For Hooker, the study of spiritual life should include three fundamental aspects: firstly, the origin of spiritual life; secondly, the way people should live spiritually in history; and thirdly, the way spiritual life is eschatologically completed beyond history, in the very life and presence of God. The most important feature of Hooker's doctrine of spiritual life is the connection between faith and Christ.

7.5.1 Faith in Christ and Life in the Presence of God

The testimony of Scripture is that Christ is the Lord of life,[83] and Hooker uses it to prove that salvation and spiritual life are closely related and are both based on the reality of the living Christ. Man cannot be said to have spiritual life apart from faith in Christ.[84] In this context, faith is not a mere notion, but a living presence which cannot be conceived without its foundation in Christ.[85] Spiritual life is the result of salvation, and salvation is the result of the work of Christ. He died for the entire world with the specific purpose of obtaining everlasting life for it.[86] Hooker uses the dialectics of life and death to explain the mystery of salvation, an idea which is also seen in Foxe.[87] The death of Christ produced the life of humanity:[88]

---

83 Atkinson, *Richard Hooker and the Authority of Scripture, Tradition and Reason*, 129; Kirby, "Richard Hooker's Theory of Natural Law in the Context of Reformation Theology", *Sixteenth Century Journal* XXX/3 (1999), 702.

84 Collinson, *Archbishop Grindal*, 41.

85 Booty, "The English Reformation: A Lively Faith and Sacramental Confession", 24; Booty, "An Elizabethan Addresses Modern Anglicanism. Richard Hooker and Theological Issues at the End of the Twentieth Century", 10.

86 For details about God's purpose in Christ, see Veatch, "The Idea of a Christian Science and Scholarship: Sense or Nonsense?", *Faith and Philosophy* I/1 (1984), 101-102.

87 Foxe, *The Acts and Monuments*, 71.

88 Lake, *Anglicans and Puritans?*, 162.

Now as the Father hath life in him selfe so to the sonne he hath given to have life in him selfe also. Joh. 6. Not so in him selfe but that other are by his quickning force and vertue made alive. For which cause peter in the third of Thapostles acts termeth him *the Lord of life.* He is *the life of the world* partly because for the world he hath suffred death to procure it eternall life; and partly for that the world being really quickned by him liveth that life which his death hath purchased.[89]

Man is the result of God's double work of creation: natural and spiritual. Hooker explains that man has a natural existence of his own due to the soul which has been given to him by God through the work of natural creation. Nevertheless, man is much more that a mere being, because he has a spiritual existence which is not his own by origin, but becomes of his own by faith in Christ. Thus, man stands between the world of nature and the world of God, and he shares both of them. But man's standing between these two worlds is somehow uneven. Ultimately, man's natural existence and his spiritual life are totally dependent upon Christ.[90] Christ is the measure of all things as far as man in concerned, and there is no life without him – be it either natural or spiritual. Hooker briefly makes use here of his doctrine of Christ's presence, as Christ must be present *in* man.[91] This means that, for the believer, there is no such thing as his own spiritual life as being separate from the presence of the life of Christ. The life of the believer, both natural and spiritual, is totally and inseparably linked to the life of Christ himself. Actually, following the testimony of Scripture, Hooker insists on the fact that Christ[92] is present *in* the believer[93] and that he lives in the heart of the believer because the new heart comes from faith, as also suggested by Tyndale[94]:

> The soul which quickneth the body is in the body, and it must be in the soul which the soul of man liveth by. Except therfore Christ be trulie in you through him ye cannot be made alive.[95]

Next, Hooker deals with the nature and the way of Christ's presence within the man who has been saved. Before expounding his own view, Hooker briefly describes two theological positions which are both

---

89   Hooker, *Pride* (*Works* V, 326.1-8).
90   Booty, "Hooker's Understanding of the Presence of Christ in the Eucharist", 133; Neelands, "Hooker on Scripture, Reason and 'Tradition'", in McGrade (ed.), *Richard Hooker and the Construction of Christian Community*, 76-83.
91   See also George, *The Protestant Mind of the English Reformation*, 348.
92   For the connection between Christ and Scripture, see also Atkinson, *Richard Hooker and the Authority of Scripture, Tradition and Reason*, 129.
93   Rupp, *Studies in the Making of the English Protestant Tradition*, 168.
94   Tyndale, *Prologue to Romans*, 123.
95   Hooker, *Pride* (*Works* V, 326.8-11).

extreme. The first is based on a rather apophatic hermeneutic, which is very pessimistic about the means of expression, and holds that Christ's presence in man is a total mystery, which is impossible to decrypt. Theological language is void of the necessary words. Although Christians are not able to comprehend this mystery at all, they must, however, believe it wholeheartedly.[96] The second is a reference to the Catholic theology of Christ's presence in man and it is described as being utterly cataphatic, with a very optimistic approach to the possibilities of language. God's Words have not been uttered in vain, therefore they are comprehensive to humans. Regarding Christ's presence in man, they hold that there is a very close link between Christ himself and humanity to the point that Christ is totally blended with man. Catholics describe this as a "mutual participation". Hooker notices that the distinction between Christ, as God and consequently as Creator, and man, as created being, is blown away by such a theology, which is supportive of a real, material (or physical) and natural mixture between the being of Christ and that of the believer:

> Others considering that for as much as the end of all speech is to impart unto others the mind of him that speaketh, the woordes which God so often uttereth concerning this point must needes be frivolous and vain if to conceave the meaning of them were a thing impossible, have therfore expounded our conjunction with Christ to be a mutuall participation wherby ech is blended with the other, his flesh and blood with ours and ours in like sort with his, even as reallie materiallie and naturallie as wax melted and blended with wax into one lump, no other difference but that this mixture may be sensiblie perceived the other not.[97]

Hooker is not at all happy with the language of a material, specifically physical, presence of Christ in the believer.[98] For him, such an attempt to describe Christ as being present in the saved man is not only against the testimony of Scripture but also against reason itself.[99] Christ and the saved person must be two different entities from the point of view of physical existence. There is an intimate union between Christ and the

96   ibid. 326.23-25.
97   ibid. 326.25-327.4.
98   Stone, A History of the Doctrine of the Holy Eucharist, 240; Booty, "Contrition in Anglican Spirituality: Hooker, Donne and Herbert", in William J. Wolf (ed.), Anglican Spirituality (Wilton: Morehouse-Barlow, 1982), 26.
99   For the relationship between Scripture and reason, see also Brockwell, "Answering to 'Known Men': Bishop Reginald Pecock and Mr. Richard Hooker", 142; Neelands, "Hooker on Scripture, Reason and 'Tradition'", in McGrade (ed.), Richard Hooker and the Construction of Christian Community, 76-80; Collinson, "Hooker and the Elizabethan Establishment", in McGrade (ed.), Richard Hooker and the Construction of Christian Community, 168.

believer but only intellectually or spiritually. As usual, Hooker starts his argument from Scripture and then fosters proofs from the ecclesiastical tradition. Thus, he uses the writings of the apostle Paul and those of Gregory Nazianzus. Basically, Hooker argues that the existence of Christ is physical. Such a theological truth is of great importance to salvation, as it builds it on solid ground. Since Christ's existence is physical, the saved knows that his own existence has a firm confirmation of future life. In addition, Hooker makes reference to the physical existence of Christ on earth as being the hermeneutical key for the proper understanding of Christ's presence in the saved person. When Christ was present in the flesh during his earthly ministry, everybody could see him as an individual. So, he was physically present among the disciples. But, as has been shown, for Hooker the presence of Christ is a matter of the intellect or of the soul, which infers a mutual participation in knowledge, not in physical terms, between Christ and the believer.[100] Christ knows the believers and they know Christ. This is mutual participation and mutual knowledge.[101] It is by means of the mind and spirit that Christ is part of the believer's life. The believer has life because he knows Christ. The believer has life because Christ knows him. Even more important for Hooker's argument is the reference to the Spirit of Christ who gives life.[102] Tyndale, for instance, had said that the Spirit also gives faith, so faith comes from the Spirit.[103] Consequently, the believer has life because he has Christ and the Spirit of Christ. It is not too far fetched an argument

---

100 See also Allchin, "The Theology of Nature in the Eastern Fathers and among Anglican Theologians", in Montefiore (ed.), *Man and Nature* (London: Collins, 1975), 151; Booty, "Contrition in Anglican Spirituality: Hooker, Donne and Herbert", in William J. Wolf (ed.), *Anglican Spirituality* (Wilton: Morehouse-Barlow, 1982), 26; Wolf, Booty, and Thomas (eds), *The Spirit of Anglicanism*, 17; Booty, "The English Reformation: A Lively Faith and Sacramental Confession", 25; Kirby, *Richard Hooker's Doctrine of Royal Supremacy*, 46; Crerar, *Positive Negatives*, 181; Gregg, "Sacramental Theology in Hooker's *Laws*: A Structural Perspective", *Anglican Theological Review* 73/2 (1991), 169-171; Booty, "The Spirituality of Participation in Richard Hooker", *Sewanee Theological Review* 38/1 (1994), 9-20; Sedgwick, "The New Shape of Anglican Identity", *Anglican Theological Review* LXXVII/2 (1995), 189; Booty, "Anglican Identity: What is This Book of Common Prayer?", *Sewanee Theological Review* 40/2 (1997), 142; Stevenson, *The Mystery of Baptism in the Anglican Tradition*, 42; Schwarz, "Dignified and Commodius: Richard Hooker's 'Mysticall Copulation' Metaphor", *Sewanee Theological Review* 43/1 (1999), 16; Newey, "The Form of Reason: Participation in the Work of Richard Hooker, Benjamin Whichcote, Ralph Cudworth and Jeremy Taylor", *Modern Theology* 18/1 (2002), 7.

101 Crerar, *Positive Negatives*, 181.

102 Hooker, *Pride* (*Works* V, 328.9-10).

103 Tyndale, *Prologue to Romans*, 123.

to say that for Hooker, the believer has life because he knows Christ and the Holy Spirit.

7.5.2 The Presence of Christ and the Work of the Holy Trinity

What Hooker wants to clarify is that the way Christ is present in the believer did not change after his resurrection and ascension in heaven. Although Christ is no longer present physically, what matters is the bond of knowledge and love which exists or existed between him and his saved people. Physical presence in the believer is totally irrelevant, but what makes intellectual and spiritual presence vital is its real character given by Christ's physical existence with God. The presence of Christ in the believer is not physical, but this does not mean it is not real. The real character of Christ's presence is given by Christ's physical existence in heaven. It is now time for Hooker to build his view of Christ's presence on his doctrine of the Trinity.[104] As already shown, Christ and the Spirit of Christ, or the Holy Spirit, have been essential to the argument.[105] For Hooker, however, this is not enough. Another element should be introduced and this is God the Father. The believer who knows and loves Christ must acknowledge and confess him as the Son of God. Although it could be argued that, before the resurrection and ascension, the real physical presence of Christ would somehow have compensated for the necessity of Christ being spiritually present in the believer, Hooker notices a vital pneumatological aspect which strengthens his doctrine of salvation and of Christ's presence in the saved person. Firstly, human nature, though saved, is still incapable of knowing God by its own natural means. This is why God has devised a means whereby the saved person should be able to know him. This is the work of the Holy Spirit. Again, regardless of its obvious importance, the physical presence of Christ is not necessarily a warranty that men would eventually know him in a soteriological way. God has planned that Christ should be present in his followers by the Holy Spirit, even if he is not physically present among them. The physical character of Christ's earthly presence does not diminish his spiritual or intellectual presence during his ministry in history or during his existence beyond the realm of created universe. Secondly, God is sovereign in salvation or in both justification and subsequent

---

104 Booty, "An Elizabethan Addresses Modern Anglicanism. Richard Hooker and Theological Issues at the End of the Twentieth Century", 10.

105 Booty, "Contrition in Anglican Spirituality: Hooker, Donne and Herbert", in William J. Wolf (ed.), *Anglican Spirituality* (Wilton: Morehouse-Barlow, 1982), 26.

aspects of the believer's life. In spite of the fact that God has design the way man should know Christ and have him present within his life, the saved person still has a duty to perform, and this is to confess that Christ is the Son of God through the work of the Spirit. For the believer, the relationship between Christ and the Spirit is equally important with the relationship between Christ and God. Thus, a person who is saved knows Christ through the Spirit and God the Father through Christ the Son. Hooker elaborates his view:

> Which grosse concept doth fight openlie against reason. For are not wee and Christ personallie distinguished? Are we not locallie devided and severed ech from other? *My little Children* saith the apostle *of whome I travail in birth againe until Christ be formed in you.* Did the blessed apostle mean materiallie and reallie to create Christ in them flesh and blood soul and bodie? No, *Christ is in us* saith Gregorie Naziazene not kata. to. faino,menon but kata. to, noou,menon not *according to that naturall substance which visiblie was seen on earth*: but *according to that intellectuall comprehension which the mind is capable of.* So that the difference between Christ on earth and Christ in us is no lesse then between a ship on the sea and in the mind of him that builded it: the one a sensible thing the other a meere shape of a thing sensible. That wherby thapostle therefore did forme Christ was the Gospell. So that Christ was formed when Christianitie was comprehended. As things which wee know and delight in are said to dwell in our mindes and possesse our harts: So Christ *knowing his sheepe* and being known of them loving and being loved is not without cause said to be in them and they in him. And foras much as wee are not on our part heereof by our own inclination capable God hath geven unto his that spirit which teaching their harts to acknowledge and *tongues to confesse Christ* the sonne of the living God is for this cause also said to quicken. [106]

The visible token of salvation is a new kind of life in the one who has faith. The saved believer has a life of his own, but what makes him truly a proof of God's work of salvation is the life of God which is manifested in him.

7.5.3 The Life of the Believer and the Life of the Proud Man

Hooker makes a very clear point of contrast between the life of the saved believer and the life of the unsaved sinner. Natural life is present in both, but spiritual life, the life of God, is only present in the saved believer. The other is dead, has no life from God and is totally estranged from the influence of divine life.[107] The matter of how divine

---

106 Hooker, *Pride* (*Works* V, 327.4-25). See also Gregory Nazianzus, *Lettres théologiques* 101.30-31 in *Sources chrétiennes* 208:48 (Paris: Editions du Cerf, 1974).
107 Morrel, "Richard Hooker, Theologian of the English Reformation", 9.

life begins in the existence of man is utterly important for Hooker. The
first step he takes in his attempt to explain the way divine life starts in
human beings has its point of departure in the notion of pride, which
has been closely associated to sin. A proud man will always live as he
himself pleases with an obvious orientation of his affections[108] towards
the immediate benefit of his own existence. Sin is the characteristic of a
man who leads a life governed by pride and all his actions are deeply
affected by such an attitude to living. Vanity, ignorance, thanklessness,
lack of mercy, of conscience, of purpose, greed and moral decay make
up a list which characterises the life of all those who live in sin and are
proud about it. Hooker's verdict is categorical: such people are not
within the beneficial sphere of the life of God:

> Touching the maner of life spirituall heere begun: Of them that walk in the
> blind vanitie of their own mindes, that *have their cogitations darkned through
> ignorance*, that *have hardned their harts*, that are conscienceless, that have
> resigned them selves over unto wantonnesse, that are gredilie set upon all
> uncleanes and sinne, of such it is plainlie determined: They are dead:
> Strangers they are from the life of God.[109]

Hooker is clear about the fact that the life of God in man begins with
regeneration, and this is perfectly in line with Bradford, in whose
theology regeneration is equalled to justification.[110] A similar approach
may also be seen in Foxe.[111] For Hooker, the essence of the life of God
which is present in the justified believer[112] has two main features.

7.5.4 The Essence of Spiritual Life in the Justified Believer

Firstly, it clearly puts forward the idea of divine dwelling,[113] which of
course is connected to the notion of divine presence that has already
been analysed. The justified man is no longer leading a life of his own,
but one which should be increasingly controlled by God. The manner
of God's presence in the believer has been mentioned before, but
Hooker chooses to make this important point again: Christ and the

---

108 For the importance of affections in Hooker, see Crerar, *Positive Negatives*, 192;
    Almasy, "They Are and Are Not Elymas: the 1641 'Causes' Notes as Postscript to
    Richard Hooker's *Of the Laws of the Ecclesiastical Polity*", in McGrade, *Richard Hooker
    and the Construction of Christian Community*, 200.
109 Hooker, *Pride* (*Works* V, 327.27-328.4).
110 Bradford, *Writings*, 217-218.
111 Foxe, *The Acts and Monuments*, 71.
112 Gregg, "Sacramental Theology in Hooker's *Laws*: A Structural Perspective", *Anglican
    Theological Review* 73/2 (1991), 173.
113 Rupp, *Studies in the Making of the English Protestant Tradition*, 168.

Spirit must live in the justified believer and this is the sign of God's presence because faith comes from the Spirit,[114] as plainly acknowledged by Tyndale.[115] This Trinitarian approach to divine life in man, which is actually his spiritual life, has an immediate practical applicability.

Thus secondly, the spiritual life of the justified should produce internal and external deeds which are pleasing to God. Inner thoughts and outward manifestations should all be acceptable in the sight of God,[116] as Hooker puts it following Tyndale.[117] The believer lives in the sight of God, and this is an essential point to make. Every aspect which belongs to his life, either natural of spiritual, is known to God and accordingly supported by him. Pneumatology again becomes an issue as Hooker explains that God upholds the lives of believers by means of the work of the Holy Spirit. The justified lives because Christ, the Son of God, gives him divine life and support through the Spirit. He had previously been a selfish being, oriented towards himself and working in such a way that only his own pleasures should be satisfied. Self-righteousness had been all he needed. This kind of life, however, ceased to be manifested as God regenerated him. Now, with the assistance of the Holy Spirit, the justified man seeks whatever is pleasing to God and consequently a righteousness which is not his own but that of God. This is how Hooker explains his views on spiritual life:

> Which life [the life of God] is nothing els but a spirituall and divine kind of being which men by regeneration attain unto, Christ and his spirit dwelling in them and as the soul of their souls moving them unto such both inward and outward actions as *in the sight of God are acceptable*. As they that life naturallie have their naturall nourishment wherewith they are sustained: So he to whome the Spirit of Christ giveth life hath whereon he also delighteth to feed. He *hungreth after righteousnes*.[118]

Justification and regeneration produce a dramatic change in the life of the believer, also advocated by Bradford,[119] which leads to obedience to Christ as in Foxe.[120] He is no longer self-centred but would rather expand his life outwards, to both God and his fellow men. As far as his

---

114 Gane, "The Exegetical Methods of Some Sixteenth Century Anglican Preachers: Latimer, Jewel, Hooker, and Andrews", 35.

115 Tyndale, *Prologue to Romans*, 123.

116 Griffith Thomas (ed.), *The Principles of Theology*, 186.

117 Tyndale, *Prologue to Romans*, 129.

118 Hooker, *Pride* (Works V, 328.4-10).

119 Bradford, *The Writings*, 218.

120 Foxe, *The Acts and Monuments*, 71.

new relationship to God is concerned,[121] the believer will seek the righteousness of God as shown – see also Barnes[122] – which will deeply affect the way he lives in community among other people. For the justified, all social barriers fall. Everybody is potentially a fellow brother in faith, and actually a creature of God towards whom love and affection should flow as proof of his new spiritual life. Distinctions like friendship-enmity are things of the past: from now on, everybody deserves love and nobody is a foe. The new ethic of love towards enemies is part of the life of God working in the believer. He will now pray for his persecutors and do whatever he can possibly achieve for his brothers. Hooker is very specific when he claims that all these are possible due to the spiritual life which is heavily backed by the presence and dwelling of Christ in the believer[123] through the Holy Spirit. Natural life will never be able to produce the fruit of the Spirit. Years, decades, centuries and even millennia do not provide enough time for a natural man to live like a spiritual man. Hooker explains why, and the answer is because human nature is stricken by sin and, unless redeemed, justified and renewed, it will never be able to lose sight of itself and live for others in love. It is not within the capabilities of sinful human nature to redeem itself.[124] The presence of Christ, the Son of God, through the indwelling of the Spirit[125] is the only means of support for the new life of the believer,[126] which is actually his justification as also suggested by Cranmer.[127] Hooker is keenly aware that a new set of gifts are bestowed (by grace)[128] upon the justified man who is thus enabled to detach himself from his old and sinful practices:

> And as the sense so the motion of him that liveth the life of God hath a peculiar kind of excellencie. His hands are not stretched out towards his enemies except it be to give them almes; his feet are slow save onlie when he traveleth for the benefit of his brethren; when he is railed upon by the wicked his voyce is not otherwise heard then the voyce of Stephen *Lord lay not this thing to their charge*. Though we could triple the yeeres of

121 Griffith Thomas (ed.), *The Principles of Theology*, 185.
122 Barnes, *The Supplication of 1531*, xciiii.b.
123 Rupp, *Studies in the Making of the English Protestant Tradition*, 168.
124 See also Marshall, *Hooker and the Anglican Tradition*, 112.
125 According to Peter Toon, this is the formal cause of sanctification in Hooker. See Toon, *Foundations for Faith*, 95.
126 Booty, "Contrition in Anglican Spirituality: Hooker, Donne and Herbert", in William J. Wolf (ed.), *Anglican Spirituality* (Wilton: Morehouse-Barlow, 1982), 26.
127 Cranmer, *The 1530 Articles*, 4.
128 Keble, *The Works*, vol. 2, 552; Secor, *Richard Hooker, Prophet of Anglicanism*, 185.

Methusalem or live as long as the moon doth endure, our naturall life without this what were it?[129]

The believer is changed inwardly so that he may perform good deeds outwardly. He begins a life which is totally abnormal to those who do not know Christ. Hooker is obviously speaking about the life of sanctification which is the visible outcome of the justification offered by God.

7.5.5 Justification, Sanctification, and Spiritual Life

The importance of the work of God in both justification and sancti-fication[130] has a tremendous significance, because God had been actively involved in the justification of the sinner, as also advocated by Barnes,[131] and he is also actively working in the new life of the justified believer. It is not that the importance of man's response is futile,[132] but what Hooker intends to underline is the fact that God's deeds in justification and subsequent sanctification are far more important then what man does. The action of God in salvation is the more important because it is the one which offers firm warranty that justification and sanctification are available for humanity. Both God's part and man's part in soteriology are important, but it is only God who secures salvation for human beings. Apart from what God does, man is totally incapable of performing whatever works which might provide the necessary righteousness of justification. There is a righteousness of justification but it cannot be attained by man.[133] Only God is able to offer it.[134] Should anyone argue that God's part is more important in justification that in sanctification, Hooker would reply that God's action is vital in both. Man is unable to carry out his new life in Christ[135]

---

129 Hooker, *Pride* (*Works* V, 328.19-27).

130 Booty, "The English Reformation: A Lively Faith and Sacramental Confession", 24; Sykes, *The Study of Anglicanism*, 67; Booty, "An Elizabethan Addresses Modern Anglicanism. Richard Hooker and Theological Issues at the End of the Twentieth Century", 14-15.

131 Barnes, *The Supplication of 1531*, xliii.a.

132 For more details about Hooker's view on man's response to God, see Booty, "Contrition in Anglican Spirituality: Hooker, Donne and Herbert", in William J. Wolf (ed.), *Anglican Spirituality* (Wilton: Morehouse-Barlow, 1982), 29.

133 Kirby, "Richard Hooker as an Apologist of the Magisterial Reformation in England", in McGrade, *Richard Hooker and the Construction of Christian Community*, 226.

134 Stanwood, "Of Prelacy and Polity in Milton and Hooker", in Margo Swiss and David Kent (eds), *Heirs of Fame. Milton and Writers of the English Renaissance*, 69.

135 Collinson, *Archbishop Grindal*, 41.

to the end by himself. The new life which he has is not his but God's. It is only because the new life of the believer is the life of God that he is able to perform outwardly the deeds which show such a high degree of abnormality to non-believing humanity. The life of God which is present in the justified believer changes every aspect of his being. Although Hooker does not say this in plain words, the way he describes the actions of the life of God which flow into the earthly life of the justified is a clear recognition of such reality. Man is totally changed by the new life which is not his. Reason, will and feeling are all divinely changed in a body which is still living on earth. If before justification, man was inwardly pushed towards bad works by his inner corrupt nature, now the new life of God will continuously urge him to do good things. Hooker is very realistic about the composition of man's life after justification. He is totally aware that God works justification and sanctification[136] in a body which is affected by corruption.[137] Should the new life of the believer be entirely his own, it would be only a short time before his sinful human nature actually begins to orient him towards evil again. But when justification occurs and is followed naturally by sanctification, as also suggested by Bradford,[138] the believer is changed by something which is not his own, but God's. This is why it is possible that he should abhorr the works of his defiled human nature, which is exactly what a sinner cannot do. The clash between these two ways of life, that of the justified sinner and that of the non-justified sinner, will inevitably result in suffering on the part of the former. In spite of the reality of such suffering, the life of God in the justified believer will continue to amaze those who are not God's by doing precisely the opposite of what the sinful world expects. Virtues like love, patience, integrity, purity, meekness and many others which Hooker so masterfully describes in simple words on the foundation of Scripture are performed by believers because their lives are not their own any more, but the life of God is the only one which rules their entire existence:

> This altereth and changeth our corrupt nature, by this wee are continuallie stirred up unto good thinges, by this wee are brought to *loath and abhor* the grosse defilements of the wicked world, constantly and patiently to suffer

---

136 Sykes, *The Study of Anglicanism*, 67; Booty, "An Elizabethan Addresses Modern Anglicanism. Richard Hooker and Theological Issues at the End of the Twentieth Century", 14-15.

137 Kirby, *Richard Hooker's Doctrine of Royal Supremacy*, 46; Bouwsma, "Hooker in the Context of European Cultural History", in Claire McEachern and Deborah Shuger (eds), *Religion and Culture in Renaissance England*, 149.

138 Bradford, *Writings*, 218.

whatsoever doth befall us though *as sheep we are led by flocks unto the slaughter*: this dispelleth the cloudes of darkness, easeth the hart of griefe, abateth hatred, *composeth strife, appeaseth anger*, ordereth our affections, ruleth our thoughtes, guideth our lives and conversations. Whence is it that we find in Abel such innocencie, in Enoch such Pietie, in Noah such equitie, in Abraham such faith, in Isaac such simplicitie, such longanimitie in Iacob such chastitie in Joseph, such meekness and tenderness of hart in Moses, in Samuel such devotion, in Daniel such humilitie, in Elias such authority, in Elizeus such zeal, such courage in prophets, in apostles such love, such patience in Martyrs, such integrity in all true Sainctes? did they not all live the life of god?[139]

The reference Hooker makes to the life of God which is already part of the believer's existence in the created world proves to be the introduction to his description of the life to come.

7.5.6 Glorification as the Eschatological Fulfillment of Spiritual Life

It is evident that in Hooker's thought justification, sanctification, and glorification are closely connected. In other words, Hooker's understanding of justification is eschatologically oriented. Justification is the event which offers the ground for a transformed life, as vividly explained by Barnes.[140] The transformed life of the believer or the life of sanctification becomes increasingly subject to the ongoing influence of the life of God. The believer's new life of sanctification is only the beginning of eternal life. The physical break between the created world and the realm of God is overtaken by the continuous spiritual *liaison* established between a sanctified life on earth and a glorified existence in heaven, on the basis of justification. Thus, in Hooker's understandding, justification seems to be the beginning of sanctification and the promise of glorification. All these seem to be linked by means of faith because it is by faith that we believe any promise which comes from God, as Tyndale also suggested.[141] In this respect, two fundamental concepts are vital to this discussion: firstly, the promise of God, and secondly, the hope of the believer. It should be noted that although justification, sanctification, and glorification are all of equal importance, the one which is most relevant to Hooker's approach at this point is sanctification. As a result of justification, the new transformed life of the believer in sanctification is totally based on Christ's promise that he

---

139 Hooker, *Pride* (*Works* V, 328.27-329.10).
140 Barnes, *The Supplication of 1531*, xlix.b.
141 Tyndale, *Prologue to Romans*, 124.

would give abundant life to those who know him.[142] It is now that Hooker makes a clear connection between justification, sanctification and their eschatological fulfilment. The believer should exercise his hope in things to come, and in life beyond death, which is also a preoccupation of Foxe.[143] Actually, he should be aware that his new life which was given to him by God as a result of his justification is, as already shown, the very life of God as, for instance, in Cranmer.[144] Thus, based on this reality, his existence does not cease in death but rather continues in the world to come. It is important to notice that the promise of God is founded on the work of Christ, which is also true in Foxe.[145] Thus, man's entire salvation is totally dependent upon what God has done[146] in order that humanity should be restored and given eternal life,[147] as also suggested by Bradford.[148] Hooker explains:

> Which life heere begun (to come to the last point) shall be in the world to come finished. Whereof wee have heretofore spoken largely. And when wee have spoken all we can speak all which we can speak is but this, He which hath it hath more then speech can possibly expresse and as much as his hart can wish: he doth abound and hàth enough. For the wourdes of the promise of life in the 10th of John are these *I came that my sheep might have life and might abound.*[149]

The promise of God goes against all human predictions. The earthly life of the justified believer is eschatologically extended beyond history, into the future world. It is important to notice that God's promise comes to the Christian from the world of God, and that the Christian is closely connected to the world of God by means of the notion of hope. Thus, justification is eschatologically oriented towards God through hope. There is a two way interaction between God and humanity in Hooker's theology. Firstly, God extends his love to us through his promise of justification, and secondly, we respond to God by means of hope. Such a hope in the world to come helps the justified in the difficulties of the present life and it also helps him when the moment of his departure from this world comes. Hooker is sure that this hope

---

142 Hooker, *Pride* (*Works* V, 329.17).
143 Foxe, *The Acts and Monuments*, 71.
144 Cranmer, *The 1538 Articles*, 4.
145 Foxe, *The Acts and Monuments*, 71.
146 This means it is dependent upon Christ and his atoning work. Booty, "Hooker's Understanding of the Presence of Christ in the Eucharist", 133; Neelands, "Hooker on Scripture, Reason and 'Tradition'", in McGrade (ed.), *Richard Hooker and the Construction of Christian Community*, 76-83.
147 Griffith Thomas (ed.), *The Principles of Theology*, 185.
148 Bradford, *Writings*, 314.
149 Hooker, *Pride* (*Works* V, 329.11-17).

reaches the world of God, and is a firm foundation for the soul. Justification, the sanctification of the justified and eschatology are all brought together by means of hope, which speaks of the inheritance that believers have in God. Hope is the support for this life, and for the moment when the justified is transferred from here to the realm of God through death. Nothing in this world is capable of frightening the Christian, as he knows – by means of hope – that a new life has been expecting him since God justified him. Scripture is again the basis of Hooker's approach:

> Seeing therfore wee are taught that life is the lot of our inheritance and that when wee have it we have enough, wherfore struggle we so much for other thinges which we may verie well want and yeat about? When wee leave the world this hope leaves us not, it doth not forsake us not unto the grave. Sundrie are the casualties of this present world, the trials manie and fearfull which wee are subject unto. But in the midst of all, this must be the chiefest *ancre unto our souls, The just shall live.* Wherfore this God setteth before the eyes of his poore afflicted people as having in it force sufficient to countervail whatsoever miserie they either did or might sustain. These dreadfull names of trobles, wars, invasions the verie mention whereof doth so much terrifie, waigh them with hartes resolved in this that *the just shall live* and what are they but panicall terrours?[150]

At this point, Hooker makes a very important step as he wants to anchor the whole of salvation and the spiritual life of the believer in the work of God alone. He does so by linking justification and the life of the justified to the concept of God's sovereignty.

7.5.7 The Sovereignty of God in Salvation

It has been proved that God's sovereignty extends over salvation and all its steps, such as justification, sanctification and the eschatological fulfilment. The Christian should know, however, that God's sovereignty is not limited to salvation but rather it encompasses every single aspect of the believer's existence. Life on earth is totally supervised by God and there is absolutely nothing which could possibly escape his vigilant eye. Everything is under close scrutiny and God is in control of all apparently insignificant aspects of life. Hooker's speech is bluntly clear but the style of his theology is softer. God is described as being our heavenly Father, so that the entire discourse on hope becomes ultimately significant as the relationship between God

---

150 *ibid.* 329.18-30.

and the justified is the same as the one between a father and his son.[151] In line with Cranmer,[152] Hooker contends that the believer can and must put his trust in his heavenly Father:[153] this will bring him, by hope, into the world of his God.

When he writes about the reality of God's control over the life of believers, Hooker resorts to the concept of God's will, which is descriptive of God's sovereignty. Hooker does not run out of biblical support and he briefly mentions that many of the saints were delivered by God in this life, which speaks with great clarity of God's constant care over his children. On the grounds of God's sovereign will, the evil plans of sinners are turned into good situations for the benefit of the saved.[154] Nevertheless, Hooker is not blissfully ignorant. Consequently, he acknowledges that life is not only a chain of happy events. Suffering is part of the believer's existence. In spite of such troubles, the promise of God stands for ever, so that the saved may have total confidence in the life and happiness which will be his when he is with God. There is a reason to trust in such a happy end, and Hooker the theologian explains doxologically that the Holy Trinity has worked out the entire plan of salvation.[155] God the Father is the one who calls the saved in union with him and makes them partakers of his everlasting life[156] on the basis of the work of his son, the Lord Jesus Christ, our Saviour – an image of Christ also used by Cranmer[157] – and through the intervention of the Holy Spirit:

> If they promise great things which are not of power and habilitie to perform the least thing promised what wise man amongst you is there whome such presumptuous promises doe not make rather to laugh then to hope? Yeat behold at the threatnings of men we trebmle though wee know that their rage is limited, that they cannot doe what they list, that *the heares of our heades are numbered*, that of so manie there falleth not one to the ground without the privitie and will of our heavenly Father. How often hath God turned those verie purposes counsels and enterprises therewith the death of his Sainctes hath bene sought both to the safetie of their lives

---

151 Griffith Thomas (ed.), *The Principles of Theology*, 185.

152 Cranmer, *The 1538 Articles*, 4.

153 Griffith Thomas (ed.), *The Principles of Theology*, 191; Booty, "The Spirituality of Participation in Richard Hooker", *Sewanee Theological Review* 38/1 (1994), 11; Sedgwick, "The New Shape of Anglican Identity", *Anglican Theological Review* LXXVII/2 (1995), 189.

154 For details about the benefits of the justified, see Morrel, "Richard Hooker, Theologian of the English Reformation", 9.

155 Booty, "An Elizabethan Addresses Modern Anglicanism. Richard Hooker and Theological Issues at the End of the Twentieth Century", 10.

156 Morrel, "Richard Hooker, Theologian of the English Reformation", 9.

157 Cranmer, *Annotations on the King's Book*, 12.

and increase also of their honours? Was it not thus in Joseph, in Moses, in David, in Daniel? If crueltie, oppression and tyrannie do so far foorth prevail that they have their desires and prosper in that which whey take in hand: the utmost of that evell which they can doe is but that verie good which the blessed apostle doth wish, *Cupio discolvi*. Thrise happie therfore are those men whome whatsoever miserie befalleth in this present world it findeth them settled in a sure expectation of that which heere God promiseth the just, felicitie and life in the world to come: Whereof God the Father make you partakers through the merits of his *onlie begotten Sonne* our blessed Saviour unto whome with the holie ghost three persons one eternall and everliving God be honour glorie and praise for ever.[158]

Hooker is not only interested in a thorough investigation of the content of salvation but also manifests a deep concern for the reason which lies beneath the very plan of salvation.

7.5.8 Carelessness as Reason for the Salvation of Humanity

Why is salvation needed in relation to humanity or, in other words, why does man need salvation at all? This question makes Hooker think of the practical reality of everyday life, which – for all people – is characterised by a more or less unconscious performance of acts against God's will. Willingly or not, man is doing things which are not according to the prescriptions of God and which consequently lead to the perdition of every man's soul. Hooker is convinced that the representatives of humanity all perform the same evil or sinful deeds and yet they all have an inner desire to live.[159] Although not clearly stated, Hooker is inferring here the fact that God punishes sin which results in death, as plainly explained by Foxe,[160] and he also infers that man is aware of this to a certain degree. In spite of his awareness of God's punishment of sin, man still does bad things while he hopes his life will somehow be kept safe. Thus, from the perspective of man's sinful daily living, Hooker identifies the core of such a destructive reality, which in his opinion is carelessness. The biggest problem man ever faces in life is total indifference, on the one hand, towards God, and on the other, towards his own sinful acts. Indifference is the way to

---

158 Hooker, *Pride* (*Works* V, 329.30-331.21). For Hooker's doxological theology, see *Believing the Church. The Corporate Nature of Faith* (London: SPCK, 1981), 98; and Booty, "The Judicious Mr. Hooker and the Authority in the Elizabethan Church", in Stephen W. Sykes (ed.), *Authority in the Anglican Communion*, 95.
159 Neelands, "Hooker on Scripture, Reason and 'Tradition'", in McGrade (ed.), *Richard Hooker and the Construction of Christian Community*, 76-83.
160 Foxe, *The Acts and Monuments*, 71.

perdition as it makes man perceive the reality of sin in the worst distorted way ever. Thus, the corrupted reasoning of his mind allows for the nonexistent possibility that his sins will not be considered against him so that his life will be spared. For Hooker, salvation is needed because man cannot have a correct judgement of his own sins. Actually, man shows a fundamental lack of interest towards his own life even if he is aware of the bad deeds he performs. Rationally, man should cease to do this if he really knows what the outcome is, but this would never happen if man is left alone. By his own powers, man is totally incapable of stopping sinning even if he knows perfectly well that his sin will lead him to death. Nevertheless, man hopes – against all odds – that his life will be preserved, although the Word of God does not give room to this possibility. This is why man needs salvation. As already shown, salvation is totally the work of God[161] practically invading the life of a man who has a distorted image of his own life, as also admitted by Foxe.[162] Unless God had himself devised salvation for humanity, men and women would never have been capable of realising that they were heading towards the perdition of their own souls. In Hooker's words:

> There never was that man so carelessly affected towards the safetie of his own soul, but knowing what salvation and life doth mean though his own waies were the verie paths of endlesse destruction yeat his secret naturall desyer must needes be not to perish but to live.[163]

Though salvation was devised by God in order that man should be correctly aware of his own sins, there is a part which belongs to man in its entirety. The Word of God contains instructions of what man must do in order to have his life preserved from perdition and cleansed from sins,[164] as also acknowledged by Frith.[165] Man should follow these instructions if he really wants to live. There is no room left for carelessness; indifference is not the answer for those who wish to gain life. God is ready to work in accordance with his Word for the benefit of humanity[166], but man must also do his part. It is clear to Hooker that the work of God is ultimately that which is fundamental to the realisation of man's salvation. Thus, salvation is closely connected to

161 Rupp, *Studies in the Making of the English Protestant Tradition*, 167.
162 Foxe, *The Acts and Monuments*, 71.
163 Hooker, *Pride* (*Works* V, 331.22-27). See also Hooker, *Pride* (*Works* V, 331.27-332.11).
164 See also Morrel, "Richard Hooker, Theologian of the English Reformation", 9; Grislis, "The Assurance of Faith according to Richard Hooker", in McGrade, *Richard Hooker and the Construction of Christian Community*, 240.
165 Frith, *A Disputation of Purgatory*, 90.
166 Morrel, "Richard Hooker, Theologian of the English Reformation", 9.

the sovereignty of God, which is described by means of phrases taken from Scripture. Everything happens under God's scrutiny so that the promise of life should be made possible for all people freely, as also suggested by Foxe.[167] It is very important to underline that, for Hooker, pneumatology is essential in his discourse. God is doing his part, man should do his own part; God's work is evidently more important than man's but even so, God does not leave man to himself: the Holy Spirit is given to man to assist him in everything he does.[168] In line with Barnes, Hooker writes that the promise of life is not only described in the Word of God but that God is actively[169] involved in the realisation of his promise by the direct intervention of his Holy Spirit in the life of man because, as also suggested by Tyndale, faith comes from the Spirit.[170] To quote Hooker:

> For whatsoever the watchfull ey of God, whatsoever his attentive ear, whatsoever deliverance out of troble; whatsoever in troble neerenes of ghostly assistance; whatsoever salvation, custody, redemption, safe preservation of their souls and bodies and verie bones from perishing doth import, the promise of life includeth all.[171]

At this point, Hooker's argument takes a very important turn by introducing the concept of justice.

7.6 The Concept of Justice

It should be mentioned here that this is also important to Frith, who said that salvation implied clothing with the justice of Christ.[172] As the leitmotif of this sermon is the life given to the just person, *"By faith the just shall live"*[173], Hooker makes a brief description of justice, which ultimately originates in God.[174] Although justice is fundamentally an attribute of God, Hooker is defining justice on the basis of the

---

167 Foxe, *The Acts and Monuments*, 71.
168 Gane, "The Exegetical Methods of Some Sixteenth Century Anglican Preachers: Latimer, Jewel, Hooker, and Andrews", 35.
169 Barnes, *The Supplication of 1531*, xliii.a.
170 Tyndale, *Prologue to Romans*, 123.
171 Hooker, *Pride* (*Works* V, 332.14-19).
172 Frith, *Patrick Places*, 30.
173 Hooker mentions Habakkuk's verse many times in the sermon as, for instance, here in Hooker, *Pride* (*Works* V, 333.15).
174 Hooker acknowledges that there is a "justice which is in God". Cf. Hooker, *Pride* (*Works* V, 333.12-13).

experience of humankind. Man's justice, however, exists as a possibility
as well as a reality only if rooted in the justice of God. It is only through
the assistance of the Holy Spirit that man is able to behave in such a
way that justice should describe all his actions. For Hooker, man is
performing the deeds of justice whenever some particular qualities are
being enacted. Thus, sincerity, disgust towards evil, bias to good
works, peace, a constant life of prayer, a contrite or a new heart (which
is very important to Tyndale who said the new heart came from
faith),[175] a humble spirit, integrity, obedience, and trust in God[176] are all
signs of justice,[177] which is also of great importance to Cranmer.[178]
Evidently, this sort of justice is part of man's life and should be the core
of his existence but ultimately it derives its origin from God because
ultimately, as Tyndale also says, justification is from God.[179] The reason
is simple because only a child of God, a justified believer, can have the
above-mentioned qualities, among which the most relevant to a
relationship with God are trust,[180] contrition of heart[181] and a full life of
prayer, which is also vitally important for Foxe.[182] Following Tyndale
again,[183] Hooker writes that the promise of God believed by faith is
linked to the notion of justice, which makes the promise even more
relevant as our justice is, in fact, deeply rooted in the justice of God:

> And those sundrie rehearsed specialties, harmlesnes and sincerity in
> speech, aversnes from evell, inclination unto good things, pursuit of peace,
> *continuance in praier, contrition of hart,* humility of Spirit, integritie,
> obedience, trust and affiance in god, what import they more then this one
> onlie name of Justice doth insinuate? Which name expresseth fullie their
> qualitie unto whome God doth promise life.[184]

---

175 Tyndale, *Prologue to Romans*, 124.
176 Booty, "The Spirituality of Participation in Richard Hooker", *Sewanee Theological Review* 38/1 (1994), 11; Sedgwick, "The New Shape of Anglican Identity", *Anglican Theological Review* LXXVII/2 (1995), 189.
177 Griffith Thomas (ed.), *The Principles of Theology*, 191.
178 Cranmer, *The 1538 Articles*, 4.
179 Tyndale, *Prologue to Romans*, 123.
180 Sedgwick, "The New Shape of Anglican Identity", *Anglican Theological Review* LXXVII/2 (1995), 189.
181 For details about Hooker's understanding of contrition, see Booty, "Contrition in Anglican Spirituality: Hooker, Donne and Herbert", in William J. Wolf (ed.), *Anglican Spirituality* (Wilton: Morehouse-Barlow, 1982), 26; Gibbs, "Richard Hooker's *Via Media* Doctrine of Repentance", *Harvard Theological Review* 84/1 (1991), 59; Booty, "The Spirituality of Participation in Richard Hooker", *Sewanee Theological Review* 38/1 (1994), 11.
182 Foxe, *The Acts and Monuments*, 77.
183 Tyndale, *Prologue to Romans*, 124.
184 Hooker, *Pride* (Works V, 332.19-25).

As Hooker defines it, justice appears to be the main distinctive characteristic of God because the very existence of God and that of humanity is totally dependant upon justice. Thus, justice influences the welfare of this world by the fact that it sustains all things which are prone towards the progress of humankind. Within the framework of this sociological definition, justice is seen as being the foundation of good life for all social categories. As such, justice guarantees help for the poor, ease for the rich, honours for leaders, and finally peace to all living creatures. Hooker then supplements his sociological description with a theological layer. He is fully aware that the theological debates of his day, and ultimately the Reformation itself, were fostered by various interpretations given to justice, so he tries to offer a definition of justice:

> Justice that which flourishing upholdeth and not prevailing disturbeth shaketh threateneth with utter desolation and ruine the whole world; justice that wherby the poore have their succour, the rich their ease, the potent their honour, the living their peace, the souls of the righteous departed their endlesse rest and quietness; justice that which God and angels and men are principallie exalted by; justice the chiefest matter contended for at this daie in the Christian world; in a wourd justice that whereon non onlie all our present happiness but in the kingdome of God our future joy dependeth, so that whether wee be in love with the one or with the other, with *thinges present or things to come*, with earth or with heaven, in that which is so greatlie available to both none can but wish to be instructed.[185]

In the realm of God, justice is an evident attribute of God himself and of angels. Justice is important not only because it is both part of God's world and of man's cosmos; justice rather derives its particular importance from the fact that it makes an obvious connection between the realm of God and that of man. Justice not only has a soteriological relevance in our world but it also has an eschatological significance as it is the core of God's future kingdom. The present and the future are knit together by justice, which is available – as Hooker acknowledges – to both the created universe and the world of God. Hooker even writes that the rest of the dead is secured by justice.

Hooker distinguishes between three main domains concerning the notion of justice. Firstly, he identifies the "nature of justice in generall", secondly the justice of God, and thirdly the justice of the believer who had been considered just – see also Tyndale[186] – or the justice of the justified believer.[187]

---

185 *ibid.* 332.30-333.11.
186 Tyndale, *Prologue to Romans*, 128.
187 Hooker, *Pride* (*Works* V, 333.11-15).

7.6.1 The Justice of Man

Hooker's analysis of the nature of justice is directed towards the justice of man and the various kinds of laws which function within creation. By introducing the concept of creation in connection to the discussion on the nature of justice, Hooker actually infers that human justice[188] is the result of a higher justice, namely the justice of God. The justice of man is rooted in the justice of God because God created the world of man. What is utterly important for the whole discussion will be disclosed later, when Hooker concludes his investigation of human justice and laws. Accordingly, he underlines the fact that the justice of man is totally dependent on the justice of God by asserting the fundamental value of the work of God in Christ.[189] The work of Christ is the highest example of God's justice being applied to the realm of humanity for the sake of every human being, as also acknowledged by Frith.[190] For Hooker, this aspect proves to be so important that he even resorts to a doxology[191] which is directly addressed to the Holy Trinity.[192] The obvious intention of such a doxology is to further stress that the justice of man is not rooted in the justice of God by means of the work of Christ only but also by means of the work of the entire Holy Trinity. The justice of the triune God is the grounds for the justice of man and also the foundation of man's salvation,[193] which is also true in Cranmer.[194]

7.6.2 The Justice of God

The fact that there is justice in God and justice in man has been proved but Hooker takes a further step into his analysis by trying to demonstrate that the justice of God is inherent in the being of God. God

---

188 When compared to the grace of God in salvation, what really matters in the end is the grace of God not the justice of man. Collinson, *Archbishop Grindal*, 41.

189 *ibid.* 41.

190 Frith, *Patrick Places*, 30.

191 For the importance of doxology in Hooker, see also Targoff, "Performing Prayer in Hooker's *Laws*: The Efficacy of Set Forms", in McGrade, *Richard Hooker and the Construction of Christian Community*, 275-282.

192 Booty, "An Elizabethan Addresses Modern Anglicanism. Richard Hooker and Theological Issues at the End of the Twentieth Century", 10.

193 Hooker, *Pride* (*Works* V, 339.26-340.5).

194 Cranmer, Works II, 130.

is and remains just even if men do not exercise properly their own justice in the world. Hooker is aware of the way the human mind functions; consequently, his concern is to prove that God is inherently just although we are not just. For instance, it could be argued that man acquired the knowledge that God was just only because he traced at least a degree of justice in the deeds of humanity. The logical conclusion would be that God is just only because man is just to a certain degree. Hooker realises that such an approach is problematic because should man be totally unjust, one might reach the conclusion that God himself is unjust too.[195] This is the main problem of natural theology which states its doctrines on the basis of an analysis of the created world. As such, although no evident statement proves it, this argument is a confutation of medieval Catholic theology. For Hooker, human logic is not always the way to the truth of ontology. It is a mistake to say that God is just only because man notices that humanity is just. This logical approach would then make room for the conclusion that God is unjust only because man notices humanity is unjust. In Hooker's thinking, however, the ontology of God is essentially separated from the experience of humanity. Although humanity tends to construe an image of God based on its limited experience, God is and remains God regardless of whether humans apprehend him correctly or not. Thus, Hooker is convinced that there is justice in God even if there were absolutely no trace of justice in the realm of humanity:

> Wherein least any man should imagin that wee term God just not because in him selfe he is so, but because the liking which we have of and love which we bear unto our selves maketh us to think God such as we ourselves are, it shall not be expedient first to prove unto you that in God there is this divine virtue called justice.[196]

In conclusion, justice is part of God's being. Nevertheless, two problems still remain. Firstly, if God is truly God, it follows that there is no higher authority than himself. Consequently, there is no higher justice than the justice of God. By which standards should God's justice be judged properly? How does man know that the justice of God is objectively just if the justice of God is not subject to any higher kind of justice? Secondly, how is it possible that the justice of God be applied to the realm of utter injustice to which humanity belongs? These two matters of disputation might be put into one single question: is there any law which regulates the actions of God, should God be, in any way, subject to any law at all? To find a proper answer to these two problems, Hooker does not resort to his philosophical acumen but he

---

195 For more details, see Hooker, *Pride* (*Works* V, 340.18-341.16).
196 Hooker, *Pride* (*Works* V, 340.7-13).

rather chooses to use the sentences of Scripture. For Hooker, the answer to these questions is the absolute will of God.[197] Thus, the absolute will of God is the warrant of God's justice and of the application of God's justice in the fallen world of men: "To this we could make no answere at all if we did hold as they do who preremptorilie avouch that there is no maner *Why* to be rendered of anie thing which God doth but onlie this, It was his absolute will to doe it."[198]

The application of the justice of God in the fallen world of humanity is basically the enacting of God's salvation which is offered to the benefit of sinful men and women.[199] Hooker also expresses his disagreement with another medieval Catholic teaching which had shaped the understanding of salvation and justification: the doctrine of merit. Man's capacity to reason is fundamentally affected by sin, which makes some think they might have more merits than others in respect to earning the salvation of God. It is within the capacities of fallen human nature to promote the merit-oriented understanding of salvation but this is contrary to the teaching of Scripture.[200]

Thus, for Hooker, the cause of salvation should not be found within any merits – because man has no merits whatsoever which could deserve God's soteriological actions – but in the mercy of God, as in Barnes,[201] and in the good character of his absolute will. It is clear that, in Hooker's thought, salvation is kept as far as possible from the reach of human achievement. God's sovereignty, expressed by means of his absolute will, is the foundation of salvation and justification. At this point, Hooker displays a Reformed understanding of salvation,[202] as this is described as being worked out by predestination[203] and adoption.[204] These two stages of salvation are evidently the work of God[205] but Hooker presents them in close connection to the historical work of Christ.

---

197 *ibid.* 341.25.

198 *ibid.* 341.22-25.

199 Morrel, "Richard Hooker, Theologian of the English Reformation", 9.

200 Hooker, *Pride* (*Works* V, 342.14-21). See also Marshall, *Hooker and the Anglican Tradition*, 112.

201 Barnes, *The Supplication of 1531*, lviii.b-lix.a.

202 See also Jordan, *The Development of Religious Toleration*, 226.

203 Cromartie, "Theology and Politics in Richard Hooker's Thought", *History of Political Thought* XXI/1 (2000), 48.

204 Malone, "The Doctrine of Predestination in the Thought of William Perkins and Richard Hooker", 109; Wallace Jr., *Puritans and Predestination*, 77.

205 For a contrary view, see Moreau, *Rome ou l'Angleterre? Les réactions politiques des catholiques anglais au moment du schisme 1529-1553*, 278.

It should be said here that Walton struggled with this problem which he solved by arguing that in God there are two wills: an antecedent and a consequent will.[206] According to God's first will, all mankind should be saved but according to God's second will only those "that did live answerable to that degree of grace which he had offered or afforded them"[207] are saved. Walton even notices that this doctrine resembles Calvin's theology, which is a powerful argument against Keble's attempt to distance Hooker from Reformed theology. Ultimately, God's decision of predestination and adoption, and the realisation of Christ's work on the cross are all caused by the sovereignty of God which, for Hooker, is best rendered through the concept of God's absolute will. This is not a hidden will but it is revealed to the benefit of humanity.[208] Hooker mentions that the absolute will of God, the cause of predestination[209] and adoption,[210] should be understood through the comforting meaning of grace,[211] which discloses God's purpose in saving according to a certain pattern. Hooker explains:

> To take down this proud opinion it is so often inculcated that whatsoever we have, the reason wherfore we have it is not our dignitie but his mercie, not the wourthiness of our merit but the goodness of his will. Yea even in that verie place where the blessed apostle setteth down our predestination and adoption thorow Christ to have bene according unto the pleasure of gods onlie will, doth not him selfe yeeld a cause of this will in God by immediatlie adding *Unto the praise of the glorie of his grace?*[212]

This pattern whereby God saves humanity could be considered, in Hooker's terms, to be a law. As a human law prescribes certain actions to be followed,[213] the same way God works out his deeds in accordance with the things which he had decided and which are so firmly established that they may be easily termed laws. In line with Cranmer,[214] Hooker is convinced that the justice of God is thus revealed in the pattern of salvation because God always acts according to the

---

206 See also Knox, *Walter Travers*, 75; Wallace Jr., *Puritans and Predestination*, 77; Lake, "Business as Usual? The Immediate Reception of Hooker's *Ecclesiastical Polity*", *The Journal of Ecclesiastical History* 52/3 (2001), 474.
207 Walton, *The Lives*, 184.
208 Morrel, "Richard Hooker, Theologian of the English Reformation", 9.
209 Cromartie, "Theology and Politics in Richard Hooker's Thought", *History of Political Thought* XXI/1 (2000), 48.
210 Wallace Jr., *Puritans and Predestination*, 77.
211 Collinson, *Archbishop Grindal*, 41.
212 Hooker, *Pride* (*Works* V, 342.21-343.1). See Ephesians 1:6.
213 See also Sabine, *A History of the Political Theory*, 441.
214 Cranmer, Works II, 130.

decisions he had taken in view of his settled soteriological purpose. The aim of God's law is the salvation of humanity and this is a clear proof of God's justice:

> Then seeing God doth wourk nothing but for some end which end is the cause of that he doth what letteth to conclude that God doth all things even in such sort as law prescribeth? Is not the end of his actions as a law? Doth it not strictly require them to be such as always they are so that if they were otherwise they could not be apt correspondent sutable unto their set and appointed end? There is no impediment therefore but that we may set it down, God is truly and properly just.[215]

The next step for Hooker is to prove that the justice of God is applied to humanity by the divine work of salvation.

7.6.3 The Application of the Justice of God to Humanity

Hooker is aware that a philosophically oriented mind might argue that the justice of God, who is utterly superior, cannot be displayed towards inferior human beings. Such an approach would only allow for the possibility that the justice of God should be applied within the Holy Trinity in a relationship of equality, because the three divine persons of the Godhead are perfectly equal.[216] Thus, Hooker knows that this way of reasoning about the application of God's justice excludes the possibility that the justice of a superior God should be manifested towards the lower levels of his created humanity. However, Hooker himself takes over this argument and acknowledges that the relationships of superiority and equality are totally part of God's realm, so the only remaining possibility is that the justice of God be applied to humanity, which exists within a relationship of inferiority with God. Hooker now explains the nature of God's dealing with humankind, as the manifestation of the justice of God in the created world comes from a superior being towards inferior creatures. When he rightly applies his justice to human beings, God acts as a Judge, Lord, and Father:

> Touching the next point how God doth exercise justice in the world, Justice exhibiteth all good which congruitie and right would have imparted unto equals inferiors or betters. Superiouritie and equalitie being excluded from all thinges as they are in relation unto god, at his handes we are to expect

---

215 Hooker, *Pride* (*Works* V, 343.1-8).
216 Booty, "An Elizabethan Addresses Modern Anglicanism. Richard Hooker and Theological Issues at the End of the Twentieth Century", 10.

onlie that which justice yeeldeth unto inferiours. In which consideration he taketh upon him the person of a Judge a Lord a Father.[217]

It is relevant to notice that, for Hooker, God himself chose to exercise his justice by means of a threefold office. In the application of justice, the image of God as Judge brings forth the reality of judgement. Nobody should imagine that the judgment of God will be delayed for ever. As already seen, God is just and he will act accordingly, by judging the world regardless of whether the judgment itself is delayed or not. Sinful people must take heed to the image of God as Judge because all their wrongdoings will eventually be assessed and rewarded in accordance with the justice of God. Hooker is a practical theologian and though sometimes his doctrines seem theoretical, nevertheless their practical applicability is also present. He has a deep knowledge of human nature and of the ways man's sinful mind tries to avoid the consequences of sin. The very fact that the judgement of God is not harshly applied immediately when any sin is committed does encourage some people to continue their sinful lives. The image of God as Judge is a serious warning to all those who think they can somehow escape the justice of God. Hooker's words are not mere theology but a sincere challenge for everybody to take the Word of God seriously and be fully convinced on the basis of the inspired Scripture[218] that God will eventually judge sin in accordance with his divine justice. To the warning is added an even more serious aspect when Hooker introduces the image of Christ the Saviour into the picture, which also proves to be of particular significance for Cranmer.[219] Some people may imagine that Christ, whose work is to save humanity from sin, will – at a certain point – work in such a way that sins will be washed away because of the encompassing love of Christ. Hooker, however, clearly encourages his readers not to be deceived by such a perilous understanding of God because Christ the Saviour is God, and God is just. Sin will be punished unless reformation of the soul occurs.[220]

The second image Hooker uses to prove that God will apply his justice to the realm of humanity is God as Lord. Such a description of God brings forth the idea of God's sovereignty, which is manifested in the life of humanity on a daily basis. The first image of God as Judge explains that God will surely judge sin when the right time comes, so that everybody should know that a time will come when God will

---

217 Hooker, *Pride (Works* V, 343.9-15).
218 McAdoo, "Richard Hooker", Geoffrey Rowell (ed.), *The English Religious Tradition and the Genius of Anglicanism*, 116.
219 Cranmer, *Annotations on the King's Book*, 12.
220 Hooker, *Pride (Works* V, 343.15-25).

judge all sins. The second image, however, that of God as Lord is
oriented towards the idea that God, in his sovereignty, has the capacity
to judge sin every single day. Hooker intended this teaching to reach a
twofold audience. Firstly, he wanted sinners to be fully convinced that
there is nothing which escapes God's awareness, because all sins are
known to him. Secondly, he intended to inform believers that sin was a
serious matter which would not go unpunished. Again, Hooker has a
well-informed pastoral knowledge of the life of believers.[221] He knows
that a justified believer still lives in a body which is affected by sin;
consequently, no believer is safe from ever committing sins. Because he
is aware that sin is a reality in the life of the believer, Hooker wants to
encourage him to give up sin, as God the Lord will judge every wrong
deed. The thought that God will somehow find a way to pardon our
sins without punishing us is a dangerous idea which not only affects
non-believers but also the justified children of God. Regardless of who
commits sins, believers or non-believers, Hooker plainly explains that
God hates sin and that he knows the deeds, the hearts and the minds of
everybody. God is Judge and he will judge sin eventually but this is not
the full picture. God is also Lord, he knows the lives of all people and
he has the capacity to punish sin daily.[222]

The third image is God as Father. This is meant to encourage both
believers who repent of their sins and all those who want to be
conformed to the prescriptions of Scripture. God is described as Father
to everyone who sincerely repents of his sins, like in Foxe.[223] God
promises to protect those who guide their lives by using his
instructions and to reward them in accordance with the good deeds
they perform.[224] As Tyndale also suggested, all these are done by faith,
the only way we can believe what God promises.[225] Within the analysis
of the image of God as Father, the concept of repentance[226] is utterly
important because it is the element which unites all three images of
God as Judge, Lord and Father. Hooker's discussion is not a theological
exercise, but an encouragement from Scripture and a fine observation
of practical divinity. Because sin is a reality for the life of any believer,

221 Allison, *The Rise of Moralism*, 4.
222 Hooker, *Pride* (*Works* V, 343.25-344.5).
223 Foxe, *The Acts and Monuments*, 77.
224 Bryan, "The Judicious Mr. Hooker and the Early Christians. The Relationship of
     Scripture and Reason in the First Century of the Christian Era", in Donald S.
     Armentrout (ed.), *This Sacred History. Anglican Reflections for John Booty*, 144.
225 Tyndale, *Prologue to Romans*, 124.
226 See also Gibbs, "Richard Hooker's *Via Media* Doctrine of Repentance", *Harvard
     Theological Review* 84/1 (1991), 59.

the true repentance and the genuine peace of mind of the justified Christian are not things which should be taken lightly. Forgiveness of any sins comes from God, as emphatically underlined by Bradford,[227] and this is an assurance which all Christians should hold to,[228] which is also present in Tyndale.[229] The image of the Father is of great value at this point because the burden of a heavy conscience triggers a lot of suffering in the life of a true and repentant believer. God the Judge and God the Lord is also God the Father. Thus he promises relief and forgiveness to all his children who manifest a genuine repentance, as also expressed in Tyndale.[230] A father will never forget his beloved child, and Hooker uses this picture for the benefit of all those who are truly sorry for their wrong deeds. This attitude reveals the complex character of God who, due to his unlimited wisdom, which is also crucial to Bradford,[231] knows how to act in such a way that his justice be shown in all his actions as Judge, Lord and Father. Writing about God as Father, Hooker himself acknowledges that "his name doth show his nature."[232] Hooker resorts to the ontological difference between God and man in order to make things even clearer. Judge, Lord and Father are words which become titles for those to whom they are ascribed. In the case of fallen human beings, they only indicate what a certain man should be, not what he is. A man can be named Judge, Lord and Father *de iure*, without being Judge, Lord and Father *de facto*. A corrupt judge has the title of a judge but he is not truly a judge. A cruel Lord is a Lord by title, not by what he really is; he is not a Lord in the true sense of the word. A father who hates his children is a father biologically, not by virtue of his qualities as a father. God, however, is different. His titles disclose what he is in reality. God is and remains just when he acts like a stern judge; his justice is equally displayed when he performs his duties as a sovereign Lord, and the same divine justice is kept intact when he behaves like a true father. In conclusion, Hooker uses the notion of righteousness to give substance to the character of God. Accordingly, God is righteous, and his righteousness is shown in the

---

227 Bradford, *Writings*, 217-218.
228 Griffith Thomas (ed.), *The Principles of Theology*, 186; Grislis, "The Assurance of Faith according to Richard Hooker", in McGrade, *Richard Hooker and the Construction of Christian Community*, 239.
229 Tyndale, *Prologue to Romans*, 125.
230 Tyndale, *The Answer to Sir Thomas More's Dialogue*, 369.
231 Bradford, *Writings*, 211.
232 Hooker, *Pride* (*Works* V, 345.6-7).

fact that his justice stays unblemished in all his dealings with sinful humanity by means of his threefold office of Judge, Lord and Father.[233]

7.6.4 The Critique of Merit and of Double Predestination

At the end of this analysis, Hooker attempts to correct two theological mistakes, which have become important ecclesiological traditions. Hooker does not identify the two traditions in clear terms but, in his opinion, both of them have developed out of a practical observation of human life. The first tradition Hooker criticises in categorical terms is Catholicism. He argues that, for Catholics, the lack of punishment and the prosperity of sin determined the application of God's justice. The practical fact of death in the case of some people who passed away immediately either after repenting from serious sins or after committing sins without any trace of remorse led Catholic theologians to infer that the deeds of such men must be rewarded by God after their death. This, however, led to the idea that works have merits in themselves, and God makes the proper retribution for every good and bad deed.[234] The other theological tradition Hooker dismisses is the Reformed doctrine of double predestination.[235] For Hooker, this tradition supports the idea that God applies his justice unto condemnation of sin[236] without any cause. Thus, God "forappointed" some people unto reprobation because the will of God had been that they should be tormented forever. Actually, Hooker denies the teaching that God had ever been actively involved in electing some to eternal punishment.[237]

The main idea which Hooker wants to make clear is that the human law of distributive justice is totally observed by the justice and righteousness of God.[238] Distributive justice is the law whereby every man receives his deserved reward in accordance with the good or bad deeds he has performed.[239] Because daily reality appears to contradict this law in the sense that evildoers are rich, while righteous people suf-

---

233 *ibid.* 344.5-345.22.
234 *ibid.* 345.23-346.9.
235 See also Hillerdal, *Reason and Revelation in Richard Hooker*, 23, and Morrel, "Richard Hooker, Theologian of the English Reformation", 9.
236 Griffith Thomas (ed.), *The Principles of Theology*, 185.
237 Hooker, *Pride* (*Works* V, 346.9-17).
238 Williams, "Richard Hooker on the Church and State Report", *The Churchman* 85/2 (1971), 102.
239 Hooker, *Pride* (*Works* V, 351.3-6).

fer from poverty, Hooker sets himself up to clarify this much debated aspect. Basically, Hooker argues that God observes the law of distributive justice by the fact that he treats his creatures, including us, much better than he dealt with his only Son, Jesus Christ. Hooker writes that even animals have their own shelters, while the Son of God did not ever have a place to rest. The inference behind the text is that God is good to his people because he gave them salvation on the basis of the work of Christ. He, who was perfect, was slain for our sins, but we, who are unrighteous, were considered righteous on the account of his death:

> How unjustlie therfore with Christ our blessed Saviour and his onlie begotten sonne who being so much more righteous then angels saw creatures far beneath men in dignitie in some parts of outward felicitie so far above him that *birds having nests and foxes holes to hide them selves the sonne of God and man had scarce where to lay his head.*[240]

The problem is not solved entirely because this text gives no reason why the unrighteous are oftentimes richer and enjoy more happiness then the righteous. The doctrine of creation partially offers the proper answer to this question. Hence, Hooker explains that both the unrighteous and the righteous are creatures of God. For instance, God allows the unrighteous to prosper on the basis of his own hard work should he be diligent enough.[241] This type of happiness, however, cannot be compared with true happiness which comes out of a genuine relationship with God.[242] The righteous should not be envious over the unrighteous, because the happiness of the former is based on things which last forever, while the joy of the latter vanishes when material possessions are lost.[243] Ultimately, the welfare of either the just or the unjust is totally dependent on the hidden will of God. He knows better if a good material position is to the benefit or to the detriment of his people. Should God think that his people could do better without worldly riches, he will not grant these to any of them. Hooker plainly writes that "the life of the just shall be long and fortunate they shall see manie and happie dayes, their prosperitie is a sequele of their pietie but with exception unlesse it be far better for them to be otherwise."[244]

It is clear from Hooker's exposition that God wants the best for his children; this is why he is and remains just in all his actions. It may be true that sometimes he allows sorrow to overwhelm them, but this is

---

240 *ibid.* 351.14-19.
241 *ibid.* 351.20-27.
242 Griffith Thomas (ed.), *The Principles of Theology*, 185.
243 For more details, see Hooker, *Pride* (*Works* V, 351.27-353.5).
244 Hooker, *Pride* (*Works* V, 354.2-5).

only in their best interest. In many cases, lest it should be said of all, suffering brings about a closer relationship to God, as Hooker mentions that "affliction is the mother of hartie devotion."[245] In the end, however, this is the plan of God, and to those who are reluctant to accept it, Hooker provides a very sensible advice when he explains that time will eventually reveal the truth: "*Truth* they say *is the daughter of time*."[246] The design and realisation of God's plan seem to be in such opposition to the natural reason of unrighteous people that it can only be appropriated by faith, with the true confidence that the mysteries of faith are hidden in God and that they are always oriented towards the benefit of his children.[247]

7.6.5 The Principles of Salvation

Towards the very end of his sermon, Hooker puts his entire doctrine of salvation into a nutshell by asserting its fundamental principles. Firstly, the foundation of salvation is the death of Christ,[248] which is so effective that brings about the forgiveness of all sins, as in Bradford.[249] Secondly, as also underlined by Frith,[250] salvation means redemption which was achieved at the cross.[251] Thirdly, all those who were saved by the redemptive work of Christ at the cross are part of "his body mysticall which is the Church."[252] Fourthly, Christians are incorporated in the Church[253] by the remission of their sins[254] on the basis of the merits of

---

245 *ibid.* 354.9-10; Targoff, "Performing Prayer in Hooker's *Laws*: The Efficacy of Set Forms", in McGrade, *Richard Hooker and the Construction of Christian Community*, 275-282.

246 Hooker, *Pride* (*Works* V, 354.25).

247 For a detailed view, see Hooker, *Pride* (*Works* V, 354.1-18), and Morrel, "Richard Hooker, Theologian of the English Reformation", 9.

248 Booty, "The English Reformation: A Lively Faith and Sacramental Confession", 24; Lake, *Anglicans and Puritans?*, 162; Booty, "An Elizabethan Addresses Modern Anglicanism. Richard Hooker and Theological Issues at the End of the Twentieth Century", 10.

249 Bradford, *Writings*, 217-218.

250 Frith, *A Disputation of Purgatory*, 90.

251 Hooker, *Pride* (*Works* V, 356.11-14).

252 *ibid.* 356.14-19; Lurbe, "Political Power and Ecclesiastical Power in Richard Hooker's *Laws of Ecclesiastical Polity*", *Cahiers Elisabéthains* 49 (1996), 19.

253 Morrel, "Richard Hooker, Theologian of the English Reformation", 10; Wolf, Booty, and Thomas (eds), *The Spirit of Anglicanism*, 29.

254 Rupp, *Studies in the Making of the English Protestant Tradition*, 166.

Christ's death[255] – also pertinently analysed by Tyndale[256] – which is an evident proof of the grace of God.[257] Fifthly, salvation has a double effect as it places the new believer both into God's favour,[258] as also underlined by Tyndale,[259] and into the fellowship of the Church.[260] The Christian becomes right with God, and, equally true, he also becomes right with his fellow people. Sixthly, as every new Christian continues to live in a body which is subject to corruption,[261] he will sooner or later sin again; accordingly, when this happens, he has access to the total remission of his sins by means of repentance,[262] which is of equal importance to Foxe.[263] Seventhly, the reality of sin is always accompanied by the reality of just desserts for sin. Nobody should deceive himself that he can escape the deserved retribution for his sins. In this respect, sins are either punished in this world or in the world to come, in accordance with the justice of God which requires that sins should be subject to punishment. Following Frith,[264] Hooker is fully convinced that all sins are rightfully punished in view of the satisfaction of God's perfect justice.[265]

---

255 *ibid.* 167; Stanwood, "Of Prelacy and Polity in Milton and Hooker", in Margo Swiss and David Kent (eds), *Heirs of Fame. Milton and Writers of the English Renaissance*, 69.

256 Tyndale, *Prologue to Romans*, 125.

257 Hooker, *Pride* (*Works* V, 356.20-28).

258 Keble, *The Works*, vol. 2, 552; Booty, "The Spirituality of Participation in Richard Hooker", *Sewanee Theological Review* 38/1 (1994), 12.

259 Tyndale, *Prologue to Romans*, 128.

260 Wolf, Booty, and Thomas (eds), *The Spirit of Anglicanism*, 18; Booty, "An Elizabethan Addresses Modern Anglicanism. Richard Hooker and Theological Issues at the End of the Twentieth Century", 10.

261 Kirby, *Richard Hooker's Doctrine of Royal Supremacy*, 46; Bouwsma, "Hooker in the Context of European Cultural History", in Claire McEachern and Deborah Shuger (eds), *Religion and Culture in Renaissance England*, 149.

262 Hooker, *Pride* (*Works* V, 356.28-357.3); Gibbs, "Richard Hooker's *Via Media* Doctrine of Repentance", *Harvard Theological Review* 84/1 (1991), 59.

263 Foxe, *The Acts and Monuments*, 80.

264 Frith, *A Disputation of Purgatory*, 90, and Cranmer, *The 1538 Articles*, 4.

265 Hooker, *Pride* (*Works* V, 360.19-28); Gibbs, "Richard Hooker and Lancelot Andrew on Priestly Absolution", in McGrade, *Richard Hooker and the Construction of Christian Community*, 272.

Conclusions

My intention in this book was to analyse Richard Hooker's doctrine of salvation and his connections to the early English reformers, whose theology he successfully continued in his sermons. It is important to underline that, in doing so, Hooker used Lutheran and Reformed insights which were characteristic of the Continental Magisterial Reformation. In the end, my demonstration is a critique of Arthur P. Monahan, who suggested Richard Hooker was a Counter-Reformation or Catholic theologian. Actually, it was Monahan's assumption that prompted me to identify the Protestant credentials of Hooker's soteriology and especially his links to the first theologians of the early English Reformation.

The first chapter is a historical study, which consists of a critical assessment of the most important works which have dealt with Hooker and his theology since the early seventeenth century. In this way, I showed that Richard Hooker scholarship is made up of a wide range of different interpretations that provide a multi-faceted image of the English reformer. The earnest academic research in the field undoubtedly shows a continued interest in Hooker. Despite of the various views of Hooker advanced by different historians, theologians, and philosophers, the somehow hidden feature of Hooker scholarship is the tendency to classify and place Hooker within a certain intellectual tradition, be it mainly theological or philosophical. Accordingly, there are some important characteristics of Hooker scholarship that emerge as a result of the present study. Firstly, there is a historical image of Hooker. As a result of recent historical studies, whatever is known of Hooker the man is grounded on solid documentary sources. No rush conclusions regarding precise information on his life and works have been advanced lately, and many of the traditionally wrong opinions about him have recently been corrected as a result of the direct interaction with primary historical sources. Secondly, there is a political image of Hooker. According to this perspective, Hooker the politician is deeply rooted in the social, historical, and political realities of the Elizabethan England. His political thinking generated a vast amount of scholarly studies which radically differ in their fundamental interpretation. Thus Hooker is seen either as a political thinker, especially prone to humanist and Renaissance political theories, or a forerunner of political liberalism. Thirdly, the image of Hooker as theologian is very important for scholarship, because this is the standpoint according to which all interpretations are assessed. The most controversial issue in the debate is whether Hooker is a Reformed theologian or merely a Catholic oriented clergyman. Fourthly, one of the most non-controversial images of Hooker is his portrait as literary writer. There is virtually no doubt about the craftsmanship of Hooker in matters of literary composition, and most discussion focuses on his style and literary devices. He is placed among the great writers of the Elizabethan period, contributing not only to English ecclesiastical literature, but also to the development of English prose. Fifthly, there is the philosophical image of Hooker, which is grounded in many serious studies as well. Hooker scholarship is not unanimous regarding the intellectual tradition to which he subscribes. Accordingly, Hooker is seen either as a rational thinker, as a Renaissance man or even as an existentialist philosopher.

The second chapter is occupied with the doctrine of salvation in the early English Reformation because this is the theology which Hooker will continue later on in his teaching and pastoral career. During the early reign of Henry VIII, the English reformers promoted a theology which was very much influenced by Lutheran teachings. Thus, in the writings of William Tyndale and John Frith, the most important feature of early Protestant theology was the sharp distinction between justification by faith and the law. Justification is not a human accomplishment, but is totally the work of God. The essence of justification is faith, which is given by the Holy Spirit. Faith should be directed towards Christ and his atoning sacrifice. As a result of faith, the Holy Spirit dwells in the believer. The major achievement of justification is the liberation of man from the bondage of sin. This divine work is given to man by means of faith, through the Holy Spirit, so faith and the Holy Spirit should never be theologically separated. Although it is the work of God, justification is manifested in history and begins with the faithful preaching of the Word of God. Justification is both declarative and redemptive: man is both declared and then made righteous by the gift of faith. Faith is not merely historical; it is fundamentally a strong trust in Christ, but it is still given by the Holy Spirit. By faith the believer is united with Christ and his sufferings. The union of the believer with Christ will generate a healthy morality in the life of the believer, who will consequently follow Christ's example and perform good works.

The sufficiency of Christ in salvation remains the major characteristic of English Protestant soteriology during the late reign of Henry VIII and Edward VI, as seen in the theology of Robert Barnes and Thomas Cranmer. The importance of Christ is actually the basis of justification. In this respect, Christ had to become flesh and accomplish the reconciliation between God and men. The essence of justification is the grace of God, which works to the remission of sins. Faith is the means by which justification is received applied to the believer. Although faith seems to have facilitated justification, the only thing that matters in soteriology is God's initiative in justification, which directly depends on election. Thus, good works are the grateful response of the believer to God's free justification, which is a solid proof that the believers were elect. Predestination effectively produces election and the consequent justification of few people, while the rest are predestined to eternal damnation. It is clear that it has been tried to separate faith from every trace of human effort. Not even faith is the grounds of justification but grace, manifested in the death of Christ. Faith is simply a means to receive justification by grace. The content of justification is the alien righteousness of Christ, which was achieved with the purpose of appeasing God's wrath and satisfying God's justice. The alien righteousness of Christ must be imputed to the believer by faith alone. Faith is the sign of the final preservation of the believer.

During the reign of Mary I, the political and religious situation was totally unfriendly to the Protestants. This historical situation seems to have influenced theology and especially the doctrine of election, which becomes crucial to soteriology. Thus, in the works of John Bradford and John Foxe, election generates justification, which consists of the forgiveness of sins. In addition, election is fundamentally good, which means that God can do only good things to the benefit of the elect. By faith, justification is made effective in the elect. It is then clear that only the elect receive justification and consequently the forgiveness of sins, which shows that God predestined the elect unto everlasting life. Hence, predestination, election and the justification were decreed by God in view of the sanctification of the elect. This reality underlines the necessity of a healthy moral life as the outcome of justification, which is due to the inner righteousness worked in the elect by the Holy Spirit through faith. After Elizabeth I ascended to throne, England entered a time of political and religious stability, which was interestingly reflected in theology by a lesser importance being given to election and an increasing focus on justification by the imputation of Christ's merits. The objective foundation of justification is the death of Christ. Man needs faith in order to be given justification effectively. Faith is the assurance of salvation and is contrasted to works. As the stress on election decreased, contrition or repentance became more important as prerequisite to justifying faith, which is ultimately given by the work of the Holy Spirit. Contrition necessarily leads to a new obedience, which makes good works a reality in the believer's moral life. Thus, justification consists of the remission of sins as a result of the non-imputation of sins to those who exercise their faith in Christ.

All these insights of the early English reformers were taken over by Richard Hooker in his sermons. Thus, the third chapter approaches the necessity of faith in Hooker's *Two Sermons upon S. Judes Epistle*. As far as the *First Sermon on S. Jude* is concerned, Hooker explains that salvation is closely linked to Scripture. Nobody can be really saved unless he or she has a proper knowledge of Scripture. However, salvation must be understood as the work of Christ, which is another obligatory condition for one's redemption. Hooker writes that the affirmation of salvation on the one hand presupposes the existence of condemnation on the other hand. The good news of salvation in Christ is there to stay with every human being but, at the same time, one should not be hopelessly unrealistic about the reality of condemnation which is equally valid. Then, in order to distinguish between salvation and condemnation, Hooker offers a brief but systematic definition of salvation. Thus, salvation consists of our reconciliation with God, which was accomplished by Christ on the basis of God's grace. Salvation is also the remission of sins by grace and satisfaction in the sight of God. Although he does not insist on the forensic aspect of salvation, Hooker nevertheless states it and then connects it to the practical level of daily living by faith.

In his *Second Sermon on S. Jude*, Hooker makes it clear that salvation should be thought of as the covenant of grace which is fundamental to the redemption of humanity. Likewise, salvation means that men and women must necessarily become united with Christ. This union with Christ cannot be achieved by everybody but only by those who believe in Christ, namely by those who display an active faith in the person and work of Christ. From the perspective of our salvation in Christ, Hooker introduces the concept of righteousness and especially of the righteousness of justification. Man is saved when considered righteous in the sight of God. This, however, cannot be done apart from the work of the Holy Spirit, who is also actively involved in the salvation of humanity.

The forth chapter deals with the epistemology of faith, which is primarily disclosed in Hooker's *Learned and Comfortable Sermon on the*

Certaintie and Perpetuitie of Faith in the Elect. The first problem that Hooker discusses is the relationship between faith and knowledge. Thus, Hooker explains that one of the most important aspects of human existence is spirituality, so he dedicates a significant amount of time to the definition of spiritual men. Then he explains the concept of science, which is foundational to human knowledge but not necessarily to the knowledge of God, and then the dual concept of certainty: of evidence and adherence. It is important, however, to notice that Hooker's analysis of the concept of certainty, of evidence and of adherence, is carefully done within the larger context of faith. Thus, even if the concept of certainty may somehow be rational, it must be approached through the perspective of faith. The next step for Hooker is to define the certainty of evidence and the certainty of adherence. The certainty of evidence is obviously connected to human reason but man's use of reason in view of discovering the spiritual things of God is limited. Reason can only assent to the truth of spiritual things, which are disclosed through God's revelation, while only faith can investigate them adequately. The certainty of adherence is also connected to faith but it does not primarily appeal to human reason but to the human heart. Within this particular context, Hooker mentions the reality of the new heart which is the result of faith but faith is also worked out by the Holy Spirit. In close connection to the certainty of adherence, the idea of faith is not only an intellectual assent but also a firm trust in spiritual things which are disclosed to men and women only by means of faith and the work of the Holy Spirit.

The second aspect of Hooker's epistemology is the relationship between faith and salvation. Thus, Hooker insists on the necessity that faith should be firm although, due to the constant reality of sin, the existence of doubt in the life of the believer cannot be denied. When it truly comes in the life of the sinner, and because it is the work of the Holy Spirit, faith becomes a permanent reality in the life of every Christian even if the reality of doubt is also present. Hooker then explains that every sinful person engages himself or herself on the difficult road which takes him or her from unbelief to faith but this is again the work of God, not of man. It is very important to realise that in spite of God's perfect salvation, which he so graciously offers to humanity, the permanence of sin is an aspect which must be fought constantly. On the other hand, those who are truly God's believing children will always persevere in faith because their justification and sanctification is not the result of their own efforts, but the very work of God.

Chapter five is concerned with the foundation of faith in Hooker's *A Learned Discourse of Justification, Workes and How the Foundation of Faith is Overthrown*. Here Hooker makes a thorough analysis of the righteousness of justification and then of the righteousness of sanctification. Regarding the righteousness of justification, Hooker deals with the imperfect righteousness of man. This is actually the starting point of his soteriology. Every human being must be totally aware that his own deeds or even his own righteousness cannot suffice for his own salvation. Man is just not good enough to save himself and his righteousness is utterly imperfect because of sin. In the end, it can be argued that man has no righteousness at all because his own status and his own existence do not qualify to save himself in the sight of God. What man needs for his salvation is not his own righteousness, which is either imperfect or even non-existent but the perfect righteousness of Christ. Hooker offers some details about the concept of righteousness and the three types of righteousness which are available to believers. Thus, God's work of salvation begins with the righteousness of justification, then continues with the righteousness of sanctification, and is completed by the righteousness of glorification. Hooker chose to insist only on the first two because they involve the current situation of man and his earthly existence. At this point, Hooker explains that Protestants share some common doctrines with Catholics but he also reveals the points of disagreement between Catholics and Protestants. Then he presents the Catholic understanding of justification which is based on the infusion of grace and on the conviction that grace is inherent to human nature. Thus, justification does not belong exclusively to Christ but also to the Christian who is able to perform good works, which can indeed count for his salvation. Unlike the Catholic understanding of salvation, the Protestant doctrine is founded on the righteousness of justification which is the righteousness of Christ and a sign of God's grace. This righteousness, however, is not inherent but fundamentally external to humanity. This is why, according to Protestant doctrine, salvation cannot be performed by man in any sense but only exclusively by God.

Hooker is also aware that the righteousness of justification must necessarily be completed by the righteousness of sanctification; thus he asserts the basic unity between justification and sanctification. Hooker insists on the necessity of good works but they must not be seen as belonging to justification, which is exclusively the work of God in Christ, but to sanctification, which is the result of the cooperation between God and man. Although sanctification is primarily and fundamentally the work of God, man has a part to play and his duty is to be faithful to God who saved him. In this context, the Christian is expected to perform good works as a confirmation of his justification. The specifically Protestant understanding of justification and salvation caused the separation between Protestants and Catholics but despite this, Hooker is convinced that some Catholics can be saved. Thus, he talks about the salvation of Catholics which is possible in spite of their ignorance. Hooker is convinced that ordinary Catholics do believe in Christ although they do not have a proper knowledge of salvation in Christ. This, however, is the fault of Catholic clergy, not of ordinary believers. So, even if ordinary Catholics do not know Christ adequately so that they are ignorant in matters pertaining to salvation, God is able and willing to save them in spite of their ignorance if they truly believe in Christ. Thus, Hooker explains that what counts for one's salvation is the foundation of faith and the true foundation of faith is Christ the Lord. Whoever believes in Christ is saved and this rule is universal; it applies to everybody, including ordinary Catholics. Salvation can become a reality only if people repent of their sins, so in Hooker the necessity of repentance is clearly stated. At this point, he also mentions the possibility that godly pagans could be saved, and in his he is in line with Erasmus and Zwingli. Without insisting too much on this particular aspect of his soteriology, Hooker proceeds to explain the theological unity between Paul and James. In fact, he stresses that Paul's insistence on justification must necessarily be completed by James' underlining of sanctification. As sanctification presupposes the observance of certain rules, Hooker continues his analysis with a presentation of the concept of law. This, however, is immediately accompanied by a discussion of the importance of Scripture, which is essential to salvation. Hooker also identifies an anthropological aspect of salvation, in the sense that human beings have an inborn desire to be saved. This is very important especially from the perspective of the fact that God's work of salvation has always been the same for all people. Thus, there is a unique foundation of faith for the Old and the New Testament. Nevertheless, it is the New Testament which completes the teachings of the Old Covenant so that we now have the chance to know Christ due to his incarnation which was realised by the active role of the Holy Spirit. The involvement of the Holy Spirit in the incarnation of Christ, which is a sign of God's plan for humanity, prompted Hooker to discuss the very important relationship between salvation and election. He also investigates the connection between faith, reason and revelation but it should be highlighted that, for Hooker, all these must be understood from the perspective of God's election. Man must rest assured that his salvation is fundamentally the result of God's work in

Christ, through the Gospel, in the power of the Holy Spirit. This is
surely not an invitation to spiritual laziness because Hooker issues a
very significant warning which concerns the presence of sin in every
true believer. Even if absolutely convinced and assured of his own
salvation in Christ, the believer must always fight his sinful condition
throughout his earthly life.

Chapter six focuses on *Master Hooker's Answer to the Supplication that
Master Travers Made to the [Privy] Counsell*. Thus, Hooker makes an
apology of faith, which is actually a defence of his own understanding
of Protestant teachings. Walter Travers accused him of having a wrong
authority for the doctrine of predestination, a wrong doctrine of
assurance, a wrong doctrine of salvation, a wrong doctrine of Scripture,
a wrong understanding of Protestant doctrines, a wrong understanding
of the Catholic doctrine of justification, and a wrong doctrine of good
works. Hooker defends himself by saying that his authority for the
doctrine of predestination is the Word of God, confirmed by the bishop
of London and the Churches which proclaim the Gospel, evidently the
Protestant Churches in Hooker's understandding. Concerning the
doctrine of assurance, Hooker insists that this must be understood in
relation to the doctrine of justification. Thus, from the perspective of
justification, the assurance of faith is part of the life of the justified
person. This assurance, however, is not perfect because of the permanent presence of sin. The doctrine of good works is, for Hooker, a
matter which must be seen again from the perspective of justification.
The assurance of faith, which may be stronger or weaker in some
people but is the confirmation of justification, results in the performance of good works. Daily prayer and spiritual discipline can increase the
assurance of faith which will surely guarantee a greater performance of
good works. Hooker explains that good works are not a condition for
the reception of justification but rather the necessary result of justification. Two of the most important good works are prayer and the study
of the Word of God which must be performed in order to increase one's
assurance of faith. Concerning his understanding of the Catholic
doctrine of justification, Hooker brings forward the differences between
Catholic and Protestant soteriologies. Thus, he explains that Protestants
differ from Catholics in at least two major areas: the essence of
salvation and the way salvation is applied. While Catholics believe that
the righteousness of man has at least a minor role in salvation and the
infusion of grace is the common way to apply salvation, Protestants
insist that man has no merit in salvation whatsoever and grace is
fundamentally imputed, not infused. He also makes reference to the
fact that Mariology is not part of the Protestant understanding of

salvation but is specifically Catholic. So any accusations against him in this respect are invalid, because he explains he has absolutely no interest in Mariology apart from the fact that Mary was a sinful human being like everybody else. In connection to his understanding of Protestant doctrines, Hooker mentions again that although some doctrines are common to both Protestants and Catholics, he chose to insist on the specific Reformed pattern of salvation which includes election and reprobation. Thus, he stresses the fact that these two realities of salvation depend on God's mercy and sovereignty. Regarding the doctrine of Scripture, Hooker underscores that his authority for the understanding of Scripture is not human reason but the reason of God.

Chapter seven is an analysis of Hooker's anthropology of faith which can be discerned from his *A Learned Sermon on the Nature of Pride*. Thus, he deals with six specific aspects. Firstly, Hooker insists on the important liaison between nature and grace. He defines the way of nature and the way of grace; the former is not helpful to salvation while the latter is essential to it. Then, he explains that faith and Christ are closely interwoven and they must be understood through the lens of election. Hooker also stresses that election itself must be interpreted by means of Christ's mediatorial office. Secondly, Hooker defines the concept of pride, which includes natural and spiritual pride, the mechanism of pride and salvation as the remedy for pride. His third interest is a concise treatment of Medieval Catholicism in general as well as Early and Late Medieval Catholicism in particular. At this point, he also enumerates the soteriological implications of the Rhemist translation of the Bible. Fourthly, Hooker approaches the permanent influence of sin in human life, which is dealt with by the mercy and sovereignty of God. He also stresses that the reality of pride is constanttly present during the believer's spiritual journey even if justification and sanctification are also truly effective in his life. Then, the relationship between pride and faith is analysed concisely with the indication that faith, which is from God, is always stronger than pride, which is from man's sinful nature. Fifthly, Hooker discusses some matters concerning the spiritual life of the believer and the presence of Christ. He seems convinced that faith in Christ leads to a life in the presence of God. The presence of Christ in the believer is a sign of the work of the Holy Trinity in the life of the believer. Hooker also makes an insightful comparison between the life of the believer and the life of the proud person. The spiritual life of the believer is important because it is the formal confirmation of his justification and sanctification. It is significant for Hooker that spiritual life does not end when a person finishes his earthly existence but goes on towards its eschatological fulfilment in glorification. This is another demonstration of God's sovereignty in salvation. According to Hooker, God was very careful with sinful human beings and decided to save them in spite of their sheer carelessness. The sixth and the last aspect of Hooker's anthropology of faith is the concept of justice. Hooker tackles the justice of man, the justice of God and the application of God's justice to humanity. He also constructs a critique of merit and of double predestination and, in the end, he briefly lists the principles of salvation.

To conclude, Hooker's doctrine of salvation is unmistakably Protestant and specifically Reformed. He continues the early tradition of the first English reformers which is evident in his treatment of some of the most important features of Lutheran and Reformed Protestantism, such as faith, justification, sanctification, glorification, election, reprobation, and the sovereignty of God.

Bibliography

Primary Sources

ANDREWS, Lancelot, *Selected Writings* (Fyfield Books, 1995);
ANDREWS, Lancelot, *Sermons* (Oxford: Clarendon Press, 1967);

BEZA, Theodore, *Letter to Jean Calvin, the 29th of July 1555*, in HOLTROP, Philip C., *The Bolsec Controversy on Predestination from 1551 to 1555. The Statements of Jerome Bolsec and the Responses of John Calvin, Theodore Beza, and Other Reformed Theologians* (Lampeter: The Edwin Mellen Press, 1993);
BRADFORD, John, *The Writings of John Bradford*, vol. I-II (Cambridge: Cambridge University Press, 1848);
BRAY, Gerald (ed.), *Documents of the English Reformation* (Cambridge: James Clark and Co. Ltd, 1994);

CALVIN, John, *Institutes of the Christian Religion*, Henry Beveridge trans. (Grand Rapids: Eerdmans, 1997);
CARTWRIGHT, Thomas, *A Commentary Upon the Epistle of St. Paul written to the Colossians* (Edinburgh: James Nichol, 1864);
CARTWRIGHT, Thomas, *A Confutation of the Rhemists Translation* (1618);
CRANMER, Thomas, *The Works of Thomas Cranmer*, in DUFFIELD, G. E. ed. (Appleford: Sutton Courtenay Press, 1964);

DOD, John, *A Plaine and Familiar Exposition of the Ten Commandments* (London: Richard Field, 1618);

FOXE, John, *The Acts and Monuments of John Foxe*, in TOWNSEND, George ed. (London: Seeley, Burnside, and Seeley, 1843);
FRITH, John, *The Work of John Frith*, WRIGHT N. T. ed. (Appleford: The Sutton Courtenay Press, 1978);

GREENHAM, Richard, *A Fruitful and Godly Sermon* (Edinburgh: Robert Waldegrave, 1595);

HILDERSHAM, Arthur, *Lectures, upon the Fourth of John* (London: G. M., 1629);
HOOKER, Richard, *Of the Laws of Ecclesiastical Polity*, McGrade Arthur Stephen ed. (Preface, Book I, Book VIII), Cambridge University Press, Cambridge, 1989;
HOOKER, Richard, *Of the Laws of the Ecclesiastical Polity*, vol. I-II (Books I-IV), Introduction by Christopher Morris (London: J. M. Dent & Sons LTD, 1907);

JANZ, Dennis (ed.), *A Reformation Reader. Primary Texts with Introductions* (Minneapolis: Fortress Press, 1999);
JEWEL, John, *An Apology of the Church of England* (New York: Cornell University Library, 1963);
JEWEL, John, *The Works of John Jewel*, John Ayre ed. (Cambridge: Cambridge University Press, 1847);
JEWEL, John, *The Works of John Jewel*, John Ayre ed. (Cambridge: Cambridge University Press, 1848);
JEWEL, John, *The Works of John Jewel*, John Ayre ed. (Cambridge: Cambridge University Press, 1850);

KEBLE, John, *The Works of that Learned and Judicious Divine, Mr. Richard Hooker, with and Account of His Life and Death by Isaac Walton*, vol. 1, 2, 3 (Oxford: Oxford University Press, 1836);

LUTHER, Martin, *Commentary on Galatians* (Grand Rapids: Kregel Publications, 1979);
LUTHER, Martin, *Commentary on Romans* (Grand Rapids: Kregel Publications, 1976);
LUTHER, Martin, *The Bondage of the Will* (Grand Rapids: Fleming H. Revell, 1999);

PARKER, J. H., *Selections from the Fifth Book of Hooker's Ecclesiastical Polity* (Oxford: Oxford University Press, 1839);

ROGERS, Richard, *A Commentary upon the Whole Book of Judges* (London: Felix Kyngston, 1615);
ROGERS, Richard, *Seven Treatises* (London: Humfrey Lownes, 1604);

SIBBS, Richard, *The Works of the Reverend Richard Sibbs* (Aberdeen: J. Chalmers & Co., 1812);
SPEED HILL, W. (ed.), *The Folger Library Edition of the Works of Richard Hooker* (Cambridge, Mass.: Harvard University Press, Belknap Press, 1977-1993);

TRAVERS, Walter, *Vindiciae Ecclesiae Anglicanae or A Justification of the Religion Professed in England* (London: TC & RC, 1630);
TYNDALE, William, *The Work of William Tyndale*, in DUFFIELD, G. E. ed. (Appleford:The Sutton Courtenay Press, 1964);

WHITGIFT, John, *The Works of John Whitgift*, John Ayre ed. (Cambridge: Cambridge University Press, 1851);
WHITGIFT, John, *The Works of John Whitgift*, John Ayre ed. (Cambridge: Cambridge University Press, 1853);

ZWINGLI, Ulrich, *Archeteles*, LXII, in ZWINGLI, Ulrich, *Early Writings* (Durham: Labyrinth Press, 1987);
ZWINGLI, Ulrich, *On Providence and Other Essays* (Durham: The Labyrinth Press, 1983);

Secondary Sources

ALEXANDER, H. G., *Religion in England 1558-1662* (London: Hodder and Stoughton, 1968);
ALLCHIN, A. M., "The Theology of Nature in the Eastern Fathers and among Anglican Theologians", in MONTEFIORE, Hugh (ed.), *Man and Nature* (London: Collins, 1975), 143-153;
ALLEN, J. W., *A History of Political Thought in the Sixteenth Century* (London: Methuen & Co. LTD, 1957);
ALLISON, C. F., *The Rise of Moralism. The Proclamation of the Gospel from Hooker to Baxter* (London: SPCK, 1966);
ALMASY, Rudolph, "The Purpose of Richard Hooker's Polemic"
ALTHAUS, Paul, *The Ethics of Martin Luther* (Philadelphia: Fortress Press, 1986);
ALTHAUS, Paul, *The Theology of Martin Luther* (Philadelphia: Fortress Press, 1966);
ANDERSON, George H., *Justification by Faith* (Minneapolis: Augsburg Publishing House, 1985);

ARCHER, Stanley, "Hooker on Apostolic Succession: The Two Voice", *The Sixteenth Century Journal* XXIV/1 (1993), 67-74;

ARCHER, Stanley, *Richard Hooker* (Boston: Twayne Publishers, 1983);

ATKINSON, Nigel, "Hooker's Theological Method and Modern Anglicanism", *Churchman* 114/1 (2000), 40-70;

ATKINSON, Nigel, *Richard Hooker and the Authority of Scripture, Tradition, and Reason. Reformed Theologian of the Church of England?* (Carlisle: Paternoster Press, 1997);

AVELING, J. C. H., "The English Clergy in the 16th and 17th Centuries", in AVELING, J. C. H.; LOADES, D. M., and McADOO, H. R. (eds.), *Rome and the Anglicans. Historical and Doctrinal Aspects of Anglican-Roman Catholic Relations* (Berlin: Walter de Gruyter, 1982);

AVIS, P. D. L., "Richard Hooker and John Calvin", *The Journal of Ecclesiastical History* 32 (1981), 19-28;

AYRIS, Paul (ed.), *Thomas Cranmer. Churchman and Scholar* (Woodbridge: The Boydell Press, 1993);

BABBAGE, Stuart Barton, *Puritanism and Richard Bancroft* (London: SPCK, 1962);

BAIRD, Henry, *Thedore Beza: Counselor of the French Reformation 1519-1605* (New York, 1899);

BAKER, William J., "Hurrel Froude and the Reformers", *Journal of Ecclesiastical History* XXI/3 (1970), 243-259;

BALL, John H., *Chronicling the Soul's Windings. Thomas Hooker and His Morphology of Conversion* (Lanham: University Press of America, 1992);

BARNIKOL, H. M., *Bucer's Lehre von der Rechtfertigung* (Diss., University of Göttingen, 1961);

BARRY, Alfred, *Masters in English Theology* (London, 1877);

BARTLETT, Alan, "What Has Richard Hooker to Say to Modern Evangelical Anglicanism?", *Anvil* 15/3 (1998), 195-206;

BATTLES, Ford Lewis, *Interpreting Jean Calvin* (Grand Rapids: Baker Books, 1996);

BAUCKHAM, Richard, "Hooker, Travers and the Church of Rome in the 1580s", *Journal of Ecclesiastical History* 29/1 (1978), 37-50;

BAUCKHAM, Richard, "Richard Hooker and John Calvin: a Comment", *Journal of Ecclesiastical History* 32/1 (1981), 29-33;

BENNETT, Gareth, "The Church of England and the Royal Supremacy", *One in Christ* XXII/4 (1986), 304-313;

BERNARD, G. W., "The Making of Religious Policy, 1533-1546: Henry VIII and the Search for the Middle Way", *The Historical Journal* 41/2 (1998), 321-349;

BETHELL, S. L., *The Cultural Revolution of the Seventeenth Century* (London: Dennis Dobson, 1963);

BETTERIDGE, Thomas, *Tudor Histories of the English Reformations 1530-1583* (Aldershot: Ashgate, 1999);

BICKNELL, E. J. (ed.), *A Theological Introduction to the Thirty-Nine Articles of the Church of England* (London: Longmans, Green and Co., 1955);

BIERMA, Lyle, "What Hath Wittenberg to Do with Heidelberg? Philip Melanchthon and the Heidelberg Catechism", in MAAG, Karin (ed.), *Melanchthon in Europe. His Work and Influence beyond Wittenberg* (Grand Rapids: Baker Books, 1999), 103-121;

BIRT, Henry Norbert, *The Elizabethan Religious Settlement* (London: George Bell and Sons, 1907);

BOOTY, John E., "An Elizabethan Addresses Modern Anglicanism. Richard Hooker and Theological Issues at the End of the Twentieth Century", *Anglican Theological Review* LXXI/1 (1989), 8-24;

BOOTY, John E., "Contrition in Anglican Spirituality: Hooker, Donne, and Herbert", 25-48, in Wolf, William J. (ed.), *Anglican Spirituality* (Wilton: Morehouse-Barlow, 1982);

BOOTY, John E., "Elizabethan Religion: Disorder Ordered", *Anglican Theological Review* 73/2 (1991), 123-138;

BOOTY, John E., "Hooker's Understanding of the Presence of Christ in the Eucharist", in BOOTY, John E. (ed.), *The Divine Drama in History and Liturgy. Essays Presented to Horton Davies on his Retirement from Princeton University* (Allison Park: Pickwick Publications, 1984), 131-148;

BOOTY, John E., "The English Reformation: A Lively Faith and Sacramental Confession", in ELMEN, Paul (ed.), *The Anglican Moral Choice* (Wilton: Morehouse-Barlow, 1983), 15-32;

BOOTY, John E., "The Judicious Mr. Hooker and Authority in the Elizabethan Church", in SYKES, Stephen W. (ed.), *Authority in the Anglican Communion* (Toronto: Anglican Book Centre, 1987);

BOOTY, John E., "The Quest for the Historical Hooker", *The Churchman* 80/3 (1966), 185-193;

BOOTY, John, "Anglican Identity: What is This Book of Common Prayer?", *Sewanee Theological Review* 40/2 (1997), 137-145;

BOOTY, John, "*Foreword*: Richard Hooker, Anglican Theologian", *Sewanee Theological Review* 36/2 (1993), 185-186;

BOOTY, John, "Hooker and Anglicanism: Into the Future", *Sewanee Theological Review* 36/2 (1993), 215-226;

BOOTY, John, "The Law of Proportion: William Meade and Richard Hooker", *St. Luke's Journal of Theology* XXXIV/2 (1991), 19-31;

BOOTY, John, "The Spirituality of Participation in Richard Hooker", *Sewanee Theological Review* 38/1 (1994), 9-20;

BOOTY, John, "Understanding the Church in Sixteenth-Century England", *Sewanee Theological Review* 42/3 (1999), 269-289;

BORNKAMM, Heinrich, *Luther in Mid-Career, 1521-1530* (London: Darton Longman & Todd, 1983);

BORSCH, Frederick H., "Ye Shall Be Holy: Reflections on the Spirituality of the Oxford Movement", in ROWELL, Geoffrey (ed.), *Tradition Renewed. The Oxford Movement Conference Papers* (London: Darton, Longman and Todd, 1986), 64-77;

BOURNE, E. C. E., *The Anglicanism of William Laud* (London: SPCK, 1947);

BOUWSMA, William J., "Hooker in the Context of European Cultural History", Claire McEACHERN, Claire; SHUGER Deborah (eds.), *Religion and Culture in Renaissance England* (Cambridge: Cambridge University Press, 1997);

BOUWSMA, William, *Jean Calvin. A Sixteenth Century Portrait* (Oxford: Oxford University Press, 1988);

BRAATEN, Carl, *Justification. The Article by Which the Church Stands or Falls* (Minneapolis: Fortress Press, 1990);

BRAATEN, Carl, *Principles of Lutheran Theology* (Philadelphia: Fortress Press, 1985);

BRADSHAW, Brendan, "Richard Hooker's *Ecclesiastical Polity*", *The Journal of Ecclesiastical History* 34 (1983), 438-444;

BRADSHAW, William, *Dissertation de Justificationis Doctrina* (John Maire, 1618);

BRAY, John S., *Theodore Beza's Doctrine of Predestination* (Nieuwkoop: B. de Graaf, 1975);

BRECHT, Martin, *Martin Luther. Shaping and Defining the Reformation 1521-1532* (Minneapolis: Fortress Press, 1990);

BREWARD, Jan (ed.), *The Works of William Perkins* (Appleford: The Sutton Courtenay Press, 1970);

BRINKLEY, Roberta Florence, *Coleridge on the Seventeenth Century* (New York: Greenwood Press, 1968);

BROCKWELL, Charles W., "Answering 'the Known Men': Bishop Reginald Pecock and Mr. Richard Hooker", in BRAUER, Jerald C.; GRANT, Robert M.; MARTY, Martin E. (eds.), *Church History*, vol. 49 (The American Society of Church History, 1980);

BROMILEY, G. W. (ed.), *Zwingli and Bullinger* (London: SCM Press, 1953);

BROMILEY, G. W., *Thomas Cranmer Theologian* (London: Lutterworth Press, 1956);

BROOK, V. J. K., *A Life of Archbishop Parker* (Oxford: Clarendon Press, 1962);

BROOK, V. J. K., *Whitgift and the English Church* (London: The English Universities Press Ltd., 1957);

BROOKS, Peter Newman, *Cranmer in Context* (Cambridge: Lutterworth Press, 1989);

BRYAN, John Michael Christopher, "The Judicious Mr. Hooker and the Early Christians. The Relationship of Scripture and Reason in the First Century of the Christian Era", in ARMENTROUT, Donald S. (ed.), *This Sacred History. Anglican Reflections for John Booty* (Cambridge, Mass.: Cowley Publications, 1990), 144-160;

BRYDON, M. A., Review of Nigel Atkinson, *Richard Hooker and the Auhority of Scripture, Tradition, and Reason: Reformed Theologian of the Church of England?* (Carlisle: Paternoster Press, 1997), in *The Seventeenth Century* XIV/1 (1999), 70-72;

BUCHANAN, James, *The Doctrine of Justification* (Edinburgh: The Banner of Truth, 1997 – first published 1867);

BURNS, Norman T., *Christian Mortalism from Tyndale to Milton* (Cambridge: Harvard University Press, 1972);

BUSH, Douglas, *English Literature in the Early Seventeenth Century 1600-1660* (Oxford: Clarendon Press, 1952);

BUSH, Sargent, *The Writings of Thomas Hooker* (London: The University of Wisconsin Press, 1980);

CAMPBELL, W. E., *Erasmus, Tyndale, and More* (London: Eyre & Spottiswoode, 1949);

CARLSON, Leland H., "Archbishop John Whitgift: His Supporters and Opponents", *Anglican and Episcopal History* LVI/3 (1987), 285-301;

CARLTON, Charles, *Archbishop William Laud* (London: Routledge and Kegan Paul, 1987);

CARTER, Patrick, "Clerical Polemic in Defence of Minister's Maintenance During the English Reformation", *Journal of Ecclesiastical History* 49/2 (1998), 236-256;

CATTERMOLE, Richard, *The Literature of the Church of England Indicated in the Selections from the Writings of Eminent Divines: With Memoirs of Their Lives, and Historical Sketches of the Times in Which They Lived*, vol. I-II (London, 1844);

CLARK, J. C. D., "Protestantism, Nationalism, and National Identity, 1660-1832", in *The Historical Journal* 43/1 (2000), 249-276;

CLEBSCH, William A., *England's Earliest Protestants 1522-1535* (New Haven: Yale University Press, 1964);

COFFEY, John, "Puritanism and Liberty Revisited: The Case for Toleration in the English Revolution", *The Historical Journal* 41/4 (1998), 961-985;

COHEN, Charles Lloyd, *God's Caress* (Oxford: Oxford University Press, 1986);

COLLINS, Jeffrey R., "Christian Ecclesiology and the Composition of *Leviathan*: A Newly Discovered Letter to Thomas Hobbes", in *The Historical Journal* 43/1 (2000), 217-231;

COLLINSON, Patrick, *Archbishop Grindal 1519-1583* (London: Jonathan Cape, 1979);

COLLINSON, Patrick, *Elizabethan Essays* (London: The Hambledon Press, 1994);

COLLINSON, Patrick, *The Birthpangs of Protestant England* (London: Macmillan Press, 1988);

COLLINSON, Patrick, *The Elizabethan Puritan Movement* (London: Jonathan Cape, 1967);

COLLINSON, Patrick, *The Religion of Protestants. The Church in English Society 1559-1625* (Oxford: Clarendon Press, 1982);

CONDREN, Conal, "The Creation of Richard Hooker's Public Authority: Rhetoric, Reputation and Reassessment", *Journal of Religious History* 21/1 (1997), 35-59;

CONSTANT, G., *The Reformation in England* (London: Sheed and Ward, 1934);

COOLIDGE, J. S., *The Pauline Renaissance in England* (Oxford: Clarendon Press, 1970);

CRAIG, John, "Reformers, Conflict, and Revisionism: The Reformation in Sixteenth-Century Hadleigh", *The Historical Journal* 42/1 (1999), 1-23;

CRANZ, Edward, *An Essay on the Development of Luther's Thought on Justice, Law, and Society* (Cambridge: Harvard University Press, 1959);

CRERAR, Douglas, *Positive Negatives. A Motif in Christian Tradition* (New York: Peter Lang, 1991);

CROFTS, Richard A., "The Defense of the Elizabethan Church: Jewel, Hooker and James I", *Anglican Theological Review* LIV/1 (1972), 20-30;

CROMARTIE, Alan, "Harringtonian Virtue: Harrington, Machiavelli, and the Method of the *Moment*", *The Historical Journal* 41/4 (1998), 987-1009;

CROMARTIE, Alan, "Theology and Politics in Richard Hooker's Thought", *History of Political Thought* XXI/1 (2000), 41-66;

CROWLEY, Weldon S., "Erastianism in England to 1640", *Journal of Church and State* 32/3 (1990), 549-566;

D'ENTRÈVES, Alessandro Passerin, *Riccardo Hooker. Contributo alla Teoria e alla Storia del Diritto Naturale* (Torino: Presso d'Instituto Giuridico della Regia Università di Torino, 1932);

D'ENTRÈVES, Alexandre Passerin, *The Medieval Contribution to Political Thought* (Oxford: Oxford University Press, 1939);

DACKSON, Wendy, "Richard Hooker and American Religious Liberty", *Journal of the Church and State* 41/1 (1999), 117-134;

DAMIAN, Grace, "Natural Law in Hooker's *Of the Laws of Ecclesiastical Polity*", *The Journal of Religious Studies*, 21/1 (1997), 10-22;

DANIELL, David, *William Tyndale. A Biography* (New Haven: Yale University Press, 1994);

DAVIES, E. T., *Episcopacy and the Royal Supremacy in the Church of England in the XVIth Century* (Oxford: Blackwell, 1950);

DE KROON, Marijn, "Martin Bucer and the Problem of Tolerance", in *The Sixteenth Century Journal* 2 (1988), 157-168;

DEAN, A. C., *Life of Thomas Cranmer* (London, 1927);

DEMAUS, R., *William Tyndale. A Biography* (Amsterdam: J. C. Gieben, 1971);

DICK, John A. R., *A Critical Edition of William Tyndale's "The Parable of the Wicked Mammon"* (Ph.D. dissertation: Yale University, 1974);

DORAN, Susan, "Elizabeth I's Religion: The Evidence of Her Letters", in *Journal of Ecclesiastical History* 51/4 (2000), 699-720;

DOWLEY, Powel Mills, *John Whitgift and the Reformation* (London: Adam & Charles Black, 1955);

DULLES, Avery, *The Assurance of Things Hoped For* (Oxford: Oxford University Press, 1994);

EBELING, Gerhard, *Luther: An Introduction to His Thought* (Collins: Fontana Library of Theology and Philosophy, 1972);

ECCLESHALL, Robert, "Richard Hooker and the Peculiarities of the English: The Reception of the *Ecclesiastical Polity* in the Seventeenth and Eighteenth Centuries", *History of Political Thought* II/1 (1981), 63-117;

EELLS, Hastings, *Martin Bucer* (London: Yale University Press, 1931);

EMERSON, Everett H., *English Puritanism from John Hooper to John Milton* (Durham, N.C.: Duke University Press, 1968);

FAULKNER, Robert K., *Richard Hooker and the Politics of a Christian England* (Berkeley: University of California Press, 1981);

FENLON, Dermot, *Heresy and Obedience in Tridentine Italy. Cardinal Pole and the Counter-Reformation* (Cambridge: Cambridge University Press, 1972);

FIELD, George C., "Critical Note: Donne and Hooker", *Anglican Theological Review* XLVIII (1966), 307-309;

FINCHAM, Kenneth (ed.), *The Early Stuart Church, 1603-1642* (MacMillan, 1993);

FITZMEYER, Joseph, A., "Justification by Faith and 'Righteousness' in the New Testament", in ANDERSON, H. George (ed.), *Justification by Faith* (Minneapolis: Augsburg Publishing House, 1985), 77-81;

FITZSIMMONS Allison, C., "The Pastoral and Political Implications of Trent on Justification: a Response to the ARCIC Agreed Statement *Salvation and the Church*", *The Saint Luke's Journal of Theology* XXXI/3 (1988), 204-222;

FORTE, Paul E., "Richard Hooker's Theory of Law", *The Journal of Medieval and Renaissance Studies* 12 (1982), 133-157;

FRAENKEL, Peter, *Testimonia Patrum. The Function of the Patristic Argument in the Theology of Philip Melanchthon* (Genève: Librairie Droz, 1961);

FULLER, Thomas, *The Church History of Britain, from the Birth of Jesus Christ until the Year MDCXLVIII*, vol. I-III (London: William Tegg, 1868);

FUNG, Ronald, "Justification in the Epistle of James", in CARSON, D.A. (ed.), *Right with God. Justification in the Bible and the World* (London: Paternoster, 1992), 147-154;

FURCHA, E. J. (ed.), *Huldrych Zwingli, 1484-1531. A Legacy of Radical Reform* (FRC/ARC, 1984);

FURCHA, E. J. (ed.), *Prophet, Pastor, Protestant* (Pennsylvania: Pickwick Publications, 1984);

GÄBLER, Ulrich, *Huldrych Zwingli. His Life and Work* (Edinburgh: T&T Clark, 1986);

GAFFIN, Richard B., "Justification in Luke-Acts", in CARSON, D.A. (ed.), *Right with God. Justification in the Bible and the World* (London: Paternoster, 1992), 106-126;

GANE, Erwin R., "The Exegetical Methods of Some Sixteenth-Century Anglican Preachers: Latimer, Jewel, Hooker, and Andrews", *Andrews University Seminary Studies* XVII/1 (1979), 23-38;

GANOCZY, Alexandre, *The Young Calvin* (Philadelphia: The Westminster Press, 1987);

GASCOIGNE, John, "Church and Stat Unified: Hooker's Rationale for the English Post-Reformation Order", *The Journal of Religious History* 21/1 (1997), 23-34;

GASCOIGNE, John, "The Unity of Church and State Challanged: Responses to Hooker from the Restauration to the Nineteenth-Century Age of Reform", *The Journal of Religious History*, 21/1 (1997) 60-79;

GEORGE, Charles H., and GEORGE, Katherine, *The Protestant Mind of the English Reformation 1570-1640* (Princeton: Princeton University Press, 1961);

GIBBS, Lee W., "Richard Hooker's *Via Media* Doctrine of Repentance", *Harvard Theological Review* 84/1 (1991), 59-74;

GIBBS, Lee W., "Richard's Hooker *Via Media* Doctrine of Justification", *Harvard Theological Review* 74/1 (1981), 211-220;

GIBBS, Lee W., "The Source of the Most Famous Quotation from Richard Hooker's *Laws of Ecclesiastical Polity*", *Sixteenth Century Journal* XXI/1 (1990), 77-86;

GIBBS, Lee W., "Theology, Logic, and Rhetoric in the Temple Controversy between Richard Hooker and Walter Travers", *Anglican Theological Review* LXV/2 (1983), 177-188;

GREEN, Ian, *The Christian's ABC. Catechisms and Catechizing in England c. 1530-1740* (Oxford: Clarendon Press, 1996);

GREEN, Lowell, *How Melanchthon Helped Luther Discover the Gospel* (Fallbrook: Verdict Publications, 1980);

GREGG, William O., "Sacramental Theology in Hooker's *Laws*: A Structural Perspective", *Anglican Theological Review* 73/2 (1991), 155-176;

GRESCHAT, Martin, *Martin Bucer. Ein Reformator und Seine Zeit* (München: Verlag C. H. Beck, 1990);

GRIFFITH THOMAS, W. H. (ed.), *The Principles of Theology. An Introduction to the Thirty-Nine Articles* (London: Vine Books, 1978);

GUY, John (ed.), *The Reign of Elizabeth I* (Cambridge: Cambridge University Press, 1995);

HAIGH, Christopher, "The Church of England, the Catholics, and the People", in MARSHALL, Peter (ed.), *The Impact of the English Reformation 1500-1640* (London: Arnold, 1997), 235-255;

HAIGH, Christopher, *English Reformations. Religion, Politics, and Society under the Tudors* (Oxford: Clarendon Press, 1993);

HALL, Basil, "Martin Bucer in England", in WRIGHT, D.F., *Martin Bucer. Reforming Church and Community* (Cambridge: Cambridge University Press, 1996), 148-149;

HALLER, William, *Liberty and Reformation in the Puritan Revolution* (New York: Columbia University Press, 1955);

HAMMANN, Gotfried, *Entre la Secte et la Cité: Le Projet d'Eglise du Réformateur Martin Bucer* (Genève: Labor et Fides, 1984);

HANCOCK, Ralph, *Calvin and the Foundations of Modern Politics* (Ithaca: Cornell University Press, 1989);

HARTH, Phillip, *Swift and Anglican Rationalism. The Religious Background of* A Tale of a Tub (Chicago: The University of Chicago Press, 1969);

HAUGAARD, William P., "Richard Hooker: Evidences of an Ecumenical Vision from a Twentieth Century Perspective", *Journal of Ecumenical Studies* XXIV/3 (1987), 427-439;

HAUGAARD, William P., "Richard Hooker: Evidences of an Ecumenical Vision from a Twentieth-Century Perspective", *Journal of Ecumenical Studies* 24/3 (1987), 427-439;

HAUGAARD, William P., "The Scriptural Hermeneutics of Richard Hooker. Historical Contextualization and Teleology", in ARMENTROUT, Donald S. (ed.), *This Sacred History. Anglican Reflections for John Booty* (Cambridge, Mass.: Cowley Publications, 1990), 161-174;

HAUGAARD, William P., "Towards an Anglican Doctrine of Ministry: Richard Hooker and the Elizabethan Church", *Anglican and Episcopal History* LVI/3 (1987), 265-284;

HAUGAARD, William P., *Elizabeth and the English Reformation* (Cambridge: Cambridge University Press, 1968);

HAUGAARD, William, "The Bible in the Anglican Reformation", in BORSCH, Frederick H. (ed.), *Anglicanism and the Bible* (Wilton: Morehouse-Barlow, 1984), 11-80;

HEAVEN, Edwin B., "The Transcendence of Order", in BRYANT, Darrol M. (ed.), *The Future of Anglican Theology* (New York and Toronto: The Edwin Mellen Press, 1984), 117-129;

HENSON, Hensley, *William Tyndale* (London: Hodder and Stoughton, n.d.);

HESSELINK, John, *Calvin's First Catechism. A Commentary* (Louisville: Westminster John Knox Press, 1997);

HICKMAN, David, "Religious Belief and Pious Practice among London's Elizabethan Elite", in *The Historical Journal* 42/4 (1999), 941-960;

HIGHAM, Florence, *Catholic and Reformed. A Study of the Anglican Church, 1559-1662* (London: SPCK, 1962);

HILDEBRANDT, Franz, *Melanchthon: Alien or Ally?* (Cambridge: Cambridge University Press, 1946);

HILL, Christopher, *Society and Puritanism in Pre-Revolutionary England* (London: Secker & Warburg, 1964);

HILLERDAL, Gunnar, *Reason and Revelation in Richard Hooker* (Lund: CWK Gleerup, 1962);

HILTON, Boyd, "*Apologia pro Vitis Veteriorum Hominum*", *Journal of Ecclesiastical History* 50/1 (1999), Review-article of Peter B. Nockles, *The Oxford Movement in Context. Anglican Churchmanship, 1760-1857* (Cambridge: Cambridge University Press, 1994), 117-130;

HINDMARSH, D. B., "The Olney Autobiographers: English Conversion Narrative in the Mid-Eighteenth Century", *Journal of Ecclesiastical History* 49/1 (1998), 61-84;

HOOPES, Robert, *Right Reason in the English Renaissance* (Cambridge, Mass.: Harvard University Press, 1962);

HUDSON, Nicholas, "Three Steps to Perfection: *Rasselas* and the Philosophy of Richard Hooker", *Eighteenth Century Life* 14/3 (1990), 29-39;

HUGHES, Philip Edgcumbe, *Faith and Works. Cranmer and Hooker on Justification* (Wilton: Morehouse-Barlow, 1982);

HUGHES, Séan F., "The Problem of 'Calvinism': English Theologies of Predestination c. 1580-1630", in WABUDA, Susan; LITZENBERGER, Caroline (eds.), *Belief and Practice in Reformation England. A Tribute to Patrick Collinson from his Students* (Aldershot: Ashgate, 1998), 229-249;

HUNT, John, *Religious Thought in England from the Reformation to the End of Last Century. A Contribution to the History of Theology*, vol. I (London: Strahan & Co. Publishers, 1870);

HUTCHINSON, F. E., *Cranmer and the English Reformation* (London: English Universities Press, 1951);

HVALVIK, Reidar, "A *Sonderweg* for Israel: A Critical Examination of a Current Interpretation of Romans 11:25-27", *Journal for the Study of the New Testament* 38 (1990);

JACKSON, Michael, "Home Cooking: British Theology and the Universal Church", *Theology* LXXXII/688 (1979), 244-251;

JONES, Serene, *Calvin and the Rhetoric of Piety* (Louisville: Westminster John Knox Press, 1995);

JORDAN, W. K., *The Development of Religious Toleration in England from the Beginning of the English Reformation to the Death of Queen Elizabeth* (London, 1932);

KAYE, Bruce N., "Richard Hooker and Australian Anglicanism", *Sewanee Theological Review* 36/2 (1993), 227-245;

KAYE, Bruce N., "What Might Alasdair MacIntyre Learn from a Reading of Richard Hooker? Rivalry, Commonality, and Their Projects", *Sewanee Theological Review* 42/3 (1999), 332-349;

KAYE, Bruce N., "Authority and the Interpretation of Scripture in Hooker's *Of the Laws of Ecclesiastical Polity*", *The Journal of Religious History* 21/1 (1997), 80-109;

KAYE, Bruce N., "Authority and the Shaping of Tradition: New Essays on Richard Hooker", *The Journal of Religious History*, 21/1 (1997), 3-9;

KENDALL, R. T., *Calvinism and English Calvinism to 1649* (Oxford: Oxford University Press, 1979);

KENNICOTT, B., *An Analysis of Hooker's Ecclesiastical Polity being a Particular Defence of the Church of England* (London, 1819);

KIRK, Terrell T., "The Meaning and Application of Reason in the Works of Richard Hooker", *The Saint Luke's Journal* IV/1 (1961), 22-35;

KITTELSON, James M., "Martin Bucer and the Sacramentarian Controversy: The Origins of his Policy of Concord", in *Archiv für Reformationsgeschichte* 64 (1973), 166-183;

KITTELSON, James, M., "Wolfgang Capito, the Council, and Reform Strasbourg", in *Archiv für Reformationsgeschichte* 63 (1972), 126-140;

KNOX, S. J., *Walter Travers, Paragon of Elizabethan Puritanism* (London: Methuen & Co. Ltd., 1962);

KNOX, S. J., *Walter Travers: Paragon of Elizabethan Puritanism* (London: Methuen & Co. LTD, 1962);

KRAPP, George Philip, *The Rise of English Literary Prose* (New York: Oxford University Press, 1915);

KREIDER, Alan, *English Chantries. The Road to Dissolution* (Cambridge, Mass.: Harvard University Press, 1979);

KRIEGER, Christian (ed.), *Martin Bucer and Sixteenth Century Europe* (Leiden: E.J. Brill, 1993);

KRÜGER, Friedhelm, "Bucer and Erasmus", *Mennonite Quarterly Review* LXVIII/1 (1994), 11-23;

KRUSE, Colin G., *Paul, the Law and Justification* (Leicester: Apollos, 1996);

KUSUKAWA, Sachiko, *The Transformation of Natural Philosophy. The case of Philip Melanchthon* (Cambridge: Cambridge University Press, 1995);

LAKE, Peter, "Business as Usual? The Immediate Reception of Hooker's *Ecclesiastical Polity*", *The Journal of Ecclesiastical History* 52/3 (2001), 456-486;

LAKE, Peter, "Calvinism and the English Church 1570-1635", in TODD, Margo (ed.), *Reformation to Revolution. Politics and Religion in Early Modern England* (London: Routledge, 1995), 179-207;

LAKE, Peter, and DOWLING, Maria, *Protestantism and the National Church in Sixteenth Century England* (London: Croom Helm, 1987);

LAKE, Peter, *Anglicans and Puritans? Presbyterians and English Conformist Thought from Whitgift to Hooker* (London: Unwin Hyman, 1988);

LAKE, Peter, *Moderate Puritanism and the Elizabethan Church* (Cambridge: Cambridge University Press, 1982);

LAMONT, William M., *Godly Rule. Politics and Religion 1603-1660* (London: Macmillan Press, 1969);

LANE, Anthony N. S., *Jean Calvin, Student of the Church Fathers* (Edinburgh: T&T Clark, 1999);

LECKY, W. E. H., *History of the Rise and Influence of the Spirit of Rationalism in Europe*, vol. I-II (London, 1865);

LECLER, Joseph, *Toleration and the Reformation*, vol. II (London: Longmans, 1960);

LEONARD, Emile, *A History of Protestantism* (London: Thomas Nelson, 1965);

LEWIS C. S., *English Literature in the Sixteenth Century Excluding Drama* (Oxford: Clarendon Press, 1954);

LIENHARD, Marc, *Luther: Witness to Jesus Christ* (Minneapolis: Augsburg Publishing House, 1982);

LITTLE, David, *Religion, Order, and Law: A Study in Pre-Revolutionary England* (New York: Harper and Row, 1969);

LOADES, David, *Revolution and Religion. The English Reformation 1530-1570* (Cardiff: University of Wales Press, 1992);

LOCHER, Gottfried, *Zwingli's Thought: New Perspectives* (Leiden: E.J. Brill, 1981);

LOCKE, Kenneth A., "Equal Ministries: Richard Hooker and Non-episcopal Ordinations", *Anvil* 14/3 (1997), 172-182;

LOCKWOOD O'DONOVAN, Joan, *Theology of Law and Authority in the English Reformation* (Atlanta: Scholars Press, 1991);

LOHSE, Bernhard, *Martin Luther's Theology. Its Historical and Systematic Development* (Edinburgh: T&T Clark, 1999);

LOSSKY, Nicholas, *Lancelot Andrewes. The Preacher 1555-1626* (Oxford: Clarendon Press, 1991);

LOUMA, John K., "Restitution and Reformation? Cartwright and Hooker on the Elizabethan Church", *Historical Magazine of the Protestant Episcopal Church* XLVI/1 (1977), 85-106;

324   Bibliography

LOUMA, John K., "Who Owns the Fathers? Hooker and Cartwright on the Authority of the Primitive Church", *The Sixteenth Century Journal* VIII/3 (1977), 45-60;

LOYER, O., "Contrat social et consentement chez Richard Hooker", *Revue des Sciences Philosophiques et Théologiques* 59/3 (1975), 369-398;

LOYER, Olivier, *L'Anglicanisme de Richard Hooker* (Paris, 1977);

LURBE, Eve, "Political Power and Ecclesiastical Power in Richard Hooker's *Laws of Ecclesiastical Polity*", *Cahiers Elisabéthains* 49 (1996), 15-21;

LYON, T., *The Theory of Religious Liberty in England 1603-1639* (New York: Octogon Books, 1976);

MacCULLOCH, Diarmaid, *The Later Reformation in England 1547-1603* (MacMillan, 2001);

MacCULLOCH, Diarmaid, *Thomas Cranmer: A Life* (New Haven: Yale University Press, 1996);

MACEK, Ellen A., *The Loyal Opposition. Tudor Traditional Polemics, 1535-1558* (New York: Peter Lang, 1996);

MALONE, Michael T., "The Doctrine of Predestination in the Thought of William Perkins and Richard Hooker", *Anglican Theological Review* LII/2 (1970), 103-117;

MALTBY, Judith, *Prayer Book and People in Elizabethan and Early Stuart England* (Cambridge: Cambridge University Press, 1998);

MAROT, D. H., "Aux origines de la théologie anglicane. Écriture et tradition chez Richard Hooker", *Irénikon* XXXIII (1960), 321-343;

MARSH, Christopher, *Popular Religion in Sixteenth-Century England. Holding Their Peace* (London: MacMillan Press, 1998);

MARSHALL, J. S., *Hooker and the Anglican Tradition. An Historical and Theological Study of Hooker's Ecclesiastical Polity* (London: Adam & Charles Black, 1963);

MARTIN, Hugh, *Puritanism and Richard Baxter* (London: SCM Press Ltd., 1954);

MARUYAMA, Tadataka, *The Ecclesiology of Thedore Beza. The Reform of the True Church* (Genève: Librairie Droz, 1978);

MASON, Thomas A., *Serving God and Mammon. William Juxton 1582-1663* (Newark: University of Delaware Press, 1985);

MAXCEY, Carl, *Bona Opera. A Study in the Development of the Doctrine of Philip Melanchthon* (Nieuwkoop: B. De Graaf, 1980);

McADOO, H. R., "The Influence of the Seventeenth Century on Contemporary Anglican Understanding of the Purpose and Function of Authority in the Church", in EVANS, G. R. (ed.),

Christian Authority. Essays in Honour of Henry Chadwick (Oxford: Clarendon Press, 1988), 251-277;

McADOO, H. R., *The Spirit of Anglicanism. A Survey of Anglican Theological Method in the Seventeenth Century* (London: Adam & Charles Black, 1965);

McADOO, Henry, "Richard Hooker", in ROWELL, Geoffrey (ed.), *The English Religious Tradition and the Genius of Anglicanism* (Ikon, 1992), 105-125;

McCULLOGH, Peter, "Making Dead Men Speak: Laudianism, Print, and the Works of Lancelot Andrews, 1626-1642", *The Historical Journal* 41/2 (1998), 401-424;

McGOLDRICK, James E., *Luther's English Connection. The Reformation Thought of Robert Barnes and William Tyndale* (Milwaukee: Northwestern Publishing House, 1979);

McGRADE, A. S., "Hooker's *Polity* and the Establishment of the English Church", in HOOKER, Richard, *Of the Laws of the Ecclesiastical Polity*, A. S. McGrade and Brian Vickers eds. (London: Sidgwick and Jackson, 1975), 11-40;

McGRADE, A. S., "Richard Hooker on the Lawful Ministry of Bishops and Kings", in SHEILS, W. J., and WOOD, Diana (eds.), *The Ministry: Clerical and Lay. Papers Read at the 1988 Summer Meeting and the 1989 Winter Meeting of the Ecclesiastical History Society* (Oxford: Blackwell, 1989), 177-184;

McGRADE, Arthur S., "The Public and the Religious in Hooker's *Polity*", in GRANT, Robert M., MARTY, Martin E., BRAUER, Gerald C. (eds.), *Church History*, vol. XXXVII (The American Society of Church History, 1968);

McGRADE, Arthur Stephen (ed.), *Richard Hooker and the Construction of Christian Community* (Tempe: Medieval and Renaissance Texts and Studies, 1997);

McGRADE, Stephen, "Richard Hooker. Apologist for All Seasons", *St. Mark's Review* 141 (1990), 12-22;

McGRATH, Alister, "Humanist Elements in the Early Reformed Doctrine of Justification" in *Archiv für Reformationsgeschichte* 73 (1982), 5-19;

McGRATH, Alister, *Iustitia Dei. A History of the Christian Doctrine of Justification* (Cambridge: Cambridge University Press, 1989);

McGRATH, Alister, *Justification by Faith. What it Means for Us Today* (Grand Rapids: Zondervan, 1988);

McGRATH, Alister, *Luther's Theology of the Cross. Martin Luther's Theological Breakthrough* (Oxford: Blackwell, 1985);

McGRATH, Patrick, *Papists and Puritans under Elizabeth I* (London: Blendford Press, 1967);

McGRATH, Peter, *Papists and Puritans under Elizabeth I* (London: Blandford Press, 1967);

McKIM, Donald K., *Ramism in William Perkins' Theology* (New York: Peter Lang, 1987);

MEYER, Carl S., *Elizabeth I and the Religious Settlement of 1559* (Saint Louis: Concordia Publishing House, 1960);

MICHAELIS, Gottfried, *Richard Hooker als politischer Denker* (Berlin: Verlag Dr. Emil Ebering, 1933);

MICKS, Marianne, "Richard Hooker as Theologian", *Theology Today* XXXVI/4 (1980), 560-563;

MILLER, Clarence H., "Seventeenth-Century Latin Translations of Two English Masterpieces: Hooker's *Polity* and Browne's *Religio Medici*", in SCHNUR, Rhoda (ed.), *Acta Conventus Neo-Latini Abulensis. Proceedings of the Tenth International Congress of Neo-Latin Studies* (Tempe: Arizona Center for Medieval and Renaissance Studies, 2000), 55-72;

MILTON, Anthony, *Catholic and Reformed. The Roman and Protestant Churches in English Protestant Thought 1600-1640* (Cambridge: Cambridge University Press, 1995);

MILWARD, Peter, *Religious Controversies of the Elizabethan Age. A Survey of Printed Sources* (London: The Scholar Press, 1977);

MOORE, Tod, "Recycling Aristotle: The Sovereignty Theory of Richard Hooker", *History of Political Thought* XIV/3 (1993), 345-359;

MOREAU, Jean-Pierre, *Rome ou L'Angleterre? Les Réactions Politiques des Catholiques Anglais au Moment du Schisme 1529-1553* (Paris: Presses Universitaires de France, 1984);

MOREY, Adrian, *The Catholic Subjects of Elizabeth I* (London: George Allen & Unwin, 1978);

MORGAN, Irvonwy, *Prince Charles's Puritan Chaplain* (London: George Allen & Unwin Ltd., 1957);

MORGAN, John, *Godly Learning* (Cambridge: Cambridge University Press, 1986);

MORREL, George, "Richard Hooker, Theologian of the English Reformation", *Christianity Today* X/24 (1966), 8-10;

MORRIS, Christopher, *Political Thought in England. Tyndale to Hooker* (London: Oxford University Press, 1953);

MOZLEY, J. F., *William Tyndale* (London: SPCK, 1937);

MUNZ, Peter, *The Place of Hooker in the History of Thought* (Westport: Greenwood Press. Publishers, 1952);

NAPHY, William, *Calvin and the Consolidation of the Genevan Reformation* (Manchester: Manchester University Press, 1994);

NELSON BURNETT, Amy, "Church Discipline and Moral Reformation in the Thought of Martin Bucer", in *The Sixteenth Century Journal* 3 (1991), 439-456;

NELSON BURNETT, Amy, *The Yoke of Christ: Martin Bucer and Christian Discipline* (Kirksville: Sixteenth Century Journal Publishers, 1994);

NEWEY, Edmund, "The Form of Reason: Participation in the Work of Richard Hooker, Benjamin Whichcote, Ralph Cudworth and Jeremy Taylor", in *Modern Theology* 18/1 (2002), 1-26;

NOCKLES, Peter Benedict, *The Oxford Movement in Context. Anglican High Churchmanship, 1760-1857* (Cambridge: Cambridge University Press, 1994);

NOCKLES, Peter, "The Oxford Movement: Historical Background 1780-1833", in ROWELL, Geoffrey (ed.), *Tradition Renewed. The Oxford Movement Conference Papers* (London: Darton, Longman and Todd, 1986), 24-50;

NORSKOV OLSEN, V., *John Foxe and the Elizabethan Church* (Berkeley: University of California Press, 1973);

NOVARR, David, *The Making of Walton's Lives* (New York: Cornell University Press, 1958);

NULL, Ashley, *Thomas Cranmer's Doctrine of Repentance. Renewing the Power to Love* (Oxford: Oxford University Press, 2000);

O'DAY, Rosemary, and HEAL, Felicity (eds.), *Christianity and Change. Personnel and Administration of the Church of England* (Leicester: Leicester University Press, 1976);

O'DAY, Rosemary, and HEAL, Felicity (eds.), *Church and Society in England. Henry VIII to James I* (London: Macmillan Press, 1977);

ORR, Robert R., *Reason and Authority. The Thought of William Chillingworth* (Oxford: Clarendon Press, 1967);

ORR, Robert, "Chillingworth Versus Hooker: A Criticism of Natural Law Theory", *The Journal of Religious History* 2/1-4 (1962-3), 120-132;

ORRÙ, Marco, "Anomy and Reason in the English Renaissance", *Journal of the History of Ideas* XLVII/2 (1986), 177-196;

OWEN, D. R. G., "Is There an Anglican Theology?", in BRYANT, Darrol M. (ed.), *The Future of Anglican Theology* (New York and Toronto: The Edwin Mellen Press, 1984);

OZMENT, Steven, *The Age of Reform 1250-1550. An Intellectual and Religious History of the Late Medieval and Reformation Europe* (London: Yale University Press, 1980);

PAGET, Francis, *An Introduction to the Fifth Book of Hooker's Treatise of the Laws of Ecclesiastical Polity* (Oxford: Clarendon Press, 1907);

PARKER, Kenneth, and CARLSON, Eric. J, *Practical Divinity. The Works and Life of Reverend Richard Greenham* (Aldershot: Ashgate, 1998);

PARKER, T. H. L., *Calvin. An Introduction to His Thought* (Geoffrey Chapman, 1995);

PARRIS, J. R., "Hooker's Doctrine of the Eucharist", *Scottish Journal of Theology* XVI (1963), 151-165;

PARRY, Glyn, "John Foxe, 'Father of Lyes', and the Papists", 302-303 in LOADES, David (ed.), *John Foxe and the English Reformation* (Scholar Press, 1997);

PAUCK, Wilhelm (ed.), *Melanchthon and Bucer* (London: SCM Press, 1969);

PEARSON, Scott, *Thomas Cartwright and Elizabethan Puritanism 1535-1603* (Cambridge: Cambridge University Press, 1925);

PELIKAN, Jaroslav, *The Christian Tradition. A History of the Development of Doctrine*, vol. 4, *Reformation of Church and Dogma 1300-1700* (Chicago: The University of Chicago Press, 1985);

PERCY, Martyn, *Introducing Richard Hooker and the Laws of Ecclesiastical Polity* (London: Darton, Longman and Todd, 1999);

PERROT, M. E. C., "Richard Hooker and the Problem of Authority in the Elizabethan Church", *Journal of Ecclesiastical History* 49/1 (1998), 29-60;

PERRY, Edith Weir, *Under Four Tudors* (London: George Allen & Unwin Ltd., 1940);

PETTEGREE, Andrew (ed.), *The Reformation World* (London: Routledge, 2000);

PETTEGREE, Andrew, *Marian Protestantism* (Aldershot: Scholar Press, 1996);

PILL, David, *The English Reformation 1529-1558* (London: University of London Press, 1973);

PINEAS, Rainer, *Thomas More and Tudor Polemics* (London: Indiana University Press, 1968);

POLLET, J. V., *Martin Bucer. Etudes sur la Correspondance*, vol. I-II (Paris: Presses Universitaires de France, 1962);

POLLET, J. V., *Martin Bucer. Etudes sur les Relations de Bucer avec les Pays-Bas, l'Eléctorat de Cologne et l'Allemagne du Nord*, vol. I-II (Leiden: E. J. Brill, 1985);

PORTER, H. C., *Reformation and Reaction in Tudor Cambridge* (Archon Books, 1972);

POTTER, G. R. (ed.), *Huldrych Zwingli* (London: Edward Arnold Publishers, 1978);

QUERE, Ralph Walter, *Melanchthon's Christum Cognoscere. Christ's Efficacious Presence in the Eucharistic Theology of Melanchthon* (Nieuwkoop: B. de Graaf, 1977);

REARDON, Bernard, *Religious Thought in the Reformation* (London: Longman, 1981);

REMNANT, Peter, "God and the Moral Law", *Canadian Journal of Theology* IV/1 (1958), 23-29;

RIDLEY, Jasper, *Thomas Cranmer* (Oxford: Clarendon Press, 1962);

RILLIET, Jean, *Zwingli: Third Man of the Reformation* (London: Lutterworth Press, 1964);

RITSCHL, Albrecht, *A Critical History of the Christian Doctrine of Justification and Reconciliation* (Edinburgh: Edmonston and Douglas, 1872);

ROSE, Elliot, *Cases of Conscience* (Cambridge: Cambridge University Press, 1975);

ROWSE, A. L., *The England of Elizabeth. The Structure of Society* (London: Macmillan, 1951);

RUPP, Gordon, *Studies in the Making of the English Protestant Tradition* (Cambridge: Cambridge University Press, 1949);

RUPP, Gordon, *The Righteousness of God* (London: Hodder and Stoughton, 1953);

SABINE, George H., *A History of the Political Theory* (London: George G. Harrap & Co. LTD., 1937);

SASEK, Lawrence A., *Images of Puritanism. A Collection of Contemporary Sources 1589-1646* (London: Louisiana State University Press, 1989);

SCARISBRICK, J. J., *The Reformation and the English People* (Oxford: Blackwell, 1984);

SCHAFF, Philip, *History of the Christian Church*, vol. 5 (Peabody: Hendrickson Publishers, 1996);

SCHAFF, Philip, *The Creeds of Christendom*, vol. III (Grand Rapids: Baker Books, 1996);

SCHENK, W., *Reginald Pole, Cardinal of England* (London: Longmans, 1950);

SCHMIDT, Martin, "Die Rechtfertigungslehre bei Richard Hooker", in ALAND, Kurt; ELTESTER, Walther; RÜCKERT Hanns (eds.), *Geist und Geschichte der Reformation* (Berlin: Walter de Gruyter, 1966), 377-396;

SCHWARZ, Robert C., "Dignified and Commodious: Richard Hooker's 'Mysticall Copulation' Metaphor", *Sewanee Theological Review* 43/1 (1999), 16-30;

SECOR, Philip B., *Richard Hooker, Prophet of Anglicanism* (Toronto: The Anglican Book Centre, 1999);

SEDGWICK, Timothy F., "Revisioning Anglican Moral Theology", *Anglican Theological Review* LXIII/1 (1981), 1-20;

SEDGWICK, Timothy, "The New Shape of Anglican Identity", *Anglican Theological Review* LXXVII/2 (1995), 187-197;

SEIFRID, Mark A., "In What Sense is 'Justification' a Declaration?", *Churchman* 114/2 (2000), 123-136;

SELINGER, Suzanne, *Calvin Against Himself. An Inquiry in Intellectual History* (Archon Books, 1984);

SELWYN, David G., *The Library of Thomas Cranmer* (Oxford: Oxford Bibliographical Society, 1996);

SHARPE, Kevin, " 'So Hard a Text?' Images of Charles I, 1612-1700", in *The Historical Journal* 43/2 (2002), 383-405;

SHAW, Marc Randolph, "The Morrow of Practical Divinity. A Study in the Theology of William Perkins" (Th.D. dissertation: Westminster Theological Seminary, 1981);

SHIRLEY, F. J., *Richard Hooker and Contemporary Political Ideas* (London: SPCK, 1949);

SHUFFLETON, Frank, *Thomas Hooker 1586-1647* (Princeton: Princeton University Press, 1977);

SHUGER, Debora, " 'Society Supernatural': the Imagined Community of Hooker's *Laws*", in McEACHERN, Claire; SHUGER, Debora (eds.), *Religion and Culture in Renaissance England* (Cambridge: Cambridge University Press, 1997);

SISSON, C. J., *The Judicious Marriage of Mr. Hooker and the Birth of The Laws of Ecclesiastical Polity* (Cambridge: Cambridge University Press, 1940);

SKEETERS, Martha, *Community and Clergy* (Oxford: Clarendon Press, 1993);

SMITHEN, Frederick J., *Continental Protestantism and the English Reformation* (London: James Clark & Co. Ltd., 1927);

SMYTHE, C. H., *Cranmer and the Reformation under Edward VI* (Cambridge, 1926);

SOMMERVILLE, J. P., "Richard Hooker, Hadrian Saravia, and the Advent of the Divine Right of Kings", *History of Political Thought* IV/2 (1983), 229-245;

SOMMERVILLE, John C., *The Secularization of Early Modern England* (Oxford: Oxford University Press, 1992);

SOMMERVILLE, M. R., "Richard Hooker and his Contemporaries on Episcopacy: an Elizabethan Consensus", *The Journal of Ecclesiastical Studies* 35 (1984), 177-187;

SPEED HILL, W. (ed.), *Studies in Richard Hooker. Essays Preliminary to an Edition of His Works* (Cleveland: The Press of Case Western Reserve University, 1972);

SPEED HILL, W., "Editing Richard Hooker: A Retrospective", *Sewanee Theological Review* 36/2 (1993), 187-199;

SPEED HILL, W., "Richard Hooker and the Rhetoric of History', *Churchman* 114/1 (2000), 7-21;

SPINKS, Brian D., *Two Faces of Elizabethan Anglican Theology* (London: Scarecrow Press, 1999);

STANWOOD, P. G., "Of Prelacy and Polity in Milton and Hooker", in SWISS, Margo; KENT, David (eds.), *Heirs of Fame. Milton and Writers of the English Renaissance* (Lewisburg: Bucknell University Press, 1995);

STANWOOD, P. G., "Stobaeus and Classical Borrowing in the Renaissance, with Special Reference to Richard Hooker and Jeremy Taylor", *Neophilologus* 59 (1975), 141-146;

STEPHENS, W.P. *The Theology of Huldrych Zwingli* (Oxford: Clarendon Press, 1986);

STEPHENS, W.P., *The Holy Spirit in the Theology of Martin Bucer* (Cambridge: Cambridge University Press, 1970);

STEPHENS, W.P., *Zwingli. An Introduction to his Thought* (Oxford: Clarendon Press, 1992);

STEVENSON, Kenneth, *The Mystery of Baptism in the Anglican Tradition* (Harrisburg: Morehouse Publishing, 1998);

STEVICK, Daniel B., "Hooker's Criteria for Liturgy", *Anglican Theological Review* 73/2 (1991), 139-154;

STONE, Darwell, *A History of the Doctrine of the Holy Eucharist*, vol. I-II (London: Longmans, Green, and Co., 1909);

STRAUSS, Leo, and CROPSEY, Joseph (eds.), *History of Political Philosophy* (Chicago: Rand McNally & Co., 1966);

STREHLE, Stephen, *The Catholic Roots of the Protestant Gospel* (Leiden: E. J. Brill, 1995);

STRYPE, John, *The Life and Acts of John Whitgift* (Oxford: Clarendon Press, 1822);

STRYPE, John, *The Life and Acts of Matthew Parker* (Oxford: Clarendon Press, 1821);

STUNT, T. C. F., "John Henry Newman and the Evangelicals", *Journal of Ecclesiastical History* XXI/1 (1970), 65-74;

STUPPERICH, Robert, *Melanchthon* (London: Lutterworth Press, 1965);

SURTZ, Edward, *The Works and Days of John Fisher* (Cambridge, Mass.: Harvard University Press, 1967);

SYKES, S. W., and GILLEY, S. W., " 'No Bishop, No Church!' The Tractarian Impact on Anglicanism", ROWELL, Geoffrey (ed.), *Tradition Renewed. The Oxford Movement Conference Papers* (London: Darton, Longman and Todd, 1986), 120-139;

SYKES, Stephen and Booty, John, *The Study of Anglicanism* (London: SPCK, 1988);

SYKES, Stephen, "Richard Hooker and the Ordination of Women to the Priesthood", *Sewanee Theological Review* 36/2 (1993), 200-214;

SYKES, Stephen, "Richard Hooker and the Ordination of Women to the Priesthood", in SOSKICE, Janet M. (ed.), *After Eve* (Collins, 1990), 119-137;

TAYLOR, John, "Introduction: The Voice of the City", *Believing in the Church: The Corporate Nature of Faith*, A Report of the Doctrine Commission of the Church of England (Wilton: Morehouse-Barlow, 1981);

TEBEAUX, Elizabeth, "Donne and Hooker on the Nature of Man: Diverging 'Middle Way'", *Restoration Quarterly*, 29-44;

THOMPSON, Bard, *Humanists and Reformers* (Grand Rapids: Eerdmans, 1996);

THORNTON, L. S., *Richard Hooker. A Study of His Theology* (London: SPCK, 1924);

TINDAL HART, A., *Clergy and Society 1600-1800* (London: SPCK, 1968);

TODD, Margo, *Christian Humanism and the Puritan Social Order* (Cambridge: Cambridge University Press, 1987);

TOLMIE, Murray, *The Triumph of the Saints* (Cambridge: Cambridge University Press, 1977);

TOON, Peter, *Foundations of Faith. Justification and Sanctification* (Westchester, Ill.: Crossway Books, 1983);

TORRANCE KIRBY Kirby, W. J., *Richard Hooker's Doctrine of the Royal Supremacy* (Leiden: E. J. Brill, 1990);

TORRANCE KIRBY, W. J., "Richard Hooker's Theory of Natural Law in the Context of Reformation Theology", *Sixteenth Century Journal* XXX/3 (1999), 681-703;

TORRANCE KIRBY, W. J., *"Supremum Caput*: Richard Hooker's Theology of Ecclesiastical Dominion", *Dionysius* XII (1988);

TORRANCE KIRBY, W. J., "The Paradigm of Chalcedonian Christology in Richard Hooker's Discourse on Grace and the Church", *Churchman* 114/1 (2000), 22-39;

TREVOR-ROPER, Hugh, *Archbishop Laud 1573-1645* (London: Macmillan Press, 1988);

TROTTER, Andrew H., "Justification in the Gospel of John", in CARSON, D.A. (ed.), *Right with God. Justification in the Bible and the World* (London: Paternoster, 1992), 126-145;

TRUEMAN, Carl R., *Luther's Legacy. Salvation and English Reformers, 1525-1556* (Oxford: Clarendon Press, 1994);

TYACKE, Nicholas (ed.), *England's Long Reformation 1500-1800* (London: UCL Press, 1998);

TYACKE, Nicholas, "Lancelot Andrewes and the Myth of Anglicanism", in LAKE, Peter and Questier, Michael (eds.), *Conformity and Orthodoxy in the English Church, c. 1560-1660* (The Boydell Press, 2000), 5-33;

URBAN, Linwood, "A Revolution in English Moral Theology", *Anglican Theological Review* LIII/1 (1971), 5-20;

VAN'T SPIJKER, Willem, *The Ecclesiastical Offices in the Thought of Martin Bucer* (Leiden: E.J. Brill, 1996);

VEATCH, Henry B., "The Idea of a Christian Science and Scholarship: Sense or Nonsense?", *Faith and Philosophy* I/1 (1984), 89-110;

VICKERS, Brian, "Hooker's Prose Style", in HOOKER, Richard, *Of the Laws of the Ecclesiastical Polity*, A. S. McGrade and Brian Vickers eds. (London: Sidgwick and Jackson, 1975), 41-59;

VOAK, Nigel, "Reason and grace in Richard Hooker" (M.Phil. Dissertation: The University of Oxford, 1994);

WALL, John N., "Hooker's 'Faire Speeche': Rhetorical Strategies in the *Laws of Ecclesiastical Polity*", in ARMENTROUT, Donald S. (ed.), *This Sacred History. Anglican Reflections for John Booty* (Cambridge, Mass.: Cowley Publications, 1990), 125-143;

WALLACE Jr., Dewey D., *Puritans and Predestination. Grace in English Protestant Theology 1525-1695* (Chapel Hill: The University of North Caroline Press, 1982);

WALSHAM, Alexandra, "'Frantick Hacket': Prophecy, Sorcery, Insanity, and the Elizabethan Puritan Movement", *The Historical Journal* 41/1 (1998), 27-66;

WALSHAM, Alexandra, "The Parochial Roots of Laudianism Revisited: Catholics, Anti-Calvinists and 'Parish Anglicans' in Early Stuart England", *Journal of Ecclesiastical History* 49/4 (1998), 620-651;

WALSHAM, Alexandra, *Providence in Early Modern England* (Oxford: Oxford University Press, 1999);

WALTON, Izaak, *The Lives of Dr. John Donne, Sir Henry Wotton, Mr. Richard Hooker, Mr. George Herbert, and Dr. Robert Sanderson* (London, 1825);

WALTON, John, "Tradition of the Middle Way: The Anglican Contribution to the American Character", *Historical Magazine of the Protestant Episcopal Church* XLIV/5 (1975), 7-32;

WALZER, Michael, *The Revolution of the Saints* (London: Weidenfeld and Nicholson, 1965);

WEBER, Max, *The Protestant Ethics and the Spirit of Capitalism* (New York: Charles Scribner's Sons, 1958);

WEBSTER, Tom, *Godly Clergy in Early Stuart England* (Cambridge: Cambridge University Press, 1997);

WENDEL, François, *Calvin. Sources et Évolution de Sa Pensée Religieuse* (Genève: Labor et Fides, 1950);

WENGERT, Timothy (ed.), *Philip Melanchthon (1497-1560) and the Commentary* (Sheffield: Sheffield Academic Press, 1997);

WENGERT, Timothy, *Human Freedom, Christian Righteousness. Philip Melanchthon's Exegetical Debate with Erasmus of Rotterdam* (Oxford: Oxford University Press, 1998);

WENGERT, Timothy, *Law and Gospel. Philip Melanchthons's Debate with John Agricola of Eisleben over Poenitentia* (Grand Rapids: Baker Books, 1997);

WHITE, Garnett Lee, "Anglican Reflections to the Council of Trent in the Reign of Queen Elizabeth I" (Ph.D. dissertation, Vanderbilt University, 1975);

WILLIAMS, C. H., *William Tyndale* (London: Thomas Nelson and Sons, 1969);

WILLIAMS, R. R., "Richard Hooker on the Church and State Report", *The Churchman* 85/2 (1971), 97-104;

WOLF, William; BOOTY, John; THOMAS, Owen, *The Spirit of Anglicanism: Hooker, Maurice, Temple* (Edinburgh: T&T Clark, 1982);

WOODHOUSE, H. F., "The Authenticity of Hooker's Book VII", in *Church History* XXII/1 (1963), 3-7;

YRI, Norvald, "Seek God's Righteousness: Righteousness in the Gospel of Matthew", 96-106, in CARSON, D.A. (ed.), *Right with God. Justification in the Bible and the World* (London: Paternoster, 1992).

Index of Subjects

102, 109, 111, 112, 115, 122,
137, 144, 147, 156, 183, 190,
192, 194, 197, 202, 206, 207,
209, 219, 222, 227, 229, 232,
247, 250, 251, 259, 261, 266-
268, 276, 278, 279, 281, 283,
288, 291, 292, 302, 305, 306,
312, 315, 322
sectarianism, 51
separation, 20, 183, 305
Sermon of the Nature of Pride, 1,
249
simul justus et peccator, 195
sin, VIII, 24, 30, 36, 53, 57, 65, 66,
68, 69, 72, 75-78, 82, 83, 87, 94,
95, 99, 100, 102-105, 115-117,
123-126, 143, 145, 147, 151,
152, 153, 154, 160-162, 163,
165, 166, 169, 171-174, 176,
180, 182, 192, 194, 195, 215,
219-223, 227, 232, 234-243, 246,
250, 255-257, 259, 262-264, 272,
274, 281, 288, 291, 292, 294,
297, 300, 303, 304, 306, 307
sinful humanity, 72, 179, 182,
234, 235, 260, 294
sinner, 30, 31, 49, 53, 76, 83, 100,
103, 170, 171, 173, 178, 180,
193, 194, 202, 206, 271, 275,
303
sinners, 32, 76, 88, 123, 125, 173,
227, 280, 292
sloth, 53
social corpus, 205
Socrates, 150
Sola Scriptura, 52
Son, 13, 51, 66, 72, 73, 76, 88, 96,
101, 122, 123, 199, 209, 219,
270, 273, 274, 295
sophister, 228
soteriology, IX, 2, 14, 18, 41, 48,
63, 64, 71, 72, 77, 78, 92, 98, 99,

130, 139, 140, 141, 143, 144,
147, 149, 152-155, 162, 168,
178, 180, 184, 185, 187, 192,
198, 203, 206, 210, 212, 213,
220-222, 234, 251, 275, 299,
301, 304, 305
sovereignty of God, VII, 91, 153,
244, 263, 283, 289, 307, 308
Spain, 108
Spanish Armada, 108
Spirit, Holy, VII, XII, XIII, 15, 31,
52, 64, 66-69, 74, 82, 84, 87, 88,
93, 95, 97, 98, 101, 102, 109,
113, 118, 126, 130, 140, 142-
145, 150, 152, 163, 187, 201,
202, 209, 210, 212, 217, 218,
220, 223, 270, 273, 274, 280,
283, 284, 300-303, 305, 331
subjective, 30, 54, 66, 71, 74, 76,
79, 81, 83, 114, 170, 191, 193
superfluous, 48, 140, 198
superior, 10, 44, 45, 174, 290
supernatural, 10, 13, 16, 24, 29,
30, 34-36, 47, 48, 50, 59, 61, 164
temporal polity, 46
testimony, VII, 34, 37, 69, 70, 72,
79, 83, 113, 125, 266, 267, 268
theologian, VII, VIII, 3, 5, 10-13,
21, 37, 39, 40, 46, 52-55, 58, 61,
62, 235, 260, 280, 291, 299, 300
theosis, 51
Thirty-Nine Articles, 1, 313, 319
to justify, 8, 49, 122, 302
Trinity, XIV, 51, 127, 270, 280,
286, 290, 307
trust, 17, 31, 66-69, 73-75, 77, 82,
89, 90, 114, 116, 120, 136, 137,
139, 146, 147, 150, 153, 155,
156, 181, 191, 204, 211, 231,
280, 284, 300, 303
*Two Sermons Upon Part of S.
Judes Epistle*, 1

Index of Names

Index of Biblical References